Canary Islands

THE BRADT TRAVEL GUIDE

THE BRADT STORY

The first Bradt travel guide was written in 1974 by George and Hilary Bradt on a river barge floating down a tributary of the Amazon, and was followed by *Backpacker's Africa* in 1977. In the 1980s and '90s the focus shifted away from hiking to broader-based guides covering new destinations – usually the first to be published on those places. In the 21st century Bradt continues to publish these ground-breaking guides, along with guides to established holiday destinations, incorporating in-depth information on culture and natural history alongside the nuts and bolts of where to stay and what to see.

Bradt authors support responsible travel, with advice not only on minimum impact but also on how to give something back through local charities. Thus a true synergy is achieved between the traveller and local communities.

*

The Canary Islands are not a typical Bradt destination, but every so often we get a proposal that completely wows us, sending us off course. Lucy Corne's infectious enthusiasm for her island home, along with her descriptions of the hidden places that most tourists never see, convinced us that these islands deserved Bradt travellers who want to do more than just lie on a beach. We are delighted with the result.

Hilary Bradt

Hilary Bradt

19 High Street, Chalfont St Peter, Bucks SL9 9QE, England
Tel: 01753 893444; fax: 01753 892333
Email: info@bradtguides.com
www.bradtguides.com

Canary Islands

THE BRADT TRAVEL GUIDE

Lucy Corne

Bradt Travel Guides Ltd, UK
The Globe Pequot Press Inc, USA

First published November 2004

Bradt Travel Guides Ltd
19 High Street, Chalfont St Peter, Bucks SL9 9QE, England
www.bradtguides.com
Published in the USA by The Globe Pequot Press Inc, 246 Goose Lane,
PO Box 480, Guilford, Connecticut 06475-0480

British Library Cataloguing in Publication Data
A catalogue record for this book is available from the British Library

ISBN-10: 1 84162 108 0
ISBN-13: 978 1 84162 108 1

Photographs
Front cover La Sorrueda Reservoir, Gran Canaria (Fototeca 9x12/Fantuz Olimpio)
Text Luis Castaneda/Tips Images (LC), Paolo Curto/Tips Images (PC),
Fernando Galván (FG), Jeanna Nash (JN), Guido Alberto Rossi/Tips Images (GAR)

Illustrations Carole Vincer
Maps Alan Whitaker

Typeset from the author's disc by Wakewing
Printed and bound in Italy by Legoprint SpA, Trento

Author/Acknowledgements

AUTHOR

Lucy Corne is a freelance journalist and part-time English teacher. As well as writing for an English newspaper in the Canary Islands, she contributes to various online travel magazines. She has lived in Las Palmas since 2001.

ACKNOWLEDGEMENTS

When writing a book like this you rely on the help of others more than you'd ever imagine and the people mentioned here are just a small number of the multitudes that made my job easier.

First, my immense thanks to Héctor Sánchez for being the first to show me what the islands have to offer. His constant moral support, fact finding and help with tricky translations have proved invaluable.

My thanks also go to Victor Siverio, Carlos Romero and especially Miriam Rodríguez at Binter Canarias and everyone at Cicar and Acantur for their help throughout the research.

In El Hierro I'd like to thank Manolo Sánchez for offering assistance that the tourist information office didn't.

Flor Falcón and colleagues in the Fuerteventura tourist information office supplied me with enough information to write a book solely about their island, and always with a smile. Thanks to everyone in La Gomera's tourist office for their help finding the answers to all my random queries and Lisdenia Benavides at La Palma's superb tourist information office for not tiring of my daily visits and endless questions. Thanks, too, to the residents of La Graciosa for giving the warmest of welcomes and providing all the info I needed in the absence of a tourist information point.

Huge thanks to David and Alex Bramwell for the sections on flora and fauna and to Jorge Naranjo in the Cabildo de Gran Canaria's environment department for enlightening me on conservation issues.

Finally, my thanks go to Emily Kingston and Jaime Coello for chasing up my loose ends and last but not least Tricia Hayne for all her support and advice throughout the various stages of the book.

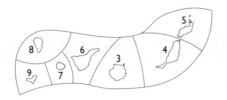

Contents

Introduction

My first visit to Gran Canaria didn't exactly expose me to the finer parts of the island. Having decided to spend a summer abroad, I found myself working as a children's representative in Puerto Rico, perhaps the Canary Islands' worst resort. I soon realised that if Britain had a better climate, many people would never bother holidaying overseas, since all anyone seemed to want was pie and chips in an English bar, watching the *EastEnders* omnibus. Most people never ventured out of the resort, and a small number never even left the hotel grounds, not even on an organised excursion. I was lucky enough to befriend a Canario who was keen to show off the island's gems on our days off. My opinion of Gran Canaria rocketed as we ate seafood in the charming Puerto de las Nieves or snorkelled in the calm seas of the capital, and for me Las Canteras remains the islands' finest beach. I must admit that I was astounded at the rugged mountains and the verdure of certain ravines, and realised that I hadn't had much of an idea about the Canary Islands before I left home. But after four months I found I'd barely seen anything of the island and returned home feeling a little disappointed with my time in the Canaries. A few years later, the opportunity arose to return, so I headed back with gusto, keen to explore Gran Canaria and perhaps the other islands. Weekends were soon taken up with hikes in the mountains or donning traditional costume to join in a small town *romería* (pilgrimage). Although they generally consider themselves Spanish, the Canarian people are proud of their heritage and I was surprised to find such a well-preserved culture. It seems that every islander has a traditional Canarian outfit stashed away and although they might usually prefer listening to chart music, none turn their nose up at a customary song, accompanied by the *timple* (a small, five-stringed guitar).

The varied landscape never ceases to amaze, and although I've been exploring the islands for over two years, there are so many villages, ravines and beaches that remain unknown to me. The rambling roads make it difficult to explore every inch, and there are many times that I've set off with plans to visit one town and found a mysterious road to follow instead. Although I'd initially known there was more to the islands than manmade beaches and high-rise hotels, I was impressed by what I found, but there was still something bugging me. Every time I returned to England and bumped into someone I knew, they'd inevitably ask me what I was doing these days. Once I told them I was living in the Canary Islands I noticed something of a look of disdain on their faces. I felt the need to quickly defend my new home, pointing out that there was much more to the archipelago than beaches and beer. I began to feel a pride in the islands that I'd never really felt about my home town, Stoke-on-Trent, and would advertise the islands' finer points whenever the opportunity arose.

It's a great pity that the vast majority of visitors never get close to exploring the islands in depth and leave believing that the Canaries are nothing more than a large tourist resort. A frightening number of people are aware only of the four islands that appear in the holiday brochures, and a tiny minority who visit are surprised to find the islands near to Africa, rather than off the Spanish coast. So I set about writing this guidebook in a hope that a few more people would discover the islands for what they are – a stunning hiking destination steeped in fascinating history, legend and a proud culture. Researching the book made me aware of the incredible variety that the islands offer, from the nightmarish resorts of southern Tenerife to La Gomera's hamlets of yesteryear; from the glorious sun-soaked beaches of Fuerteventura to Teide's snow-capped peak. The latter remains a source of much frustration to me, since my attempts to conquer it have both been thwarted by the weather. Although I tell my friends I'm never walking up there again, deep down I know that I'm not leaving the Canary Islands until I've appreciated the stunning views that you apparently get from the summit.

Many of my Canarian friends have yet to explore their islands in depth and although they joke that I now know more about their home than they do, I continue to explore, looking for those towns I missed last time. I hope that after reading this book you'll look past the stereotype and join me.

FEEDBACK REQUEST

I have strived to ensure that this book is as accurate and up-to-date as possible. However, places change and feedback from readers is invaluable for future editions. If you have any comments, please send them to Lucy Corne, c/o Bradt Travel Guides, 19 High St, Chalfont St Peter, Bucks SL9 9QE or email info@bradtguides.com.
Many thanks!
Lucy

Part One

General Information

CANARY ISLANDS AT A GLANCE

Location In the Atlantic Ocean, approximately 100km west of Morocco and 1,100km southwest of Spain

Islands Gran Canaria, Fuerteventura, Lanzarote, Tenerife, La Gomera, La Palma, El Hierro

Size/area 7,447km^2. Largest island Tenerife (2034km^2), smallest El Hierro (278km^2)

Climate Temperate, with year-round temperatures between 18°C and 30°C

Status One of Spain's autonomous communities, split into two provinces, that of Santa Cruz (Tenerife, La Gomera, La Palma, El Hierro) and Las Palmas (Gran Canaria, Fuerteventura, Lanzarote)

Population 1.67m

Capital (and population) Alternates between Las Palmas (400,000) and Santa Cruz de Tenerife (230,000)

Other main towns La Laguna (Tenerife), Telde (Gran Canaria), Arrecife (Lanzarote), Puerto del Rosario (Fuerteventura), Santa Cruz de La Palma, San Sebastián (La Gomera), Valverde (El Hierro)

Life expectancy 78 years

Economy Main earner is tourism, though ship building, construction and agriculture are also of importance

GDP US$219m

Language Spanish

Religion Roman Catholic

Currency Euro

Exchange rate (October 2004) €1 = £0.69, £1 = €1.45

Airline/airports Binter Canarias and Islas Airways. Each island has an airport, but those on La Gomera and El Hierro cater only for inter-island flights.

International telephone code +34

Time GMT

Electrical voltage 220V, 50Hz

Weights and measures Metric

Flag Yellow, white and blue tricolour

National plant Dragon tree (*Dracaena draco*)

National bird/animal Giant lizard

National sport Lucha Canaria (wrestling)

Public holidays January 1, Good Friday, May 1, August 15, October 12, November 1, December 6, December 25 plus a further six chosen by local authorities

Background Information

It is rather difficult to offer an accurate description of the Canarian landscape. It is necessary to visit this privileged land in order to admire sights unique in the world. When touring any of these islands we are offered a new landscape with every turn of the road; from the Egyptian décor to the lush postcard from the West Indies; from the rugged northern landscape to the soft plains where sugar cane and palm trees grow.

Alexander von Humboldt

HISTORY
Origins

It would surprise many to find that there are three schools of thought on the origins of the islands. The most widely accepted hypothesis is that the islands are volcanic in origin and represent the tiniest part of huge volcanoes below the sea. A theory that wins little support these days is that the archipelago was once joined to Africa, or was part of a huge continent that stretched from Africa to the Americas. This idea is based on the fact that there are examples of flora from both Africa and America in the Canary Islands, though botanists dismiss it as pure nonsense, saying that the archipelago's plantlife arrived by chance. The third and perhaps least credible idea is that the islands, along with Cape Verde, Madeira and the Azores, are in fact the remains of the legendary sunken continent, Atlantis. However, all but the dreamers agree that the islands are the result of volcanic activity and are basically the peaks of a massive subaquatic mountain range. Millions of years ago as the African continental plate drifted eastwards it came to an abrupt halt, forming large cracks in the seabed. Lava flowed through these crevices and eventually formed the islands that we see today. It's estimated that Fuerteventura, Lanzarote and Chinijo were formed 30–40 million years ago, Gran Canaria, La Gomera and Tenerife 10–15 million years ago and La Palma and El Hierro between one and five million years ago. The best place to get a taste of the islands' origins is in the Parque Nacional de Timanfaya in Lanzarote, where underground temperatures reach 400°C. There have not been any volcanic rumblings on most of the islands for a few centuries, though Teide continues to emit the pungent aroma of sulphur. It last erupted in the early 20th century, but on a rather unimpressive scale. La Palma was the site of the most recent volcanic activity in the archipelago when, in 1971, Volcán Teneguía spewed out fiery lava. Certain observers believe that the island's turn is coming and that Teide will erupt in the foreseeable future.

WHICH CAME FIRST, THE ISLANDS OR THE BIRDS?

The more you read about the Canary Islands' history, the less you feel you know. Everything about the archipelago sparks debate, from their formation to the origins of the men that first inhabited them. No-one can even agree on where the Canaries got their name. Although many people would immediately say that the islands are named after dogs, not everyone is so sure. For centuries new theories as to the origin of the archipelago's name have been emerging, some more fantastic than others. If you go for the theory that the first islanders were Berbers from the Sahara, it's logical that they would have named their new homeland after their old tribe – the Canarii. While some believe that the archipelago was named after the sweet-voiced birds thought to originate there, most agree that canaries have something in common with champagne – they take their name from the region.

The theory with most followers is that the islands take their names from the fearsome dogs that once roamed free in the mountains. Amongst the first known visitors to the islanders were a group of Mauritanian explorers who reached Canarian shores in the 1st century BC. They were impressed by the dramatic landscape but more so by the hundreds of strong but friendly dogs. The explorers took a couple of puppies for their boy king, Juba II and knowledge of the fine animals spread. The islands were soon referred to as Canaria, from *canis*, Latin for dog. Then there are some who believe that, while the islands are named after canines, it's more for the natives' fondness for eating dog meat than the abundance of the animals. Most dismiss this theory, popularised by historian José Viera y Clavijo, since there is no archaeological evidence to suggest that the islanders ate dogs. Another idea that's the object of ridicule is that Italian explorers arriving on the islands decided to christen them Cranaria, in honour of their kings Crana and Cranus. There are so many theories circulating that if none of the above appeal, you could always invent one to your liking: I'm sure you wouldn't be the first.

Early inhabitants

> They lived in huts and caves ... the men went about naked except for shirts made of goat or sheep skin ... they ate their meat roasted and boiled rather than raw ... they had no iron tools or other objects made of iron or any other metal.
>
> Abreu Galindo, *Historia de las siete islas de Canaria*, 1602

The origins of the islands' first inhabitants are a topic of much discussion and speculation. Some believe they were blond-haired Scandinavians, the result of a Viking adventure which got lost; others relate them to Egyptians due to their similar mummification methods, while dreamers like to think that they were ancestors of the citizens of Atlantis. Most, however, consider these explanations nothing more than romantic fairy tales. For a long time, the general consensus was that the aboriginal Canarians were Cro-Magnons who came over from northwest Africa some time around 1000–2500 BC. The Cro-Magnon race lived in the southwest of France in the quaternary age, but moved south when they found their way of life under threat from encounters with new people and the ever-changing European climate. Evidence has been found that they ended up in Morocco,

Tunisia and Algeria, a mere leap from the Canary Islands. Today another theory is winning greater support – that the islands' inhabitants are descendants of the Canarii tribe, a Berber people living in the Sahara. Similarities in their art, appearance and customs suggest a link and it would certainly explain where the islands got their name. Cultural differences, the varied rock engravings and pottery styles have led archaeologists to agree that the islands were populated by more than one group. Further influxes of immigrants later on probably also came from North Africa.

How the first inhabitants arrived is an even greater mystery, since there is no evidence that they had any knowledge of navigation or shipbuilding and there is a suggestion that on certain islands the natives couldn't even swim.

The first residents are generally referred to as Guanches, although in reality the Guanches were from Tenerife (in their language, *guan* meant descendant and *chinech* or *Achinech* was their name for Tenerife). However, this term is now acceptably used to talk about the indigenous people from all of the islands for simplification. In truth, the first inhabitants were known as Bimbaches in El Hierro, Benahoaritas in La Palma, Gomeros in La Gomera, Guanches in Tenerife, Canarios in Gran Canaria and Mahos in Fuerteventura and Lanzarote.

Accounts of early visitors to the islands described the Guanches as an attractive people – tall, robust and good-looking with clear, rosy skin, fair hair and blue eyes. They were pastoral cave dwellers who lived from minimal farming and fishing. Food was scarce and frugal, with the most important crops being wheat and barley, which they toasted to make *gofio*, still an intrinsic part of Canarian culture and cuisine. Their diet was also heavy on goat, though they occasionally ate pork and lamb. They dressed in animal skins, though often went naked due to the climate and used to shed their clothes in times of war to aid movement, something that shocked the European conquerors. They essentially lived as men had during the Stone Age, since the limitations of their land stopped progression – there's not a speck of metal to be found anywhere in the Canary Islands.

While some islands were split into different cantons, each governed by a *mencey* or *guanarteme* (king), others counted on one ruler for the whole island. Each island had some kind of legal system and decisions were made by a council (*sabor*) in a construction known as a *Tagoror*. As with all aspects of early Canarian culture, laws were different on each island. On Gran Canaria thieves were sent to prison, while on La Palma they were admired for their intelligence and on El Hierro they had an eye removed. Murderers in Fuerteventura were taken to the shore and beaten about the head with a rock, while Tenerife's Guanches were terrified of blood and instead took the rather less gruesome measure of giving the culprit's livestock to the family of the victim. As for religion, it is difficult to tell if the Guanches worshipped just one god, as the chroniclers wrote, or many (as the presence of various idols suggests). They did worship the sun, which they called *Magec*, and feared Mount Teide, which they believed to be hell. Historian Abreu Galindo, in his account of the conquest, wrote that the Guanches worshipped a god called Achaman, which meant *He that Sustains Heaven and Earth*. The Catholic priests that chronicled the conquest commented that the islanders' religion consisted of little more than rainmaking and fertility rituals and that they worshipped Alcorán, the sky god.

Although the majority of the Guanches' culture was lost soon after the conquest, their main leisure activities have survived in some form. The *tajaraste* dance is still practised in La Gomera and their favourite sport, a form of two-man wrestling, was the basis for the present-day *Lucha Canaria*. Their most important festival, the Benyesmen (harvest) is still celebrated in certain areas of the islands, such as the Barranco de Guayadeque in Gran Canaria.

LOVE AND MARRIAGE

Women played an important role in the early Canarian society and were highly respected, so much so that a man couldn't touch, converse with or even look at a woman unless she made the first move and breaking these rules could lead to serious punishments. The attitudes towards women varied considerably from island to island though, and in La Gomera they were considered common property. If a man dropped in on an early Gomero home he'd as likely be offered the host's wife as a plate of *gofio* and a glass of goat's milk. Marriage existed on all of the islands, but attitudes towards it varied. According to Bethencourt's chroniclers, it was common practice for women in Lanzarote to have three husbands – an interesting twist and an effective way to curb the population growth in a poverty-stricken island. In Gran Canaria, when a woman was due to get married, she stayed in bed for a month, eating as much as possible so that she would be fat and therefore beautiful on the big day. On her wedding night the first man to take her to bed wouldn't be her husband but the *guanarteme*, or one of his advisers if he wasn't in the mood.

Arranged marriages weren't common, although the woman had little say in the matter in El Hierro. Once a man had spotted his potential bride he showered gifts upon her family in an attempt to win their approval. Marriage was a little more democratic in Gran Canaria and Tenerife, where both parties got to have their say. Monogamy was of the utmost importance to Tenerife's Guanches, though a form of divorce existed if things went wrong. Either party could instigate the separation, though their children would thereafter be considered illegitimate. The early islanders could marry any woman except for their mother or sister, though this rule was waived for royals.

And although the women essentially worked in the home raising the children, they also helped in agricultural tasks and played their part in the conquest. Accounts of the conquest tell of brave, Amazonian women fighting alongside their men folk, particularly in La Palma.

When the Europeans arrived they soon realised that although the Guanches were a peaceful people if left alone, they were strong and capable of atrocities if their freedom was under threat. Unfortunately they had no access to metal and their primitive wooden weapons were no match for the European invaders.

Early visitors

It's not really known when the outside world discovered that the Canary Islands existed. In ancient Greek literature, Homer wrote of a group of islands further away than the Pillars of Hercules (the Straits of Gibraltar) and gave them the name the Garden of Hespérides. It is debatable whether the ancient Greeks ever ventured this far but what seems certain is that stories of these islands were passed down through the generations and were considered a kind of paradise on Earth. Naturally other archipelagos in the area, such as the Azores and Cape Verde, claim to be Elysium, the place where the righteous spent their afterlife; and who knows to which islands Homer was referring?

In the 1st century AD, natural historian Pliny the Elder furnished the Romans with a seemingly accurate report of what he called 'the Fortunate Islands'. His writings were based on the accounts of King Juba of Mauritania's visit to the islands a century earlier. He described a group of islands close to the African coast with a white mountain rising up from them and while there are no guarantees, many believe that the islands he referred to were the Canary Islands and that the white mountain was Teide. During the Middle Ages, sailors didn't venture into the Atlantic due to the belief that the waters were infested with dragons, so knowledge of the islands was somewhat lost until the mid 13th century when explorers from Spain, Italy and Portugal began to arrive. Around 1330, Italian Lancelloto Malocello landed on Lanzarote's coast, surely giving the island its name. An important Portuguese expedition in 1341 provided the first detailed look at the islands and the first time that they had been correctly marked on a map. Other visitors around this time included merchants and gold hunters, wrongly believing that the fabled source of Saharan gold lay at the latitude of the Canary Islands.

Around this time, the labour force was diminishing in Europe due to war and disease, so sailors turned their hand to the capture and sale of slaves, seeing the Canary Islands as a good shopping ground. It was one such expedition that led to the eventual colonisation of the islands and the end of the Guanches' way of life.

The not-so-fortunate isles – the conquest, part one

By the end of the 14th century the islands were well known and became sought-after property. As the new century dawned it brought with it 100 years of bungling, incompetence, treachery, lies and murder as Spain attempted to take the islands as their own and convert the heathen natives into God-fearing citizens. In 1402 Frenchman Jean de Bethencourt saw the fruits of a Spanish voyage to the islands in the form of a few captured natives. Impressed by their strength and by stories of the fertility of the land, he decided this was just the break he'd been looking for and set his heart on conquering them. Out for fame and glory, he set sail with 250 soldiers, most of them Frenchmen, but less than a quarter made it the 1,000km to the archipelago thanks to disease and desertion. On arrival at the most northeastern island, Lanzarote, they were welcomed by ruler Guadarfía. Respecting their friendly greeting, Jean de Bethencourt promised protection to Guadarfía and his subjects.

Once their camp was set up at Playa de las Coloradas, the conquistadors set out to explore the neighbouring island, Fuerteventura. Finding that the most populous and verdant settlement was in the west, they named it Río de Palmas (Palm River). They also discovered that they would need more troops if they were to conquer the island. Bethencourt headed to Spain to appeal to the king for sponsorship and back-up troops, leaving Gadifer de la Salle in command at the Lanzarote camp. But in Bethencourt's absence things began to turn sour. Supplies were short and while Gadifer was busy seal hunting on Isla de Lobos, one of the men, Berneval, launched a revolt, stealing supplies and capturing Lanzaroteños with plans to sell them as slaves. Having wounded some of his countrymen, Berneval fled on a passing pirate boat. But the damage had already been done and the islanders no longer trusted the invaders and launched their own revolt, albeit a short-lived affair. When Bethencourt arrived with the reinforcements in 1404, Gadifer set off to investigate the other islands, while Bethencourt set his sights on Fuerteventura. As the island had been well explored in the two years that the Europeans had been in the archipelago, they knew its weak points and the best place to attack. After an initial tussle, the island's two kings, Guize of Maxorata (in the north) and Ayoze of Jandía (south) soon saw that fighting was futile and surrendered. Along with some of their subjects they were baptised, Guize becoming Luis and Ayoze renamed Alfonso.

Success went to Bethencourt's head and he quickly set his sights on Gran Canaria, but his attempt failed. As one of his boats docked, it was attacked so fiercely that they were forced to retreat and rethink their plans. Things were turning sour between the two commanders as Gadifer became jealous of Bethencourt and was irritated at Bethencourt's habit of claiming all the glory for himself.

A failed attempt on La Palma revealed that the Benahoaritas were fearless warriors and Bethencourt's men were soon beaten back and some mortally injured. Despairing of the unexpected difficulties that the conquest was posing, Bethencourt turned his attentions to the smallest island, El Hierro. It was an unfair battle, since the island's population had been greatly reduced by slave traders in previous years and although the normally peaceful and impassive Herreños mounted some resistance, their primitive weapons were no match for the Normans. The island's ruler at the time was Armiche, whose brother Auguerón had been captured a few years earlier. Auguerón was now part of Bethencourt's crew and he managed to convince the *mencey* (ruler of the region) to discuss a peaceful settlement with Bethencourt. On Armiche's surrender, Bethencourt went back on his word, taking over 100 Bimbaches (the first inhabitants of El Hierro) as prisoners, most of them ending up as slaves. He left 120 families on El Hierro, people who'd come from Normandy seeking the legendary eternal spring and fertile lands for which the islands were famed.

Details of the conquest of La Gomera are sketchy, but it appears that the island was not taken by force. There is no record in the chronicles that Bethencourt and his men conquered the island and it's thought that over a period of time the Gomeros saw what was happening on their neighbouring islands and just came to accept the conquerors as a normal part of life. Jean de Bethencourt died in Normandy in 1425, his lieutenant and nephew Maciot de Bethencourt taking over as governor of the Canary Islands. Although at first Maciot was a compassionate ruler, his reign later became a time of feuding and unrest. He smothered a revolt in El Hierro triggered by poor treatment of the islanders by their captors. He also condoned the slave trade, regularly landing on the shores of Gran Canaria and Tenerife to capture natives and sell them to the highest bidder. His rule was short-lived as disputes over the ownership of the islands abounded. The islands changed hands countless times with Guillén de las Casas taking over in 1430, leaving Maciot as lord of Lanzarote. In a final act of treachery, Maciot sold his lordship over Lanzarote to the Portuguese, causing anger and panic in the Spanish. The islands eventually fell to Fernán Peraza el Viejo by means of his wife, Inés de las Casas. Peraza invaded Lanzarote in 1445, planning to take control of all of the conquered islands, but failed to expel the Portuguese so he settled in La Gomera. The Portuguese remained on Lanzarote for two years, until they were ousted by the native people. However, the Portuguese remained interested in the islands, acting on orders from Enrique el Navigante who wanted to conquer everything in his path from Portugal to South Africa.

Fernán Peraza's reign over La Gomera marked the start of an era of brutality from both him and his descendants. The following years saw no advances in the conquest of the remaining islands, with a few failed and often bloody attempts to take La Palma, Gran Canaria and Tenerife. On learning about the Portuguese interest in the archipelago, the *Reyes Católicas* (monarchs) began to pay more attention to the islands. In 1477 they gave Diego García de Herrera (a descendant of Peraza) the right of conquest, allowing him to attack the remaining islands. In return for their efforts the Herrera Peraza family received money and the title of 'Count of La Gomera' for them and their ancestors. Lanzarote, Fuerteventura, El Hierro and La Gomera were called the *señorio* (lordship) and were governed locally, rather than by the Castilian crown.

Conquering the three biggies: Gran Canaria, La Palma, Tenerife

The conquest of Gran Canaria was a drawn-out affair, delayed greatly by disagreements between the two men chosen for the job, Juan Rejón and Juan Bermúdez, dean of Rubicón. They arrived in what is now the capital in 1478 with 600 troops and soon let their power be known, quashing an attack by the natives. High hopes of a quick conquest were dampened by growing rivalry between Rejón and Bermúdez and by 1480 their squabbling meant that they had made no progress in conquering the island in the two years they'd been there. When word of their incompetence reached the ears of the Catholic monarchs, they dispatched Pedro de Vera to sort things out. Following the deceitful lead of his predecessors, de Vera set about removing some of the Canarios from the equation. He bundled them on to boats, promising a new life in the neighbouring island of Tenerife, though his real plan was to take them to the mainland to be sold as slaves. Somehow they got wind of the plan and launched a mutiny near Lanzarote, where they were unloaded and left.

Back in Gran Canaria, de Vera attacked the island's capital, Gáldar. The town's *guanarteme*, Tenesor Semidan, was captured and sent to Spain to be baptised. He later returned to Gran Canaria and played a part in the conquest of his homeland, convincing his fellow islanders to give in to the Spanish. Pedro de Vera and his men continued to attack settlements across the island and met resistance from fearless warrior Doramas, though he too met a sticky end eventually. The date generally used to mark the end of the Gran Canaria conquest is April 29 1483, though the island wasn't officially part of the Spanish crown until 1487.

Following the death of Diego García de Herrera in 1485, the *señorío* was divided between his sons. Fernán Peraza (the younger) received La Gomera and El Hierro, while Lanzarote and Fuerteventura were divided between the other sons. Times had been tough in these islands and the citizens were constantly revolting in protest at the despotic way in which they were ruled. Unfortunately, things were not going to get any better under new rulers, especially for the Gomeros, who suffered under Fernán Peraza. Juan Rejón was back on the scene again, this time with his sights set on La Palma. However, strong winds forced his vessel off course and he landed on the northern shores of La Gomera. When Peraza learned of his arrival he had Rejón murdered, perhaps fearing he would take the island due to an old feud. Peraza was tried for this crime in Spain but let off, probably thanks to his family's connections. He was, however, ordered by Queen Isabel to marry Beatriz de Bobadilla, a maid of the court.

In La Gomera, the islanders could not take any more of Peraza's cruelty and launched a rebellion, forcing Peraza and his new wife to take refuge in the Torre del Conde. They appealed to Pedro de Vera for help and he quashed the uprising, hanging the ringleaders and taking many Gomeros as slaves. But the islanders were intent on seeing the end of Peraza and achieved their aim in 1488. On one of his clandestine meetings with his indigenous lover Iballa, Peraza was attacked and killed by the Mulagua tribe. On hearing the news of her husband's death, Beatriz de Bobadilla once more retreated to the tower to await help from Gran Canaria's governor. De Vera returned seeking revenge and quashed the uprising with a cruelty that knew no bounds. He coaxed the Gomeros from their mountain hideouts with promises of a pardon and an agreement to put the past behind them. The majority were soon captured and anyone above the age of 15 was executed in some unspeakable way. A few got off lightly and were deported as slaves. Vera also decided to kill the Gomeros now living in Gran Canaria, since he figured that they'd probably been in on it too.

Horrified complaints of de Vera's conduct reached the Catholic monarchs and he was soon withdrawn from the islands, to be replaced by Alonso Fernández de Lugo. His military career spoke for itself and his participation in the conquest of Gran Canaria suggested that he was the man to finally finish off the occupation of the archipelago. He was given the authorisation to attack La Palma and Tenerife and set off with his new-found troops and funds. He also took a large number of Canarios to conquer La Palma. In 1492 he landed on the coast of Tazacorte and made his way to Tedote (now Santa Cruz de La Palma), soon overpowering the inhabitants of Los Sauces, Barlovento and Garafía. The natives offered little or no resistance other than Tanausú, the *mencey* of Taburiente. He and his subjects fought bravely to protect the *caldera*, but Alonso de Lugo, like many of the islands' conquerors before him, resorted to underhand tricks. With the help of a relative of the king, Juan de Palma, he arranged to meet the great *mencey* alone to discuss a settlement, but took with him a substantial number of troops ready to ambush Tanausú. He and many of his men (and women, for the female Benahoaritas were known for their strength and bravery) were captured and destined to be sold into slavery. Loath to accept a life of servitude, Tanausú chose to starve himself to death, dying on the boat destined for the mainland. The conquest of La Palma ended in May 1493.

Following his success in La Palma, de Lugo returned to the mainland to obtain permission to invade the last and largest of the islands, Tenerife. Lured by promises of land and goods, many citizens of the surrounding islands joined with de Lugo's huge army to take Tenerife. De Lugo first arrived on Tenerife in 1494 with 1,000 armed men and a few hundred Canarians, all of whom were surprised at the warm welcome they received. Of course, they soon found that not everyone on the island was pleased to see them. Tenerife was essentially split into two types of canton – the peaceful and the warring. While the peaceful Guanches were ready to assist the invaders, the warriors put up a brave defence and the outsiders suffered a bloody defeat. Undeterred, de Lugo and his men returned the following year, this time with more success. Though the Guanches under the command of their *mencey*, Bencomo, tried to fight off the attackers, de Lugo had returned with reinforcements and the natives were no match for them. Following the death of Bencomo, the Guanches became resigned to the fact that they could not beat the better-equipped Spaniards and accepted their fate as slaves. The conquest of Tenerife ended on July 25 1496, marking the end of a 94-year struggle to take the islands from the ill-equipped but fiercely proud Guanches.

The natives continued to be a source of Spanish headaches even after the conquest. They refused to live in the towns, preferring to maintain their pastoral lives in the mountains where their agility and knowledge of the landscape kept them safe. In 1499 de Lugo launched yet another attack on the poor Guanches of Tenerife who had fled to the mountains and were harbouring fugitive slaves. There was particular unrest in Tenerife as those who had aided the Spanish were no longer being protected but maltreated and threatened with slavery along with the rest.

The conquistadors showed little respect for the natives and their traditions, meaning that little of their culture survived. Within a century their language had all but disappeared and today all that remain are a few odd words and numerous place names. The Guanches themselves were also under threat of extinction, what with murders, new diseases and their mixing with the Europeans.

Colonisation

Once the islands were all officially under control of Spain, the next problem facing Alonso de Lugo was their colonisation. The islands needed a government and a viable economy. Soon the *Cabildos* (Island Councils) were founded on Tenerife, Gran Canaria and La Palma. The other islands had their own town halls but were still governed by the lords rather than the Spanish crown. A series of laws was established, though since each island was self-governed there was plenty of autonomy (and no lack of corruption). The *Cabildos* were responsible for things like water supply, developing hospitals and ports, tax collection and providing incentives for new settlers, since the population increase was slow. This system remained in place until the 18th century when other less successful systems were tried out. The *Cabildos* returned in 1912, though they had little power and almost nothing in common with their 16th-century counterparts.

The 16th century – unwelcome visitors

The 16th century brought with it a new kind of trouble. The increasing success of the islands' ports and the considerable amount of maritime traffic passing through on its way to America and Africa brought new wealth to the islands; but it also brought disaster. The islands soon became a regular target for pirates and numerous towns were reduced to rubble in pirate attacks. In an attempt to overcome these attacks, Felipe II appointed a Captain General to co-ordinate the military efforts across the islands. Castles and towers began to shoot up on the coasts and hilltops but their success in warding off attack was limited to say the least.

Despite a slow start, the population of the islands grew steadily with many immigrants coming from Galicia, Andalucía and above all Portugal. In the absence of further slaves to sell, the Canary Islands needed a new pillar for their economy. The archipelago had almost nothing to trade and so the new settlers began to bring seeds and livestock from the continent. Sugar cane was introduced from Madeira and it soon became big business in Gran Canaria. Thanks to this bustling trade, Las Palmas's port began to thrive, leading some of the other islands to jump on the sugar-cane bandwagon. Competition from Africa and America in the mid 16th century brought the end of the sugar trade, but the islanders already had a plan B. The Portuguese had brought over the first vines earlier that century and by the late 1500s, a thriving wine trade existed between the Canary Islands and England.

17th and 18th centuries – vines and volcanoes

The vineyards thrived and the islands enjoyed a new prosperity. The demand for Canarian wine in England was great and this led to strong and unbreakable ties being formed between the two. The first British settlers arrived at Puerto de la Cruz in Tenerife in the middle of the 17th century and promptly tried to monopolise the wine trade. In 1666 the Garachico winemakers revolted, tipping the Brits' wine away and destroying their cellars. Frequent droughts, locust plagues and volcanic activity had seriously damaged other possible sources of income at the start of the century, so the islanders were grateful for the introduction of new crops from America, namely potatoes and corn. The former was to become a staple of the Canarios' diet and economy as well as an identifying part of their language (see box, page 21). This century also saw various publications on the Canary Islands. Following Leonardo Torriani's *Descripción de las islas Canarias* in 1590, came Juan de Abreu Galindo's *Historia de la conquista de las siete islas de Canaria* in 1602 and *Le Canarien*, the chronicle of Bethencourt's conquest, published in 1630.

Although the route to the New World had opened up trade for the islands, it also spelled disaster once the Americas were ready to do business. In the 1770s, Canarian wine merchants suffered the same fate as the sugar traders had a couple of centuries before. They simply couldn't compete with the American prices and the Canarian wine trade dwindled away. In desperation, thousands of the islanders emigrated to the New World searching a more prosperous life. Those who stayed behind had bigger things to worry about than market competition. Volcanic eruptions in Tenerife destroyed Güímar in 1704 and Garachico in 1706, the latter obliterating an important port and a good part of the town. Then 1730 saw the start of violent eruptions of Timanfaya in Lanzarote which lasted seven years. This brought disaster to the already poor farmers of the island, who would have to cope with unfertile land as well as the severe lack of water. Disheartened farmers from Fuerteventura and Lanzarote moved to the more prosperous western islands to replace those that had left for the Americas.

Towards the end of the century, the archipelago started to experience something of a cultural revolution, with the creation of the first local newspapers, the opening of the university in La Laguna, the creation of the first museums and an increasing number of schools, which had previously been available only to the privileged. This era is known as the 'golden century' for Canarians and produced a few illustrious writers such as historian José Viera y Clavijo. In 1799 botanist and explorer Alexander von Humboldt briefly passed through Tenerife on his way to Latin America. On seeing the Orotava Valley, he declared it 'the most enchanting view that eyes have ever seen'. His unabashed praise of the islands probably helped their popularity, with the first tourists arriving not long afterwards, though at this stage a trip to the Canaries was for the richest classes only.

19th century – internal conflict
With the pirates finally out of the way, the 19th century saw the start of an internal conflict that would remain alive in the Canary Islands until the present day – the bitter rivalry between Gran Canaria and Tenerife. Competition arose between the archipelago's two main cities, Las Palmas and Santa Cruz, with both vying to become capital of the province. The naming of Santa Cruz de Tenerife as capital in 1823 did nothing to alleviate the rivalry, although Gran Canaria temporarily abandoned its idea of becoming capital. Meanwhile, El Hierro, Fuerteventura, La Gomera and Lanzarote experienced a boost when the *señorios* were abandoned and they became part of the Canary Islands province. The land was distributed amongst the farmers and the descendants of the islands' first inhabitants were given the opportunity to work, meaning a better quality of life for all. The crops of the century were the banana and the tomato, both of which play an important role in the islands' economy today. Cochineal was also introduced, a parasitic beetle that lives on certain cactus plants and can be used to create a natural red dye. It thrived in Lanzarote and Fuerteventura and provided a short-term prosperity that the eastern islands had not experienced before. The cochineal boom reached its height in the middle of the century, but dropped off towards 1900 due to the introduction of manmade dyes. Lack of food and employment meant that emigration figures remained high in the second half of the century but, despite that, the population of the islands grew from 200,000 to a little over 350,000 by the start of the 20th century. Following the arrival of the first printing press in the 18th century, the islands finally got their own newspaper with the first copy of *El Guanche* printed in 1897. By the end of the century, tourism, which had been gradually developing in Puerto de la Cruz and Las Palmas, was becoming a viable part of the economy.

20th century – an economic saviour arrives?
The British presence in the islands increased with the maritime traffic and companies such as Fyffe's set up in Gran Canaria. World War I meant a cease in

maritime traffic, which created shortages of essential provisions and badly damaged the banana trade. But the 1920s brought fortune in the form of new governor Miguel Primo de Rivera. Supplies and road systems improved, new political parties emerged and in 1912 the *Cabildos* returned in the form that they take today. In 1936, the Spanish government exiled a right-wing soldier to Tenerife, fearful that he was plotting to set up a dictatorship and wanting to get him off the scene. Their plan wasn't successful though and in July of that year General Francisco Franco, along with a few allies, started an uprising. The repression began almost immediately, with teachers, writers, left-wing politicians and artists mysteriously disappearing. The Spanish Civil War lasted until 1939 and killed an estimated 350,000 Spaniards. Although the war had ended, times were still tough in the Canary Islands; the 1940s brought with them food shortages, rationing and a thriving black market

World War II created further troubles because of an Anglo–American plan to invade the islands and use them as a doorway into Africa and southern Europe. During this period the Canaries lost their usual trade partners in Europe and banana exports went solely to mainland Spain. Not until the 1960s did the Canarian economy pick up with the arrival of what would become the backbone of their economy for many years to come: tourism.

In 1982 the Canary Islands became an autonomous community and in an attempt to ease the rivalry between Las Palmas and Santa Cruz, the government base alternated between the two cities, creating two capitals. The population quadrupled in the 20th century, mainly due to a pause in emigration in the 1960s as jobs were now being created at home in tourism. For the first time, the islands were experiencing mass immigration thanks to a sudden stable economy and one that for once could probably stand outside competition, since there are few countries that can compete with the Canary Islands' weather.

GEOGRAPHY
Physical
The Canary Islands are made up of seven islands and six islets which lie off the west coast of Africa, the closest being just 100km from the Moroccan coast. They form a part of Macronesia (from the Greek Makaron Nesoi, meaning Fortunate Islands), along with the Azores, Madeira and the Cape Verde islands. The seven islands are all inhabited, as is one of the islets, La Graciosa, with a surface area of just 27km^2. The largest island is Tenerife at 2,034km^2 with the Roque del Oeste a mere pinprick in the ocean and totally devoid of life. The total area of the archipelago is 7,447km^2, covering a marine area of 100,000km^2. There are just 11km between the two closest islands, Lanzarote and Fuerteventura, while 400km separates Lanzarote from the baby of the group, El Hierro. The easternmost islands of Lanzarote and Fuerteventura have desert-like landscapes, with their highest peaks measuring 670m and 807m respectively. Their arid scrubland is a far cry from the pine and laurel forests scattered throughout the high peaks of the more westerly islands. The highest point in the archipelago is Mount Teide, also Spain's highest mountain at 3,718m. The height difference in the islands is an indicator of their age and the amount of erosion that has taken place. Perhaps if you pop back in 20 million years or so El Hierro will more closely resemble its big brother Fuerteventura.

There are few permanent sources of running water in the islands, though you can find year-round trickles in Caldera de Taburiente (La Palma), Barranco del Infierno (Tenerife), Barranco de Cernícalos (Gran Canaria) and Barranco del Cedro (La Gomera).

Social

The total population is almost 1,700,000, 5% of which are foreign residents. The islands are a favourite amongst northern Europeans, with 39% of the foreign residents originally from the UK and Germany. Around 13% are from Latin America and 5% from Morocco, though these are the official figures – there are thousands of illegal immigrants in the islands, most coming from Morocco, Senegal and Mauritania. In the '40s, '50s and '60s around 100,000 Canarians emigrated, but the same number of immigrants has arrived every five years since the 1980s.

Overpopulation is something of a problem; Gran Canaria is the most densely populated island, with 468 inhabitants per km², while El Hierro, the smallest island, has a mere 31 people per km². As an average, the archipelago has 224 inhabitants per km², almost three times the figure for mainland Spain. The rise in population since 1900 when the islands had just 49 inhabitants per km² is quite incredible. None of these figures account for the ten million tourists that visit the islands each year.

CLIMATE

'Eternal spring', 'the best climate in the world', 'always sunny'. There's no denying that the Canary Islands have the perfect climate and it's something that the holiday brochures won't let you forget. The climate is the reason for their unerring success as a tourist destination, providing a winter haven for northern Europeans seeking to escape the cold winters. And the ideal weather hasn't just recently been noticed; it was a contributing factor to the title of Fortunate Islands bestowed on the archipelago and the myth of the Garden of Hespérides. The average annual temperature is 25°C, with the mercury rarely rising above 35°C in summer or dropping below 18°C in winter. Average annual rainfall is 324mm, though this is considerably lower in the arid eastern isles.

Due to the location, just north of the Tropic of Cancer, you might well expect the weather to be hotter but a number of factors keep the climate pleasant without being uncomfortably warm. The main contributors are the trade winds, known as the *alisios*, which blow from the high-pressure area above the Azores and arrive loaded with humidity. On impact with the higher points of the Canary Islands (between 1,000 and 1,800m) they condense and form a cape of mist known as the *mar de nubes* ('sea of clouds'). You'll hear much talk of the *mar de nubes*, which keeps things humid below and allow certain types of vegetation to thrive. The effect of the *alisios* is more intense in the summer, when the high-pressure area is further from the Canaries. This is when the *panza de burro* ('donkey's belly') hangs over northern parts of the islands and stops the sun from appearing. Since Fuerteventura and Lanzarote aren't high enough to be affected by the *alisios*, it's rare to see clouds forming there and rainfall is particularly low. In the past, prolonged droughts, sometimes lasting years, have caused mass emigration and famines in the eastern islands.

Cold currents from the Gulf of Mexico also play their part in keeping the climate bearable. The cool seas keep coastal temperatures down and cool the air, stopping it from rising to form clouds, hence the low rainfall.

Other factors affecting the climate are warm winds blowing from the Sahara (sirocco), bringing hot weather and an unpleasant dust that lingers in the air and covers everything. This is known as *calima*, and locals joke that it happens when the Moroccans are doing their spring cleaning. Occasionally these winds also bring plagues of locusts and they always bring problems for asthma sufferers and leave you wondering if this is what the end of the world would look like. Winds blowing from the North Pole sprinkle the higher peaks (above 1,500m) with snow in winter, while winds from the tropical south sometimes bring heavy rains. While the rain is much needed, heavy downpours can cause chaos in the islands, quickly flooding roads and homes.

While the climate offers little variation throughout the year, there is a surprising amount of change within each island. If you're holidaying in Tenerife, don't be surprised if it's raining in La Laguna, cloudy in Santa Cruz and gloriously sunny in Candelaria. Take the advice of the citizens of La Palma – if the weather is not to your liking, change to the other side of the island and you'll surely find what you're looking for.

NATURAL HISTORY
Flora
David Bramwell, author of numerous books on Canarian flora, including Flora of the Canary Islands *(see Further Reading, page 333)*

The Canary Islands are something of a Lost World when it comes to their exceptional plants. Over 650 unique species grow only on the islands, a living museum descended from the flora of the Mediterranean extinguished thousands of years ago by the ice ages and the expanding Sahara Desert. Protected by the Atlantic Ocean they survived only on the Canaries and nearby islands and are now as biologically important and unique as the tortoises of the Galapagos Islands or the marsupials of Australia. Some, such as the Euphorbias, Echiums and Aeoniums or houseleeks have since diversified into a multitude of species growing in different niches on the islands. Others, such as the dragon trees, have remained largely unchanged for 20 million years.

There is a lot of truth in the statement that anything will grow on the Canaries provided it is watered. Literally thousands of cacti and aloes are cultivated in hotel gardens, parks and even on the roadsides. Bougainvillea, hibiscus, passion flowers and any number of creepers and shrubs thrive along with jacaranda, flame and palm trees. Many species have become naturalised on the islands, such as the prickly-pear cactus and agaves. Fruit trees are planted extensively and markets on the islands offer one of the widest range of fruit and vegetables anywhere.

Many species flower after the winter rains and before the hot, dry summer and this is when the islands become a mass of colours and scents. It is at this time that the true diversity of plantlife on the islands can be best appreciated. A drive around the islands at this time of year is a must-do activity for any visitor. Every small change in altitude or orientation produces a complete change in the plants present and almost every bend in the road will produce a new surprise. Here we provide a brief guide to the plants you may encounter.

Close to the sea, salt-tolerant species such as the sea lavender and Canary samphire dominate. Growing in the sand dunes are Canary palms and tamarisks and Fuerteventura even boasts a crocus that grows only in the sand dunes. Higher up, spurges predominate, especially the candlestick plant *Euphorbia canariensis* which protects more delicate species such as the *Sonchus*, or giant sow thistles, from grazing goats, the biggest threat to most Canary plants.

As the altitude increases the scrub zone gives way to lowland forests made up wild olive and Pistacia trees or junipers. This area harbours some spectacular plants such as *Convolvulus floridus*, a shrub that produces masses of white flowers and would be a star in any garden. Further up the forests become taller and are dominated by the Canarian laurels and other trees such as the strawberry tree. Shaded by the trees, cinerarias and foxgloves thrive along with the beautiful orange-flowered Canarian bellflower, *Canarina canariensis*. The laurel forests of La Gomera are so important that they have been declared a World Heritage Site by the UN.

On Gran Canaria, Tenerife, El Hierro and La Palma the mountains are covered by Canary pine trees growing in open, savanna-like forests. Brooms and trefoils grow in between the pines, which are vital to the islands as their long needles collect water from the frequent mists. Large areas of pine forest were chopped down in the past but reforestation projects are slowly replacing what was lost.

Above the pines we come to the high mountain zone, dominated by brooms, flixweeds, scabiouses, daisies and a range of other endemic plants such as *Echium wildepretti* from Tenerife, which produces a huge spike of red flowers during the spring. At the highest altitudes almost nothing grows except for the tiny Tenerife violet which has to put up with snow and ice during the winter and summer temperatures of up to 40°C.

Plants to watch out for

The aeoniums or rock roses are a Canarian speciality. Well over 30 species of these strange plants with their rosettes of fleshy leaves grow on the islands. Some, such as *Aeonium gomerense,* grow only on a tiny patch of a single island while others grow extensively over large areas. Many species produce huge yellow, white or red inflorescences.

The echiums or viper's buglosses are another exceptional group of plants on the islands. About 25 species are known and some are now cultivated in gardens all over the world for their attractive hairy leaves and spectacular white, blue or purple flowers. Echium flowers attract large numbers of butterflies and bees to feed on their nectar.

The spurges are a very varied group of succulent plants that grow all over the Canaries. While euphorbias species are typically desert and scrubland plants, *Euphorbia mellifera* from Tenerife, La Palma and La Gomera is a forest species that grows into a tree up to 15m high. More typical are the cactus-like *Euphorbia canariensis* and *Euphorbia handiensis,* the latter growing only in the south of Fuerteventura and is now close to extinction. All spurges produce poisonous, milky sap if damaged and should not be handled.

A few years ago a brand-new species of dragon tree, *Dracaena tamaranae*, was discovered in the mountains of Gran Canaria and instantly became one of the rarest trees on Earth. There are only about 20 growing on the island, all on inaccessible cliff ledges. The more common Canary dragon tree, *Dracaena draco*, has now been planted extensively in parks and gardens on the islands. It can be recognised easily thanks to its rotund trunk and branches, and rosettes of long, triangular leaves. Every few years, each tree produces bunches of orange fruits which are used on the islands as a treatment for coughs. The huge dragon tree at Icod de Los Vinos on Tenerife is thought to be thousands of years old.

Sea daisies, daisies and tansies are all small shrubs that produce masses of yellow or white flowers. For all their beauty many grow only in tiny areas and are threatened in the wild by overgrazing by goats and building work in their habitats. Fortunately, many are now grown in gardens around the world.

For almost 120 years the red-flowered dove's bill, *Lotus berthelotii,* from the pine forest cliffs of the island of Tenerife, was the only known member of its group. In 1970, however, a second, yellow-orange flowered species, *L. maculates,* was discovered on the northern sea cliffs of the same island. Now four of these beautiful ground-covering plants are known and can be seen growing in gardens and along the roadsides of most of the islands.

Fauna
Alex Bramwell

The animals of the Canaries are a curious mix of the African and the European. Garden favourites like the blue tit and goldfinch live alongside decidedly more exotic birds like the Egyptian vulture and the hoopoe. In the sea, whales are abundant and turtles visit regularly to feed along with huge schools of tuna fish and some of the biggest marlin and swordfish in the world.

Birds

The Canaries are an important breeding site for a number of seabirds such as shearwaters and petrels. The small islets of the Chinijo Archipelago off northern Lanzarote are also one of the few breeding sites of the enigmatic Eleonora's falcon. This colonial hawk takes advantage of the mass of migrating songbirds passing through the islands during the spring to feed its young and then migrates to faraway Madagascar to pass the winter.

The most famous birds of the islands are the blue chaffinches and laurel pigeons. Two closely related races of the blue chaffinch live in the pine forests of Gran Canaria and Tenerife, relying heavily on the pines for food and shelter. These beautiful slate-blue birds, larger than the European chaffinch, have suffered from the felling of these forests and the Gran Canaria race is close to extinction. The two laurel pigeon species, superficially resembling wood pigeons, live in the laurel forests of Tenerife and the western islands and are probably the last survivors of a once widespread species. Other unique birds include Meade-waldo's stonechat, a small, charismatic bird found only on Fuerteventura, the Canarian chiffchaff, common on all the islands, the fast-running Berthelot's pipit, the plain swift and of course the canary. Rather than the bright yellow creature familiar as a caged bird, the wild canary is a green-brown bird and only the males have a bright yellow breast. Their beautiful song, however, is instantly recognisable.

On the dry, stony plains of Lanzarote and Fuerteventura we find a selection of very African birds such as the Houbara bustard, cream-coloured courser and black-bellied sandgrouse. Flocks of trumpeter bullfinch also range over these islands searching for seeds and stopping to drink at the few streams that flow in the barrancos. Parrots, waxbills, mynah birds, guineafowl and even an ibis have been introduced to the islands in recent years, giving the Canaries an exotic touch without as yet harming any of the native species.

Mammals and reptiles

Except for bats and a tiny, recently discovered shrew there are no native mammals on the islands, although rats, mice, hedgehogs, cats, rabbits, wild sheep and even a ground squirrel have been introduced by man. Niches occupied elsewhere by small mammals are taken up in the Canaries by a range of lizards, skinks and geckos. The geckos are often seen feeding on walls close to streetlights at night and have the ability to change colour to suit their background. The giant Gran Canaria lizard remains common and can be seen almost anywhere on the island basking in the sun. Similar lizards, all of which grew to over 50cm, were feared to have died out on the other islands due to predation by cats and rats. However, tiny populations of these lizards have recently been rediscovered on cliffs in Tenerife, La Gomera and El Hierro. The La Gomera lizard, which has a pure white belly, is the rarest as only about ten have ever been found. Fortunately they are now being bred in captivity and their habitats protected.

Insects and invertebrates

Among the smaller wildlife, praying mantises lurk in the bushes and large flightless beetles wander through the dunes. There are thousands of endemic insects and other invertebrates, including the islands' only poisonous animal: a nocturnal and rarely seen centipede. Large orange-and-black monarch butterflies, which colonised the islands from America, the white African migrant and familiar red admirals and painted ladies visit flowers in parks and gardens. On Lanzarote, at Los Jameos de Agua, a colony of pure white blind crabs lives only in one small pool inside a lava tube.

Cetaceans

Up to 26 species of whale and dolphin have been seen around the Canary Islands, more than almost anywhere else on Earth. The waters between La Gomera and Tenerife boast a colony of about 500 short-finned pilot whales which grow up to 7m long, as well as regular sightings of sperm whales and the rare and little-known beaked whales. This has made boat trips out to see these whales increasingly popular and conservationists have warned that the whales may be being disturbed or even harmed. There are now strict regulations preventing boats from approaching the whales too closely and anyone wanting to see the whales should be sure to choose a licensed boat supervised by trained guides.

Other sealife

Under water there is a whole other world waiting to be discovered by snorkellers and scuba divers, with 553 documented species of fish in the Canarian seas. Barracuda, moray eels and brightly coloured parrot fish are common along with a myriad of small and brightly coloured wrasse and damsel fish. In ports and harbours look out for grey mullet with their white lips and the plumper salemas, with fine yellow stripes. Close to the harbour walls, bright blue damsel fish and the multicoloured peacock wrasse will be in evidence, along with white-faced Atlantic blennies and the occasional puffer or triggerfish. The lucky may even spot an octopus tentacle protruding from a cave or even the ugly head of a moray eel! There are sharks in these waters, though not dangerous ones. Hammerhead sharks are a common sight off the coast of La Gomera in summer and elsewhere you're most likely to spot the angel shark. There are five species of turtle to be found in the seas surrounding the Canary Islands, all on the endangered list. The green turtle (*Chelonia mydas*) is the most common though if you're particularly lucky you might get to see a loggerhead turtle (*Caretta caretta*), Kemp's Ridley turtle (*Lepidochelys kempi*), hawksbill turtle (*Eretmochelys imbricata*) or leathery turtle (*Dermochelys coriacea*). The main threat to these creatures comes from fishing and they are often caught in nets or found dead on the shore, with hooks lodged in their mouths.

ECOLOGY AND CONSERVATION

Pollution is not a serious issue in the Canary Islands and other than the two petrol refineries, the ecologists have little cause to complain on this score. The biggest problems are overpopulation and uncontrolled construction, particularly in Gran Canaria and Tenerife. It's not uncommon to see slogans such as '*Canarias tiene un límite, ni una cama turística más*' ('Canaries have a limit, not one more tourist bed') in protest to the out-of-control building projects in tourist resorts.

The other big problem is the lack of water, especially in the eastern islands where rainfall is particularly low. Desalination in the islands accounts for 2% of the world's desalinated water (almost all tap water on Fuerteventura and Lanzarote is refined sea water). Rainfall is low and more than half of it evaporates, leaving the Canarians to invent ever-more ingenious ways of preserving the water they have left. And as if the lack of water wasn't enough, in the summer months forest fires ravage all but Lanzarote and Fuerteventura, where there are no trees to destroy.

According to ecology association Ben-Magec, 75% of the archipelago's endemic flora is endangered and the organisation spearheads campaigns to protect the natural environment. There are also a few endangered reptiles, such as the giant lizards in El Hierro, La Gomera and Tenerife and all five species of tortoise found in the islands' waters. The main threats to the islands' flora and fauna are destruction of habitat and the introduction of foreign species, such as wild cats, Barbary sheep and squirrels. On the up side, there are recuperation projects under way for the particularly endangered El Hierro giant lizard (*Gallotia simonyi machadoi*) and the Houbara bustard (*Chlamydotis undulata fuertaventurae*), found in the eastern islands. Other species which have prompted conservation programmes are the Gran Canaria blue chaffinch and the Tenerife great spotted woodpecker whose habitats are slowly being destroyed by the annual forest fires. The monk seal (*Monachus monachus*), which once swam in the waters around Isla de Lobos, disappeared from these waters long ago but a current plan hopes to reintroduce the species. There are currently small colonies of the seal in Madeira and Mauritania, though with just 500 examples in the world it's considered one of our most endangered marine mammals.

And it's not the only sea mammals that cause concern. While whale- and dolphin-watching excursions may be a good money-spinner, they pose a threat to the 26 species of cetacean that frequent the waters south of Tenerife. Be wary of unscrupulous companies who get too close.

Four of Spain's ten national parks are in the Canary Islands and an impressive 42% of the archipelago's total area falls under some level of protection (national parks, nature parks, special or integrated nature reserves, protected landscapes, natural monuments, rural parks and sites of scientific interest). The Parque Nacional de Timanfaya in Lanzarote has the highest level of protection, with much of the park off-limits to visitors.

GOVERNMENT AND POLITICS

The Canary Islands are split into two provinces: Gran Canaria, Lanzarote and Fuerteventura belong to the province of Las Palmas, while Tenerife, La Palma, La Gomera and El Hierro form the Santa Cruz province. Together they make up one of Spain's autonomous communities. The administration within the islands is complex and gives rise to nightmarish bureaucracy where nothing ever gets done as no-one is sure who's job it is. Each town has an *ayuntamiento* (town hall) for deciding local matters such as road works, parks, public resources etc. The *Cabildo* (island council) on each island co-ordinates the work of the town halls and deals with the economic interests of the island. The *Gobierno de Canarias* deals with the legislation of education, culture, fiestas, public health, social services, works and so on but there is generally plenty of overlap between the three levels, meaning you never quite know in which office you should be.

Police

There are three types of police officer in Spain: the Guardia Civil, the Policía Nacional and the Policía Local. The Guardia Civil dress in green uniforms and occupy themselves with matters in the countryside, speeding drivers and prisons. The Policía Nacional cover large cities and deal with serious crime such as terrorism, drug pushing and murder. Hopefully, you'll have no cause to deal with them unless you want to stay in Spain – they also deal with foreigners' paperwork. The Policía Local can be found in smaller cities, towns and villages and deal with minor offences like traffic and parking. They also patrol the beaches, dressed for the part in shorts, baseball caps and trainers. These are the guys you'll most likely speak to if you should have anything stolen. Where relevant, the locations of police stations for all three strands are given in this book, just so that you can head for the closest in a real emergency.

ECONOMY

Throughout the years, the islands have relied on various exports as a means of income. When the Spanish arrived the only commodity they could find was people, so a bustling slave trade emerged in the 15th century. After the conquest, slaves were replaced with a new commodity: sugar cane, brought to the islands from Madeira by Pedro de Vera. Sugar exports reached their peak in the mid 16th century when the islands were known briefly as the Sugar Islands. Competition from Africa and Latin America meant that the Canaries had to think of a plan B, so they turned their hand to wine production. The first vines had been transported to the islands in the 15th century by the Portuguese and by the end of the century Canarian wine was in great demand, particularly in England where it had been given the seal of approval by Shakespeare, Defoe and Lord Byron amongst others. Once again, stiff competition meant that the not-so-fortunate islands had to look elsewhere for income. In the 18th century, potatoes, tomatoes and bananas were introduced from Latin America and became important exports. Wine made a short-lived comeback in the 19th century, though the commodity of the century was cochineal, a parasitic beetle used as a natural dye.

These days the archipelago still exports large number of tomatoes, bananas and potatoes, but there is no arguing that the main pillar of the economy is tourism. The perfect climate and dramatic landscape mean that it's unlikely that the islands will have to search for a new industry any time soon. In the past the islands have relied rather too much on package deals and the horrors of certain resorts are testament to this, but rural tourism is gradually taking off and the islands are slowly becoming known as a perfect golf destination.

Industry in the islands is weak due to the lack of natural resources and inconvenient transport links. The main industries are construction, drinks and tobacco, with the vast majority of industry (80%) concentrated in Gran Canaria and Tenerife.

PEOPLE AND CULTURE
People

> You may travel the world and will be hard pressed to find anywhere
> people more handsome and striking than those of the islands, men and
> women both, to say nothing of their fine understanding, which only needs
> cultivating.

So wrote Padres Bontier and Le Verrier, the chroniclers of Bethencourt's expedition, of the aboriginal inhabitants. Although there's not much of the aboriginal culture to be seen these days, Canarians are still a personable lot, applying a laid-back Latin American attitude to life. You'll find the people friendly, though their insular way of life means it can sometimes be difficult to infiltrate a group. That said, once you are in you can be sure that you've found a group of friends for life.

Though elements of their early traditions remain, there's no arguing that the culture is Spanish. Saying hello is a complicated business. Some Canarians greet with just one kiss (on the right cheek), while others stick with the Spanish standard of two kisses. This can cause embarrassment as you go in for the second kiss and the other person steps away, or you retreat after the first kiss and they grab you for a second. It's the norm to kiss everyone on arrival, so just as you've done the rounds, someone else arrives and you have to start again. Just saying *hola* can be a lengthy process in the Canary Islands and then you have to go through the same rigmarole when people start leaving.

Language

The language is Spanish (or Castilian), though with some peculiarities. Aside from the variations in vocabulary (see box), the grammar and pronunciation differ somewhat from Spanish spoken on the mainland. Canarians eat the *s* at the end of a word, or in the middle if followed by a consonant, but not completely. It becomes what they call an aspirated *s*, sounding similar to an *h*, so the ubiquitous potato side order becomes *papah arrugadah* and you wouldn't be the first to get confused between the island of La Palma and the city of *Lah Palmah*. They also avoid the lisping pronunciation of *c* and *z*, so *gracias* is pronounced *grasias*, rather than *grathias* as it would be on the mainland. If you're used to mainland Spanish, you'll notice that Canarians don't use the *vosotros* form (plural version of 'you'). Instead they opt for the *ustedes* form, usually reserved for talking to groups of

PAPAS *AND* GUAGUAS

Although the islanders speak Spanish (or Castilian), it sometimes has more similarities with the South American language than that of mainland Spain. As well as the pronunciation and grammatical differences mentioned above, there are a few quirks in the Canarian vocabulary. You wouldn't be the first person to feel a little silly asking what time the next *guagua* (pronounced *wawa*) leaves, but if you want to be accepted by the locals, avoid the mainland terminology (*autobus*). No-one is quite sure where the local word for 'bus' came from, but a reasonable theory is that it was brought over from Cuba with an influx of immigrants. The Canarians' Caribbean counterparts used to use the word 'wagon' to talk about public transport and there aren't many steps from wagon to *wawa*, if you allow for a bit of laziness and odd pronunciation.

Odd words, such as *gofio* and *baifo* (young goat), date back to Guanche times, while others have found their way into the local language from other countries. Throughout the islands' long relationship with Britain, a few English words have seeped into the language, although with Spanish spelling. On their birthdays, Canarians blow out the candles on their *queque* and cut it into slices using a *naife*.

If there's one other word that's emblematic of the Canarians it's *papas*. Potatoes arrived on Canarian shores from Peru, where they were known as *papas*. This presented something of a problem for Catholic Spain, since *papa* is the Castilian word for pope. The powers that be agreed that it wasn't acceptable to call a vegetable by the same name as the head of the Catholic Church and came up with *patatas*. Always keen to maintain their distance from the mainland, the Canary Islands stuck with *papas* and it's become something of an identifying word for them. When referring to the islanders' often lax pronunciation, mainlanders say that they talk *con papas en la boca*, presumably meaning that they sound as though they have potatoes in their mouths, not the head of their Church...

If you're ever stuck for something to say in the Canary Islands, you need learn just one word: *chacho*. It's a shortening of the word *muchacho* (boy) but its meaning stretches much further. To sum up, a local joke goes something like this: A mainlander sees someone sitting on his car and says 'Hey, what are you doing on my car mate? Please get off as I would like to use it' while if a Canarian sees a stranger on his bonnet he says 'chacho chacho chacho'!

strangers. It is widely agreed that the Herreños speak the 'best' Spanish, perhaps because their society has received fewer immigrants throughout the years.

For basic words and phrases, see *Appendix 1*, page 327.

Religion

As in the rest of Spain, the religion of the Canary Islands is overwhelmingly Catholic. Of course, they weren't always God-fearing citizens; the Guanches appeared to have beliefs which included rainmaking and fertility rites, with the pretext for the conquest being to convert the heathen natives into good Catholic citizens. Though many Canarians are baptised and confirmed, less than half go to church for anything other than weddings and funerals. These days Sunday's most popular meeting point is the football ground.

Festivals

Canarians really know how to enjoy themselves and there's no lack of fiestas on any of the islands. One of my favourite things is that you can always find some kind of party or gig happening and the climate allows year-round music concerts in the open air. Each town has its special *romería* (pilgrimage), an all-day party that starts with traditional dancing followed by a procession and then the all-important late, late *verbena* (street party). Most people dig out their traditional costume for the event, though you won't be frowned upon if you don't partake. Undoubtedly the biggest party is carnival and there's nowhere better to experience it than Santa Cruz de Tenerife (although some Gran Canarians would disagree). A month of partying sees *comparsas* (dance troops) and *murgas* (off-key chants with saucy lyrics, usually

FIESTAS – THE WEIRD AND THE WONDERFUL

It won't take you long to realise that the Canarians love a good party but what you might not notice straight away is just how odd some of those parties are. The islanders seem to have something of a penchant for throwing things at each other and the messier the better. If there's nothing on hand to throw, they're not adverse to hitting each other for fun either. Here's a run down of a few peculiar parties you might like to attend (though perhaps not!):

Lomo Magullo is the unlikely location for one of Gran Canaria's craziest fiestas, the **Traída del Agua** ('the Bringing of the Water'). The streets (all two of them) of this tiny village are packed full of young people with only one thing on their mind – getting as wet as possible. It's basically a five-hour water fight, with people using anything from an empty beer can to a pesticide container (not necessarily rinsed out) to soak their fellow revellers. Although its origins are in a Guanche rainmaking ritual, the party took its present form in the 1970s. If you want to partake, get your water pistol ready in the second week of August (the date changes annually).

The **Fiesta del Charco** in Playa de la Aldea (Gran Canaria) is another one for water babies. The pond, usually devoid of marine life, is filled with fish and revellers jump in, trying to catch as many fish as possible using their hands. It's celebrated on September 11.

If throwing water isn't messy enough, perhaps the **Traída del Gofio** in Agüimes (Gran Canaria) is more your style. The theme is similar to that of Lomo Magullo's festival but includes a healthy portion of *gofio* just to make it a bit messier. It starts with a traditional procession and ends with a late *verbena* (street party). Catch it on the last Saturday in September.

of a political nature and particularly difficult to understand). Later in the festivities you can witness the crowning of the senior citizens' queen, the children's queen, the overall carnival queen and the ever-popular drag queen. Children and parents enjoy the spectacle of the *cabalgata* (parade), while the 20-somethings prefer to celebrate in the *mogollón* (a street party with makeshift bars). Each island generally celebrates carnival at a slightly different time so you can continue partying for six weeks if you so desire. La Palma's carnival celebrations are also well known and lots of fun. *Semana Santa* (Easter) sees sombre processions making their way through the streets while Corpus Christi is celebrated with impressive flower-petal carpets, a tradition that's been all but lost on the mainland. The best places to see these magnificent works of performance art are Mazo in La Palma and La Laguna and La Orotava in Tenerife. Other fiestas celebrated across the archipelago are Kings' Day on January 6, where the three kings ride through the towns on camels, throwing sweets to the crowds; the Fiestas del Carmen (patron saint of sailors) on July 16 and San Juan on June 24. Each island has its own big events, which are described in the individual island chapters.

Architecture

Things have certainly changed since the conquerors arrived and found the Guanches living in a combination of natural and manmade caves or a few ramshackle houses (see box, page 25). It's tricky to specify what is 'typical Canarian architecture' since Spanish, Portuguese, British and Flemish influences have all played their part. There are often different styles represented in one building – perhaps the back of the church is Gothic, but then pirates ransacked

On September 29, the small town of Valsequillo celebrates the San Miguel festival in which you can see the **Suelta del Perro Maldito** (literally, 'the Release of the Cursed Dog'). This 200-year old battle between good and evil sees the normally deserted streets filled with people dressed as the Grim Reaper and the devil, prancing around to a soundtrack of impressive fireworks. Devilishly good fun.

It's not only Canariones that like getting messy. In Santa Cruz de La Palma, **carnival** takes on an unusual theme. While dressed up as Palmeros returning from Latin America, the whole city, young and old, throws talc at each other all night to the tune of Cuban salsa music. It's said that the origins of this whiteout lie in the 19th century when a boat carrying sacks of flour had to unload in the port as its cargo was going off. Locals decided the flour might as well be used for something and incorporated it into their carnival celebrations.

Carnival in Tenerife and Gran Canaria might have all the fame, but they're never going to make it on to the oddball fiesta list. Not true for the pre-Lent celebrations in Teguise on Lanzarote, where people dressed as devils terrorise locals, hitting them with a goatskin whip.

Just down the road in the island's capital, Arrecife, carnival includes the scary-sounding **Parranda de los Buches**. In this winner of the weird festivals Oscars, seafarers whack onlookers with dried, inflated fish bladders.

Another carnival oddity is in Frontera, El Hierro: the **Fiesta del Carnero**. If you've ever had a yearning to see Canarian men wearing dried sheepskins (usually of the stinky variety) and running after townsfolk, this is your fiesta. If you avoid being charged at by the madman, you probably won't be so lucky at dodging the black dye that the shepherds hurl at onlookers.

the front and it was rebuilt in baroque style. This makes it rather difficult to categorise the buildings in terms of style and they are generally talked about in terms of usage.

Civic architecture
Military
The archipelago's location has always made it appeal to travellers, though they weren't always such a friendly bunch. When pirates were frequenting the islands, numerous towers and castles were constructed, in a generally not very successful attempt to ward off the bandits. They were rough, thick-walled constructions, usually with a lookout point at the corners. The finest examples of military architecture are on Lanzarote and Fuerteventura, such as Arrecife's Castillo de San José and Castillo de San Gabriel and the Castillo de El Tostón in El Cotillo. Las Palmas has the Castillo de la Luz, while the ruins of the Castillo de San Andrés near Santa Cruz de Tenerife are interesting. However, the most striking example was built not to deter pirates, but to save the island's governors from rioting Guanches. The Torre del Conde in San Sebastián de La Gomera was built in the 15th century and is the island's most emblematic building. Most of the military structures are open to the public and many double as some form of museum or art gallery.

Religious
Many of the churches and hermitages date from the 16th and 17th centuries and contain a mixture of styles. If you want to get a good overall view, La Laguna and La Orotava in Tenerife have an excellent variety of well-maintained religious buildings from different eras. If you're looking for something more specific, the interior of the Catedrál de Santa Ana in Las Palmas is the best example of Gothic style (or Atlantic Gothic as it is known) and the Iglesia de Santa Maria in Betancuria (Fuerteventura) is an *almost* pure piece of baroque architecture, rebuilt in the 17th century. Some of the most photographed religious buildings are much more recent, such as the ever-impressive Iglesia de San Juan in Arucas (Gran Canaria). While it may look like the real thing, the church was actually built in 1917 in neo-Gothic style. There are some fine Flemish paintings and sculptures within the islands' churches, especially in La Palma.

Urban architecture
Balconies and patios
The most emblematic aspects of Canarian architecture are the internal patios and wooden balconies. Examples of the latter can be seen scattered around most towns, though the finest are certainly in Santa Cruz de La Palma. Early rural houses were very basic, often with just one room and a rudimentary straw roof. Few examples of this type of home remain, though there are a few traditional *pueblos* in El Hierro. The richer classes started to build houses with two floors in the 16th century and this is when the balconies and patios made their debut. By the 18th century these types of dwelling were more widespread and many homes, both urban and rural, sported impressive balconies. Wood became an integral part of Canarian construction and some of the carved balconies, doors and stairways you'll see are true works of art. The balconies vary considerably from island to island – in Las Palmas's Vegueta barrio they tend not to have roofs, as in Lanzarote where the style is much simpler. Some are painted in bright colours, while others have a more natural appearance. Other than the Avenida Marítima in Santa Cruz de La Palma, there are superb examples in La Laguna and La Orotava (Tenerife) and Teror (Gran Canaria).

The 1960s

Since the 1960s a rather less picturesque style of architecture has dominated the landscape – tower blocks. Although there are some that are relatively pleasant to look at, the majority are ugly masses of brick and glass but a necessary part of life on the densely populated islands. The construction-mania in the tourist resorts has long been a cause of concern and most agree that the high-rise hotels are a serious blot on the landscape. An exception to the rule is Puerto de Mogán in Gran Canaria. It's a low complex, draped in bougainvillea and built in the 1980s. Unfortunately, by then it was already too late for most resorts and two-floor hotels wouldn't come close to housing the 10 million tourists that descend on the islands each year.

Of course, not all architecture took the form of 20-floor towers. It was around this time that Lanzaroteño artist César Manrique returned to his home soil and began to put Lanzarote on the map. His penchant for using natural materials to create structures in line with their surroundings earned him the name 'the ecological artist' and led to the island being used as a model for sustainable tourism. His finest works are the Jameos del Agua and his own house, built around five lava caves and now open to visitors. On other islands he built the Parque Marítimo in Santa Cruz de Tenerife, the Lago Martiánez in Puerto de la Cruz , the Mirador de la Peña in El Hierro and the Mirador de Palmarejo in Valle Gran Rey (La Gomera). Manrique's vision was to work in harmony with nature, rather than creating sculptures that destroyed their surroundings. The trademark of his work is the use of volcanic materials, easily found in the Canarian archipelago.

Painting and sculpture

Aboriginal art

The finest example of aboriginal art is to be found in the Cueva Pintada (Painted Cave) in Gáldar, northern Gran Canaria. It's a series of brightly coloured geometrical

CAVE LIVING

The early Canarians were blessed with rugged mountains lined with countless caves so they felt no need to construct their own dwellings. The caves were used not only as living quarters but also as tombs. The latter were generally located far away from the settlements – at the top of cliffs or at the end of ravines. In Lanzarote people took advantage of the volcanic landscape and lived underground in the many tunnels and *jameos* that flowing lava had created. However, when the conquerors arrived they were surprised to find a mixture of caves and clumsily constructed stone houses. Throughout the years, new immigrants had arrived and brought with them knowledge of construction, but although the different settlers learned from each other in certain respects, they also maintained their own traditions. Archaeologist Diego Cuscoy recorded: 'The cave dwellers lie alongside the house dwellers and burial sites in caves alongside burials in tombs.'

There are plenty of opportunities to visit caves around the islands: Cueva de Belmaco in La Palma is a natural cave with some well-preserved stone etchings – it is now a museum. Gran Canaria has the finest selection, both manmade and natural. Examples of both are to be found near the rim of the Bandama crater, while Cuatro Puertas, near Telde, is one of the most impressive manmade caves in the archipelago. The carefully decorated Cueva Pintada ('Painted Cave') in Gáldar may have been a royal residence and don't miss the Cenobio de Valerón, an ancient grain store in the north of the island.

shapes painted on to the walls of a large cave. The site was uncovered in the mid 19th century, though it's not known when the designs were etched. Generally, the Guanches seemed to prefer carving their designs on to rocks and there are engravings from different eras across the islands. The most notable sites are El Júlan in El Hierro, La Zarza and Cueva de Belmaco in La Palma and Montaña Tindaya in Fuerteventura. Their most common etchings were spirals and semicircles and to date no-one has managed to work out their meaning. Aboriginal art still serves as an identifier for Canarians and the designs that the Guanches scraped on to their cave walls are frequently seen emblazoned across T-shirts or crafted into necklaces.

On certain islands, the pottery could also be considered a work of art, particularly on Gran Canaria and La Palma, where great care was taken to add patterns to the pots. The finest sculpture from Guanche times is the Ídolo de Tara, found in Gran Canaria. It's a curvy feminine figure and much has been made of the importance of women in Guanche society because of this idol.

Early artists

For many years after the conquest, art in the Canary Islands was imported from other lands, notably Belgium. There are fine examples of Flemish paintings and sculptures in Canarian churches, and it wasn't until the late 17th century that the islands began to produce their own works of art. Gaspar de Quevedo (1616–?) is generally considered to be the archipelago's first artist, with Juan de Miranda (1723–1805) following soon after. They both produced religious paintings, with de Miranda's *La Adoración de los Pastores* (the adoration of the shepherds) standing above the rest. It is housed in the Iglesia de la Concepción in Santa Cruz de Tenerife. One of the first painters to move away from religious art was Gumersindo Robayna (1829–98). He painted some fascinating pictures depicting key events in the conquest which are now a permanent fixture in the Museo de Bellas Artes in Santa Cruz de Tenerife.

The 20th century

The 20th century was an altogether more fruitful period for Canarian art. Gran Canarian Néstor de la Torre (1887–1938) was one of the first artists of the new century and is the islands' most important modernist painter. Above all he produced some extraordinary murals, which can be seen in the Museo Néstor in Las Palmas. Later artists showed regionalist tendencies, such as Fuerteventura's Jorge Oramas (1911–35). His colourful depictions of Canarian villages clinging to cliffs have been defined as 'magic realism'; most of his works now belong to private collectors. Antonio Padrón (1920–68) managed to convey the essence of Canarian country life in his expressionist paintings and sculptures which are on show in a museum dedicated to the artist in his birthplace, Gáldar (Gran Canaria). Felo Monzón (1910–89) also started out as an expressionist painter but progressed to surrealism, perhaps spurred on by Óscar Domínguez (1906–57), the Canarian surrealist painter *par excellence*. The latter's work was included in Spain's first surrealist art exhibition and is well known outside the archipelago. Although more often thought of as a sculptor or architect, César Manrique (1919–92) also painted some magnificent abstract works, such as *Mil años de Jable*. The finest abstract artist is considered to be Manolo Millares (1926–72). His paintings and sculptures are heavily influenced by aboriginal art, with spirals being an integral element.

Sculpture

A striking thing about the Canary Islands is the number of sculptures to be found in the streets, parks, squares and on city roundabouts. They are generally crafted by local artists and provide something to look at when you're trapped in city traffic. While the islands boast a fair number of sculptors today, plenty of years passed after the conquest before the first emerged.

Many of the religious sculptures you'll see in Canarian churches are Flemish, although the islanders have turned out a couple of statues of their own. Luján Pérez (1756–1815) was the first and certainly the most important local sculptor. His finest works are *El Cristo de la Sala Capitular* in Las Palmas's cathedral and *El Cristo de la Columna*, found in the church in Teror (Gran Canaria). Other pieces can be seen in churches in La Laguna, Puerto de la Cruz and in various towns around Gran Canaria. His student Fernando Estévanez (1788–1854) continued the tradition of fine religious sculpture. His work showed neoclassical influences and his best is the dark-skinned figure of *Nuestra Señora de la Candelaria*, housed in the church of the same name (Tenerife). Other sculptors of note are modernists Eduardo Gregorio (1903–74) and Plácido Fleitas (1915–72). Their work was heavily influenced by aboriginal art and rural Canarian life.

Nowadays, the best known Canarian sculptor is Martín Chirino, born in 1925. He often uses the Canarian symbol, the spiral, as a base for his art, though his most famous pieces are a series of sculptures called the *Ladies*. These huge iron figures can be seen at key points throughout the islands, such as *Lady Harimaguada* which guards the entrance of Las Palmas. Deserving a third mention is César Manrique, whose sculptures are dotted around his native island, Lanzarote. The most famous is the Monumento al Campesino, a tribute to Lanzarote's farmers which sits in the centre of the island.

Handicrafts and public art

The craftwork on the islands is excellent and much of it could be classed as works of art. The Canaries are famed for their excellent embroidered tablecloths, found in La Orotava (Tenerife), Ingenio (Gran Canaria) and Mazo (La Palma). El Paso (La Palma) is the place for intricate handmade silk goods and basketry is excellent across the archipelago. Sticking close to their roots, the women of El Cercado (La Gomera) turn out some excellent imitation Guanche pottery and carpenters in Teguise (Lanzarote) make the finest *timples* (small string instrument similar to a ukelele, a symbol of the Canary Islands).

Most of the islands' festivals could be classed as works of art, but none more so than carnival, when the streets become a stage and every citizen a player. Finally, the stunning Corpus Christi carpets, made with flower petals and volcanic earth, are the ultimate in street art.

Literature

The Canary Islands' first step into literature is relatively recent, since the Guanches appeared to have no knowledge of writing. That said, Leonardo Torriani in his description of the islands transcribed some of the natives' songs and poems, which survive to this day. The first recorded poem in the Canary Islands' history was known as *Las Endechas a Guillén Peraza*, a melancholy verse written after Peraza's bloody death attempting to conquer La Palma. The archipelago has long had a tradition of songs and poems which have been passed down through generations but never written. Throughout the years, there has always been a high level of illiteracy, so while songs and poems existed, it would be years before they were recorded.

The first written passages about the islands were written by the priests who chronicled the conquest and their work, *Le Canarien*, is considered one of the most important in the islands' history. Another painstaking early work was Torriani's

16th-century *Descripción de las Islas Canarias*, which he wrote based on the chronicles of the conquest (although the former was actually published first). Juan de Abreu Galindo finished his *Historia de la Conquista de las Siete Islas de Canaria* in the early 17th century.

The islands' first poet was priest Bartolomé Cairasco (1538–1610), known for his religious and epic poems. Antonio de Viana (1578–?) combined history, legend and a touch of imagination to produce some excellent prose and poetry with true Canarian roots. His masterpiece was *Antigüedades de las Islas Afortunadas*, whose main theme was the conquest of Tenerife.

Tinerfeño José de Viera y Clavijo (1731–1813) wrote poetry but is better known for his meticulous work, *Noticias de la Historia General de Canarias*, an excellent account of the islands' history, which took 20 years to complete. His fellow islander Tomás de Iriarte (1750–91) was best known for his *Fábulas Literarias* and is considered the top fable writer in Spanish literature. Another Tinerfeño, José Plácido Sansón (1815–75) was an instigator in the Canarian romanticism movement. His poetry covered many topics, though he's most noted for his verses about Guanche heroes such as Bencomo. This patriotism for the islands led to the beginnings of a new type of poetry known as regionalism. Probably the most important poet in this school was Gran Canarian Nicolás Estévanez (1838–1914). Although he spent much of his life out of the islands, it was clear where his heart lay; his finest work is considered to be *Canarias*, a poem that tells the story of the conquest and clearly conveys his sympathies for the Guanches.

The most important figure in Canarian literature is undoubtedly Benito Pérez Galdós (1843–1920). As well as being a source of pride for Canarians, Pérez Galdós is considered one of the most important figures in Spanish literature. His social critiques and excellent descriptions of 19th-century Spain (not the Canary Islands) have led him to be compared to Charles Dickens and won him international acclaim as an author. His most celebrated works are the 46 books making up the *Episodios Nacionales* and the four-part novel *Fortunata y Jacinta*, dubbed the finest Spanish literary work of the 19th century. There is a museum dedicated to the author based in his childhood home in Las Palmas.

Tomás Morales (1885–1921) was the first of the islands' modernist poets and by many considered the finest of Canarian bards. He too has a museum in his honour, based in his home town Moya (Gran Canaria). His contemporary Alonso Quesada (1886–1925) also wrote some important modernist poetry.

José Luis Correa (born 1962) is upholding the tradition of Canarian literature with his acclaimed series of detective novels set in Las Palmas.

As well as producing a few notable writers, the islands have served as a source of inspiration to visiting authors. While exiled to Fuerteventura, Spaniard Miguel de Unamuno (1864–1936) paid the islands a large compliment by putting them into his prose works. Agatha Christie was so fond of the islands that two of her novels were set there: *The Mysterious Mr Quinn* was based in La Orotava while Agaete was the setting for *Miss Marple and the 13 Problems*.

You won't find much Canarian poetry or prose that has been translated into English, other than the works of Pérez Galdós. There is an anthology of 20th-century poetry which has been translated (see *Further Reading*, page 334).

Music and dance

The first inhabitants of the islands loved a good dance as much as the next man, though they had to use primitive instruments to provide their music. Sticks, bones, makeshift drums, snails' shells and pots filled with stones made up the Guanche orchestra. They generally danced with partners, though there are also records of competitive dances involving furious jumping. The best known and widespread is El Canario, a lively number where partners faced each other in two lines. The fiercely traditional Tajaraste, danced to the beat of a drum, is still popular in La Gomera. El Baile del Vivo, a bizarre pantomime dance, can be witnessed in El Hierro. Danced in pairs, the woman carries out a series of exaggerated actions which the man copies. Her aim is to swipe her partner's hat from his head, while his goal is to keep her dancing as long as possible. Rain dances were also an important part of Guanche life, since the lack of water is not a new problem in the archipelago. You'll still see the odd rack of bones in a few houses, though the most famous Canarian instrument today is the *timple*. It's like a tiny guitar (not dissimilar to a ukulele) with five strings and is an essential part of any display of Canarian folk music. As it's such a representative instrument it's tempting to think that it has pre-Hispanic roots but in fact it seems to have come from Africa post conquest. A similar instrument called a *kouco* is used in northern Africa. You can catch performances at any *romería* (pilgrimage) or big fiesta and on Sunday nights on TVE2, when the locally filmed live music programme *Tenderete* is aired.

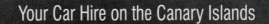

Practical Information

WHEN TO VISIT

The main reason behind the Canary Islands' success as a tourist destination is the unchanging climate, meaning that the archipelago can be visited at any time of the year. Certain months are busier, so finding accommodation may be more difficult and prices will probably be hiked up. You'll find the accommodation most in demand during carnival (February), *Semana Santa* (Easter), and Christmas. The summer months can also get busy and temperatures regularly exceed 30°C, so you might want to visit at a cooler, quieter time. Most agree that the islands are at their best in January and February, after light rainfall has brought a touch of verdure to the usually arid mountains. Other things to take into account depend on your chosen activity – windsurfing is better in the summer months while hiking is more enjoyable in spring and autumn, without the stifling heat or possibility of rain. If you're hell-bent on climbing Teide, don't go in winter; temperatures drop below freezing and the mountain hut is likely to be closed. If you want to join in some local fiesta, August and September are the busiest months with something happening somewhere pretty much every day.

HIGHLIGHTS

A recent survey of holidaymakers showed that 92% of British tourists and 79% of Germans visited the Canary Islands in search of sun and sand. It's a sad fact that few people think of the islands as much more than a beach with a few bars but there's a lot more on offer than package holidays. One of the finest activities is **hiking** and since the islands are still not known as a walking destination, you'll often wander for hours without seeing another soul. The finest island for walking is probably La Palma and you shouldn't miss the *Ruta de los Volcanes*, a long walk that takes you through the recently formed volcanoes in the south of the island. No trip to Tenerife would be complete without a visit to Mount Teide. Walk it if you can, though driving and taking the cable car are worthy alternatives if you're not up to the tough hike to the summit.

If you're looking for a party, then **carnival** in Santa Cruz is the biggest and best, considered second only to Rio de Janeiro. Other important events are the Fiestas del Carmen in Fuerteventura, Bajada de la Rama and Fiesta del Pino in Gran Canaria, Bajada de la Virgen de los Reyes in El Hierro, the Fiesta de San Ginés in Lanzarote, Bajada de la Virgen de las Nieves in La Palma and the Fiesta de Nuestra Señora del Guadalupe in La Gomera. Of course, if you're looking for something a little more local and intimate, there is almost always some kind of *romería* or street party somewhere on any island, with summer being the busiest time for fiestas.

The islands are slowly gaining popularity as a **golfing** destination. Gran Canaria and Tenerife have a number of excellent courses, while Fuerteventura, Lanzarote and La Gomera count on one each.

Diving enthusiasts will enjoy the south of El Hierro and the west of Tenerife, though the sport is practised to some extent on every island. Fuerteventura boasts some of the world's best **windsurfing** and you'll also find places to learn or practise in Lanzarote, Tenerife and Gran Canaria.

If you want to partake of the islands' most popular tourist activity, there's no lack of **beaches** and no shortage of sun. Fuerteventura has the finest golden *playas*, stretching for miles without high-rise hotels as a backdrop (a real luxury in the Canary Islands). Lanzarote also has a handful of excellent golden beaches in the south, which are well off the beaten track. Gran Canaria has the marvellous Maspalomas sand dunes and Las Canteras, a city beach *par excellence*, known for its perfectly calm waters. The other islands offer a mixture of crowded artificial beaches and delightful black-sand coves.

There is some scope for **surfing** on all of the islands, but the biggest and best waves are at Caleta de Famara in the north of Lanzarote, apparently known as the Hawaii of Europe.

If you're looking to learn a bit about the **culture** and history of the islands, head for the cities of Las Palmas, Santa Cruz de Tenerife and La Laguna, where you'll find some stunning architecture and interesting museums. Fuerteventura also has a network of delightful ethnographic museums, while Lanzarote's landscape is scattered with the works of César Manrique.

The **western islands** of El Hierro, La Gomera and to a lesser extent La Palma offer the simple pleasures of good local food, well preserved traditions and island hospitality.

POSSIBLE ITINERARIES

What you see depends largely on how much time you plan to spend in the Canaries. If you can spare only one week then you should stick to one island. Obviously your choice of island depends on your interests – if you're a keen windsurfer or sunseeker you'll be quite happy in Fuerteventura, whereas if you want to hike you'd be better off in La Palma. El Hierro and La Gomera offer the quiet life, while Lanzarote will appeal to art lovers. Your ability to pack in a few islands also depends on your budget. If you're trying to cut costs by taking boats and buses you'll need to allow more time since certain boat journeys take 24 hours and you could spend a lot of time waiting for buses.

Probably, your best bet for a **one-week** stay as a first visit would be either Tenerife or Gran Canaria, which offer the most variety and will give the best overview of the islands.

With **two weeks** you could certainly take in two islands without rushing. Tenerife would be a good place to start and from there you'll find frequent boats to La Gomera or La Palma. This way you can take in Mount Teide and some of Tenerife's urban treasures, then move to one of the smaller islands for some hiking and small-town hospitality.

In **three or four weeks** you could probably fit in the Santa Cruz province (Tenerife, La Palma, La Gomera and El Hierro) or the Las Palmas province (Gran Canaria, Fuerteventura and Lanzarote) although you might be in a bit of a rush.

You could comfortably see all the islands (including Lobos and La Graciosa) in six weeks or even better, two months. As a vague guide you'd see plenty with ten days in Tenerife, Gran Canaria and La Palma, a week each in Fuerteventura and Lanzarote and five days in La Gomera and El Hierro.

In some of the chapters, you'll find descriptions of drives around the islands. If you're really pushed for time, each of these drives could be done in a day, though it wouldn't allow you to get out of the car for long. Drives are not mentioned for

Tenerife, Gran Canaria or La Palma as it would be a crime to spend only a day or two on any of them.

ACTIVITIES

Although the Canary Islands are not a place to practise dangerous sports, there are certainly enough activities to keep even the most energetic traveller occupied. The activities on offer tend to make the most of the islands' natural assets: sun, wind, mountain and clear waters. There are dozens of companies in the tourist resorts offering diving packages, windsurfing lessons, hiking tours and boat trips, so shop around for prices.

Adventure sports

Although adrenalin junkies will perhaps get bored, there are a few options for riskier sports. Most islands offer the chance to go potholing, canyoning and climbing and there are a few companies offering these activities. If you can't find what you're looking for ask in a hiking agency as they usually have other activities on offer. You can do a parachute jump over the Maspalomas sand dunes in Gran Canaria and *parapente* is quite popular throughout the archipelago if you fancy being strapped to an instructor and hurling yourself off a cliff.

Beaches

Although some of the resort beaches are overcrowded horrors backed by high-rise concrete hotels, there are plenty of quiet, unspoilt beaches if you care to look for them. Fuerteventura has by far the finest beaches, though there are a few gems in the south of Lanzarote and Gran Canaria. The western islands have some lovely little coves if you don't find black sand off-putting. Remember that the sea tends to get pretty rough in the north of the islands and swimming isn't generally recommended, especially in winter. If there's no lifeguard and no-one else on the beach, please be content with paddling up to your ankles. As a general rule, watch what the locals do and follow suit if you must but go no further.

Boat trips

There are boat trips for all tastes, from the all-you-can-drink booze cruises to whale-watching trips and private yachts available for charter. Only La Gomera has a passenger boat service around the island although Naviera Armas operates a boat that does a full circuit around Gran Canaria. In the main tourist resorts touts will try to hassle you into buying some kind of boat trip, probably promising sightings of whales. The best whale- and dolphin-watching area is between Tenerife and La Gomera, but be wary of dodgy outfits that get too close to the animals. The short trips from Fuerteventura to Isla de Lobos and from Lanzarote to La Graciosa are cheap and worthwhile.

Diving

Like the culture, the seas around the island represent a meeting of three continents meaning a stunning variety of underwater life. Add to that visibility of 25–30m and average water temperatures of 18–24°C year-round and you can understand why the archipelago is a popular place to dive. Expect to see groupers, barracudas, octopus, angel sharks, parrotfish and sweepers and occasional encounters with manta rays, pilot whales, sunfish and dolphins. There are scores of diving schools throughout the islands though it is generally agreed that El Hierro has the most fascinating seas and the best visibility. The coastal platform here is almost non-existent, so you don't have to stray far from the shore to reach great depths. The

Archipelago is also a superb diving zone as the ban on fishing leaves huge numbers of marine creatures for you to see. Diving here presents problems, though, as the waters are part of a marine reserve and permits are usually required. Gran Canaria has a large number of wrecks around its coast and recent volcanic eruptions in the south of La Palma have created fascinating underwater scenery. There are diving schools on every island, most of which offer courses in a variety of languages. Visibility is best in summer. All diving outfits offer PADI courses for beginners. The course lasts from five to eight days and costs around €300. A trial or discovery dive (known as a *bautizo*) costs about €50 and packages are available for about €25 per dive if you are already qualified.

Fishing

If you have your own equipment, the opportunities for fishing are countless and you'd have a lovely peaceful break in El Hierro or La Gomera. Surprisingly, there aren't too many companies offering fishing trips though you'll always find them in the tourist resorts. Fishing around La Graciosa is superb but you need to go with a local who can tell you where it's legal to fish.

Golf

The Real Club de Las Palmas in Gran Canaria was Spain's first golf course, built in 1891. Since then another dozen or so have been built around the islands. As with most activities, the excellent climate attracts golfers wanting to play all year round. There are courses on five of the islands (only El Hierro and La Palma are golf-free zones). Green fees vary, but €60 for 18 holes is an average figure (with an extra €15 to hire clubs).

Hiking

The western islands are more interesting for walking since Lanzarote and Fuerteventura have little in the way of mountains or vegetation. The heat and lack of shade there can also make hiking uncomfortable. That said, a guided walk in the Timanfaya National Park in Lanzarote is fascinating and well worth it. For variety and sheer beauty, La Palma is unrivalled and also has the best information available, with many of the walks well signposted. There are some spectacular hikes on Tenerife and Gran Canaria, though getting hold of maps and information can sometimes be more of a challenge than doing the walk itself. The Teide National Park offers a dozen different routes, many of them pretty hard going. If you want something a little greener, there are scores of walks and plenty of solitude in the rural parks of Teno and Anaga (Tenerife). Gran Canaria's finest walks take you through the Tamadaba pine forest and along the Barranco de Cernícalos, with its year-round running water. The Garajonay National Park in La Gomera offers shade, spectacular scenery and good views: my personal favourite in the whole archipelago. El Hierro's walks afford superb vistas of the coast, but are mostly tough out-and-back walks which take you from sea level to the top of the island and back again.

Some walks are detailed in this book though there are hundreds more possibilities. Maps and descriptions are available from town halls and/or *Cabildos*, but you'll need a good command of Spanish and a large supply of patience if you hope to get anything from them. Reasonable maps and information are available from the tourist information offices in La Palma, El Hierro and La Gomera. In Tenerife you'll have no trouble finding information about Teide or Anaga while in the other islands you'd be wise to do your research before arriving. Do seek advice before you undertake a walk. I've been caught out on more than one occasion when

I've discovered that a route has become overgrown, making it impossible to pass. It's not much fun retracing your steps up that 5km hill just because you never thought to ask if the routes had been checked recently. The Town Hall should have this information. Routes that are frequented by the walking companies will be fine.

Getting to the start of the walk can also be a problem, particularly for the non-circular routes since leaving your hire car and collecting it another day is unlikely to appeal. Where relevant, bus routes to reach the start of each walk are mentioned in this book, with the other alternative being slightly less interesting out-and-back walks which at least return you to your car. When cost and inconvenience are taken into account, it might be just as well to hook up with a hiking company. There are plenty of companies offering walking trips on every island; their details are given in each chapter. Bear in mind that, generally, the lower the price the higher the number of walkers in your group will be.

Walks in this book are given a difficulty rating from one to five, with things such as gradient, underfoot conditions and the need to scramble over rocks taken into account. The times stated are an average for a not-super-fit person who takes regular breaks to enjoy the surroundings, take photographs, eat snacks and tend to calls of nature.

1 Easy walk with few or no uphill stretches and easy underfoot conditions.
2 A few mild uphill and/or steep downhill sections. Possibility of rough paths.
3 Suitable for most reasonably fit people. Some steep sections but much of the walk flat.
4 Difficult walk with steep slopes and difficult underfoot conditions such as sand, volcanic ash or slippery rocks.
5 Particularly difficult walk, probably all uphill. Requires some scrambling. For experienced walkers only.

Surfing
The good surfing beaches tend to be in the north of the islands, in the areas where you probably wouldn't want to go swimming. The favourites are La Pared in Fuerteventura, Playa de la Caleta and El Frontón in the north of Gran Canaria and, above all, Caleta de Famara in Lanzarote. You won't find as many surf schools as you will diving companies but there are a few and they usually cater for all levels.

Theme parks
If you have a hankering to visit a naff theme park you will be in heaven in Gran Canaria and Tenerife and to a lesser extent La Palma and Fuerteventura. There are numerous zoos, botanical gardens, water parks and countless random theme parks that seem to bear no relation to the Canary Islands at all such as Sioux City, the wild west town in Gran Canaria. There are also several opportunities to ride a camel, should the urge take you. The theme parks all tend to be overpriced.

Windsurfing
The Canary Islands offer some of the world's finest windsurfing, especially Fuerteventura, where the international championships are held each year. Other popular haunts are Pozo Izquierdo in Gran Canaria, El Médano in Tenerife and Costa Teguise in Lanzarote. There are also ample opportunities for beginners to learn in Fuerteventura and Lanzarote. Summer is the best time for windsurfing if you're looking for strong winds (though beginners might prefer other times of year). Kiteboarding is also taking off and you'll generally find opportunities to hire equipment or take lessons wherever there is a windsurfing school.

Wine tasting

Tourist boards like to make a big deal of the fact that Shakespeare enjoyed a drop of Canarian plonk, so much so that he mentioned it in more than one of his plays. In *The Merry Wives of Windsor* (Act III), the innkeeper says: 'Farewell my hearts, I will drink to my honest knight Falstaff and drink Canary with him.' Each island will tell you that the bard was talking about its wine, though you might not notice much difference in the tastes from island to island. Lanzarote has the oldest bodega, El Grifo, and certainly the most picturesque vineyards. There is an excellent museum where you can taste wine on Tenerife, while on the other islands you'll just have to drive around and visit the individual cellars. The red wines are rather disappointing but there are some tasty whites on offer, particularly the *malvasía*, reportedly Shakespeare's personal favourite.

TOUR OPERATORS

Most mainstream tour operators in the UK, Germany and Scandinavia offers trips to the Canaries. The biggest are mentioned here, along with a few niche outfits.

Canarian Dreams Silver Spring Farm, Constantine, Falmouth, UK; tel: 0870 7705378; fax: 0870 7705379; email: info@canariandreams.com; www.canariandreams.com. As well as routine package deals, they offer nudist and surfing holidays.

Casas Canarias 106 Savernake Rd, London, UK; tel 020 7485 4387; fax: 020 7267 4384; email: info@casascanarias.co.uk; www.casascanarias.co.uk. Arrange stays in rural accommodation, upmarket hotels and apartments in off-the-beaten-track locations in La Gomera and Tenerife. Can arrange car hire and have lots of information on hiking. While they don't book your flights, they will sort out the ferry from Tenerife to La Gomera.

Island Wandering 51a London Rd, Hurst Green, East Sussex, UK; tel: 01580 860733; fax: 01580 860282; email: enquiries@islandwandering.com; www.islandwandering.com. A hiking company that offers tailor-made tours. You can book accommodation only or a full package with flights and walks included. They go to all of the islands.

Mantrav-Dasi International 58 New Walk, Totnes TQ9 5WE, UK; tel: 0870 787 6848; fax: 01803 867 763; email: info@mantrav.co.uk; www.mantrav.com. There is also an office in the USA: PO Box 2307, Seal Beach, CA 90740; tel: 877 276 6636; fax: 562 430 0031; email: dasi@mantrav.com; www.mantrav.com. Specialise in gay-friendly or gay-exclusive accommodation in Gran Canaria.

My Travel www.uk.mytravel.com (UK); www.fti.de (Germany); www.mytravel.dk (Denmark); www.mytravel.nl (Netherlands); www.mytravel.se (Sweden). Lots of flights and package deals to most of the islands.

Sportif International Spathem Lane, Ditching, Sussex, UK; tel: 01273 844919, fax: 01273 844914; email: info@sportif-uk.com; www.sportif-uk.com. Windsurfing or kiteboarding trips to Fuerteventura, Gran Canaria and Tenerife.

Thomas Cook Tel: 0870 7488 493; www.thomascook.co.uk; www.thomascook.com (Germany). Large company incorporating other operators in the UK and Germany.

Throb Holidays Atlas House, Mulberry Court, Frome, Somerset, UK; tel: 01373 453550; fax: 0870 120 8604; email: res@throb.co.uk; www.throb.co.uk. Gay tour operator serving Fuerteventura, Gran Canaria and Tenerife.

Tui Tel: 0511 566 1901 (Germany); www.tui.com. Tui has all manner of tour operators, airlines and hotel groups, many of which serve the Canary Islands. They tend to be mainstream package deals to the tourist resorts.

Wildlife Worldwide 30 Marsh Wall, London E14 9FY, UK; tel: 020 8667 9158; www.wildlifeworldwide.com. Classic tailor-made wildlife holidays to destinations around the world.

RED TAPE

Citizens of EU countries and those that as part of the Schengen convention (most EU countries plus Iceland and Norway) do not need a visa to visit Spain. Nationals of Switzerland, the USA, Canada, Japan, Australia and New Zealand can spend up to 90 days in Spain without a visa, provided the purpose of the trip is tourism. Nationals of other countries should check with their local Spanish consulate before setting off for the Canary Islands. You should also contact the consulate if you plan to study or work while in Spain. Most tourist visas issued are for up to 90 days, ample time to see the Canaries in depth. Visas must be obtained before you arrive in Spain and can't generally be extended.

EMBASSIES AND CONSULATES
Spanish embassies abroad

Australia 31 Market Street, Sydney; tel: (61) 92 61 24 33; fax: (61) 92 83 16 95; email: cqspainsydney@mail.mae.es

Canada 74 Stanley Av, Ottawa; tel: (1) 613 747 22 52; fax: (1) 613 744 12 24; email: embespca@mail.mae.es

Denmark Kristianiagade 21, Copenhagen; tel: (45) 35 42 47 00; fax: (45) 35 26 30 99; email: embespdk@mail.mae.es

France 22 Av Marceau, Paris; tel: (33) 144 43 18 00; fax: (33) 147 20 56 69; email: ambespfr@mail.mae.es

Germany Lichtensteinallee 1, Berlin; tel: (49) 30 254 00 70; fax: (49) 30 257 95 57; email: embespde@correo.mae.es

Ireland 17a Melyn Park, Ballsbridge, Dublin; tel: (353) 269 16 40; fax: (353) 269 18 54; email: embespie@mail.mae.es

Morocco Rue Aïn Khalouiya, Rte Des Zaërs km 5.3, Rabat; tel: (212) 63 39 00; fax: (212) 63 06 00; email: ambespma@mail.mae.es

Netherlands Lange Voorhout 50, The Hague; tel: (31) 302 49 99; fax: (31) 361 79 59; email: ambespnl@correo.mae.es

Norway Oscarsgate 35, Oslo; tel: (47) 22 92 66 80; fax: (47) 22 55 98 22; email: embespno@mail.mae.es

Senegal 18–20 Av Nelson Mandela; tel: (221) 821 30 81; fax: (221) 821 68 45; email: ambespsn@mail.mae.es

South Africa 169 Pine St, Arcadia, Pretoria; tel: (27) 344 38 75; fax: (27) 343 48 91; email: embespza@mail.mae.es

Sweden Djurgardsvägen 21, Stockholm; tel: (46) 667 94 30; fax: (46) 663 79 65; email: embespse@mail.mae.es

UK 39 Chesham Place, London; tel: (44) 0207 235 5555; fax: (44) 0207 235 9905; email: embespuk@mail.mae.es

USA 2375 Pennsylvania Av, Washington DC; tel: (1) 2 728 2335; email: embespus@mail.mae.es

Consulates in the Canary Islands

The consulates all observe a similar timetable; none are open on weekends or in the afternoon. To be sure to catch someone there, you need to call between 09.00 and 14.00. The main embassies are all in Madrid.

Gran Canaria

Austria Av Gran Canaria 26, Playa del Inglés; tel: 928 76 25 00
Belgium Calle Leopoldo Matos 22, Las Palmas; tel: 928 23 07 01
Denmark Calle Albareda 48, Las Palmas; tel: 928 26 47 64
Finland Calle Franchy y Roca 5, Las Palmas; tel: 928 22 43 58

France Calle Néstor de la Torre 12, Las Palmas; tel: 928 29 23 71
Germany Calle Franchy y Roca 5, Las Palmas; tel: 928, 27 52 70
Iceland Calle Juan de Escobedo 5, Las Palmas; tel: 928 25 22 92
Ireland Calle León y Castillo 244, office 209, Las Palmas; tel: 928 23 04 60
Netherlands Calle León y Castillo 244, 6th floor, Las Palmas; tel: 928 24 23 82
Norway Calle Luis Morote 6, Las Palmas; tel: 928 49 50 35
South Africa Calle Franchy y Roca 5, Las Palmas; tel: 928 22 60 04
Sweden Calle Luis Morote 6, Las Palmas; tel: 928 26 08 84
United Kingdom Calle Luis Morote 6, Las Palmas; tel: 928 26 25 08
USA Calle Los Martínez de Escobar 3, Las Palmas; tel: 928 22 25 52

Tenerife
Belgium Calle Villalba Hervás 4, Santa Cruz; tel: 922 24 11 93
Denmark Calle Villalva Hervás 5, Santa Cruz; tel: 922 27 57 57
Finland Calle Villalva Hervás 3, Santa Cruz; tel: 922 28 09 55
France Calle José María de Villa 1; tel: 922 23 27 10
Germany Avenida de Anaga 45, Santa Cruz; tel: 922 28 48 12
Ireland Calle Castillo 8, Santa Cruz; tel: 922 24 56 71
Netherlands Calle La Marina 7, Santa Cruz; tel: 922 24 35 75
Norway Edificio Fred Olsen, Poligono Industrial Añaza, Santa Cruz; tel: 922 62 83 71
Portugal Calle Velázquez 11; tel: 922 23 72 50
Sweden Calle Villalva Hervás 5, Santa Cruz; tel: 922 27 74 56
UK Plaza del General Weyler 8, Santa Cruz; tel: 922 28 66 53

GETTING THERE AND AWAY
By sea
Trasmediterránea Tel: 902 45 46 45; www.trasmediterranea.es. There is one ferry a week leaving Cádiz in the south of Spain, calling at Lanzarote, Gran Canaria, Tenerife and La Palma. The journey takes almost 2 full days and is a rough ride; the only reason to arrive by boat is if you really need to take your car. It's not a cheap way to arrive either, with fares averaging €400 per person (one way).

Cruise boats
Costa Cruises Email: info@us.costa.it; www.costacruise.com. Their trips take in 3 or 4 islands as well as southern Spain. Boats leave from Savona, north Italy.
My Travel For contact details see *Tour operators*, page 36. Offer fly and cruise packages originating from numerous European countries.
P&O Cruises Richmond House, Terminus Terr, Southampton, UK; tel: 0845 3555 333; fax: 023 8052 3720; www.pocruises.com. A good selection of cruises taking in a few islands and usually mainland Spain and Madeira too.

By air
From Spain
There are three companies operating scheduled flights between mainland Spain and the Canary Islands and they all have the same prices, give or take a euro. If you're lucky you'll find a return fare for €150, but in peak times expect to pay at least twice this.

Air Europa Tel: (34) 902 40 15 01; www.aireuropa.com. A dozen flights a day connecting the islands with Madrid and further services to Bilbao, Málaga, Barcelona and Alicante. There are also a few flights a week from the mainland to Lanzarote and lots of international connections once you get to mainland Spain.

Iberia Tel: (34) 902 400 500; www.iberia.com. Numerous daily flights from Madrid, Barcelona and Seville to all but El Hierro and La Gomera.
Spanair Tel: (34) 902 13 14 15; www.spanair.com. There are regular flights connecting Fuerteventura, Gran Canaria, Lanzarote and Tenerife with Madrid and a few to other large Spanish cities including Barcelona and Valencia.

From the UK
There is no lack of charter flights connecting Britain and the Canary Islands. In low season you could be lucky enough to find a flight for under £100 but at Christmas and in summer you should be happy with anything under £250.

Excel Airways Tel: 08709 98 98 98; www.excelairways.com. This new charter airline usually has good deals, touting themselves as the 'with frills' budget airline (their planes have leather seats, in-flight entertainment and hot meals). You'll easily find a return for £150.
British Airways Tel: 0845 6060747; www.britishairways.com. Various direct flights to Gran Canaria, Lanzarote and Fuerteventura. Return flights from around £200.

From the rest of Europe
Braathens Tel: (47) 815 20 000; www.braathens.no. Three direct flights a week from Oslo to Las Palmas, costing anywhere between €200 and €500 for a return flight.
LTU Tel: (49) 211 9418 333; www.ltu.de. Flights from all major German cities; if you're lucky you could get a return flight for €200.
My Travel www.mytravel.dk (Denmark); www.mytravel.se (Sweden). Regular charter flights from Copenhagen and Stockholm to Tenerife and Gran Canaria, with some flights to Lanzarote and Fuerteventura.
Transavia Tel: 0900 0700; www.transavia.nl. There are numerous flights from Amsterdam to Gran Canaria, Tenerife, Fuerteventura and a couple to La Palma. Prices start at €140 for a return flight.

From the USA
If coming from the USA, you'll have to go first to one of the larger European cities before getting to the Canary Islands. For example, you could fly to London and then take a charter flight or you could head for Madrid and then use one of the three Spanish companies that fly between the islands and the mainland. You can arrange the whole flight through Iberia, Air Europa or Spanair, all of which fly to numerous American cities. You should be able to get a return flight for around $700.

From Africa
Air Mauritanie Tel: 525 22 16; www.airmauritanie.mr. Operate 3 flights a week to Las Palmas from Nouadhibou in Mauritania. If you're going the other way there are onward flights to various West African countries. Flights are often cancelled if there's not enough interest. A return flight is around €300.
Royal Air Maroc Tel: 09000 0800; www.royalairmaroc.com. One flight a day from Laayoune in the Western Sahara to Gran Canaria. Daily flights to and from Agadir and Casablanca. You can pick up a return for around €300, or €150 to Laayoune.

From Latin America
Santa Barbara Airlines Tel: +58 212 20 44 100; www.santabarbaraairlines.com. There is 1 direct flight a week from Caracas to Tenerife and 4 that go via Madrid. Return flights cost around €600.

GETTING AROUND
Between the islands
By air
Air travel between the islands is excellent, though it can be pricey. There are two airlines now, however, meaning there is at least a little competition and you can pick up the odd bargain here and there if you check the newspapers. Normally, though, you'd be very lucky to find a one-way flight for less than €40. Friday afternoon is a very popular time to fly so make sure you book ahead if you must travel then. The quietest day is Saturday, when you're most likely to pick up a bargain. The longest flight is no more than 50 minutes, though you'll usually be in the air for half of that. Flying offers some superb views of the islands, especially if you're flying over Tenerife. If you take off from Tenerife North Airport and are heading west, sit on the left-hand side of the plane and you'll get some stunning views of Teide poking up through the clouds. The 20-seater planes that service La Gomera are also worth taking.

Binter Canarias Tel: 902 39 13 92; www.bintercanarias.es. Long-established and very professional company with plenty of flights to all the islands.
Isla Airways Tel: 902 47 74 78; www.islasairways.com. The new kid on the block. While their timetable isn't as comprehensive as Binter's they are constantly adding new flights and their prices tend to be a few euros cheaper.

A guide to the number of flights between the islands is given in each chapter.

By sea
Some journeys are ridiculously long and leave you with no alternative but to pay the extra for a plane fare. Prices vary greatly depending on the length of the trip and therefore on the type of boat you opt for; as an idea the three-hour Armas boat from Las Palmas to Santa Cruz de Tenerife costs €15, the Fred Olsen fast ferry takes 1½ hours but you need to get to Agaete as well (the bus is included in the price; it costs €30). The one-hour jetfoil connecting the two capitals would set you back €40 (all prices are for a one-way ticket). You can pay for a cabin on longer journeys but it's probably an unnecessary expense, since the seats on deck are usually comfortable enough.

Fred Olsen Tel: 902 10 01 07; email: reserves@fredolsen.es; www.fredolsen.es
Trasmediterránea Tel: 902 45 46 45; www.trasmediterranea.es
Naviera Armas Tel: 902 45 65 00; email: narmas@naviera-armas.com; www.naviera-armas.com

There are also smaller companies servicing La Graciosa, Isla de Lobos and to get around La Gomera. See the relevant chapters for details. A guide to the number of boats between the islands is given in each chapter.

Within an island
Buses
Each island has a public bus service, ranging from the comprehensive systems of Tenerife and Gran Canaria, which serve even the tiniest of *pueblos*, to the one-a-day timetable in El Hierro. In the main islands you could travel entirely on public transport as long as you have plenty of time, but in El Hierro and La Gomera you need to hire a car if you want to see anything of the countryside and don't want to be stuck in a less-than-inspiring village all day waiting for the next bus. If you plan to do more than a couple of journeys, a *bono* or *tarjeta insular* is a good investment. It's a ticket that gives you hefty discounts on longer bus journeys. You put it in the

machine on the bus, tell the driver where you want to go and the correct amount is deducted from your card. They're available in all the islands except El Hierro and La Gomera and can be purchased from bus stations and some newsagents.

Car rental
There are numerous car-hire companies in all of the airports and ports and you'll have no problem finding a car anywhere where there are tourists. You have the choice of the mammoth multi-national companies, the large Canarian companies that cover a few islands or a local firm with just the one office, though prices tend to be pretty similar for all. If you just want a car for one day, expect to pay around €30 for the smallest model on offer. The longer you keep a car, the cheaper it becomes per day. Most companies make a note of the petrol level and ask you to leave it at the same level when you return the car, though some ask for a deposit on the petrol in the car, returnable if you give the car back with the same amount of petrol. If you're heading to El Hierro, it's wise to book a car in advance, even if it's low season. There aren't many hire cars on the island and it would be hard work seeing much without one.

Hitchhiking
Although never entirely recommendable, hitchhiking is a necessary and recognised way of getting about on some islands. In El Hierro and La Gomera you'll have no trouble getting a lift and will find that in some cases, people will go out of their way to deliver you to your destination. It's far more difficult on the larger islands, though, even in out of the way places. Hitchhiking is illegal on the *autovías* and *autopistas* (motorways).

Taxis
You'll probably be amazed by the volume of taxis in the Canary Islands, particularly in the tourist resorts and cities. Although you might find a few unlicensed cars at airports, the majority are legal cabs (they are white with a green light on the roof). They're relatively cheap and tipping isn't compulsory, though I doubt any Canarian cabbie would turn his nose up at a 10% gratuity.

Bicycle
There are opportunities to rent bicycles on most islands, though cycling in the Canaries can be a tad masochistic, especially in the summer. Obviously the easiest places to get around on two wheels are virtually flat Fuerteventura and Lanzarote. Cycling on La Graciosa is joyous and necessary since there are no cars or buses. If you're up for a challenge, cycling in the mountainous western islands is beautiful, especially when you reach the top and get to freewheel back down again!

TOURIST INFORMATION
Virtually all largish towns have some form of tourist information office, though how useful it will be is another matter. The annoying thing about them is that they can only provide information on their town or municipality, which means that you have to go to the *oficina de información turística* in every town you visit to find anything out. There is a main office in each of the capitals where, in theory, you should be able to pick up a reasonable amount of knowledge about the whole island, though some islands' facilities are better than others. It might surprise you to know that the smaller islands have more useful info on offer than Gran Canaria and Tenerife (the latter has the most frustrating system, with virtually no information in the main office). Opening times vary greatly, though most are open

on weekdays only, obviously working on the premise that tourists take weekends off. There is some form of information office in all of the airports except in La Gomera, but very few of the ports.

TIME
The Canary Islands observe GMT and daylight saving time (or BST). The clocks are put forward an hour on the last Sunday in March and back again on the last Sunday in October. This means that the time is the same as in the UK, though always an hour behind mainland Spain.

HEALTH
Generally, the islands are a healthy place to be, though the climatic conditions might cause problems. Most tap water is desalinated, tastes foul and might upset your stomach, so stick to bottled water like the locals do. In the mountains the tap water may be drinkable as it could come from a spring – ask locally. If you want to drink from a spring or fountain, look for a sign saying *agua potable*. If there's no sign, there's no guarantee that the water is safe. There are no insect-borne diseases to worry about and no poisonous snakes.

Immunisations
No jabs are necessary for a visit to the Canary Islands, though it's always advisable to be up to date with tetanus, polio, and diphtheria. Longer-term visitors should consider being vaccinated for hepatitis A and typhoid. A single dose of hepatitis A vaccine (eg: Havrix Monodose, Avaxim) provides protection for a year and can be boosted to extend protection to ten years. The newer typhoid vaccines have much better efficacy than previously and do not have the unpleasant side effects either. A single injection will last for up to three years.

Dehydration
Drink plenty of water, especially if you're hiking or doing some other energetic activity that will make you sweat. As a bare minimum you need to drink 1½ litres a day, but you should triple that if doing a long hike in the midday sun. Ease gently into sun worshipping, starting with less than an hour on the first day or two. Dehydration can lead to heat exhaustion.

Sunburn and prickly heat
While the islands are famed for their good weather, there's often a layer of cloud, which fools tourists into believing they won't get burnt. You wouldn't be the first bright-pink traveller wandering around the Canaries, so take precautions. Cover up with light-coloured, cotton clothes and have a high-factor sunscreen at hand. Try to stay out of the sun between 12.00 and 16.00 and if you're out for a tan, build up slowly, perhaps starting with 30 minutes for the first couple of days. Wearing a hat when hiking is essential (and no less so when lying on the beach). If you do get burnt, apply after-sun or camomile lotion and stay out of the sun for a few days.

Prickly heat is an itchy red rash. If you think you have it, stay out of the heat, take care to dry yourself properly after a shower and use prickly heat powder to ease the itching. Talc will do if the former is not available.

Heat exhaustion and heatstroke
Caused by dehydration and over-exposure to the sun, heat exhaustion is your first warning to move indoors. Symptoms include lethargy, headaches, shallow

breathing, a weak pulse and muscle cramps. Get out of the sun and drink plenty of non-alcoholic liquids.

Heatstroke is a serious condition caused by spending long periods in very hot conditions and not drinking enough, making your body temperature rise to dangerous levels. Symptoms include a high temperature, lack of sweating and generally feeling ill. More serious symptoms are blinding headaches, confusion, lack of co-ordination and unconsciousness. Get the sufferer out of the sun, strip them off and cover in wet towels or sheets. Hospitalisation or medical assistance is necessary and the condition can be fatal if not treated.

Motion sickness

Other than heat-related problems, this is the main gripe from visitors to the Canary Islands. Motion sickness occurs when your eyes give your brain a piece of information which the balance organs in the inner ear don't agree with. In the western islands, the endless mountain roads could have even the sturdiest traveller feeling green and some of the ferry crossings between islands can be choppy. To reduce the chances of nausea, eat lightly before the journey, avoid alcohol, fizzy drinks and greasy foods and either fix your eyes on some non-moving point or keep them closed. Reading and cigarette smoke will probably make things worse. Ginger is said to help, or taking a tablet before the journey will probably stop the discomfort if you take it long enough before setting off.

Altitude sickness

Altitude sickness occurs at heights greater than 2,500m and the only place in the islands that you might be at risk is at the top of Mount Teide in Tenerife. Symptoms include headaches, nausea, vomiting, dizziness and insomnia. If you feel the signs of altitude sickness coming on, immediate descent is required – 500m should do it, though 1,000m is recommended if symptoms are serious. To avoid altitude sickness, ascend slowly and avoid over-exertion and alcohol. People with cardiovascular or pulmonary problems should consult their doctor before attempting to conquer Mount Teide.

Swimming

More than a few tourists a year drown in the false belief that the seas are calm, but what appears to be a gentle ocean harbours strong and unpredictable currents below its surface. As a general rule, the south is safer than the north. Particularly dangerous beaches include Playa de Nogales in La Palma and the perilous Playa de la Concha on La Graciosa. Look where the locals are swimming, pay attention to flags and signs and, if in doubt, only go in up to your ankles (or not at all). If you do find yourself unable to get back to shore, try to swim parallel to the beach rather than toward it; this way you should be able to swim around the current. There are no dangerous sharks around the islands, though there are jellyfish. If you are stung, rinse the sting with sea water or ideally vinegar. Hospitalisation may be necessary if the victim shows signs of nausea, abdominal pain or fever.

Travel clinics and health information

A full list of current travel clinic websites worldwide is available on www.istm.org/. For other journey preparation information, consult www.tripprep.com. Information about various medications may be found on www.emedicine.com/wild/topiclist.htm.

UK

Berkeley Travel Clinic 32 Berkeley St, London W1J 8EL (near Green Park tube station); tel: 020 7629 6233

British Airways Travel Clinic and Immunisation Service There are two BA clinics in London, both on tel: 0845 600 2236; www.britishairways.com/travelclinics. Appointments only at 111 Cheapside; or walk-in service Mon--Sat at 156 Regent St. Apart from providing inoculations and malaria prevention, they sell a variety of health-related goods.

The Travel Clinic, Cambridge 48a Mill Rd, Cambridge CB1 2AS; tel: 01223 367362; fax: 01223 368021; email: enquiries@travelcliniccambridge.co.uk; www.travelcliniccambridge.co.uk. Open 12.0–19.00 Tue–Fri, 10.00–16.00 Sat.

Edinburgh Travel Clinic Regional Infectious Diseases Unit, Ward 41 OPD, Western General Hospital, Crewe Rd South, Edinburgh EH4 2UX; tel: 0131 537 2822. Travel helpline open 09.00–12.00 weekdays. Provides inoculations and anti-malarial prophylaxis and advises on travel-related health risks.

Fleet Street Travel Clinic 29 Fleet St, London EC4Y 1AA; tel: 020 7353 5678; www.fleetstreet.com. Injections, travel products and latest advice.

Hospital for Tropical Diseases Travel Clinic Mortimer Market Centre, 2nd Floor, Capper St (off Tottenham Ct Rd), London WC1E 6AU; tel: 020 7388 9600; www.thhtd.org. Offers consultations and advice, and is able to provide all necessary drugs and vaccines for travellers. Runs a healthline (09061 337733) for country-specific information and health hazards. Also stocks nets, water purification equipment and personal protection measures.

MASTA (Medical Advisory Service for Travellers Abroad), at the London School of Hygiene and Tropical Medicine, Keppel St, London WC1 7HT; tel: 09068 224100. This is a premium-line number, charged at 60p per minute. For a fee, they will provide an individually tailored health brief, with up-to-date information on how to stay healthy, inoculations and what to bring.

MASTA pre-travel clinics Tel: 01276 685040. Call for the nearest; there are currently 30 in Britain. Also sell malaria prophylaxis memory cards, treatment kits, bednets, net treatment kits.

NHS travel website, www.fitfortravel.scot.nhs.uk, provides country-by-country advice on immunisation and malaria, plus details of recent developments, and a list of relevant health organisations.

Nomad Travel Store 3–4 Wellington Terrace, Turnpike Lane, London N8 0PX; tel: 020 8889 7014; fax: 020 8889 9528; email: sales@nomadtravel.co.uk; www.nomadtravel.co.uk. Also at 40 Bernard St, London WC1N 1LJ; tel: 020 7833 4114; fax: 020 7833 4470 and 43 Queens Rd, Bristol BS8 1QH; tel: 0117 922 6567; fax: 0117 922 7789. As well as dispensing health advice, Nomad stocks mosquito nets and other anti-bug devices, and an excellent range of adventure travel gear.

Thames Medical 157 Waterloo Rd, London SE1 8US; tel: 020 7902 9000. Competitively priced, one-stop travel health service. All profits go to their affiliated company, InterHealth, which provides health care for overseas workers on Christian projects.

Trailfinders Immunisation Centre 194 Kensington High St, London W8 7RG; tel: 020 7938 3999.

Travelpharm The Travelpharm website, www.travelpharm.com, offers up-to-date guidance on travel-related health and has a range of medications available through their online mini-pharmacy.

Irish Republic
Tropical Medical Bureau Grafton Street Medical Centre, Grafton Buildings, 34 Grafton St, Dublin 2; tel: 1 671 9200. Has a useful website specific to tropical destinations: www.tmb.ie.

USA
Centers for Disease Control 1600 Clifton Rd, Atlanta, GA 30333; tel: 888 232 3228 (toll free and available 24 hours) or 800 311 3435; fax: 877 FYI TRIP; www.cdc.gov/travel. The

central source of travel information in the USA. Each summer they publish the invaluable Health Information for International Travel, available from the Division of Quarantine at the above address.

Connaught Laboratories PO Box 187, Swiftwater, PA 18370; tel: 800 822 2463. They will send a free list of specialist tropical-medicine physicians in your state.

IAMAT (International Association for Medical Assistance to Travelers) 417 Center St, Lewiston, NY 14092; tel: 716 754 4883; email: info@iamat.org; www.iamat.org. A non-profit organisation that provides lists of English-speaking doctors abroad.

Canada

IAMAT (International Association for Medical Assistance to Travellers) Suite 1, 1287 St Clair Av W, Toronto, Ontario M6E 1B8; tel: 416 652 0137; www.iamat.org

TMVC (Travel Doctors Group) Sulphur Springs Rd, Ancaster, Ontario; tel: 905 648 1112; www.tmvc.com.au

Australia, New Zealand, Thailand

TMVC Tel: 1300 65 88 44; www.tmvc.com.au. Twenty-two clinics in Australia, New Zealand and Thailand, including:

Auckland Canterbury Arcade, 170 Queen St, Auckland; tel: 9 373 3531

Brisbane Dr Deborah Mills, Qantas Domestic Building, 6th floor, 247 Adelaide St, Brisbane, QLD 4000; tel: 7 3221 9066; fax: 7 3321 7076

Melbourne Dr Sonny Lau, 393 Little Bourke St, 2nd floor, Melbourne, VIC 3000; tel: 3 9602 5788; fax: 3 9670 8394

Sydney Dr Mandy Hu, Dymocks Building, 7th Floor, 428 George St, Sydney, NSW 2000; tel: 2 221 7133; fax: 2 221 8401

IAMAT PO Box 5049, Christchurch 5, New Zealand; www.iamat.org

South Africa

SAA-Netcare Travel Clinics PO Box 786692, Sandton 2146; fax: 011 883 6152; www.travelclinic.co.za or www.malaria.co.za. Clinics throughout South Africa.

TMVC 113 DF Malan Drive, Roosevelt Park, Johannesburg; tel: 011 888 7488; www.tmvc.com.au. Consult the website for details of clinics in South Africa.

Switzerland

IAMAT 57 Voirets, 1212 Grand Lancy, Geneva; www.iamat.org

SAFETY
Crime

The Canary Islands are generally safe, though Las Palmas and Santa Cruz are not immune to the normal problems of largish cities. Keep an eye on your bag while you're on the beaches (particularly where there are most tourists); you wouldn't be the first to have your belongings swiped while enjoying a siesta in the sun.

Hassle

The biggest hassle you'll face is again to be found in the large tourist resorts and it comes in the form of timeshare touts. Of course, they're easy enough to ignore, but you'd be forgiven for losing your patience when being approached for the 50th time in a day. There are a few beggars in Las Palmas and Santa Cruz de Tenerife and one in Santa Cruz de La Palma. Arrecife has more than its share of dodgy-looking characters but they are unlikely to bother you.

Women travellers

The Canary Islands don't pose any particular dangers to female travellers, though you might stir up a bit of interest if travelling alone in smaller *pueblos*. Still, the attention you'll receive is likely to be friendly rather than threatening. Be ready for regular calls of *rubia* ('blonde', and it doesn't matter if you're not – the word applies to anyone whose hair isn't jet black) and *guapa* ('attractive'). Reply with a smile and a cheery *hola* and you'll probably make someone's day. It does get tiresome after a while but it could be worse; I used to complain about these macho remarks until someone shouted *fea* ('ugly') from a car window!

WHAT TO TAKE

Don't panic too much about remembering to pack everything – you can buy anything that you've forgotten when you arrive, and probably at a lower price than at home. If you're planning to travel on a budget, you might want to pack your own towels, since many of the *pensiones* don't provide them (or soap). Sheets are almost always clean, so there's no need for a sleeping bag unless you're planning to camp. Don't be fooled by the islands' image as a year-round sunny destination – evenings can get chilly and it's downright cold up in the mountains once the sun goes down. The plug is the standard European two pin and the electricity supply is 220V, 50Hz.

MONEY

The Canary Islands are a part of Spain and so switched from pesetas to euros in 2002. Credit cards are widely accepted and even the tiniest *pueblo* has at least one ATM. You can change travellers' cheques at change bureaux (*casas de cambio*) and most banks, with the latter offering better rates. Banks open at around 08.30 until lunchtime from Monday to Saturday. The savings banks (known as *cajas*) are closed on Saturdays but open for a couple of hours on Thursday evenings instead. The extra hours (Thursdays and Saturdays) are not observed during the summer months (April to September inclusive). If you're in a bind and really need someone to send you money, you can do a transfer with Western Union in most post offices. It takes couple of days and commission varies depending on the amount of money sent.

Budget

In general, the Canary Islands are cheaper than mainland Spain though prices rocket once you get into the tourist resorts. Budget travel is possible, but you might miss out on a few activities. Travelling alone, using buses, staying in the most basic of *pensiones*, perhaps eating out once a day and keeping activities and museums to a minimum, you might just get by on €30–35 a day (€15 for a single room, supermarket breakfast €2, menu of the day lunch €6, transport €3, sandwich and drink for dinner €3, museum entrance €3). Obviously this would be slightly less if travelling as a pair. If you're a couple wanting to stay in a reasonable hotel, eat out twice a day, enjoy a few of the activities on offer and occasionally hire a car you should budget for around €50–60 per day each. For two people eating in restaurants three times a day, regularly hiring a car, indulging in some pricey pastime like golf or diving and staying in an upmarket hotel you'd be looking at a minimum of €100 per day per person and could easily spend twice that. Your spendings will rise considerably if you want to take in more than one island, since inter-island travel is a costly business.

The Canary Islands for free

It's not impossible to see a bit of the archipelago without forking out for it, though you'll have to stick to just one island unless you intend to become a stowaway. Two of the finest activities won't cost you a penny – sunning yourself on a beach or hiking in the mountains. There are plenty of free campsites around too, so you could feasibly hike and camp for as long as you wanted. Bear in mind that you can't just pitch a tent anywhere and that you usually need a permit (free) to camp on the government-run sites. There are plenty of museums and art galleries in Las Palmas and Santa Cruz where entry is gratis, especially if you visit on Sundays. Some of the finest fiestas can also be enjoyed free of charge, such as Carnival, WOMAD and the countless *romerías* around the islands. Finally, walking around the old parts of town and admiring the varieties of architecture is enjoyable and costs nothing.

ACCOMMODATION

Booking ahead isn't always necessary but highly recommended at busy times such as Easter, Carnival, August, Christmas and around popular festivals. Reservations are always recommended on El Hierro and La Graciosa, where accommodation is limited.

All prices quoted are per night unless otherwise stated.

Hotels and apartments

In the main cities and large resorts there is an abundance of accommodation, almost all of it in self-catering apartments or expensive hotels. In certain resorts you'll struggle to find anything, since the majority of beds are taken by tour operators. Each island has a parador, a government-run hotel, which is usually luxurious and in an enviable position, though you'll pay for it. Most places have varying prices depending on the season. All prices quoted in this book are high-season rates (high season is the end of July until the beginning of September and late November until Christmas). Prices rocket over Christmas week and Semana Santa. You'll find apartments to rent in even the tiniest of coastal villages, though smaller operations often request a minimum stay of three nights. Prices for hotels can vary from around €40 up to €2,000 for a double, though a more usual price is €50–100. Apartments are around €40 per night for up to three people, though they'll be more expensive in the large resorts.

Cottages

One increasingly popular way to spend a night is staying in a *casa rural* (rural house). These are often family-run and to be found in stunning locations, such as clinging to the side of a ravine or nestled in a forest. The majority are better equipped than many people's homes and offer excellent value for money. Some ask for a minimum stay of three nights, though you'll probably want to stay longer. Most *casas rurales* belong to one of the various associations, mentioned in each island chapter. Acantur co-ordinate cottages on all but Lanzarote and have an excellent webpage: www.ecoturismocanarias.com. Prices range from €40 to €70 for two people per night. Some cottages sleep four or six.

Budget accommodation

Many people complain at the lack of budget accommodation but there is a reasonable amount if you avoid the main tourist centres. Budget places are called *pensiones*, *residencias* or *hostales* and all offer the same level of comfort. Some have private bathrooms while in the majority you'll have to share the facilities with the rest of the corridor (though that's sometimes just two or three other rooms). All have hot water and the odd one or two have extras like balconies, TV or even a minibar. In many of them you cannot book in advance so you just have to turn up and hope for the best. They expect you to pay up front; try to negotiate a discount if you're staying a few days. The cheapest deals are in Tenerife and Gran Canaria, though some of Las Palmas's *pensiones* are less than appealing. An average price is €18/25 for a single/double room, though there are a few bargains to be had.

Camping and hostels

There are plenty of campsites in the islands, both privately owned and government-run. The former tend to have all the facilities you'll need while the latter are often free but offer the most basic amenities or sometimes nothing at all. You will need a permit to camp at the government campsites, obtainable from the environment department (*medio ambiente*) of each island's *Cabildo* (contact details given in each island's *Where to stay* chapter). Bear in mind that it is illegal to pitch a tent wherever you want to, though in practice there's unlikely to be anyone checking in out of the way places.

There are a few hostels scattered around, most of them geared towards hikers and so are in *very* out of the way locations. Tenerife has two marvellous hostels, known as *albergues*, in the Teno and Anaga rural parks. Gran Canaria has one near Valleseco and another at Pozo Izquierdo, aimed at windsurfers. There's also a species of hostel (more like a hikers' hut) in the north of La Palma. You'll find a *refugio* (mountain hut) near the peak of Mount Teide, offering cold water (or sometimes frozen pipes), dirty sheets and one toilet for all to share. While you may see other *albergues*, most are reserved for large groups such as school trips and are not open to individual customers. A night in a hostel costs around €12.

EATING AND DRINKING
Food

Although it would be unfair to call Canarian cuisine poor, it has been shaped by a history of hardship and poverty. One of its tastiest dishes, *ropa vieja* ('old clothes'), was devised as a way to disguise yesterday's leftovers. It's a chick-pea stew with various vegetables, herbs and some kind of meat, though you're unlikely to find two chefs who make it the same way. Another hearty dish is *potaje de berros*, a watercress stew made with whatever vegetables are at hand (and sometimes with meat as well).

Gofio is a staple accompaniment to many meals though you might find it a bit hard to swallow; in which case, you'll be looking for something else to fill up on, so look no further than the ubiquitous *papas arrugadas* ('wrinkly potatoes'). If you find any menu that doesn't offer these small potatoes, boiled in their skins with an abundance of salt, please let me know! They're delicious and usually served with some kind of *mojo*, a spicy sauce that can be made with chillies, coriander or basil. As in other areas once suffering food shortages, *mojo* was designed to hide the often unpleasant flavours of local fodder, hence its potent taste.

Although these days you'll find many Spanish and international restaurants, if you're looking for true Canarian fare you should sample the rabbit, pork and above all goat dishes. Naturally the seafood is also excellent. Vegetarians might have problems, especially if they can't be tempted by some fresh fish. Omelettes, salads and of course *papas arrugadas* will probably make up your diet. Tapas are as popular and varied as on the mainland, although you won't get any free nibbles with your drinks in the Canary Islands. Most supermarkets will make you a sandwich if you're planning a picnic lunch.

Breakfast in the Canary Islands is a low-key affair, as in Spain, and a cup of strong coffee with some kind of cake or a *sandwich mixto* (cheese and ham toasted sandwich) usually suffices. *Churrerías* (cafés that specialise in churros) fill up on weekend mornings when people opt for the unhealthiest of breakfasts: deep-fried,

AS CANARIAN AS GOFIO

Many non Canarios can't understand the fuss about *gofio* (toasted maize), but it was once all that was available, especially in the eastern islands, and is an intrinsic element of Canarian cooking. *El pan de los Canarios* ('the bread of the Canarios') is used as a starter, an accompaniment, a dessert or, in particularly hard times, was eaten alone. It's served in a surprising number of ways: mixed with milk for a hearty start to the day, with water and vegetables as an accompaniment to a meal, mashed with banana as a dessert and even added to fish stew to make *gofio escaldado*. You can taste *gofio* liquor, *gofio* ice-cream, *gofio* mousse…

For outsiders, it's rather bland and stodgy and could be likened to Marmite in that you'll either love it or loathe it. In either case, there is no doubt that it has always formed a part of Canarian life. Scores of rudimentary handmills, dating back to aborigine times have been found across the islands and *gofio* is no less important now than it was then. It has even made its mark on the local language, so that something pleasing can be described as *está de gofio* and after a hard day at the mill you might hear someone proclaim *estoy hecho gofio*. Whether it sounds or looks unappealing, you should certainly try it while you're in the islands. Any locally run place will have some at hand or you can buy your own at markets or from the few remaining mills.

sausage-shaped pieces of batter called *churros,* which are served with a cup of thick hot chocolate.

The best way to get an overview of the local food (and the cheapest way to fill up) is with a *menu del día* (menu of the day). For around €7 you can eat a three-course meal with wine or water. They're most abundant in the larger towns and cities and seemingly every restaurant in Las Palmas has the offer. Elsewhere, expect to pay around €8 for a main meal and a similar amount for a few tapas dishes if you're sharing with someone else.

You won't be left disappointed if you're after something sweet to round off your meal – Canarians are renowned *golosos* (ie: with a sweet tooth). The desserts usually contain almonds and honey in some form, with the most well-known being *bienmesabe*, a sickly sweet cake made with almonds, sugar, cinnamon and some more sugar. It's also sold as a sauce in some places. Literally, *bienmesabe* means 'it tastes good to me'.

Each island also has its specialities and these are described in the relevant chapter.

Drink

Since the tap water is not recommended for consumption (it tastes foul and will probably upset your stomach), stick to bottled water; it's dirt cheap and there are countless local brands on offer.

Vines were first brought to the islands by the Portuguese at the end of the 15th century and the Canaries soon took their place in the international wine trade. Lord Byron, Robert Louis Stevenson and Shakespeare all complimented the Canarian *malvasía* and if it was good enough for them… There are places for wine tasting on every island and many supermarkets sell the local brew. Of course, if you're looking for something a little stronger, the Canarian rum is a tasty tipple. It comes in white, gold, dark and honey varieties and is a cheap way to get drunk.

HINTS ON PHOTOGRAPHY
Nick Garbutt and John Jones

All sorts of photographic opportunities present themselves in the islands, from simple holiday snaps to that one-off encounter with a blue iguana. For the best results, give some thought to the following tips.

- As a general rule, if it doesn't look good through the viewfinder, it will never look good as a picture. Don't take photographs for the sake of taking them; be patient and wait until the image looks right.
- Photographing **people** is never easy and more often than not it requires a fair share of luck. If you want to take a portrait shot of a stranger, it is always best to ask first. Focus on the eyes of your subject since they are the most powerful ingredient of any portrait, and be prepared for the unexpected.
- There is no mystique to good **wildlife** photography. The secret is getting into the right place at the right time and then knowing what to do when you are there. Look for striking poses, aspects of behaviour and distinctive features. Try not only to take pictures of the species itself, but also to illustrate it within the context of its environment. Alternatively, focus in close on a characteristic which can be emphasised.
- Photographically, the eyes are the most important part of an animal – focus on these, make sure they are sharp and try to ensure they contain a highlight.
- Look at the surroundings – there is nothing worse than a distracting twig or highlighted leaf lurking in the background. Getting this right is often the difference between a mediocre and a memorable image.
- A powerful flashgun adds the option of punching in extra light to transform an otherwise dreary picture. Artificial light is no substitute for natural light, though, so use it judiciously.

For something softer, there are a few locally brewed beers. Naturally, Tinerfeños will tell you that their offering, Dorada, is the finest, while Canariones will vote for Gran Canaria's Tropical. Personally, I find both a little flat and prefer the smooth and oft-forgotten Reina (brewed in Tenerife, incidentally). Don't forget to finish your meal with a Palmero cigar, second only to those made in Havana.

FIESTAS

Eight bank holidays are set by the Spanish government and then a further six are chosen locally, be it by the *Gobierno de Canarias*, the *Cabildos* or *ayuntamientos*, so public holidays can vary a little from island to island. Unlike in some countries, the holiday is held on the exact date and not moved to a more convenient day. This can go in the workers' favour since when a holiday falls on a Thursday they take a *puente* (bridge) and will often have Friday off work too. Of course, it also means that holidays can fall on a Saturday or Sunday.

The following dates are set by the Spanish government and so are observed throughout Spain:

January 1	Año Nuevo (New Year's Day)
March/April	Viernes Santo (Good Friday). On Good Friday most towns stage a sombre procession.
May 1	Día del Trabajador (Labour Day)
August 15	La Asunción de la Virgen

- Getting close to the subject correspondingly reduces the depth of field. At camera-to-subject distances of less than a metre, apertures between f16 and f32 are necessary to ensure adequate depth of field. This means using flash to provide enough light. If possible, use one or two small flashguns to illuminate the subject from the side.

Landscapes are forever changing, even on a daily basis. Good landscape photography is all about good light and capturing mood. Generally the first and last two hours of daylight are best, or when peculiar climatic conditions add drama or emphasise distinctive features. Never place the horizon in the centre – in your mind's eye divide the frame into thirds and either exaggerate the land or the sky.

Film
If you're using conventional film (as against a digital camera), select the right film for your needs. Film speed (ISO number) indicates the sensitivity of the film to light. The lower the number, the less sensitive the film, but the better quality the final image.

For general print film, ISO 100 or 200 fit the bill perfectly. If you are using transparencies for home use or for lectures, then again ISO 100 or 200 film is fine. However, if you want to get your work published, the superior quality of ISO 25 to 100 film is best.

- Try to keep your film cool. Never leave it in direct sunlight.
- Don't allow fast film (ISO 800 and above) to pass through X-ray machines.
- Under weak light conditions use a faster film (ISO 200 or 400).

October 12	Día de la Hispanidad (Spanish National Day)
November 1	Día de Todos Santos (All Saints' Day)
December 6	Día de la Constitución
December 25	Día de Navidad (Christmas Day)

Other holidays are decided locally and vary from island to island or even within an island. Sometimes workers in Las Palmas will be enjoying a day off while their counterparts in Maspalomas are slaving away. These fiestas often depend on when a town's patron saint's day falls and when the Town Hall decides to celebrate carnival. As a rough guide, the following fiestas are widely observed:

January 6	Día de los Reyes Magos (Three Kings' Day). This is when Spanish children receive their presents, rather than December 25. On the eve of Kings' Day Melchior, Caspar and Balthazar ride through the streets on camels and throw sweets to onlookers.
February/March	Carnival Tuesday (the date changes depending on when Easter falls)
March/April	Jueves Santo (Maundy Thursday)
May 30	Día de las Islas Canarias (Canary Islands' Day). A good time to witness displays of traditional music and dance and sample some Canarian food.
June 24	Día de San Juan (St John's Day)
July 25	Día de Santiago Apóstol (St James the Apostle, patron saint of Spain)
December 8	Immaculate Conception

SHOPPING

Las Palmas and Santa Cruz have mammoth shopping centres crammed with chain stores and fast-food joints. If you're looking for something with a bit more local character, head for one of the many farmers' markets. They're a great place to pick up some Canarian edibles and most have at least a few crafts on sale. In the resorts you'll find a frightening amount of tacky souvenir stores selling all manner of tat that you wouldn't buy for your worst enemy. If you're looking for a gift or a memento of your trip you're most likely to find it at one of the aforementioned markets. Some spicy *mojo*, a jar of Gomeran *almogrote* or an assortment of Palmeran sweets all make great gifts, since they can't be found elsewhere. Amongst the finer crafts are embroidered tablecloths and placemats, dolls made from palm or banana leaves and some imitation Guanche pottery.

Opening hours

Smaller shops close for siesta in the middle of the day. A typical timetable is 09.00–13.00 and 17.00–20.00, though it varies from shop to shop. Chain stores generally stay open all day, as do larger supermarkets. Banks open until the early afternoon and sometimes on Thursday evenings or Saturday mornings. Pretty much everything is closed on Sundays, except in the run-up to Christmas.

ENTERTAINMENT

One of the finest things about the islands is that there is always something happening – it might be anything from a local festival or a small outdoor concert in a town square to a massive international music festival. There are three magnificent auditoriums: the Alfredo Kraus in Las Palmas, the Jameos de Agua in Lanzarote and the striking new auditorium in Santa Cruz de Tenerife. There are also a growing number of regular arts festivals within the islands, such as WOMAD in Gran Canaria, 'El Festivalito' (digital film festival) in La Palma, the opera seasons in Las Palmas and Santa Cruz de Tenerife and the annual film festival held in Las Palmas. The latest events are always advertised in the main regional newspapers (see below). For more details on the archipelago's big parties, see *Festivals*, page 22.

Spectator sports

While you're in the islands, you should try to catch one of the more traditional sports in action (see box opposite) but there are possibilities if you fancy something more modern. Football is the local passion and while you're likely to find a match happening just about anywhere, the two big teams are UD Las Palmas and CD Tenerife, both of which are in the Spanish second division. The rivalry between the two islands is never stronger than when their teams meet on the pitch. Other favourites include basketball, volleyball and handball, all of which are played to a professional level on the main islands. Ask at tourist information offices for details of any important games happening during your stay.

Vela Latina Canaria, a local form of sailing, is popular in Gran Canaria. It dates back to the late 19th century when sailors in Puerto de la Luz were employed to shuttle goods and crews from their boats to the shore. In quiet times these seamen held mini regattas and these continue today, albeit very occasionally. Keep your eye on the Spanish press and just turn up on Las Palmas's Avenida Marítima to watch the action with the rest of the city.

MEDIA AND COMMUNICATIONS

English and German newspapers and radio stations abound, though how many of them you'd want to read or listen to is another matter. Of the newspapers, *Island*

CURIOUS CANARIAN SPORTS

They're a competitive bunch, the Canarians, and over the years they have devised more and more unusual ways of proving their superior strength or sporting prowess.

The best-known and best-loved Canarian sport is **Lucha Canaria**, considered the most important legacy left behind by the Guanches. Nowadays the fights are held in a sand-covered ring measuring 10m in diameter. This ancient form of wrestling involves two competitors trying to throw each other off balance, and the first to touch the floor with any part of his body other than the soles of his feet is declared the loser. Though it was once an individual sport, fighters now play in teams of a dozen and the team with the most victories at the end of the 12 *bregas* (bouts) is declared the winner. *Lucha Canaria* matches are often aired on TV and you can usually find some fighting at local fiestas, particularly in El Hierro and Fuerteventura. If you're particularly keen to see it, ask at the tourist information offices for details of competitions or see the Lucha Canaria Federation's website: www.federacionluchacanaria.com.

Juego de palo (literally, the stick game) is a kind of fencing but in the absence of metal on the islands, 2m-long sticks are used instead of swords. Competitors try to score points without hitting their opponent, though the sport wasn't always so tame. It was the Guanche equivalent to a duel, with the aim being to injure and not just outclass the opponent. It was considered too dangerous and was banned after the conquest but is enjoying a small-scale comeback now as the islanders fight to keep their heritage. Your best chance to catch it is at a fiesta.

Although not really a sport, the **salto de pastor** makes interesting viewing. It wasn't invented as a form of entertainment though, more a way of making life easier for goat herders on the craggy islands. While goats are used to mountain living, it's often a little more difficult for their keepers to maintain the pace, so they used to use long sticks to aid them as they jumped down steep cliffs and ravines. It dates back to pre-Hispanic times and probably took on a competitive slant between herders to pass the hours as the goats grazed. It is now mainly for display, and you'll probably get to see it at most small-town *romerías,* though there are herders who still carry the 3m-long stick, just in case.

Other lesser-known sports include **levantamiento del arado** ('plough lifting') and **levantamiento de piedra** ('stone lifting'), both tests of brute strength; **pina**, a team game where the aim was to hit a wooden ball into the goal using sticks; and **pelotomano**, an early form of handball.

These days, however, traditional games tend to be reserved for special occasions and the sport closest to every Canarian's heart is undoubtedly football. To the extent that, when a good friend of mine broke his leg in the middle of a game, his friends asked if he'd mind waiting until they finished the match before taking him to hospital!

Connections covers the whole archipelago in theory, though in practice much of their news is from Tenerife. The only other English-language rag worth reading is *Tenerife News*, a fortnightly newspaper. In Spanish, *Canarias 7* and *La Provincia* are the two daily papers for the Las Palmas province, while *La Opinión* and *El Día* cater for the Santa Cruz province. Each island also has its own regional paper where you're likely to find out forthcoming events, cinema times etc. As well as the four national television stations, the islands have numerous local channels which range from the professional Televisión Canaria (available across the islands) to Las Palmas's bizarre and hilarious Channel 25, which constantly shows the Canarian equivalent to a tea dance, filmed with a shaky camcorder. The foreign-language radio stations tend to be very much centred in the main resorts, so they're OK if you want to know where there's karaoke on but you're unlikely to find much information about the rest of the island.

Telephone and internet

There are internet cafés in the larger towns, cities and tourist resorts, but thankfully the quaintest villages have not yet been overrun by *cibers*. Expect to pay between €1.50 and €2.50, or triple that in a resort. *Locutorios* are the place to make overseas telephone calls. Prices vary greatly but as a guide, a call to Europe or the USA will probably set you back about €0.15 per minute. They also sell telephone cards, which are the cheapest way to phone home. You can get two hours of calls to the UK or USA for €6 with a phonecard.

Post

You'll find a post office in all but the smallest of towns, though whether you'll find it open is another matter. In the cities the post offices stay open all day, but in towns they close at 14.30 on weekdays and 13.00 on Saturdays. In smaller villages, the post offices open for just an hour or two each morning. Post is generally reliable, but send it recorded delivery (*correo certificado*) if it's even slightly important. Sending a light letter or postcard within Europe costs €0.45, or €0.75 to the USA.

LIVING, WORKING AND STUDYING IN THE CANARY ISLANDS

Anyone planning to stay in Spain for longer than 90 days should apply for a residence card. It's a tiresome process for EU citizens but nightmarish for nationals of other countries. Non-EU citizens first need to apply for a Spanish residence visa in their own country and come armed with large amounts of patience. What tends to happen is that you spend hours waiting to be seen and then get turned away because you're missing a photocopy. Make sure you know what you need before you arrive. It all has to be done in person and not over the telephone or by post.

Studying Spanish

There are surprisingly few places that offer Spanish courses to holidaymakers or visitors, perhaps because they're working on the false premise that people who come to the Canaries have no interest in learning the lingo. You'll find decent set-ups in Las Palmas, La Laguna, Puerto de la Cruz and Valle Gran Rey, though there are others scattered around.

The Escuela Oficial de Idiomas (the official, government-run language school) has courses in Spanish for foreigners but they last a full academic year. You need to apply in May and if you're not a beginner, sit the level test in September. Places are extremely limited though, so don't pin your hopes on getting in. You could also try for the German, English or French courses. If all else fails you could opt for a private teacher (expect to pay €10–12 per hour) or find an *intercambio* partner. This means you advertise for someone interested in learning your language and spend part of the time chatting in Spanish and the rest in your mother tongue. The best way to find a partner is by putting up a sign in the official language school (there are schools on every island).

Working

EU citizens and those from Iceland and Norway can work without a visa, though you're supposed to apply for the *tarjeta de residencia* if you plan to stay for more than three months. As a bare minimum you need an NIF (foreigner's identification number) in order to get a work contract. Go to the Policía Nacional to fill in the paperwork and be patient – it takes at least two months before you receive your number (though you can work in the interim). Nationals of other countries need to apply for a working visa before they arrive – a complicated process and almost impossible if you haven't already got a job lined up. Of course, there are always opportunities to work *sin papeles* to avoid the paperwork and queues.

Tourist resorts

Outside the resorts, opportunities are limited for those who don't speak Spanish. However, there are ample possibilities to work in bars and restaurants in the tourist resorts or, if you're really hard up, there are *always* jobs in timeshare. The foreign-language press advertises local jobs, most of them in sales or dodgy nightclubs. A more reliable job would be to work for a tour operator, though this usually needs to be arranged before you leave home.

TEFL (Teaching English as a Foreign Language)

Not many people would think of the islands when looking for a job in TEFL but there are ample opportunities, at least in the larger islands. A certificate in English-language teaching will be a big help, though in needy times most schools will take the unqualified. For a list of language schools consult the *Spanish Yellow Pages* online, www.paginasamarillas.es, and search for *academias de idiomas*. Schools pay around €9 an hour and you can live quite nicely working 20 hours a week. There is also plenty of scope for giving private classes, charging anything from €10 to €30 an hour depending on your customers (though a normal price is €15). There are also possibilities for teaching German and French.

GIVING SOMETHING BACK

You might think that the Canary Islands are rich enough and are not in need of your help, and on many counts you'd be right. However, the archipelago has been damaged considerably over the years as mass tourism has taken hold. The following charities and organisations deal with environmental issues, so you might like to repair some of the damage that a previous traveller has helped to cause. In many cases, your assistance might be as welcome as your money – contact the organisations to find out what events they have planned and to see how you can help.

Los Burros Felices Tel: 922 55 15 11; fax: 922 55 13 24; email: burros@arrakis.es; www.burrosfelices.com. As the rural lifestyle diminishes in the islands, the number of abandoned donkeys is increasing rapidly. Los Burros Felices ('the Happy Donkeys') is a privately funded sanctuary based in the north of El Hierro caring for some terribly mistreated animals. Some of them have spent years carrying tourists around while others have spent a lifetime helping farmers in steep ravines. If you want to help, you can simply make a donation, or opt to sponsor a donkey for a year. You can also visit the stables and stay in a *casa rural* nearby (profits from your stay in the cottage will also help the charity).
Ben Magec Tel: 922 63 10 18/928 36 22 33; email: ecologistas@benmagec.org; www.benmagec.org. An ecological group which co-ordinates conservation projects and environmental groups in all seven islands. Amongst other things they support plans for renewable energy, water conservation, protecting the many endangered species in the

islands and, of course, environmental education. You can help them with signatures and by supporting their protests or you can subscribe to their monthly magazine for US$50 per year. Donations are always welcome.

Canarias por una Costa Viva Tel: 922 533 297; fax: 922 53 20 43; email: info@canariasporunacostaviva.org; www.canariasporunacostaviva.org. If you want to do a bit of hands-on help, this group organises beach clean-ups amongst other things. They are supported by the WWF (Worldwide Fund for Nature).

Bradt Travel Guides is a partner to the 'know before you go' campaign, masterminded by the UK Foreign and Commonwealth Office to promote the importance of finding out about a destination before you travel. By combining the up-to-date advice of the FCO with the in-depth knowledge of Bradt authors, you'll ensure that your trip will be as trouble-free as possible.

www.fco.gov.uk/knowbeforeyougo

Part Two

The Islands

KEY TO STANDARD SYMBOLS — Bradt

- - - - -	National park boundary
✈	Airport (international)
✈	Airport (other)
✛	Airstrip
⬳	Helicopter service
🚗	Car ferry
🚢	Passenger ferry
⧫	Bridge/ tunnel mouth
....	Footpath
⛽	Petrol station or garage
P	Car park
🚌	Bus station etc
🚲	Cycle hire
⌂	Hotel, inn etc
☆	Night club
♉	Wine bar
✕	Restaurant, café etc
✉	Post office
e	Internet access
✚	Hospital, clinic etc
✚	Health centre/pharmacy
⚱	Museum
i	Tourist information
$	Bank
⚑	Statue or monument
∴	Archaeological or historic site
▒	Urban park (town plans)
⊞	Historic building
⛫	Castle/fortress
✝	Church or cathedral
🏃	Stadium
⚐	Golf course
⚙	Windmill
•	Other place of interest
▲	Summit (height in metres)
☼	Volcanic crater
⌂	Cave/Rock shelter
▭	Cable car, teleférico
▰	Main urban sprawl
●	Main town/city
○	Small town/village
═══	Primary road
═══	Dual carriageway road
═══	Main road
═══	Other road
═══	Minor road
======	Track (4 x 4 etc)
⇥	Mountain pass
☀	Scenic viewpoint
❀	Botanical site
♣	Specific woodland feature
⚑	Lighthouse
⚊	Marsh
➚	Beach
≈≈	Coral reef
⚓	Scuba diving
🐟	Fishing sites

Other map symbols are sometimes shown in separate key boxes with individual explanations for their meanings.

Gran Canaria

Land of Gran Canaria, colourless …
The sun striking full on the crags
And the sea … as though inviting to the
    impossible!

Alonso Quesada, *Tierras de Gran Canaria*
('Lands of Gran Canaria') 1915

Many people (although not those from Tenerife) think that if you're going to visit only one island, then Gran Canaria should be it. Its slogan is 'the continent in miniature', referring to the variation in climate between north and south and the diverse landscape this creates. OK, so its beaches can't quite compare to those of Fuerteventura, its peaks are dwarfed by Teide, its villages not quite as quaint as those in La Gomera and its craters pale into comparison if you've been to Lanzarote, but if you've got time for only one island, Gran Canaria gives you a good taste of all that's on offer. It lies around 100km from Tenerife and 100km from Fuerteventura and its climate is a mix of the two – hot and dry in the south, cloudy and wet in the north. As well as offering world-class windsurfing, a fine city and some good hiking spots, Gran Canaria has Europe's biggest gay resort, Playa del Inglés.

HIGHLIGHTS

Enjoy one of the world's finest city beaches, Las Canteras, after a hard day's shopping in one of Las Palmas's many malls. The island's other not-to-be-missed beach is the 6km stretch in Maspalomas, with the stunning sand dunes stretching out behind. There are plenty of charming villages and towns on the island, notably Fataga and Temisas in the south, Teror, Guía and Firgas in the north. Keen divers will find an unusually high number of wrecks not far off the coast and some of the world's finest windsurfing is to be had around Pozo del Izquierdo. Roque Nublo and the nearby towns of Tejeda and Artenara offer some spectacular vistas, while driving the west coast provides a vertiginous view of the craggy cliffs.

BACKGROUND INFORMATION
History

Although the island's first inhabitants knew it as Tamarán, it has been known as Canaria by outsiders for centuries, though no-one is 100% sure why (see box, page 4). The first inhabitants, known to the outside world as Canarios, were happily living in their caves when in 1478 Juan Rejón and Dean Bermúdez landed on the shores of La Isleta. While looking for a suitable camp, the Spaniards encountered an elderly woman who ushered them to the entrance of the Barranco de Guiniguada (near the nowadays Plaza de Santa Ana), something that the conquerors considered to be divine intervention. An army of 2,000 natives soon attacked the camp under the command of fearless leader Doramas and although

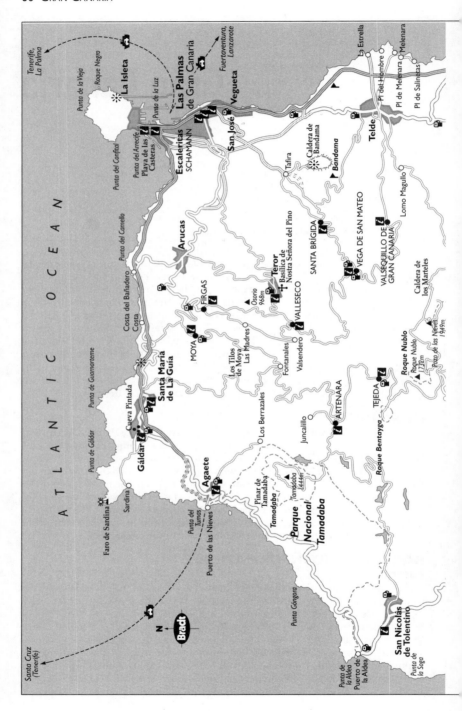

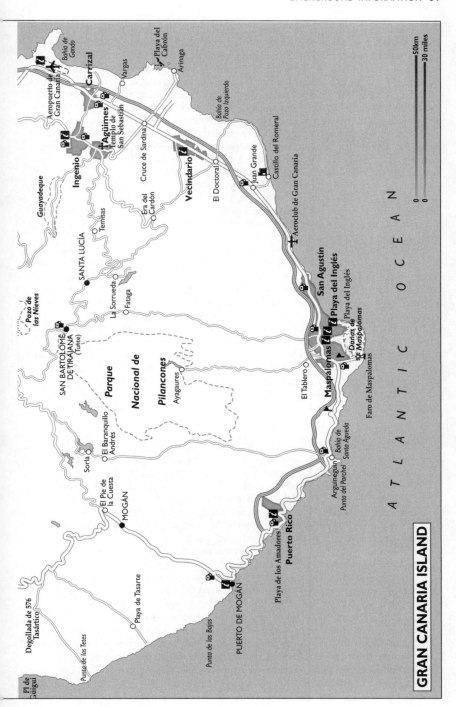

GRAN CANARIA ISLAND

the Spaniards were unprepared they fought back and soon won, leaving 300 Canarios dead (records show that only seven of the invaders lost their lives). Following the attack, Rejón immediately ordered that the Real de las Palmas, as they had called their settlement, be fortified. Disagreements soon broke out between Rejón and Bermúdez which were made worse on the arrival of Pedro de Algarba and Bishop Frías in 1479, the former having been handed the title of Governor of Gran Canaria. Rejón quickly made an enemy of the new governor and was sent back to the mainland in chains but managed to clear his name and soon returned to wreak his revenge. He captured the governor, decapitated him and banished Bermúdez to Lanzarote. These events delayed the conquest attempt considerably; in the two years that the Spanish had been on the island, they had barely strayed from their camp. News of Rejón's behaviour reached the Catholic kings, who sent another army to the island under control of Jerez-born Pedro de Vera, the island's new governor. Once de Vera had prosecuted Rejón and sent him back to Spain he began to make up for lost time, conning the Canarios on to boats, pledging to help them start a new and better life in Tenerife, when in fact they were destined to become slaves.

De Vera was planning to take control of Gáldar, the then capital of the island. The Canarios fought bravely under Doramas, but even he wasn't immune to de Vera's dirty dealings. Doramas challenged the Spaniards to fight but, warned against going it alone, de Vera took along an ally who attacked Doramas from behind, killing him. Tenesor Semidan, *guanarteme* of Gáldar, was captured in a later battle and sent to Spain with a number of his subjects as testament to the success of the conquest. He was baptised by the Catholic monarchs and became known as Fernando Guanarteme. He later returned to Gran Canaria and played a part in the conquest of his homeland, convincing his fellow islanders to give in to the Spanish. Pedro de Vera and his men continued to attack settlements across the island; the last Canarios surrendered in the Tirajana mountains in 1483.

The population has grown from 8,000 in the 17th century to almost 800,000 today, making it the most populous island in the Canaries. Immigrants account for

PINTADERAS

There's many a young Canarian who sports a necklace with an aboriginal motif, but it would be interesting to find how many actually know where the designs come from. These symbols form an important part of the Canarian identity and while some are taken from the various *grabados* (rock engravings) found around the archipelago, the majority of the designs come from the mysterious *pintaderas*. Hundreds of these clay stamps, sporting circular and triangular designs, have been found across Gran Canaria and naturally there are various theories as to their use. Early historians believed that the Guanches smeared the *pintaderas* with some kind of paint and then used them to stamp designs on their skin – a kind of temporary tattoo. Other theories suggested that they were used to add interest to clothes or pottery, or that they were actually oversized pendants, meant to be worn around the neck. In 1942 Georges Marcy came up with the theory that the *pintaderas* were used to place a seal of identification on grain stores. His assumption was based on similar artefacts used by mountain populations in Algeria and this is the most generally accepted theory today. You can see a good selection of *pintaderas* in Las Palmas's Museo Canario.

around 5% of the population, with the majority coming from Colombia, Germany and the United Kingdom.

Geography

Around 80% of Gran Canaria emerged from the sea some 15 million years ago, with the remainder of what we see today formed around four million years ago. It's the third largest island at 1,532km^2 and can be cut into two distinct parts by drawing an imaginary line from Guía to Agüimes, with the old part of the island falling southwest of that line. It is known as *la isla redonda* ('the round island') and only the northwest spoils the island's circular shape, looking like someone has taken a bite out of it. The arid south of the island has almost year-round sun, with just a few cloudy or rainy days, while the north has a slightly cooler climate and counts on considerable rain in the winter months, creating verdant forests and mountains. The *panza de burro* ('donkey's belly'), formed by the *alisios* winds, hangs over the capital in summer months but disappears as you drive south, as do the rain clouds in winter. In the coldest months half the island flocks to the island's highest point, Pico de las Nieves (1,950m), to enjoy the light covering of snow that falls there. Get there early if you want to partake, for it soon becomes dirty sludge. Gran Canaria's largest volcanic crater is Bandama, not far from the capital, at 800m in diameter and 200m deep. The average rainfall in Gran Canaria is 300mm a year.

Economy

Gran Canaria is the island with the most diversity in terms of industry: construction is an important earner, though also a cause of concern for environmental groups. The ship-building industry is of considerable importance and much of the island's income is generated by Las Palmas's outsized port. Of course, the biggest money-maker is tourism, evident in the sprawl of the southern tourist resorts. To the despair of many, new hotels are still shooting up everywhere, though tourism chiefs are trying to encourage quality tourism rather than stick to the traditional bums-on-seats approach. Tomatoes, bananas and fishing also create a reasonable revenue.

Flora and fauna

There are 80 species of flora that are endemic to the island and a further 124 that are found only in the archipelago. Gran Canaria's unique plants include the Tenteniguada viper's bugloss (*Limonium sventenii*) and the beautiful but rare Gran Canaria sea lavender (*Echium callithyrsum*) There are important areas of Canarian pine in Tamadaba and Pilancones and a small, somewhat dishevelled laurel forest in the north of the island, Los Tilos de Moya. You might find a few dragon trees in inaccessible ravines like Arguineguín and Fataga. The great spotted woodpecker (*Dendrocopos major*) lives in the pine forests, as does the chaffinch (see *Conservation*, below). There are some interesting migratory birds to be found around the Charco de Maspalomas.

Conservation

As in other islands, Gran Canaria's biggest problem is lack of water. Although it rains more than in the eastern islands, only 25% of the rainfall is used, with desalination providing the rest of the tap water. There are over 60 dams on the island and more than 2,000 wells, though more than half of the latter are dry. The island racks up an impressive 32 protected spaces, including the Maspalomas sand dunes special nature reserve. There is considerable concern for the Gran Canaria blue chaffinch (*Fringilla teydea polatzeki*), and a conservation programme has been started. The bird is in danger of extinction due to the lack of water, increased number of human visitors to its habitat and the annual forest fires that damage large areas of Canarian pine.

Festivals
Carnival is a lavish affair, though not quite as impressive as Santa Cruz's celebration (however, you won't find many Canariones who'll admit that). The celebrations centre on Parque Santa Catalina, with the parade crossing the entire city and usually lasting more than five hours. The other biggie in Gran Canaria is the *Bajada de la Rama* (the Descent of the Branch), a rainmaking festival with its roots in aboriginal times. A procession collects branches from the Tamadaba region and then heads to Agaete and then on to the coast to beat the sea with the branches. The real fun is the *verbena* (street party) on August 4 in Agaete, though its popularity is getting out of control and the tiny town can barely hold the thousands of revellers. The celebrations in honour of the island's patron saint (Nuestra Señora del Pino) also attract large numbers of revellers who flock to the normally deserted town of Teror on September 7 and 8. In the south of the island, gay pride is a big event, with a procession and plenty of parties and events.

Food
The island offers all the usual Canarian favourites, though there are a few specialities that will appeal to sweet-toothed travellers. Cakes and biscuits using almonds are big business in Tejeda and Valsequillo, while islanders come from miles around to stock up on Moya's tasty *bizcochos*, a crispy sponge, like the ones used in British trifle.

GETTING THERE AND AWAY
By air
Binter Canarias Tel: 902 39 13 92; www.bintercanarias.es. *El Hierro:* 4 a week.
Fuerteventura: 10 a day. *La Gomera:* 2 a day. *La Palma:* 2 a day. *Lanzarote:* 8–10 a day. *Tenerife North:* 15 a day during the week and 10 on weekends. *Tenerife South:* 2 a day.
Islas Airways Tel: 902 47 74 48; www.islasairways.com. *Fuerteventura:* 5 a day. *La Palma:* 2 a day. *Tenerife North:* 1 a day.

By sea
Fred Olsen Tel: 902 10 01 07; email: reserves@fredolsen.es; www.fredolsen.es. *Tenerife:* 6 a day (from Agaete, includes free bus from Las Palmas).
Trasmediterránea Tel: 902 45 46 54; www.trasmediterranea.es. *Fuerteventura:* 1 jetfoil per day (to Morro Jable); 3 ferries a week to Puerto del Rosario. *La Palma:* 1 a week. *Lanzarote:* 3 a week (to Arrecife). *Tenerife:* 3 jetfoils a day and 1 slower ferry (all to Santa Cruz). *Cádiz:* 1 a week
Naviera Armas Tel: 902 45 65 00; www.naviera-armas.com. *Lanzarote:* 3 a week. *Tenerife:* 2 a day.

GETTING AROUND
Public transport
The bus service is comprehensive and you could quite happily move around *en guagua* (by bus) for the duration of your stay, provided you don't mind waiting around a bit. Fares to get around the island aren't cheap and it's definitely worth buying a *tarjeta insular* (see page 40) if you plan to do more than a couple of journeys. The card gives you a 20% discount.

Car hire
Avis Tel: 928 57 95 78 (airport); 928 26 55 67 (Las Palmas)
Betacar Tel: 928 57 42 44 (airport); 928 26 36 97 (Las Palmas); 928 76 55 00 (Playa del Inglés)
Cicar Tel: 928 57 44 24 (airport); 928 26 40 89 (Las Palmas); 928 76 76 50 (Playa del Inglés)
Hertz Tel: 928 57 95 77 (airport); 928 22 88 46 (Las Palmas); 928 76 30 26 (Playa del Inglés)
Reisen Tel: 928 57 91 59 (airport)
Union Rent Tel: 928 29 67 01 (Las Palmas); 928 77 82 80 (Playa del Inglés)

WHERE TO STAY
Las Palmas has ample accommodation for all budgets, from some pretty seedy guesthouses to the five-star magnificence of the Hotel Santa Catalina. Accommodation would seem to be in abundance in the southern tourist resorts, but the majority of the garish buildings you'll see are tour operator-owned apartments. In other towns accommodation is limited, though there are a few family-run hotels or *pensiones* around. As in all the islands, the finest accommodation option is renting a rural house. In Artenara don't miss the chance to stay in a converted cave house, bookable through **Retur** (tel: 928 66 16 68; fax: 928 66 15 60; www.returcanarias.com). They have other houses across the island if you don't fancy sleeping in a cave. Prices vary but expect to pay around €60 per night for up to four people. **Gran Canaria Rural** (tel: 928 46 25 47; fax: 928 46 08 89; email: info@grancanariarural.com; www.grancanariarural.com) have a couple of dozen cottages, mostly in the lush north. Prices average €75 for two people and €105 for four; many of their properties have swimming pools. The agency with most houses is **Gran Tural** (tel: 902 15 72 81; fax: 928 39 01 70; email: grancanaria@ecoturismocanarias.com; www.ecoturismocanarias.com/grancanaria). Prices average €50–70 for two people and €70–90 for four.

There are **campsites** across the island which are free although facilities are basic. You need to obtain a permit from the environment department of the *Cabildo*, tel: 928 38 41 65. Their office is in the OIAC building behind Calle Venegas, on the first floor. There are two hostels on the island, one in Valleseco that's ideal for hikers and another on the coast at Pozo Izquierdo, Gran Canaria's windsurfing Mecca.

ACTIVITIES
Hiking
Two of the finest barrancos for walking are Guayadeque in the south and Cernícalos, near Telde. The Tamadaba and Pilancones regions harbour surprising areas of pine forest, while there is tough but rewarding walking to be done in the mountains. The greenest area is the north, between Teror, Valleseco and Moya, where a small laurel forest still survives. A walk from your car to the base of Roque Nublo is short but worthwhile.

There are numerous companies offering hiking tours throughout the island, most of which are based in the south. Bear in mind that trips are often cancelled in July and August due to the extreme heat.

Canariaventura Based in Playa del Inglés; tel: 928 76 61 68; www.canariaventura.com. Hikes are €28 per person, including water and a snack. They also organise climbing, canoeing, archery, canyoning, bungee jumping and kayaking for around €50 per person.
Grupo Montañero Mogán Tel: 928 73 53 26; email: trekking.mogan@terra.es. Probably

the best range of tours on offer, many of them way off the beaten track. Walks leave every Sunday from the meeting point in Arguineguín. Tours cost €20 per person and must be booked by lunchtime on Friday.

Happy Biking Based in Playa del Inglés; tel: 928 76 68 32; email: info@happy-biking.com; www.happy-biking.com. Hiking trips are €37 per person including lunch and a drink; bike tours are €42 and include transport to the start of the route and a picnic lunch.

Rutas Canarias Based in Las Palmas; tel: 928 67 00 72; email: rutas_canarias@hotmail.com; http://rutascanarias.iespana.es. Highly informative walks every Sunday. Groups tend to be huge which is why they are considerably cheaper than the rest at €12 per person.

Viajes Drago Based in Playa del Inglés; tel: 928 72 03 03. They offer some original routes that many of the other companies don't have, including the barrancos of Guayadeque, Santa Lucía and the unmissable Cernícalos. They also run bus tours around the island for €35 per person.

Viajes Las Palomas Also known as Eurotrekking, Centro Comercial San Agustín; tel: 928 76 41 95; email: vpalomas@accesocero.es. A good variety of routes for €29 per person.

Boat trips

Naviera Armas offer an excellent excursion around the island, leaving from the harbour at Arguineguín. The boat does a complete circuit around the island, which takes about seven hours. While on board you get lunch and drinks and use of the swimming pool. Excursions leave every Tuesday and Thursday at 10.00, with a free bus leaving Las Palmas at 08.00. Tickets are €54 and can be bought from hotel receptions or at the harbour. There are plenty of boat trips on offer in the tourist resorts, particularly Puerto Rico.

Diving

The main attraction of diving around Gran Canaria is the large number of shipwrecks around its coast. The port in Las Palmas has been an important one since the 15th century, though the safety record hasn't always been as good as it is now. There are reckoned to be about a dozen sunken boats near the capital and a few scattered elsewhere around the island. If you're not looking for a wreck, the most interesting underwater life is around Playa del Cabrón.

As well as a reasonable number of companies in the resorts (see relevant chapters for details), there is an excellent diving school in the capital:

Buceo Canarias Calle Bernardo de la Torre in Las Palmas; tel: 928 26 27 86. The PADI open-water diver course costs €300 and takes a minimum of a week. They operate dives around the island.

Fishing

Although it's probably not somewhere you'd want to spend your trip, there is a good selection of fishing trips available in Puerto Rico. Expect to pay €40–60 for a full day out, usually including lunch.

Golf

There are six golf courses in Gran Canaria, including the oldest course in Spain, near the crater of Bandama. Three are in the north, close to Las Palmas, while the other three are near the tourist areas in the south of the island. Two of the courses (Real Club and El Cortijo) are for members only in the afternoons and on weekends. Eighteen holes costs between €50 and €80, depending on the course. www.grancanariagolf.org; email: info@grancanariagolf.org.

Helicopter rides

You can take a chopper ride to admire Gran Canaria's varied landscape. A short trip around the south of the island is €50 per person, while a long excursion starting in the south and flying over Roque Nublo before returning to the take-off point is €150 per person. **Blue Canarias Helicopters** are based at the Aeródromo El Berriel in San Agustín; tel: 928 15 72 15; www.bluecanarias.com.

Skydiving

There are certainly worse places to jump out of a plane than over the *dunas de Maspalomas*. After a 20-minute flight you jump with an instructor from a height of 3,500m and freefall for 45 seconds. It costs €210 (or €190 if there's more than one person). You can get photos and a video of your jump for an extra €80. Tel: 670 80 81 02; email: skydivegrancanaria@mundivia.es; www.skydivegrancanaria.es.

Windsurfing and surfing

Surfers tend to stick to the north, with the top spots being the north end of Las Canteras, El Frontón on the Gáldar coast and Playa de la Caleta in the Moya municipality, the site of an international long-board competition in November. Pozo Izquierdo is probably the second finest place for windsurfing in the archipelago (after Sotavento in Fuerteventura), though it's not at all suitable for beginners. There is a large windsurfing school there that caters to all levels and ferries novices off to calmer waters to learn. There are plenty of beaches suitable for windsurfing between Las Palmas and Maspalomas.

LAS PALMAS

With almost 400,000 inhabitants, Las Palmas is the only place in the Canary Islands with that big-city feel. The settlement was founded in 1478 by Juan Rejón and obtained city status in 1515 at the insistence of Queen Juana. She bestowed the title of 'most noble and loyal city' on Las Palmas. By the end of the 16th century it had more than 80 houses and its first cartographer, Torriani, described it as 'illustrious and renowned'. Although once a walled city – an attempt to keep the pirates out – the walls came down in the mid 19th century, perhaps because of the increasing number of tourists visiting. Las Palmas is essentially split into five sections. The southernmost area, Vegueta, is the old part of town and the site of the original settlement. Its narrow cobbled roads are reminiscent of a small Spanish town and it boasts the cathedral and a number of museums. It's a delightful area and is worth paying a visit to Las Palmas for. The next section is one of the city's main shopping areas, Triana, which stretches from the Teatro de Pérez Galdós to the bus station and San Telmo park. The area from the bus station to Avenida Juan XXIII is a grotty commercial and residential area with nothing of interest to tourists. From the avenida, the architecture changes completely as you reach Ciudad Jardín (Garden City), an area of mansions built in the 18th and 19th centuries by British settlers. On reaching the old football stadium, you'll find the other main shopping area starts, with Avenida Mesa y López being the main place for hitting the shops. From there it's only a five-minute walk to a fine city beach, Las Canteras.

Getting there and around
From the airport
There are regular buses between the airport and the capital (number 60), running from 06.00 until 02.00. A taxi will cost around €20.

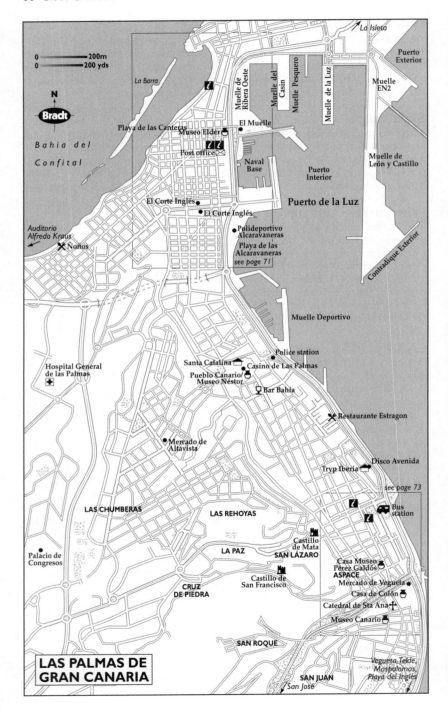

LAS PALMAS DE GRAN CANARIA

By car

While it's possible to drive around the city, it's not recommended unless you enjoy heavy traffic and getting lost in one-way streets. Parking is an absolute nightmare. Take the bus instead.

By bus

There is a good service around Las Palmas with frequent buses taking you to all points of the city. Any journey costs €0.90 or you can buy a *bono de guagua* which gives you ten journeys for €5.10. These are available from the bus station and from some newsagents.

By taxi

You might be amazed at the sheer number of taxis in the capital. It's not difficult to find a cab and journeys are not expensive.

Where to stay
Upmarket

Hotel Fataga Calle Nestor de la Torre 21; tel: 928 29 0614; fax: 928 29 27 86; email: hotel@hotelfatga.com; www.hotelfataga.com. Really a business hotel, though perfectly equipped for tourists too. Each floor is decorated to represent a different Canary Island. There are no single rooms. Double €80, including breakfast.

Hotel Imperial Playa Calle Ferreras 1; tel: 928 46 88 54; fax: 928 46 94 42; www.nh-hoteles.com. At the La Isleta end of Las Canteras and boasting the best views of any Las Palmas hotel. Rooms are modern and every one comes equipped with a PlayStation. Single €95; double €105; breakfast €9 extra.

Hotel Meliá Las Palmas Playa de las Canteras; tel: 928 26 91 50; fax: 928 26 84 11; email: melia.las.palmas@solmelia.com; www.solmelia.com. Excellent location, though the rooms and service are a little disappointing for a 5-star hotel. Has an excellent restaurant specialising in seafood and rice. Single €100; double €150; suites from €230 to €450.

Hotel Parque Calle Muelle de Las Palmas 2; tel: 928 36 80 00; fax: 928 36 88 56; email: comercial@hparque.com; www.hparque.com. Good location near Triana and the old part of town and right next to the bus station. Has extra thick windows to keep the noise from the road out. Single €62; double €70.

Hotel Santa Catalina Calle León y Castillo 227; tel: 928 24 30 40; fax: 928 24 27 64; www.hotelsantacatalina.com. Without doubt the city's finest hotel, frequented by the rich and famous. Built in the late 19th century and quite recently renovated, it sits in the Parque Doramas and is set back from the road, so it's a pretty quiet place. Rooms are large and elegant, all with views of the park. Single €120; double €185.

Hotel Tryp Iberia Calle Alcalde Ramírez Bethencourt 8; tel: 928 36 11 33; fax: 928 36 13 44; email: tryp.iberia@solmelia.com; www.solmelia.com. Not in the best area of the city for tourists and it's really a business hotel. Some rooms have excellent sea and city views, though you do have to work a little to ignore the busy Avenida Marítima between you and the ocean. Staff are very friendly. Single €95; double €120.

Mid-range

Aparthotel Las Lanzas Calle Bernardo de la Torre 79; tel: 928 26 55 04; fax: 928 26 55 08; email: laslanzas@inicia.com. Clean, close to the beach and doesn't seem to have been decorated since the '60s. Studio apartment for 2 people €40.

Hotel Faycán Calle Nicolás Estévanez 61; tel: 928 27 06 50; fax: 928 27 91 23; email: hfaycan@infonegocio.com. Only a minute's walk from the beach. All rooms have TV and fridge. Single €38; double €51; triple €61, including breakfast. Also have studio apartments available for €5 extra.

Hotel Olympia Calle Dr Grau Bassas 1; tel: 928 26 17 20; fax: 928 26 26 17. Small family-run hotel near the beach. Rooms are nothing spectacular but are comfortable and service is friendly. Single €36; double €42; triple €54.

Hotel Valencia Calle Valencia 64; tel: 928 29 25 84; fax: 928 23 09 29. The hotel is old and could do with a makeover, but it's perfectly acceptable for a few days. Some rooms have a balcony. It's a slightly noisy location, right next to the market, but very convenient for shopping and nightlife and not far from the beach. Single €34; double €45; triple €60.

Budget

Hostal Alcaravaneras Calle Luis Antúnez; tel: 928 24 89 14; email: hostalalcaravaneras@telefonica.es. One of the best budget options. Bright rooms, some with private bathroom. Single €15; double €18/€20 without/with bathroom.

Hotel El Cisne Calle Ferreras 19; tel: 928 46 88 20. It's a bit run-down but rooms are clean with TV and private bathroom. You won't find another budget option this good so close to the beach. Single €22; double €25; triple €35.

Pensión España Calle Domingo J Navarro 34; tel: 928 36 09 60. Nice old building with high ceilings and big windows but rooms are a bit grotty. Quiet location in the Triana side streets. Single €8; double €16, with shared bathroom.

Pensión Falow Calle Alfredo Calderón 25; tel: 928 23 06 27. Boasts hot and cold water! Rooms at the back are a bit dark and all rooms are quite small. Some have a bathroom, which is more of a cubicle with walls that don't quite reach the ceiling. Single €12; double €20.

Pensión Perojo Calle Perojo 1; tel: 928 37 13 87. Cheerful rooms in a marvellous old building near the main Triana shopping street. Bathrooms are shared. Single €15; double €24.

Where to eat
North

Casa Carmelo At the far end of Las Canteras, next to the Hotel Imperial. One of Las Palmas's best meat restaurants.

Carusso Plazoleta de Farray. You can indulge in a bit of people-watching while you enjoy their extensive tapas menu. Also has a good choice of breakfasts and all at very reasonable prices.

El Anexo Calle Salvador Cuyás; tel: 928 27 26 45. Specialises in rice dishes, including the not very pretty to look at but delicious *arroz negro* ('black rice' – rice cooked in squid ink with squid rings). Closed on Sundays.

El Coto Calle Alfredo Calderón; tel: 928 24 67 76. Romantic, cosy place serving excellent Lebanese food. At €12 and above for a main course it's not cheap but definitely worth it.

El Quiquere Calle Valencia; tel: 928 24 08 71. A bit bright and garish, but is the best place in this area to eat tapas. Always very popular so it's wise to book, especially on weekend nights.

La Pizza Calle Tomás Miller; tel: 928 26 85 79. A cosy, romantic place to eat pizza and the oldest pizzeria in the archipelago. The pizzas are cooked on a wood fire, giving them a better taste than most.

Mexico Tex Calle Tomás A Edison; tel: 928 22 02 23. Extensive menu of Mexican dishes and a few less spicy choices. Portions are huge so go easy on the starters. Booking ahead is advisable on weekends. Open for lunch and dinner; main meals are around €10.

Nabila Calle Leon Tolstoy; tel: 928 47 27 67. Popular Moroccan restaurant with excellent food and service, seriously comfy seats and demonstrations of belly-dancing at weekends. Expect to pay €15 for a main course. Closed Sunday evenings.

Ñoños Paseo de las Canteras, near the auditorium. The tapas is excellent, especially the seafood, but the bar's not much to look at. It gets pretty busy but you can't book – you take

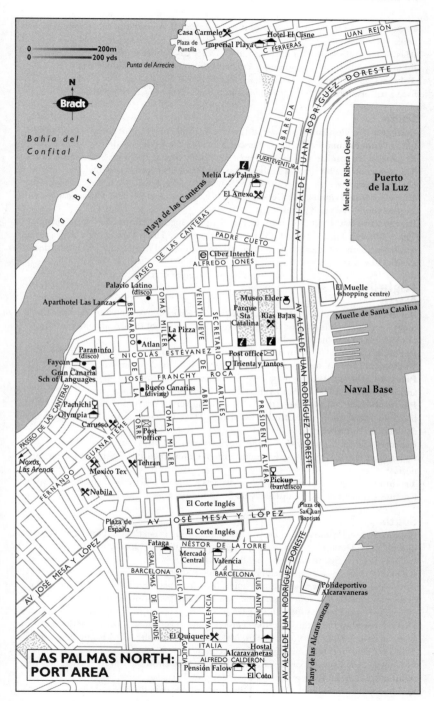

LAS PALMAS NORTH: PORT AREA

a ticket on arrival and wait for your number to be called. At least you can admire the view while you wait.

Rías Bajas Calle Simón Bolivar; tel: 928 27 13 16. Las Palmas's top restaurant, serving the finest seafood in town, but don't expect change from €60 for a meal for two.

Tehran Calle Bernardo de la Torre; tel: 928 22 28 17. Family-run Persian restaurant. The food is excellent though service can be a little slow. Gets busy at weekends.

South

Bodegón Pueblo Canario Tapas and typical Spanish cuisine. Not cheap at around €10 for a main meal, but the Pueblo Canario is a lovely place to sit outside.

El Rincón de Joselito Calle Cano Peregrina. Fancy cuisine based on Spanish favourites. The restaurant is a bit bright and the décor is cold but it's popular nonetheless. Main meals €12 and above.

La Rebaná de Triana Calle Constantina, off Calle Mayor de Triana. Cosy tapas bar with a varied menu and good prices.

Restaurante Estragon Av Marítima. Popular place serving Basque and Riojan cuisine.

Tasca Sillares Tucked away in the back streets near the Hotel Parque, they have a varied menu with some good salads, Canarian tapas, some original main meals and a tasty dessert menu. Closed on Sundays.

Nightlife
North

Bar Bahía Av Juan XXIII. By day it's a below average café, frequented by the over 70s. By night it's a 'start the night' bar full of young people who want to take advantage of the outdoor tables and cheap drinks.

Pachichi Calle 2 de Mayo, near Las Canteras. Another early bar with cheap drinks. It's a bit dingy and has no music but gets very busy and has a studeny crowd.

Palacio Latino Calle Luis Morote. As the name suggests this place plays Latin rhythms and stays open until 06.00. Sometimes attracts a few unsavoury characters.

Paraninfo Calle Nicolás Estévanez. This is the university disco so it's a bit shabby but plays good rock music and often has live bands. There is a cover charge but you get a ticket that entitles you to a drink.

Pickup Calle Montevideo. Gets going at about 03.00 and plays chart music. Lively and with a good crowd. Expect to pay a minimum of €5 for any drink. There are similar bars nearby.

Treinta y tantos Calle Franchy y Roca. Attracts a slightly older crowd and has reasonable live music on Friday and Saturday nights from midnight.

South

Casino de Las Palmas If you fancy a flutter the casino is next to the Hotel Santa Catalina in the Parque Doramas. Open to all as long as you're over 18. Open every day 16.00–04.00; entrance is €3 or free for those staying in the hotel.

Cuasquías Live music venue behind the Monopol shopping centre. It has rock, jazz and Latin bands every Friday and Saturday night (but don't get there too early as bands often don't start until 02.00). Drinks are quite expensive and there is sometimes an entry charge, depending on the band. Open until 06.00.

Disco Avenida Under the Tryp Iberia Hotel. Plays '60s, '70s and '80s music and gets going at about 02.00 (open until 06.00). Make sure you visit the ATM before you arrive – drinks are extortionately priced.

El Monje Calle Espiritú Santo. Early-ish bar, very popular in the summer when they put tables outside in the shadow of the cathedral.

La Floridita Calle Remedios. One of the cheesiest places in the city and also one of the

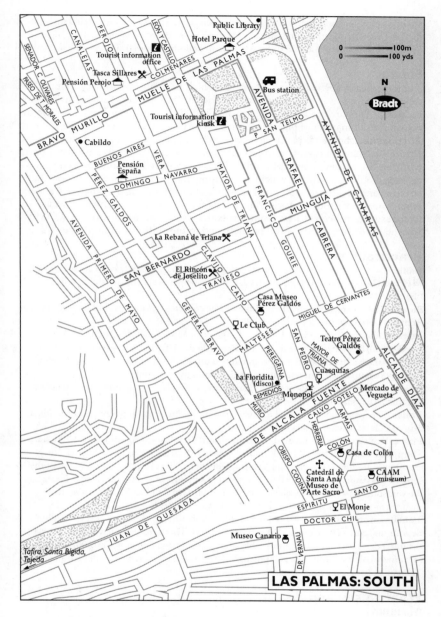

LAS PALMAS: SOUTH

largest, with numerous floors, patios and gardens. It's full of middle-aged men in smart suits and there's a strict dress code. Plays all kinds of pop music.

Le Club Calle Dr Rafael González. Small, claustrophobic and always packed out. Plays house and techno music and stays open until around 04.00.

Monopol Plaza de las Ranas. The basement of the shopping centre is full of life on weekend nights when the dozen or so tiny bars open their doors. There's a good atmosphere if you can concentrate on shutting out the music from the surrounding bars – they're a bit close together. And they all share a toilet, so expect to spend half the night queuing. Drinks are around €3 and the bars stay open until about 04.00.

Fiestas

The main party in Las Palmas is carnival, which happens in February/March. The crowning of the various queens takes place in the Parque Santa Catalina and makeshift bars are set up in the surrounding area. Everyone dresses up for the occasion in all manner of bizarre costumes. The party culminates with the Entierro de la Sardina, a funeral procession where the citizens dress up as widows to bid farewell to the sardine for another year. The giant fish is put in a boat and burnt while an impressive fireworks display fills the sky over Las Canteras. On June 24 the beach fills up with revellers celebrating the San Juan fiesta. People build bonfires and challenge each other to jump over the flames and there's a general atmosphere of merriment. Parque Santa Catalina becomes a stage in October/November as bands from across the world visit to perform in WOMAD and the Las Palmas film festival is celebrated in the auditorium in March.

Practicalities

Banks There are banks everywhere, though you'll find a particularly good choice on Calle Mayor de Triana, Avenida Mesa y López, Calle Franchy y Roca and around Parque Santa Catalina.

Health The Hospital Dr Negrin is in the El Horno district of the city, not far from the Las Arenas shopping centre; tel: 928 45 00 00.

Internet Ciber Interbit, Calle Alfredo L Jones, open Mon–Fri 10.00–24.00, Sat–Sun 10.30–24.00; €1.50 per hour; Atlan, Calle Bernardo de la Torre, open every day 12.00–24.00; €1.20 per hour; there is free access on the ground floor of the main library, next to the bus station, but you can stay online for only 15 minutes.

Pharmacy There are scores of them everywhere, all displaying the timetable of where you can find a late pharmacy.

Police The main police station is a rather magnificent building on the Avenida Marítima, near the Hotel Santa Catalina.

Post office On Calle Bernardo de la Torre; Mon–Fri 08.30–20.30, Sat 09.30–13.00.

Shopping The shopper who can't find what they're looking for in Las Palmas is a fussy one. There are four large shopping centres: La Ballena, Siete Palmas (both way out of the centre), Las Arenas and El Muelle. Other main shopping areas are Calle Mesa y López and the surrounding streets and Calle Mayor de Triana. There's a handicrafts market in Vegueta most Sunday mornings where you can also witness folk music.

Tourist information The main tourist information office is on Calle León y Castillo, near Parque San Telmo, open Mon–Fri 08.00–15.00. There are also a few kiosks around the town that observe the same timetable (though some don't open until 09.00). Kiosks are to be found on the Las Canteras promenade, in Parque Santa Catalina and in Parque San Telmo.

What to see and do

Museums

CAAM (Centro Atlántico de Arte Moderno)

Calle Los Balcones, Vegueta

The EU's southernmost modern art gallery, with temporary exhibitions changing every month or so. The exhibitions are usually from European, Latin American and African artists, emphasising the fact that the islands are a link between the three continents. There is a smaller gallery near the Casa de Colón which has temporary exhibitions by Canarian artists. Open Tue–Sat 10.00–21.00, Sun 10.00–14.00; entrance is free.

Casa de Colón
Calle de Colón, Vegueta
If you have any questions about Christopher Columbus and his relationship with the archipelago, you'll find the answers in this well laid out museum, which was the house of the island's first governors. Columbus is said to have stayed here in 1492 when he docked in Las Palmas to repair a ship. The museum also has information on the history of Las Palmas, an area dedicated to pre-Columbian America and some fascinating old maps. Open Mon–Fri 09.00–19.00, Sat–Sun 09.00–15.00; entrance is free.

Casa Museo Pérez Galdós
Calle Cano, Triana
The museum is dedicated to Gran Canaria's most famous writer, Benito Pérez Galdós, and is based in what was his childhood house. Open Mon–Fri 09.00–19.00; Sat 10.00–17.00; Sun 10.00–14.00; all visits are guided and leave on the hour; entrance is free.

Catedrál de Santa Ana and Museo de Arte Sacro
Plaza de Santa Ana, Vegueta
The Cathedral is open to the public Mon–Sat 08.00–10.00, Sun 08.30–13.30, 18.00–20.00 and entrance is free. You can also take the lift to the top of the tower for a good view over the old part of town. It costs €1.50 and is open Mon–Fri 09.15–18.00, Sat 09.15–14.45. The museum houses religious sculptures and paintings from the 16th to the 19th centuries. It's around the right-hand side of the cathedral and is open Mon–Fri 10.00–16.30, Sat 10.00–13.30; entrance is €3.

Museo Canario
Calle Dr Verneau, Vegueta
Rather an old-fashioned museum but with decent information on the prehistory, archaeology and natural history of the islands. They boast the largest collection of Cromanoide mummies in the world and there's a terrifying room full of skulls. It's considered the most complete collection on pre-Hispanic Canary Islands culture. Open Mon–Fri 10.00–20.00, Sat–Sun 10.00–14.00; entrance €3.

Museo Elder
Parque Santa Catalina
The slogan of this science and technology museum is 'prohibido no tocar' ('forbidden not to touch'). It has some interesting interactive exhibits, though it's not a patch on the Science and Cosmos Museum in Tenerife. There is also an IMAX cinema with a daily showing in English (you need to book in advance). Open Tue–Sat 10.00–20.00; entrance is €3 for adults and €2.10 for under 18s; a ticket for the IMAX is €4.50 for adults, €3 for children.

Pueblo Canario
Ciudad Jardín
Built in the middle of the 20th century in what is known as neo-Canarian style, the Pueblo Canario is now a quiet place to have lunch, do a bit of handicraft shopping or visit the museum. The shop is open Mon–Fri 09.30–13.30, 17.30–20.30, Sun

10.00–14.00. On Sundays there is a display of traditional Canarian music and dance in the courtyard at 11.30.

Museo Néstor
In the Pueblo Canario
This is another of the museums paying homage to famous residents, this time to the early 20th-century artist Néstor de la Torre, one of Spain's most important symbolist painters. Mon–Sat 10.00–20.00, Sun 10.30–14.30; entrance is €2, free for children and students.

Learn Spanish
The Gran Canaria School of Languages Calle Grau Bassas 27; tel: 928 26 79 71; fax: 928 27 89 80; email: office@grancanariaschool.com; www.grancanariaschool.com. Intensive Spanish courses from one to four weeks (20 hours per week). Courses for absolute beginners start on the first Monday of every month and other levels can start on any Monday of the year. You can attend a free taster class to make sure that you like their method.

TAFIRA
Jardín Botánico Canario Viera y Clavijo
Spain's largest botanical garden is just 7km from the capital, on the way to Santa Brígida. As well as the endemic and native species, there are also examples of flora that have been introduced into the archipelago, including an impressive selection of cacti and succulent plants. It's well designed and a pleasure to visit, especially in the winter months when the rains have been. Open every day 09.00–18.00; entrance is free.

SANTA BRÍGIDA
Santa Brígida has a large park, a reasonable farmers' market and a well-stocked tourist information office but is nothing to write home about. The real interest lies in the surrounding area, since this is Gran Canaria's wine district. The tourist information office has a leaflet detailing the bodegas in the area and when they are open to the public. There are also plans to open a wine museum in the town.

Getting there
Bus 303 leaves Las Palmas every half-hour on its way to San Mateo. Line 311 leaves the Santa Catalina bus station about every hour, passing through Bandama and La Atalaya before reaching Santa Brígida.

Where to stay
Hotel Rural Villa del Monte Calle Castaño Bajo 9; tel: 928 64 43 89; fax: 928 64 15 88; email: pwonisch@teleline.es; www.hotelvilladelmonte.com. Although it's an old house, the décor is contemporary, if a little mismatched. The quiet location and gardens make it the ideal place for a relaxing break as long as you don't mind large dogs roaming around. Single €50; double €65; suite €100.
Hotel Escuela Calle Real de Coello; tel: 828 01 04 00; fax: 828 01 04 01; email: hesb@hecansa.com; www.hecansa.com. Peaceful place out of the town on the road to Tafira. Rooms are large and there are nice gardens to lounge around in. Single €100; double €125.

Where to eat
Bar Restaurante Parque Tapas and sandwiches. Has a terrace overlooking the park.
Pizzería California Calle Manuel Hernández Muñoz. Decent pizza menu and a few pasta dishes.

Restaurante Chino Internacional Further down the same road. Average Chinese restaurant, also with a take-away service.

Restaurante La Cuchara de Plata Circunvalación. Undoubtedly Santa Brígida's best restaurant, specialising in Spanish cuisine made with all natural ingredients.

Practicalities

Banks La Caixa, Calle 18 de Julio, open Mon–Fri 08.15–14.00, Thu 16.30–19.45; Santander Central Hispano, opposite the post office, open Mon–Fri 08.30–14.00, Sat 08.30–13.00; La Caja de Canarias, next door, open Mon–Fri 08.00–14.00, Thu 17.30–19.30.

Health The Health Centre is on Calle 18 de Julio.

Internet Cyber Jayma, Calle Manuel Hernández Muñoz, open Mon–Sat 11.00–23.00, Sun 12.00–15.00, 16.00–23.00; €2.10 per hour.

Pharmacy On Calle Alfereces Provisionales.

Police The Policía Local is on Av Palmeral.

Post office On Calle José Antonio Primo de Rivera, open Mon–Fri 08.30–14.30, Sat 09.30–13.00.

Shopping There is a farmers' market on Calle 18 de Julio; Sat 07.30–20.00, Sun 07.30–14.00.

Tourist information On Calle 18 de Julio, open Mon–Fri 08.00–15.00, 16.00–20.00.

What to see and do
Parque Agrícola del Guiniguada
This large park is great for kids, since it has a few farm animals scattered here and there. It's also a nice place to eat the picnic you've bought from the market. Open daily 08.30–19.00; entrance is free.

LA ATALAYA
La Atalaya has a long history of ceramic production, which is being preserved at the **Centro Locero de La Atalaya**. The pottery on show has all been made using traditional methods and you can buy whatever takes your fancy. The centre is open Mon–Fri 09.00–14.00, 17.00–21.00, Sat 10.00–14.00. Nearby and with the same opening hours is **Ecomuseo Casa Alfar**, once the cave house and workshop of La Atalaya's best-loved potter, Panchito. Bus 311 runs between Las Palmas and La Atalaya (see Santa Brígida for times).

VEGA DE SAN MATEO
San Mateo is basically a few shops and houses scattered along a busy main road, so it's not the most charming place to hang out. Its small church is a block behind the main road but it's not worth stopping here just for that. There's a reasonable **ethnographic museum** on the main road, **La Cantonera**, which has decent exhibits on the history and handicrafts of the island. Open Mon–Sat 10.00–16.00; entrance €3.60 which includes a glass of wine and some nibbles. The main reason to visit San Mateo is to browse around its excellent farmers' market, held behind the bus station on Saturday and Sunday mornings. If you do want to stick around you could do worse than stay in the **Hotel Rural La Cantonera** (Av Tinamar 17; tel: 928 66 17 95; fax: 928 66 17 77). It has the air of a honeymoon hotel, with its cosy rooms set in an old mansion. There's also a sauna, jacuzzi and beauty salon. Single €38; double €100 including breakfast. There is also a nice restaurant at the hotel serving typical Canarian fare. There are buses every half an hour to and from Las Palmas.

VALSEQUILLO
There's no arguing that Valsequillo boasts a stunning location which rivals even that of Tejeda. It's surrounded by steep ravine walls enveloped in green vegetation

in the winter months. Traditional buildings line the narrow streets, leading to the rather oversized San Miguel Church, built in the early 20th century. One thing you'll notice about Valsequillo is a lack of people and someone has seen fit to scatter a few statues here and there in everyday positions (such as a small boy relieving himself against a lamppost), perhaps to give the tiny town more of a feeling of life. Other than enjoy the utter silence and do a bit of shopping at the Sunday market, there is nothing to do, although there are some excellent handicraft and cheese shops in surrounding villages. It's worth visiting in early February when the almond trees are in flower or on September 29 for the bizarre Fiesta de San Miguel (see box, page 22).

TELDE

Gran Canaria's second city pales in comparison with most towns on the island and most people don't bother to visit. However, it would probably surprise a large number of Canarios that Telde actually has a charming historic quarter, at least as appealing as Vegueta in Las Palmas. A labyrinth of narrow alleys and cobbled streets lies just south of the old town's main road, Calle León y Castillo. If you're a fan of Canarian architecture or shady little plazas, Telde is as good a place as any to while away an hour or so. The **Museo de León y Castillo** is a delightful old building, though the museum's interest really lies solely in the architecture. It pays homage to Telde's most famous resident, politician Fernando de León y Castillo, and is based in his childhood home. The museum is filled with his writings and possessions, a few paintings and general bits and bobs related to the islands. Information is in Spanish only. It's open Mon–Fri 09.00–20.00, Sat 10.00–20.00, Sun 10.00–13.00; entrance is free. Staff at the museum also arrange free walking tours around the town as well as visits to Telde's most important archaeological sites, Cuatro Puertas and Tufia. There's a decent tourist information office a little further down the same road (open Mon–Fri 08.00–15.00), just before you reach the large church square. Ambling through the streets behind the 18th-century **Basílica de San Juan** is also pleasant, as is a wander around the impressive **Parque Urbano de San Juan**. At the far end of Calle León y Castillo, the **Iglesia de San Pedro Mártir** houses temporary exhibitions. The rest of Telde is a dull commercial zone with nothing of interest to the traveller.

INGENIO

Ingenio is known for its handicrafts and is the best place on the island to pick up ceramics or the famous embroidered tablecloths. The best place to buy is the **Museo de Piedras y Artesanía Canaria**. There's a small museum with a few random artefacts, a nice patio and some particularly smelly goats, but the shop is well stocked and sells craftwork from across the archipelago. It's out of the centre, but well signposted; open Mon–Sat 08.00–18.30; entrance is free. Other than that, Ingenio has a large, pleasant square and some picturesque narrow streets to get lost in. Follow signs for the *Casco Histórico* and church, since the rest of the town is rather ugly. If you're stopping for lunch you should sample the local speciality, Sopa de la Virgen, a thick soup made with beef, bread, eggs, chick-peas and cinnamon.

GUAYADEQUE

Although it's getting rather touristy these days, you can't dispute that the Barranco de Guayadeque is one of Gran Canaria's finest ravines. It stretches some 20km from the Caldera de los Marteles to the coast and boasts archaeological finds, some interesting endemic species and, due to its isolated position, a well-preserved culture. Entrance to the ravine is between Agüimes and Ingenio (signposted from both towns), and leads you to the village of Montaña de las Tierras, a small troglodyte settlement. A series of footpaths leads past the cave dwellings and you can pop your head round the door of the tiny church carved into the rock. You should eat in one of the cave restaurants while you are there. **Restaurante Tagoror** (tel: 928 17 20 13), another ten minutes' drive from the village, offers good Canarian cuisine and is amazingly cheap considering its popularity and the fact that it's well on the tourist trail. Main meals are about €6. Bookings are recommended, though if you turn up without one at least you can admire the view while you wait. There is also a visitor centre near the start of the ravine (as you enter from Ingenio), where the formation, aboriginal occupation and current importance of the ravine are explained; open Tue–Sat 09.00–17.00, Sun 10.00–18.00.

AGÜIMES

As you approach Agüimes from Ingenio, the dominating sight is the magnificent Templo de San Sebastián, declared a national historic and artistic monument in 1981. Founded in 1487, the town is one of Gran Canaria's finest as long as you head straight for the old part (follow signs for the *casco histórico*). Cobbled streets connect the numerous squares and there are plenty of pavement cafés where you can enjoy Agüimes' tranquillity. On the last Saturday in September the town pays homage to that Canarian favourite, *gofio*, in a wild party called the Traída del Agua y del Gofio. Dressed in traditional costume, revellers fetch bags of *gofio* from a nearby mill and return to the town square to hurl it at each other. It's a way of saying thank you for plenty of rain and a good harvest and is an excellent chance to see a truly Canarian celebration.

Getting there

There are buses from Las Palmas every half an hour which pass through Ingenio before reaching Agüimes.

Where to stay

There are two hotels in town, both run by the same company. There are also a number of *casas rurales*; contact the tourist information office for an up-to-date list.

Hotel Rural Casa de los Camellos Calle Progreso; tel: 928 78 50 03; fax: 928 78 50 53; email: hrcamellos@hecansa.com; www.hecansa.com. Rooms are a little chintzy but the shared facilities are good and it's a charming, intimate establishment. Single €50, double €70, breakfast is extra.
Hotel Rural Villa de Agüimes Calle El Sol; contact through the Hotel los Camellos. Another lovely little place, with just 6 bedrooms. The hotel is in traditional 19th-century style with an interior balcony. It used to serve as the Town Hall. Single €45; double €60, breakfast is extra.

Where to eat and drink

Agüimes is famed for its bread, so much so that a local phrase, 'better than bread from Agüimes', is used to describe something particularly superior. Of course, there are some charming places to sit out if you fancy something a bit more exciting than dry bread.

Bar La Esquina Calle Dr Joaquín Artiles. Popular choice with locals, serving all the usuals and a fair range of pizzas.
Bar La Juventud Plaza del Rosario. Opens evenings only and attracts a youngish crowd. More of a drinking place although there are a few snack foods on offer.

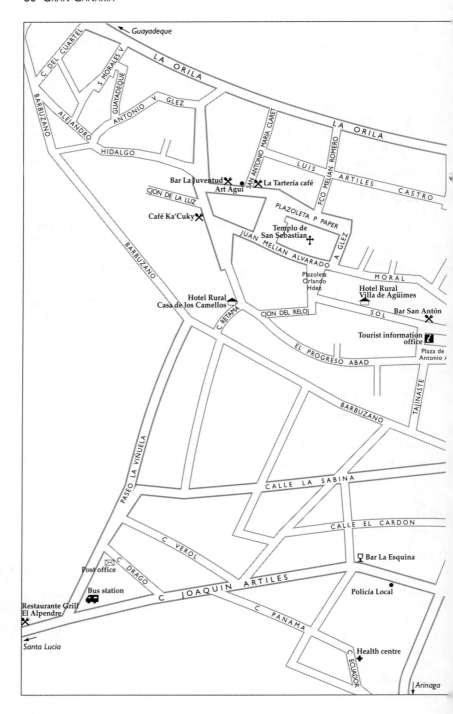

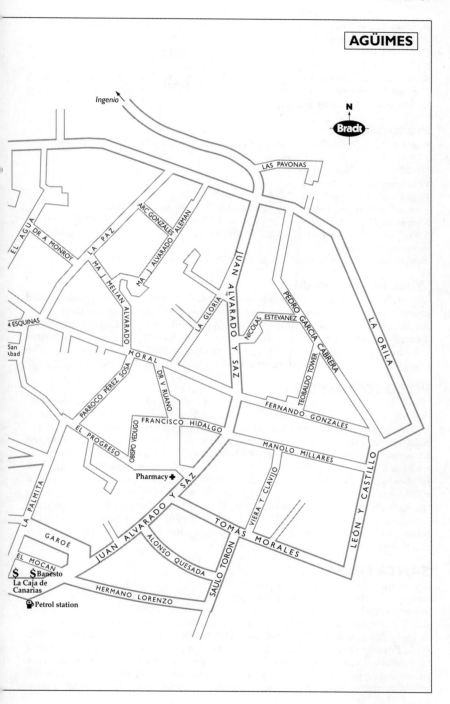

AGÜIMES

Ingenio

N

Bradt

LAS PAVONAS

EL AGUA
DR A MONROY
LA PAZ
ARC GONZALES
MA J ALVARADO ALEMAN
MA J MELIAN ALVARADO
LA GLORIA
JUAN ALVARADO Y SAZ
NICOLAS ESTEVANEZ
PEDRO GARCIA CABRERA
TEOBALDO TOWER
LA ORILA

4 ESQUINAS
San Abad
MORAL
PARROCO PEREZ SOSA
DR V RUANO
FERNANDO GONZALES

OBISPO VEDUGO
FRANCISCO HIDALGO
EL PROGRESO
MANOLO MILLARES
LEON Y CASTILLO

Pharmacy ✚

JUAN ALVARADO Y SAZ
VIERA Y CLAVIJO

LA PALMITA
GAROÉ
TOMÁS MORALES
EL MOCAN
ALONSO QUESADA
SAULO TORON
$ $ Banesto
La Caja de Canarias
HERMANO LORENZO
⛽ Petrol station

Bar San Antón Next to the tourist information office. The menu is far from exciting but it's a delightful place to sit out for a coffee or a plate of *papas arrugadas*.

Café Ka' Cuky Plaza del Rosario. Friendly places serving tapas and sandwiches.

La Tartería Plaza del Rosario. Excellent coffee and cakes.

Restaurante El Alpendre Calle Dr Joaquín Artiles, next to the swimming pool; tel: 928 78 67 83. Rather touristy but with good reason. There's a large terrace where you can enjoy the Canarian and international specials.

Practicalities

Banks La Caja de Canarias, on the town's main junction, open Mon–Fri 08.00–14.00, Thu 17.30–19.30; Banesto is next door, open Mon–Fri 08.30–14.00, Sat 08.30–13.00.

Health The Health Centre is on Calle Ecuador.

Pharmacy On Calle El Progreso.

Police In a small square just off Calle Dr Joaquín Artiles.

Post office On Calle Drago, open Mon–Fri 08.30–14.30; Sat 09.30–13.00.

Shopping There's a farmers' market opposite the bus station on Thursday 09.00–14.00. There's also a decent shop in Plaza del Rosario where you can get craftwork and typical foodstuffs (Art-Agüí).

Tourist information In Plaza de San Antón, open Tue–Sun 10.00–15.00.

What to see and do

The delight of Agüimes is really just wandering through its old quarter and enjoying the quiet. There is a small museum in the tourist information centre detailing the history of the town; entrance is free. It's worth visiting the impressive **Templo Parroquial de San Sebastián**, a church with the air of a cathedral. Construction was started in 1796 and completed in 1940 in neoclassic style. The church houses some interesting art including some Luján Pérez sculptures

POZO IZQUIERDO

There is only one reason to visit this windswept coastal town – windsurfing. Although not as celebrated as Sotavento in Fuerteventura, Pozo Izquierdo is making headway as an international windsurfing destination, with championships held there each summer. You can learn from the best at the **Centro Internacional de Windsurfing**, which offers courses for all levels. Beginners are taken off to a slightly less scary area of the coast, while experts stay in Pozo Izquierdo. Courses last a month and cost €100 if you want two sessions a week or €120 for three sessions a week. The centre is in a complex just out of the town, on the seafront. There is also a **hostel** (tel: 928 12 14 00), charging €16 per night for a bunk in an eight-bed room. The facilities are decent with a restaurant, television room and even a swimming pool. The complex also has internet access, late bar and diving school.

SANTA LUCÍA

The natural fortress south of Santa Lucía, Ansite, saw the last battles between the natives and the conquerors in the late 15th century. This area was once quite densely populated but these days everyone has moved south to find work. The first thing you'll spot in Santa Lucía if you're approaching from the east is a rather tacky-looking castle on the main road. This building houses the **Museo Castillo de la Fortaleza**, a real hotchpotch of a place that doesn't seem to know what kind of museum it wants to be. Amongst other things you'll find skeletons found in the municipality, paintings from modern Canarian artists, shells, rocks and a room full of old weapons presided over by none other than General Franco (well, a large portrait of him). There's also a room dedicated to the Santa Lucía celebrations in Sweden. The museum is open Mon–Fri 09.00–17.00, Sat 12.00–18.00, Sun 09.00–15.00; entrance is €2. Other than that and the early 20th-century church overlooking the town, there's no reason to stop unless it's December 13. On this day (or the closest Saturday to it) the normally sleepy town is host to one of the island's most popular *romerías*, that of Santa Lucía.

SAN BARTOLOMÉ
There are a few restaurants and shops aimed at tourists and San Bartolomé is a good place to buy a bottle of plonk. There is also a magnificent place to stay nearby, **Hotel Las Tirajanas** (tel: 928 12 300 00; fax: 928 12 30 23; email: informacion@hotel-lastirajanas.com; www.hotel-lastirajanas.com). Hotels don't come in better locations than this, with superb views over the southern barrancos. Rooms are no less impressive and there are good facilities, including a health spa. Single €58; double €116; suite €130, including breakfast. The hotel also has a decent restaurant, serving Canarian cuisine with an unbeatable view. Main meals start at €12. Reservations are recommended, tel: 928 12 30 00. There is a museum in the town showing middle-class life in times gone by (though no-one seems quite sure which century). It's open only to groups of ten and above and you need to book a visit; tel: 696 43 00 92.

FATAGA
There's no finer village on the island than Fataga and few friendlier people. Of course, there's nothing to do other than get lost in the maze of narrow alleys but it's well worth a stop. There are a few tasty and reasonably priced restaurants on the main road and a small bodega hidden in the depths of the hamlet. If you're a woman looking for the quiet life, you'd be welcomed in Fataga since the village has a rather male-dominated population. The year 2003 saw the first 'Love Caravan' roll in to town – an all-day matchmaking fiesta in which a few of the menfolk found romance. Organisers are considering making it an annual event.

MASPALOMAS AND PLAYA DEL INGLÉS
Playa del Inglés is the island's largest resort and also Europe's biggest and best gay holiday destination, while Maspalomas is quieter and tends to appeal more to families. There's not a lot of reason to stick around unless you're looking for some serious nightlife, although you should definitely visit *las dunas*, Gran Canaria's finest beach and one of the best in the Canary Islands.

Getting there
There are dozens of buses connecting the resorts with Las Palmas, some of which continue to Puerto Rico and Puerto de Mogán.

Where to stay
Upmarket
Hotel Caserío Av de Italia 8, Playa del Inglés; tel: 928 77 40 50; fax: 928 77 41 50. Modern rooms with good views either of the sand dunes and ocean or of the mountains behind. The hotel has a pool, gym, sauna and can organise a variety of sports and activities. Single €100; double €115.
Hotel Catarina Av de Tirajana 1, Playa del Inglés; tel: 928 76 28 12; fax: 928 76 06 15; email: reservas@creativhotel.com; www.creativhotel.com. The reception area is so modern and minimalist that it feels rather cold, though rooms have a bit more character. The pools are set in tropical gardens and it's very close to the dunes. Single €75; double €100.

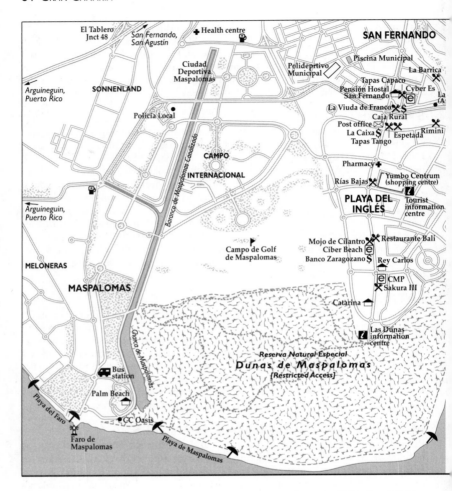

Hotel Gloria Palace Calle Las Margaritas, San Agustín; tel: 928 12 85 00; fax: 928 76 79 29; email: gloriapalace@hvsl.es; www.hotelgloriapalace.com. Rooms are what you'd expect from a 4-star hotel. The real attraction here is the thalassotherapy centre that is attached to the hotel. See page 88 for details. Single €90; double €125, including breakfast.

Hotel Gran Canaria Princess Av Gran Canaria 18, Playa del Inglés; tel: 928 76 81 32; fax: 928 76 41 60; email: centralreservas@princess-hotels.com; www.princess-hotels.com. Typical high-rise hotel that resembles all the others, though its rooms are larger than many and it does have nice grounds. Single €90; double €145, including breakfast.

Hotel Meliá Tamarindos Calle las Retamas 3, San Agustín; tel: 928 77 40 90; fax: 928 77 40 91; email: melia.tamarindos@solmelia.com; www.solmelia.com. Rooms are quite small for a 5-star establishment but well equipped and with good sea or mountain views. The casino is next door. Single €105; double €150, including breakfast.

Hotel Palm Beach Av del Oasis, Maspalomas; tel: 928 72 10 32; fax: 928 14 18 08; email: info@hotel-palm-beach.com; www.seaside-hotels.com. If you're going to splash out on a

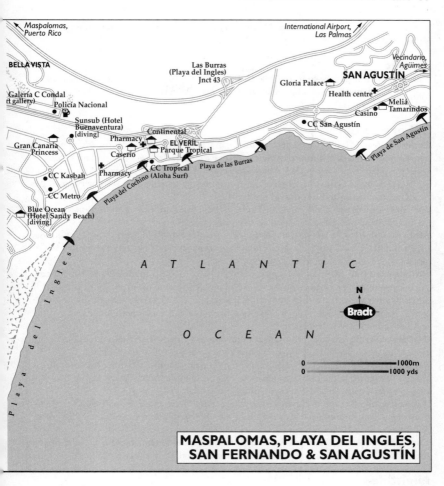

MASPALOMAS, PLAYA DEL INGLÉS,
SAN FERNANDO & SAN AGUSTÍN

good hotel, this should be on your shortlist. The décor is contemporary and the hotel feels more homely than many. Single €220; double €310; suites from €500 to €700 for two people.

Hotel Parque Tropical Av de Italia 1, Playa del Inglés; tel: 928 77 40 12; fax: 928 76 81 37; email: reservas@hotelparquetropical.com; www.hotelparquetropical.com. Easily the hotel with the most charm in the resort, built in Canarian style with high-beamed ceilings, Canarian balconies and pleasant gardens. Each room also has a lounge area. Single €70; double €140, including breakfast.

Hotel Rey Carlos Av de Tirajana 14, Playa del Inglés; tel: 928 76 01 16; fax: 928 76 29 45. The décor is a little over the top but rooms are excellent. It's a suite hotel, so every room has a separate lounge area and a fridge. Single €75; double €110, including breakfast.

Mid-range

Hotel Continental Av de Italia 2, Playa del Inglés; tel: 928 76 02 49; fax: 928 77 14 84; email: continental@ifacanarias.es. Rooms are quite small and a bit hot due to the carpeted floors. They have a reasonable-sized balcony and sea views if you stand on your tiptoes and squint. Single €60; double €95.

Budget
Pensión Hostal San Fernando Calle La Palma 16; tel: 928 76 39 06. Located in a tower block in San Fernando, it's a bit seedy and very basic. All rooms have shared bathrooms. Single €12.50; double €18.50.

Where to eat
Espetada Av de Gran Canaria, next to the Gran Chaparal shopping centre. Not a place for vegetarians. It's an Argentine restaurant with an excellent selection of steaks and kebabs, most of which come char grilled. There are a couple of token fish dishes.

La Barrica Av de Gáldar, San Fernando. A surprisingly charming tapas bar serving all the best Canarian wines and some good meat dishes.

La Viuda de Franco Calle Alcalde Marcial Franco, San Fernando. Nothing spectacular about the menu but the locals swear by this place.

Mojo de Cilantro Av de Tirajana. A tapas bar frequented by old Spanish men is nothing unusual in the *pueblos* but it's a rare find in the tourist resorts. The choice is limited but it's all tasty.

Restaurante Bali Avenida de Tirajana; tel: 928 76 32 61. This Indonesian restaurant can get busy so reserving a table wouldn't be a bad idea. Closed on Sundays.

Restaurante Rimini Avenida de Gran Canaria; tel: 928 76 41 87. Perhaps the best Italian restaurant around, though there's probably not much competition. There's another branch on Av de Tenerife.

Rías Bajas Av de Estados Unidos, next to the Yumbo Centrum. Although it doesn't come close to its namesake in Las Palmas, it's not a bad place to eat fish and seafood.

Sakura III Av de Tirajana. Popular Japanese restaurant that has two other branches in Las Palmas. It's aimed at the novice in Japanese cuisine, with pictures of every dish and a variety of set menus so you can taste a bit of everything.

Tapas Capaco Next to the *pensión* in San Fernando. Plenty of choice and with a few Canarian dishes thrown in. It's a delightful little place with plenty of character. Closed on Sundays.

Tapas Tango Av de Gran Canaria. They have more than 40 choices, so it's a good place to get an overall idea of tapas and you're sure to find something you like.

Nightlife
If you're looking for late, late nightlife then you're in the right place. There's not much in the way of quality live music but there are lots of clubs and a very lively gay scene (everyone welcome). The Yumbo Centrum is where you'll find the largest concentration of gay venues, though singling any out would be as unfair as it is pointless. There are scores of bars to choose from, so delve in until you find something you like.

The other main area for nightlife is the Centro Comercial Kasbah on Avenida de Tenerife and Centro Comercial Metro, behind it. There are plenty of bars and a few discos that stay open until 06.00 or 07.00.

If you fancy a flutter, the **Casino Gran Canaria** is on Calle las Retamas, next to the Hotel Meliá Tamarindos. It's open daily from 21.00–04.00; entrance is free but you need some form of ID to get in.

Practicalities
Banks You'll find branches of just about every bank in Spain in the Yumbo Centrum. Apart from that, La Caixa is on the corner of Av de Tirajana and Av de Gran Canaria: open

Above Playa de Las Salinetas, Gran Canaria (FG)

Below Dunas de Maspalomas, Gran Canaria (FG)

Above Lago Martiánez, Puerto de la Cruz, Tenerife (GAR)

Below left Refreshments overlooking the Caldera de Taburiente, La Palma (JN)

Below right Jameos del Agua, Lanzarote (JN)

Mon–Fri 08.15–14.00, Thu 16.30–19.45; Banco Zaragozano is further down the same road, open Mon–Fri 08.30–14.00, Sat 08.30–13.00; Caja Rural, next to La Viuda de Franco, is open Mon–Fri 08.30–14.00, Thu 17.00–19.30.

Health There are plenty of private Health Centres around, with English and German-speaking doctors. The public Health Centre is north of Maspalomas, close to the GC1.

Internet Ciber Beach is on Av de Tirajana; €2.50 per hour; open Mon–Sat 17.00–22.00; CMP is a little further down the same road; €1 for 15 minutes; open Mon–Fri 09.00–22.00, Sat 11.00–21.00. Cyber Es is behind the *pensión* in San Fernando and charges €3 per hour; open Mon–Fri 11.00–22.00, Sat 13.00–22.00.

Pharmacy In Playa del Inglés you'll find plenty of pharmacies, mostly in the shopping centres. There's one in the CC Oasis in Maspalomas and one on Av Italia in the CC San Agustín.

Police The Policía Nacional is on Calle Moya, between Playa del Inglés and San Fernando; the Policía Local is on Av Touroperador Tui in Maspalomas.

Post office In the Edificio Mercurio on Av de Tirajana. Mon–Fri 08.30–20.30, Sat 09.30–13.00.

Shopping The resorts are awash with naff souvenir shops and overpriced supermarkets. If you're looking for something a bit more 'authentic' you'll have to head to a smaller town such as Agüimes or Ingenio.

Tourist information In a rather impressive red building on Calle Estados Unidos, near the Yumbo Centrum; open Mon–Fri 09.00–21.00, Sat 09.00–13.00. There's a smaller office near the golf course in Maspalomas, open Mon–Fri 09.00–16.00.

What to see and do
Las Dunas
Construction in the '60s and '70s sadly destroyed part of these magnificent dunes and they were declared a Special Nature Reserve in 1994 to prevent any further destruction. The sand dunes cover an area of 4km^2 and, contrary to popular belief, the sand is of marine origin and hasn't blown over from the Sahara. The reserve also contains a small palm grove and lagoon (El Charco) replenished with water from the Fataga ravine. The area surrounding the Charco is a nesting site for over 20 species of birds while guppies and eels thrive in the lagoon. There are three walks through the dunes; please stick to them and don't make new paths as the plantlife is fragile. If you want to learn more about the dunes, there's an information centre behind the RIU Hotel in Plaza Fuerteventura, open Mon–Fri 09.00–13.00, 16.00–20.00.

Diving
Sunsub Hotel Buenaventura, Playa del Inglés; tel: 928 77 81 65; email: webmaster@sunsub.com; www.sunsub.com. A 1-day discovery course is €60 while the 4-day PADI open-water diver course costs €325. There are plenty of other packages available, including courses just for kids. They also rent out equipment to qualified divers.

Blue Ocean Based in Hotel Sandy Beach, Playa del Inglés; tel: 928 77 05 46; email: info@bodive.com; www.bodive.com. An introduction to diving costs €60, a short course to become qualified is €225 and they offer a variety of adventure dives for around €50. They also run snorkelling trips for €15 per person.

Golf
Campo de Golf Maspalomas Tel: 928 76 25 81; email: reservas@maspalomasgolf.net; www.maspalomasgolf.net. Impressive location for a golf course, near the sand dunes and with sea views. It's an 18-hole, par 73 course with driving range, putting green and lessons available. Green fees €75 plus €13 for clubs rental.

Art gallery

La Galería – Casa Condal Calle Alcalde Marcial Franco, San Fernando. If you want to escape the madness of the tourist resort, you could visit this small art gallery which hosts temporary exhibitions by local artists. There is also a permanent exhibition looking at the history of Maspalomas. Open Tue–Sat 10.00–20.00; entrance is free.

Surfing

It's a good place for beginners, since the waves aren't too scary. **Aloha Surf** (Centro Comercial Tropical, Playa del Inglés; tel: 639 12 68 24) rents out boards for €15 per day and offers courses of one or three days, costing €90 per day, although there are reductions if there is more than one person. Prices include transfers.

Thalassotherapy

San Agustín has Europe's largest thalassotherapy centre, based in the Gloria Palace Hotel. In case you're wondering, it's an anti-stress treatment using sea water heated to body temperature. It doesn't come cheap though at €17 for a two-hour session in the 'get in shape' pool. It is relaxing but is a bit repetitive as the treatment basically involves body massage with warm jets of water. The centre also offers all sorts of beauty and health treatments from a €12 manicure to a €500, six-day relaxation treatment. Open daily 10.00–21.00.

PUERTO RICO

This garish, overdeveloped resort has little in its favour and virtually nothing for the independent traveller. Not too long ago it was a quiet fishing village but you'd be hard pushed to find much evidence of it now – there aren't even good fish restaurants to visit. It's a perfect example of over-construction and bad planning, with the tiny beach not coming close to accommodating the thousands of tourists that descend on the resort daily, making it just about the most crowded beach in the archipelago. The authorities have recently extended the motorway, meaning you can bypass Puerto Rico completely if you want to. However, if you fancy a boat trip, this is where you'll find the best choice on the island. Many of them are rather naff, although there are a few quality outfits and one boat that will take you to the secluded Güi-güí beach on the west coast.

PUERTO DE MOGÁN

Although the waterfront is entirely taken over by a tourist complex, it's worlds apart from neighbouring Puerto Rico. Designed by Raphael Neville in 1980, the uniform buildings have two or three floors and are draped in flowers and plants, giving a rather quaint feel. True, the town has expanded considerably in recent years and a large hotel is under construction on the outskirts, causing the locals to worry. But the narrow streets around the harbour are oozing with charm and it makes me wonder why they haven't adapted the same building style to other resorts. If you want to see Puerto de Mogán at its best, get there early when the fishermen are returning and the waiters are setting up their chairs for the day. At 10 o'clock the tour buses start to arrive and the tranquillity is broken.

Getting there
By boat

There are regular boats connecting Puerto de Mogán with Puerto Rico and Arguineguín. It's a glass-bottom ferry and there is a small possibility of seeing dolphins en route. At any rate, if you're staying in one of the resorts and want to

visit Puerto de Mogán, it sure beats driving around the winding roads. Boats leave every hour and cost €9 return to Puerto Rico and €18 to Arguineguín.

By bus
Bus number 1 leaves Las Palmas every 20 minutes, stopping absolutely everywhere on its way to Puerto de Mogán. There are also a couple of buses a day to and from Gáldar.

Where to stay
As well as the places mentioned here, you're likely to find apartments for rent everywhere. Most ask for a minimum stay of a week and charge around €25 per night.

Mid-range
Club de Mar Urb Puerto de Mogán; tel: 928 56 50 66; fax: 928 56 54 38; email: clubdemar@clubdemar.com; www.clubdemar.com. Pretty standard rooms but with good-sized terraces and it's in the nicest part of the village. Also has a spa and restaurant. Single €60; double €85, including breakfast. Apartments for up to 3 people €50.
La Venecia de Canarias Urb Puerto de Mogán, Local 328; tel: 928 56 56 00; fax: 928 56 57 14; www.laveneciadecanarias.net. Apartments are a trifle small but very bright and have

more of a homely feel than most holiday apartments. Friendly staff. Apartment with 1 bedroom €50; 2 bedrooms €80.

Budget

Pensión Eva Lomoquiebre 35; tel: 928 56 52 35. You'll see the *pensión* from the road, about a kilometre out of the port on the way to the *pueblo*. The rooms are basic and bathrooms shared but there's a large communal area with a kitchen and you can't complain at these prices. Single/double €15; triple €20.

Pensión Juan Deniz Lomoquiebre 20; tel: 928 56 55 39. In the narrow streets above Pensión Eva, this place offers a similar deal though the rooms are slightly nicer. All have shared bathrooms and access to a kitchen and large terrace. Single/double €15.

Pensión Salvador Calle La Corriente 13; tel: 928 56 53 74. Basic place with shared bathrooms hidden away in the steep alleyways behind the Plaza Pedro Betancor. Single/double €15.

Where to eat

Bar Churrería Balillo Av Castillete. This is the locals' choice, serving up good Canarian fodder, the catch of the day or just a plate of *churros* for breakfast.

Heladería Ferrari Pasaje de los Pescadores. Chilled-out place for ice-cream and coffee.

La Taberna del Puerto On the seafront behind the main harbour. Another fresh fish joint, with main meals at around €10.

La Cicala Behind the beach. An excellent menu of pasta, *paninis* and wraps with fine views of the town and beach.

Qué Tal Near the plaza; tel: 928 56 55 34. Puerto de Mogán's gourmet restaurant, with a 3-course menu for €30 or a menu that allows you to sample everything for €50. Reservations recommended.

Restaurante Cocina Creativa In the plaza next to the bandstand. Boasts 'gourmet tapas' for those tired of the usual Canarian offering. They have tasters of food from Japan, Italy, North Africa and Scandinavia and it's all 'freestyle, with a lot of fantasy'.

Restaurante El Pescador In the plaza. Fresh fish and seafood at excellent prices. You can get a main dish for €5.

Seemuschel Between La Venecia de Canarias and Club de Mar; tel: 928 56 54 86. A classy little place claiming to offer 90 different fish and seafood dishes. Main meals start at €10. Open evenings only.

Tu Casa Behind the beach. A charming building with a large terrace. *Menú del día* €8.

Nightlife

The wild nights out are to be had down the road in Puerto Rico and there's very little in the way of night-time entertainment in Puerto de Mogán. If you must go out, **Nico**, just off Avenida Castillete, is a smart and trendy bar which seems totally out of place here. The other place with a bit of Friday night action is **Paradise Tattoo** on the road leading to the Health Centre, where you can partake of the karaoke and sample 'the cheapest bar in Mogán'.

Practicalities

Banks Banca March, Plaza Pedro Betancor, open Mon–Fri 08.30–14.00, Sat 08.30–13.00; La Caja de Canarias, Pasaje de los Pescadores, open Mon–Fri 08.00–14.00, Thu 17.30–19.30; La Caixa, further along the same road, open Mon–Fri 08.15–14.00, Thu 16.30–19.45.

Health The Health Centre is on the same road as the church.

Internet Access at Internet Mogán (in a street behind La Taberna del Puerto) is €4 per hour, open Mon–Fri 10.00–15.00, 17.30–20.00, Sun 10.00–13.00. A better option is Recreativo Mogán, Plaza Pedro Betancor, open every day 09.00–23.00; €2 per hour.

Pharmacy Just out of Plaza Pedro Betancor on the Subida a los Riscos.
Police In the *pueblo* of Mogán, a 30-minute drive away.
Post office The closest is in the *pueblo*.
Shopping Other than the numerous supermarkets and souvenir shops, there is a market on Friday mornings.
Tourist information None, though you can pick up information on boat trips and watersports in the harbour office; open every day 09.00–20.00.

What to see and do
Boat trips
As well as the regular glass-bottom boats between Puerto de Mogán and Puerto Rico (see *Getting there*), there are a few other sea excursions leaving the harbour. **Yellow Submarine** is the most popular, with hourly departures to have a look at what's going on 25m under the sea. The trip takes 45 minutes and costs €27 for adults; €13 for children. Their office is next to Internet Mogán. There are other boats offering dolphin-watching trips; ask around in the harbour.

Diving
Atlantik Diving Hotel Club de Mar; tel: 689 35 20 49; email: atdiving@clubdemar.com. Excursions to 12 different dive sites and a variety of courses on offer. Discovery dive €90, open-water diver course (four days) €390; dives are €40 per person including all equipment.

SAN NICOLÁS DE TOLENTINO
The pre-Hispanic name of this town is unknown as it was christened San Nicolás de Tolentino in the middle of the 14th century by a group of Mallorcan explorers. The church that they constructed in honour of the Italian saint was one of the first in the islands and a sign that Christianity was on its way. The area was already populated, with the majority of residents living in the valley, away from the risk of pirate attacks. Nowadays it's a quiet place, quite cut off from the rest of the island due to the meandering roads and poor bus service. The town, which is also known as La Aldea ('The Hamlet') has a few places to stay and a couple of average museums, while the coast is an excellent place to eat fresh fish. You should probably have some kind of tomato dish too, since this is the backbone of the local economy. If you want to visit when there's a bit of action, you'd better turn up for the Fiesta del Charco, one of Gran Canaria's oddest festivals, held at Playa de La Aldea on September 11. Thousands of people turn up from across the island to writhe around in a pond, trying to catch as many fish as they can using just their hands, as their ancestors would have done. Bizarre.

Getting there
Bus number 38 leaves Puerto de Mogán five times a day (four times on weekends) on its way to Gáldar. San Nicolás is one of those places where the travelling is more impressive than the arriving, whether you come from the north or the south, though the roads are hard work.

Where to stay
Other than the options in the town centre, there are also numerous *casas rurales* and a campsite in the vicinity. See *Where to stay*, page 65 for contact details.

Hotel Cascajos Calle Los Cascajos 9; tel: 928 89 11 65; www.la-aldea.com/hotel. Basic rooms with TV and own bathroom. They also have some large 2-bedroom apartments for

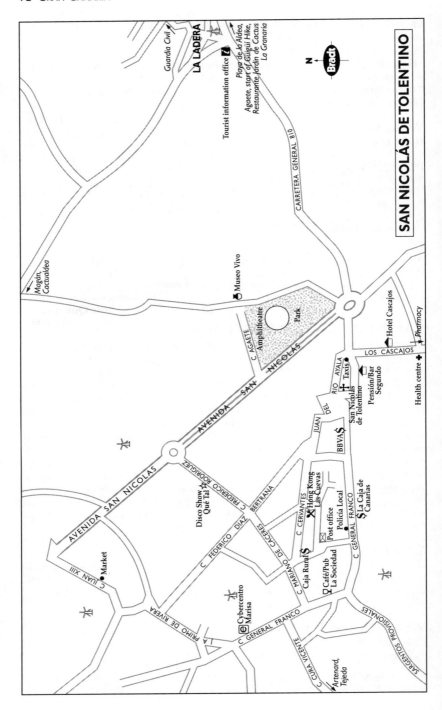

SAN NICOLÁS DE TOLENTINO

up to 5 people. Single €30; double €40. Apartments are €30 per night for a minimum of 7 nights.

Pensión Segundo Calle Alfonso XIII; tel: 928 89 09 01. Good location opposite the church and above a café. All rooms have own bathroom. If there's no-one around, go to the Hotel Cascajos to enquire about rooms. Single €20; double €30.

Where to eat

There's not much on offer in the way of gourmet cuisine in the town. You'd be better off driving out to Playa/Puerto de La Aldea where you'll find a few good seafood restaurants. The local speciality is *ropa vieja de pulpo* – a chick-pea stew with octopus.

Bar Restaurante Segundo Next to the *pensión*; they have a limited tapas menu but serve reasonable breakfasts.

Restaurante Hong Kong Las Cuevas Calle Francisco León. Not the finest Chinese restaurant, but at least it offers something different to the other bars and restaurants in town.

Restaurante Jardín de Cactus La Gañanía On the main road from the *pueblo* to the coast. Typical Canarian fare in pleasant surroundings.

Nightlife

As you can guess, there's not much in the way of night-time entertainment, though you could try **Café Pub La Sociedad**, open 19.00–23.00 during the week and until 03.30 on Friday and Saturday. Everyone moves on to **Disco Show Qué Tal** once the bars have closed. It's open Fridays and Saturdays from midnight until 05.00.

Practicalities

Banks La Caja de Canarias, Calle General Franco, open Mon–Fri 08.00–14.00, Thu 17.30–19.30; Caja Rural, Calle Herrería, open Mon–Fri 08.30–14.00; BBVA, Calle General Franco, open Mon–Fri 08.30–14.15, Sat 08.30–13.00.

Health The Health Centre is near the hotel.

Internet There is access in Café Pub La Sociedad, on Calle General Franco 56, open Mon–Thu 19.00–23.00, Fri–Sat until 03.30. Also Cybercentro Marisa, Calle General Franco, open Mon–Fri 09.00–13.00, 16.00–20.00, Sat 09.00–13.00; access €2 per hour.

Pharmacy Just out of town on Calle Los Cascajos, past the hotel.

Police The Policía Local is next to the Town Hall on Calle General Franco. The Guardia Civil is out of the centre in the La Ladera *barrio*.

Post office On Calle Herrería, open Mon–Fri 08.30–14.30, Sat 09.30–13.00.

Shopping There's a farmers' market on Calle Juan XIII, open Sunday mornings, 09.00–14.00. The town is known for is basketry and palm-leaf handicrafts.

Tourist information In the windmill, which is on the main road from the coast, open Mon–Fri 09.00–12.00.

What to see and do
Cactualdea

This cactus garden has over 200 species of cactus on display, both native to the islands and from abroad. Also some exotic birds (thankfully not riding bikes) and some rather depressed-looking camels. It's on the road to Mogán. Open every day 10.00–18.00; entrance €6.

Museo Vivo

Out of the town centre on Calle Barranquillo de la Plaza; tel 928 89 24 85.
A working museum, demonstrating the traditional Canarian life. You can sample

bread made in a traditional oven, watch the animals working in the fields, try your hand at milking cows and enjoy some live folk music. There's also a *gofio* tasting session. You must call in advance to make an appointment.

Playa de Güi-güí

On the coast between Playa de La Aldea and Mogán is one of the Canary Islands' most secluded beaches, Playa de Güi-güí. The majority of Gran Canarians have never been to this smallish stretch of black sand backed by imposing cliffs. There are only two ways to get there and neither of them is easy. If you're up for a challenge, you could hike; it's around a five-hour trek from San Nicolás and is suitable for experienced hikers only. The walk starts on the road between the town and the harbour (it's signposted) and is easy to follow. Do not attempt the hike in wet weather. The more relaxing but pricey alternative is to go by boat. Dorama, a local fisherman, is the only person willing to take people to Güi-güí, and he doesn't come cheap. Up to 20 people can fit in the boat and it costs €150 each way. He'll drop you off one day and pick you up the next if you want to spend the night (bear in mind that, strictly speaking, you're not allowed to camp on the beach, though the chances of anyone ejecting you are very slim). The boat leaves Playa de La Aldea in good weather only; tel: 928 89 04 37. There are a couple of boats that leave Puerto Rico for Güi-güí, but they don't allow you to spend any time on the beach.

PARQUE NATURAL DE TAMADABA

This natural park is one of the finest areas of Gran Canaria. Its pine forest is the largest on the island, covering 8km², and the many *miradors* offer spectacular views of the mountainous centre of the island and Mount Teide on Tenerife if the weather is good. The best way to explore is on foot, visiting the almost-abandoned hamlets and keeping an eye out for endangered birds such as the blue chaffinch and great spotted woodpecker. There is a reasonable network of roads through the park and ample opportunities to park up and stretch your legs

AGAETE

Agaete has all the amenities and a fair dose of charm, but nearby Puerto de las Nieves is where you're supposed to be. If you find yourself in Agaete, you've probably taken a wrong turn, since there's nothing here at all, other than a pretty Town Hall and some narrow streets that will have you fretting for the paintwork of your hire car. It is the site of one of the island's biggest fiestas, the *Bajada de la Rama* on August 4. There is also a fine garden, the Huerto de Flores, on Calle Huertas, open Mon–Fri 09.00–14.00; entrance is free.

PUERTO DE LAS NIEVES

This was one of the first places I ever visited on Gran Canaria and one of the reasons I fell in love with the island. The houses are a uniform white with vivid blue paintwork and the sleepy atmosphere is interrupted only by the boat passengers arriving from Tenerife. Fishing is the root of the economy and there are some top-notch seafood restaurants. Canarios are understandably worried about the future of the village, as it finds itself on more and more coach-tour schedules and the bars gradually translate their menus into seven different languages. Still, there's a long way to go before it reaches the heights (or plummets the depths) of Puerto Rico and tourists are unlikely ever to flock to its pebbly beach and rough sea. There's a weird rock formation just off the shore, which vaguely resembles a pointing digit, earning it the name 'Dedo de Dios' ('God's Finger'). Puerto de las Nieves is also the launching point for Fred Olsen ferries to and from Tenerife.

Getting there

Bus 103 leaves Las Palmas every hour, heading for Puerto de las Nieves and passing through Agaete. For details of boats to Tenerife, see *Getting there and away*, page 64.

Where to stay

Hotel Puerto de las Nieves Av Alcalde José de Armas; tel: 928 88 62 56; fax: 928 88 62 67; email: hpnieves@idecnet.com; www.hotelpuertodelasnieves.com. Rooms are large and welcoming, as are the staff (well, they're welcoming anyway). Single €60; double €100. The hotel also has a health spa and all the beauty treatments you could ever need. A session in the relaxation circuit costs €12; treatments start from €15. Relaxation packages including treatments and accommodation are also available.

Where to eat

There is certainly no shortage of restaurants in Puerto de las Nieves and they all have a very similar menu which basically consists of some of the best fish and seafood you'll eat on the island.

Casa Ramos On the *paseo* with tables outside.
Cofradía de Pescadores Stands alone at the end of the promenade and comes highly recommended. It's often agreed that the *cofradía* (fishermen's association) is the best place to eat fish.
Restaurante Dedo de Dios Has one of the best locations. It's on the beach, so you can admire the view while eating your lunch.
Restaurante El Oliver Also on the *paseo* and with an excellent value *menú del día* for €5.50.
Restaurante La Palmita On the road from Puerto de las Nieves to Agaete. The large terrace and children's play area make this an appealing place. Has an extensive menu if you're looking for something other than fish.

Practicalities

Banks The closest banks are La Caixa, open Mon–Fri 08.15–14.00, Thu 16.30–19.45 and La Caja de Canarias, open Mon–Fri 08.00–14.00, Thu 17.30–19.30. Both are on Calle Concepción in Agaete.
Health The Health Centre is in Agaete.
Pharmacy On Calle Francisco de Palomares.
Police Both the Policía Local and the Guardia Civil are in Agaete.
Post office In Agaete, open Mon–Fri 08.30–14.30, Sat 09.30–13.00.
Shopping There are a couple of handicraft shops on Calle Nuestra Señora de las Nieves.
Tourist information On Calle Nuestra Señora de las Nieves, open Mon–Fri 09.30–16.30, Sat 09.30–12.00.

What to see and do

There's nothing to do other than relax on the pebbly beach and enjoy some good food, but it's probably the most pleasant place to base yourself if you want to explore the north of the island and is convenient for an excursion to Tenerife.

GÁLDAR

Gran Canaria was once divided into ten cantons, each with its own tribe and leader, but the islanders were united by Queen Andamana in the 14th century. She married Gumidafe and together they set up court in Agáldar (as it was then known). The queen died at the end of the century and although the island split into two kingdoms, Agáldar retained the title of capital. While it has little of its former importance, the town centre is a nice place to amble around and once the Cueva Pintada (Painted Cave) is open to the public, the tourists will be flocking. It's perhaps the most important archaeological find in the islands, housing one of the few examples of aborigine art.

Getting there
There are regular buses to Gáldar from Las Palmas and a few a day that go from Gáldar to Puerto de Mogán, passing through San Nicolás..

What to see and do
Casa Museo Antonio Padrón
Calle Drago. This is one of the finer house-museums on the island due to the fact that it is filled with the marvellous expressionist paintings and sculptures of Gáldar's most famous resident, Antonio Padrón. Open Mon–Fri 09.00–15.00; entrance is free.

Parque Arqueológico de la Cueva Pintada
Historians are not sure whether this large cave was used as a dwelling, a place of worship or a burial site, and some believe that it was the royal residence. The cave was discovered in 1860 and opened to the public in 1970 but was closed the following decade as the humidity from nearby farmland and the influx of visitors were damaging the paintings in the interior of the cave. It has remained closed until today, although the powers that be have been threatening to open it to the public for some years. A painstaking excavation project has taken place and it's almost ready to be opened as a visitor centre. Latest estimates suggest that the cave should be open by early 2005.

Poblado del Agujero y Necrópolis de la Guancha
This is one of Gran Canaria's most important historical sites, though unless you're a real archaeology buff it's a trifle disappointing up close (though aerial photos of the site are quite stunning). Rediscovered in 1935, it was once an important settlement and burial site though nowadays it's little more than a pile of rocks (covering an area of 2.4km²). It's free to visit the site but you must call and make an appointment first, unless you just want to look at it through a fence. Tel: 928 21 94 21. It's on the Gáldar to El Agujero road, on the north coast.

SANTA MARÍA DE LA GUÍA
There is a nice surprise waiting in the middle of Guía's ugly urban sprawl. The centre of the *pueblo* is one of the most attractive on the island, and was declared of historical artistic interest in 1982 due to its mix of architecture styles. There is a rather pitiful market on Thursday mornings in the town square. Don't leave without trying the local *queso de flor*, a delicious sheep's cheese blended with the flowers of the Cardo Azul (blue thistle) giving a unique flavour. Casa Arturo, on Calle Lomo Guillén (as you enter Guía from the GC2) has a wide selection of local cheeses and you can try before you buy. The shop is open Mon–Fri 09.00–14.00, 16.00–21.00, Sat–Sun 09.00–15.00.

VALLESECO
Valleseco ('Dry Valley') appears to be one of the most inappropriately named *pueblos* in the archipelago; it has in fact the highest annual rainfall on Gran Canaria. The lush vegetation in the surrounding ravines includes small areas of laurel forest, making this one of the island's finest spots to go walking. The town itself could just

about keep you occupied for ten minutes (or an hour if you visit for the enjoyable Sunday morning market); it basically consists of two main roads separated by a church and a handful of people mooching around. Still, there's no denying that the surrounding area is gorgeous and at least the authorities have recognised that – the Town Hall organises free walks in the municipality once a month (call 928 61 87 40 for information and to book a place). On the outskirts of the town there are numerous villages with quality craftwork on sale and there's a pleasant recreation area, La Laguna, on the road to Teror. There's a **hostel** near Valleseco, in Valsendero, perfectly located for hiking in the Parque Rural de Doramas. Lodging in a dormitory is €9 per night which includes breakfast; tel: 928 61 88 75; email: pimarobe@terra.es.

TEROR

This is the typical Canarian town *par excellence* – if there was a Canarian section in Disney World's Epcot Centre, it would look just like Teror. This area is known as 'the green heart of Gran Canaria' and is stunning in the spring when the surrounding valley walls are draped in greenery. Its location means that the town suffers from extreme temperatures, unusual on the island – the mercury can reach 40°C in summer and drop as low as 4°C in the winter. To be honest, Teror is a little lacking on attractions, but you should visit nonetheless. During the week and on weekend afternoons the centre is like a ghost town, which for many will add to its appeal. However, if you fancy seeing it with a bit of life you should visit on Sunday morning when the island's oldest **market**, though certainly not its best, is held around the church (08.00–15.00). There's a lot of tat on offer, large amounts of religious memorabilia and some freaky wax limbs. However, the selection of food is good, a blessing since the town is renowned for its impressive lack of decent places to eat. Stock up on locally produced cakes and biscuits and you mustn't leave without trying *chorizo de Teror*, a spicy sausage made with enough garlic to keep vampires from your door for a good while. You must have a look, too, at the **Basílica de Nuestra Señora del Pino**, home to Gran Canaria's patron saint. Legend has it that the image of the virgin appeared atop a pine tree in the nearby Aterura forest during the conquest and was soon moved to a hermitage. This hermitage later became the church that today dominates the centre of Teror. It's not one of the island's prettiest, but worth a visit for its religious importance and to see the virgin surrounded by all the glitz befitting a patron saint. The church was first built in 1767, but restored on numerous occasions, most notably in the late 1960s. There is a useful **tourist information office** in the square, open Mon–Fri 09.30–16.30. Opposite the office you'll find the **Casa Museo de los Patronos de la Virgen**, a house devoted to preserving 18th-century Canarian life, open Mon–Sat 11.00–18.00, Sun 10.00–14.00. There are usually art exhibitions in the Casa de Cultura; ask in the tourist information office for details.

If you enjoy the traditional architecture of Teror but the lack of life freaks you out, you'd do well to visit during the festivities devoted to Nuestra Señora del Pino on September 8. On the eve of the fiesta, a *romería* attracts revellers from all 21 municipalities of the island as well as a fair number of tourists. You'll also find a livestock fair, folklore festival and plenty of music and dancing, both traditional and modern.

Near Teror, on the GC23 to Arucas, is a real jewel, the **Finca de Osorio**. Once a series of privately owned farms, the area was taken over by the *Cabildo* in the 1980s and is now used for education purposes and for weekend walkers and picnickers. It offers orchards, farm animals, a small laurel forest and some wonderful views from the top of Pico de Osorio. There's a small information centre a short walk from the car park and a good network of footpaths too, meaning you can explore at your leisure. Open every day 09.00–17.00; entrance is free.

MOYA

Moya is worth a stop for a couple of hours. One of its main attractions is the 20th-century church, **Iglesia de Nuestra Señora de la Candelaria**, built in a spectacularly precarious position, which will probably give you vertigo just looking at it. There are good views of the Barranco de Sangre from behind the church (but don't look down). The town also has a small museum, **Casa Museo Tomás Morales**, based in the former house of the local poet. It's not terribly exciting, in fact it's nothing more than a reconstruction of the poet's house, though there are a few examples of his work displayed there. It's open Mon–Sat 10.00–20.00, Sun 10.00–14.00; entrance is free. There is a rather useless tourist office near the museum, allegedly open Mon–Fri 08.00–15.00, but you might have to ask in the Town Hall for someone to open up. While you're here you should try the two local specialities, *bizcocho* and *suspiros* (the former is a hard sponge cake like that used in trifle, the latter a small meringue-like sweet). You'll find them in any of the local bars or bakeries or at the Sunday morning market, an excellent place to pick up some craftwork, especially musical instruments and wooden articles. Not far from Moya, along the GC150, is Gran Canaria's laurel forest, Los Tilos – not a bad place to do a bit of hiking.

FIRGAS

The most remarkable thing about Firgas is its main avenue which has fountains and scale models of all seven islands. There is also a working mill where you can see the corn being ground and then purchase freshly made *gofio*. It's open Mon–Sat 11.00–16.00, Sun 11.00–14.30, closed on Tuesdays. There is a tourist information office in the square, open Mon–Fri 09.00–14.00.

ARUCAS

The old Arehucas became Arucas after the conquest and found fortune in the sugar-cane industry. Today it's well known for its rum, which retains the town's aboriginal name. Arucas is a small, sleepy town and if you turn up during siesta time you might wonder if anyone lives there at all. But you should visit, if only to admire the imposing Iglesia de San Juan. The neo-Gothic church was completed in 1917 and is one of the most renowned in the Canary Islands and surely their finest example of 20th-century religious architecture. There are a few good examples of traditional Canarian houses in the old part of town too, especially the Casa de la Cultura on Calle Gourie. The main street is Calle León y Castillo and this is where you'll find the majority of the shops and bars; it also leads you to the pretty municipal park. The park is definitely worth a visit when the flowers are in bloom; Arucas isn't known as *la ciudad de las flores* ('the city of the flowers') for nothing.

Getting there and around

There are regular buses between Las Palmas and Arucas. If the steep streets of Arucas don't appeal, you could catch the Plátano Express, a mini train that shuttles tourists around the town's main attractions for €10. It leaves from in front of the church every hour and a quarter from 10.00 to 16.15.

Where to stay

Hotel Rural La Hacienda del Buen Suceso Ctra de Arucas a Bañaderos km 1; tel: 928 62 29 45; fax: 928 62 29 42; email: hacienda@idecnet.com; http://hotelhacienda.sitio.net.

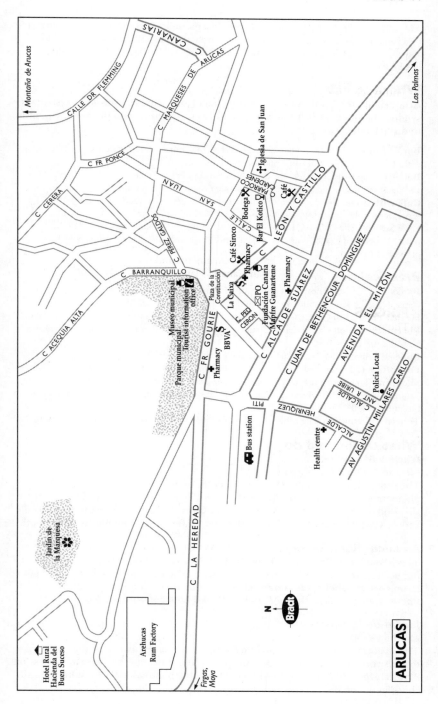

ARUCAS

The only place to stay near Arucas and one of the nicest hotels on the island. Surrounded by a banana plantation and in a 19th-century farmhouse, the hotel offers all the comfort and amenities of a 5-star hotel (although it isn't). Single €105; double €150, including breakfast.

Where to eat

Arucas is another of those towns that suffers from acute lack-of-good-restaurants syndrome. There are half a dozen or so places scattered around the town with little to distinguish between them.

Bar El Kotico Has tables outside, at the side of the church. A fair variety of food on offer, including tapas, pizza and some good seafood dishes.

Bodega Calle Parroco Cárdenes. Probably your best bet for a sit-down meal. Serves tapas and Spanish cuisine, has a covered patio inside or you can sit out next to the church.

Café with no name No gourmet cuisine but the largest selection of snacks on offer. They serve tacos and crêpes as well as the usual *bocadillos* and tapas. It's on Calle León y Castillo.

Café Siroco Calle León y Castillo. Its photo menu doesn't look too appetising but the food must be good as the place is always packed. Nice décor and not such a macho clientele as a few of the bars in town.

Practicalities

Banks BBVA, Calle Francisco Gourie, open Mon–Fri 08.30–14.15, Sat 08.30–13.00; La Caixa, Calle León y Castillo, open Mon–Fri 08.15–14.00, Thu 16.30–19.45.

Health The Health Centre is on Calle Alcalde Henríquez Piti, just south of the bus station.

Pharmacy One on Calle León y Castillo, another on Calle Francisco Gourie and another on Calle Alcalde Suárez.

Police Av Agustín Millares Carlo, near the Health Centre.

Post office Calle Servando Blancos; Mon–Fri 08.30–14.30, Sat 09.30–13.00.

Shopping There are a few nice shops on Calle León y Castillo, which is also the site of the Saturday street market where you can pick up some handicrafts, foodstuffs and a few other bits and bobs; 08.00–14.00.

Tourist information The office is in the park, next to the museum; Mon–Fri 08.00–16.00.

What to see and do

Museo Municipal

Next to the tourist information office.

The museum hosts temporary art exhibitions, often by local painters, sculptors and photographers. Open Mon–Fri 10.00–13.00, 17.00–20.00, Sat 10.00–13.00. You can also find art exhibitions in the Fundación Canaria Mapfre Guanarteme on Calle León y Castillo, open Mon–Fri 09.00–13.00, 17.00–21.00. Entrance is free to both.

Arehucas Rum Factory

The island's favourite tipple is brewed in Arucas and the factory is open to the public. The tour around the factory isn't particularly informative but you do get a tasting session afterwards and the chance to buy their produce cheaper than you'll find it anywhere else. Open Mon–Fri 09.00–14.00; entrance is free.

Jardín de la Marquesa

On the GC30, near the hotel.

The majority of the flora in this lovely botanical garden is from other countries, though you will find a few Canarian species too. It belongs to the marchioness of Arucas. Open Mon–Fri 09.00–12.00, 14.00–18.00; entrance €5 for adults, €2 for children under 10.

TEJEDA

Although there's not much to Tejeda, it attracts a fair number of visitors who come for the unbeatable views and to sample the delicious almond cakes and biscuits. The town sits at 1,050m above sea level, though the surrounding mountains reach much higher. It's a pretty place with good views of the island's most famous rocks, Roque Nublo and Roque Bentayga. The main road winds through the houses, museums and past the small church square. Almond trees line the streets and the best time to visit is February when the town celebrates the Almond in Bloom festival. In summer the heat is stifling, while if you visit in winter you'll need some warm clothing. Other than the attractions mentioned below, there are two *Cabildo*-run museums due to open at the end of 2004: the Museo de las Tradiciones, a look into local customs, and the Museo de Plantas Medicinales.

Getting there

There are just two buses a day between Tejeda and the capital, leaving Las Palmas at 07.15 and 16.15 and returning at 09.15 and 18.15. Bus number 18 leaves Maspalomas at 08.00, 10.00, 14.00 and 16.00 every day, returning at 07.30, 11.30, 13.30 and 17.30.

Where to stay

Apartamentos Gayfa Calle Cruz Blanca 34; tel: 928 66 62 30. Large apartments for two people, most with good views. They have all mod cons, including washing machine. €32 per night or €28 if you stay for more than 3 nights.
Hotel Rural El Refugio Cruz de Tejeda; tel: 928 66 65 13; fax: 928 66 65 20; email: elrefugio@canariasonline.com. Small, cosy hotel decorated in Canarian style. Also has a swimming pool, though it's often too nippy to use it up at Cruz de Tejeda. Single €53; double €68, breakfast is €4.50 extra.

Where to eat

Bar Restaurante Cueva de la Tea On the main road. Usual menu of tapas and Canarian specials.
Dulcería Nublo On the main road. While in Tejeda you should try the cakes and desserts, famous across the island, and this is a good place to start. Wide selection including *bienmesabe*, marzipan and other goodies containing the locally grown ingredient: almonds.
Restaurante La Esquina On the main road. Possibly the restaurant with the best view on the island. Good hearty cuisine including goat stew, watercress stew and rice pudding for dessert.

Practicalities

Banks La Caja de Canarias, open Mon–Fri 08.00–14.00, Thu 17.30–19.30.
Health The Health Centre is just out of the centre, on the road to La Degollada.
Pharmacy Off the main road, behind the Museo Abraham Cárdenes.
Police The Policía Local is in the Town Hall, next to the church.
Post office On the main road, open Mon–Fri 09.30–12.30, Sat 11.00–12.30.
Shopping There is a small market every morning at Cruz de Tejeda. A lot of it is tourist tat, though you might find some good craftwork and certainly some of the local cakes and biscuits.
Tourist information In the Museo Abraham Cárdenes and with the same opening hours.

What to see and do
Roque Nublo

The archipelago's most famous monolith reaches 1,813m above sea level, though it's actually just 70m high. The four-million-year-old rock is all that's left of a volcano that once dominated these parts. Roque Nublo can be admired from afar but it's worth the half-hour walk to get up close, especially on a clear day when the views are spectacular. From Tejeda you can either head towards Cruz de Tejeda and then take the GC150, later joining the GC600, or a slightly longer but even more impressive route is to take the GC60 to Ayacata and then join the GC600. You'll know when you've reached the starting point for the walk as there are always cars and buses lining the road. The walk is steep in parts but is short.

Museo Abraham Cárdenes
This small museum showcases work by local sculptor Abraham Cárdenes Guerra. Open Mon–Fri 11.00–14.30, Sat 11.30–14.30, Sun 11.30–16.00; entrance is free.

ARTENARA
Artenara is the island's highest town at 1,270m and has been populated since ancient times. The residents are keen not to lose their heritage and a considerable number still live in cave dwellings, although these days they often come with running water and satellite dishes. The tourist information centre and hermitage are both situated in caves and while there are no hotels or *pensiones* in Artenara or the surrounding area, there is a unique accommodation option on offer – the chance to stay in a cave. These unique *casas rurales* are in the surrounding villages of Las Arvejas and El Caidero. Expect to pay €50–70 per night for up to four people; tel: 928 66 16 68; www.returcanarias.com. If you don't get the chance to stay in a cave, you can visit a mock-up of a typical Artenara dwelling in the tourist information office, open Mon–Fri 09.00–16.00 (if it's closed, ask around and someone will open up for you).

Everything is based around the large square, though whether anything will be open is another matter. Residents complain that they are the forgotten municipality and that *Cabildo* money never reaches them, perhaps explaining why the *pensión* and museum are both closed with no news of if or when they will ever reopen. Still, the town's trump card is the **Ermita de la Virgen de la Cuevita**, a tiny church excavated into the hillside. It was constructed in the 18th century and its pews, pulpit and confessional are all crafted from stone. The hermitage is a ten-minute walk from the town and is signposted from the square. Also worth a visit is the **Restaurante Mesón La Silla**, built into the mountainside and serving hearty stews and meat dishes. The views from here are pretty impressive; tel: 928 66 61 08. There are a reasonable number of buses from Teror to Artenara and the return leg takes you all the way back to Las Palmas.

HIKES
Bandama – the crater floor and caves
Distance: 3¹/₂km; time: 2¹/₂ hours; difficulty: 3–4
Many people visit Bandama and admire the huge crater, but few explore further. The 5,000-year-old volcano has a diameter of 800m, is 200m deep and almost every inch can be explored on foot. There are three main walks you can undertake: the peak, the rim and the crater floor. The last is explained here. To get to Bandama, take the GC110 from Las Palmas heading towards Tafira. Once you get to a roundabout with a turn-off for Santa Brígida, you need to follow the signposts for Bandama. To reach the peak of the crater, follow the GC822. But to do the walk described here, look for the point where the road splits and opt for the GC 802. Immediately after the turn-off you'll see a few houses, a church and a restaurant; this is the start of the walk. If you're taking the bus, you need to get the 311 from Las Palmas and get off outside the restaurant. The start of the walk is signposted, taking you through the houses and past the church. As

you pass through the iron gate, take the cobbled path to your left rather than the gravel path on the right that leads to a lookout point. The path soon becomes loose stone. After a couple of minutes you'll reach a fork; bear right, heading for a rickety *mirador*, and then follow the path until you reach the crater floor. The walk down is about half an hour and can be very slippery. On reaching a huge boulder at the bottom, look for a path heading off to the right. This will take you around the edge of the crater floor. If you miss the path, you'll find yourself in a small cluster of disused buildings. Just backtrack and search a little; the path is there, it's just well-hidden.

The walk around the crater floor is easy, with no ups or downs, though watch out for wild donkeys! Once you complete the circle (where you'll encounter a man that actually lives down there) it's time for the difficult part – climbing back up. Retrace your steps until you reach that original fork in the path, very near the top. Just a couple of metres above the fork you'll see a very narrow trail leading off to the right. Take this path for the best part of the walk. It's very narrow and the gravel is loose; be warned and be careful. After about five minutes you'll come to a cave, although with its levelled floor and ceiling it looks more like a 20th-century dwelling than an aboriginal home. Continue for another ten minutes, following the narrow path until you cannot go any further, to reach the real gem of the hike: La Cueva de los Canarios. At the bottom of the path look for a hole above your head in one of the rocks. Climb up the makeshift steps through the hole to explore the caves further; it's worth the effort. Head back the way you came. The walk is not advisable in wet or windy weather.

Barranco de Cernícalos
Distance: 6km; time: 3 hours; difficulty: 2
This is about the only place in Gran Canaria where you can still find year-round running water. You'll also see some unique flora and a wide variety of birds. The 12km ravine is situated between Telde and Lomo Magullo. Once in Telde head for Lomo Magullo, park wherever you can and follow the sign for the start of the route. At the start of the walk, take the path to the left and throughout try to follow the water pipes that run the length of the ravine.

The hike is relatively easy, with just a few steep sections. For the most part the path follows the stream and it's necessary to cross it several times. After about an hour you will reach a precipice with inaccessible caves; take the path to the right and pass an overhang about four or five metres above the river. Don't continue to the wall as the path here becomes very difficult to follow. There is one accessible cave here, though it is well hidden. The descent from the cave is difficult and not recommended.

Keep following the path along the valley floor until the small waterfalls become closer together and greater in number. The river becomes flanked by two natural stone walls. Keep following the river until it is impossible to go further. Don't be fooled by a route that looks difficult: when you have really reached the end, you will know.

The final waterfall is about 10m high – quite a rare sight in Gran Canaria. It's impossible to pass, so relax and enjoy the view before returning along the same path.

Cruz de Tejeda–Teror
Distance: 11¹/₂km; time: 5 hours; difficulty: 3 (though the downhill stretches might play havoc with your knees)
There are two buses a day from Las Palmas and three from Maspalomas (see Tejeda entry for details). There is plenty of space to park a car if you don't mind catching the bus to collect it later.

Once you reach Cruz de Tejeda, walk up the road to the right of the cross, passing the stalls on your right. Just after the *parador* that is under construction on the left, take a hidden, cobbled path, which takes you up and behind the electricity sub-station. It's a mild uphill stretch (one of few on the walk) and in around 20 minutes you'll reach the road. From here you get a magnificent view of Roque Nublo and the valley beneath it.

Cross the road and find the path heading down into a pine forest, where you'll find running water in winter. Keep descending into the valley and when you reach a fork in the path, turn right (on to a downhill trail). If you manage to choose a clear day you'll get magnificent views from here, over the Barranco de Charquillo. Ten or fifteen minutes later you emerge from the Canarian pine and reach a rocky outcrop with a sheep pen on the right. Here look for the track leading off to the left, ignoring the downhill path. Once more you'll reach the road; turn right and you'll see a fork in the road and a stone bridge overhead. To the left of the road signs is a cobbled path ascending the mountainside; keep following this path and ignore a minor track leading off to the right.

After passing a farmhouse you join the road once again; turn left and 50m further on, take a right (it's signposted for Madrelagua). Continue through the houses for about 15 minutes until the road takes a sharp turn to the left. This is Calle el Lomo, but don't follow the road down the steep hill. Instead continue straight ahead on to a dirt track leading upwards. After just a couple of metres look for a well-hidden path on your right. If you pass the first house you have gone too far and need to backtrack to find the overgrown track. Make sure you don't opt for the path that leads into someone's garden.

The track descends into the lush Barranco del Charquillo Madrelagua, from where you can see Las Palmas in the distance, weather permitting. The overgrown path continues to a two-house hamlet, through the houses and over a footbridge. A set of stone steps leads you to a short stretch of road. Turn left here and follow the road until it becomes a dirt track. Keep an eye out for a stone garage on your right and then take a steep concrete driveway on your left, almost doubling back on yourself.

Not for the first time you'll feel as though you've made a mistake and are heading for someone's private property. Don't worry, a narrow path leads to the valley floor and from here the walk is flat and easy to follow. The cactus-lined track gives way to a stone path and eventually takes you to the hamlet of Las Rosadas. On reaching the road, turn right and follow the concrete path down to the village of Los Llanos. On leaving Los Llanos join the main road (GC21) and follow signs for Teror. Bus number 216 leaves Teror for Las Palmas every hour.

Los Pilancones

Distance: 6km to do the direct walk, 14km if you intend to visit the mammoth pine tree; time: 2¹/₂ hours (direct), add another 4 hours if you opt for the extended walk; difficulty: 3 if you're doing the basic walk, 4 if you head for the big tree

This walk takes you to an area that many Gran Canarians themselves have never visited, dismissing it as barren and dull. The truth couldn't be more different, since the area has a stunning pine forest and some incredible views. OK, so the pine isn't as dense or impressive as in Tamadaba, but compared with what you'd expect to find it's pretty remarkable. The walk takes you from the Hotel Tirajana, just outside San Bartolomé, to Cruz Grande (though it can be done in reverse, making the walk much easier.) Setting out from the hotel car park, join the road and turn left. After a minute or so you'll see a road leading off to the right, signposted Camino del Pinar. Follow this road which soon becomes a dirt track and passes a farm (you'll know you're on the right track if you can smell the animals!). The path takes you steeply up the hillside for about an hour on what is certainly the toughest stretch of the walk. When you reach the top, opt for the right-hand fork in the road. This flat track, wide enough for a car, snakes around the mountain for a little over an hour, at which point you'll come to a fork in the path with a signpost pointing to Los Bailaderos. If you're planning to camp, or want to visit a massive pine tree, opt for this path, otherwise continue straight ahead – it's about half an hour to Cruz Grande on a pretty flat road, with no possibility of getting lost. If you opt to head for Los Bailaderos, it's a 45-minute walk downhill (coming back up later is a killer and will easily take an hour). Once you get to the campsite, dump your bags before attempting to reach the pine tree. It's all downhill to the tree and takes a little over two hours there and back.

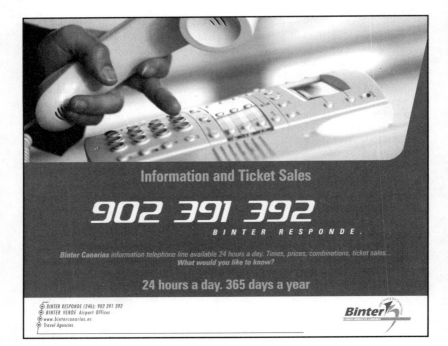

Fuerteventura

Fuerteventura…
Eden to die in, endless tomb.
Your fishermen slowly plough to the sea –
There's no hurry to live or die.

Pedro Lezcano, *Oda a Fuerteventura*
('Ode to Fuerteventura'), 1965

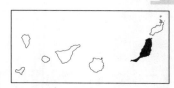

During his exile on the island, Spanish writer Miguel Unamuno referred to it as 'an oasis in the middle of civilisation's desert', and perhaps its tag *'la isla tranquila'* ('the calm island') comes from this homage. The island's residents probably wouldn't mind a few more oases in the desert of Fuerteventura, since its lack of rain has caused no end of hardships in the past. It's just 100km from the African continent and has more in common with the nearby Sahara than the rest of the Canary Islands. The pace of life couldn't be any slower, and the most exciting thing you're apt to see is the locals' response if it rains. With few natural resources and no industry, Fuerteventura has long been the poorest of the islands. One thing it doesn't lack though is sun – 2,800 hours of it a year to be precise, so it's no surprise that tourism is the number one earner, with holidaymakers flocking to the pristine golden beaches. And despite the constant increase in tourist numbers, you can still find long stretches of sand with not a soul in sight, perhaps something you'd more associate with the Caribbean than the Canaries.

HIGHLIGHTS

While the forests and mountains may attract you to the other islands, there is really one reason that you'll want to visit Fuerteventura: its beaches. There are 152 to choose from, many of them undeveloped stretches of golden sand (although there is 25km of black sand) edged by clear waters. The best beaches are undoubtedly in the south of the island, on the Jandía peninsula. Fuerteventura is a haven for professional windsurfers and there are also some excellent schools based in calmer waters, ideal for beginners. Driving is a pleasure since it's flat and you can see for miles. There is a good network of interesting museums, most dedicated to the history and culture of the island or else paying homage to Fuerteventura's famous sons. You must sample the Majorero cheese and if there's one island where you should eat goat, this is it. If you're after lush vegetation or beautiful, demanding hikes, you'd be better of on one of the western islands, though a walk around Isla de Lobos is worthwhile.

BACKGROUND INFORMATION
History

The original inhabitants, the Majoreros, knew the island as Mahoh meaning 'My Country', though it has also been known as 'Capraria' for its abundance of goats

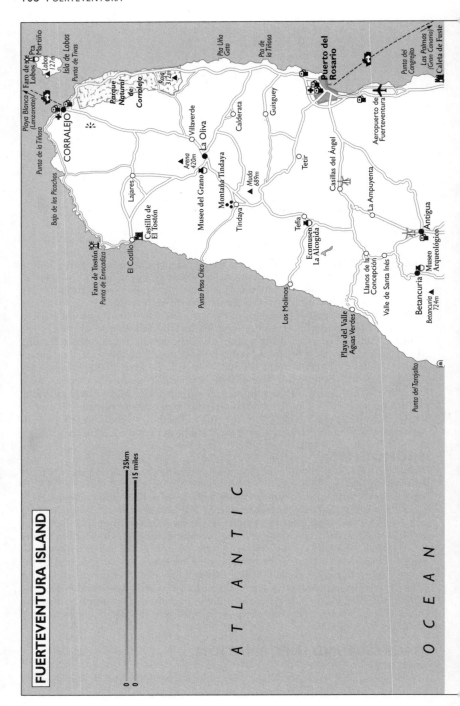

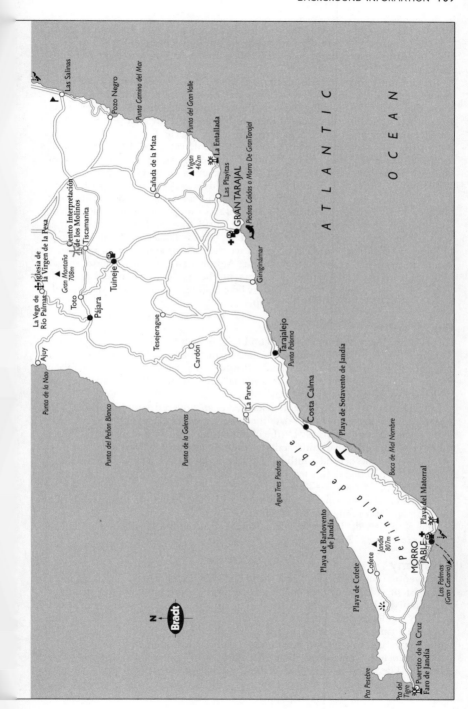

and as 'Planaria' due to its flatness. No-one knows who gave Fuerteventura its current moniker or where the name comes from, but it seems to relate to some kind of difficult expedition to the island (*fuerte* means 'strong' and *aventura* means 'adventure').

In aboriginal times Fuerteventura was more densely populated than other islands and was split into two rival kingdoms: Maxorata and Jandía, separated by a low 6km wall. The hostility between the two kingdoms meant they were used to conflict, something that helped them to fight against the first pirates landing on the island. They managed to ward off a few attacks but the might of the conquerors was too much and the islanders were defeated in 1405 with the two kings, Guize and Ayoze, being baptised. Once on the map, Fuerteventura suffered pirate attacks, though not nearly as many as neighbouring Lanzarote. While military architects would like to think this was because of the castles and forts erected on the island, it really had more to do with the poverty that has always dogged Fuerteventura – the pirates simply weren't interested. Traditionally the island lived from meagre agriculture and livestock farming, with all the most important settlements being inland. Today, the traditional way of life is rapidly disappearing as people leave their towns and head for the coasts where tourism has created employment. Although in the past Fuerteventura suffered from mass emigration, these days another problem has reared its head. Not a week goes by without some rickety boat landing on the island's shores with a cargo of people looking for a better life.

Geography

At 1,658km² Fuerteventura is the second largest island in the archipelago (after Tenerife) and has the longest coastline at 340km. Amongst the many names that have been bestowed upon the island, 'Planaria' is perhaps the most apt (*plano* means 'flat'); its highest point is Pico de la Zarza at just 807m. It's the island which most resembles the nearby African coast and no less than 22% of Fuerteventura is beach. Geologists have discovered unique rocks on Fuerteventura that seem to pre-date those on any other island and it's reckoned to be around 38 million years old (the oldest island, along with Lanzarote). While there is no record of volcanic activity, there is evidence of various eruptions, particularly in the central south of the island, known as Malpaís Grande and Malpaís Chico. The average temperature is 25°C and the average annual rainfall barely reaches 100mm, the lowest of any of the islands. You can't fail to notice the presence of goats on Fuerteventura – there are 75,000 of them, while the human population only reaches 69,500.

The 5km² Isla de Lobos lies 2km from Fuerteventura, its highest point, La Caldera reaching 127m.

Economy

Fuerteventura has never been a rich island due to its aridness. Agriculture is almost non-existent and although the cochineal plant was a good earner once, demand for the natural dye is low nowadays. Farmers have fought against the scarce rainfall and the salty underground streams by inventing *gavias*, a series of underground irrigation channels. The island missed out on the economic booms brought by the wine, sugar cane, tomato and potato trades and seemed doomed to be always the poor cousin until someone realised that the lack of rain could actually be their salvation. The island now has the highest number of tourist beds per inhabitant and has experienced the second fastest growth in tourist industry within the islands. If the Canary Islands are popular for their excellent weather, Fuerteventura is the place where you can almost guarantee to get a tan, so its popularity as a holiday destination is unlikely to diminish.

Flora and fauna

The flora and fauna bear many similarities to that found in Lanzarote. You'll soon notice the lack of trees and low-lying plants such as the tabaiba, with brushwood vegetation dominating instead. Fuerteventura hosts a dozen endemic species, the majority of which are in the Jandía peninsula, such as Jandía thistle (*Euphorbia handiensis*), which grows up to a metre high and sprouts small red flowers. Salt tolerant plants are to be found in the salt marshes of Playa del Matorral, near Morro Jable. Many consider Fuerteventura to be the best island for birdwatchers, with sightings of shearwater, egret and ringed plover quite common. You might also glimpse the great bustard, probably one of the most endangered birds within the islands although it's widely distributed in the rest of the world. The seas are rich with life, boasting somewhere in the region of 350 species of fish. The only mammals are bats, rabbits, hedgehogs and the brown squirrel, recently introduced from Africa and having a destructive effect on the environment.

Conservation

There are 13 protected areas including Isla de Lobos. The *Cabildo* has a few conservation projects under way, the most important being measures to save the Canary Island stonechat (*Saxicola dacotiae*), a highly endangered species found only on Fuerteventura. There is also a plan to protect the Houbara bustard. As in Lanzarote, the biggest problem is lack of water. Rainfall is low and the warm winds from the Sahara cause high evaporation.

Festivals

The most important fiesta is that of Nuestra Señora de la Peña, patron saint of the island. On the third Saturday in September a church service is held in La Vega de Río Palmas and then the party adjourns to Betancuria for a full scale *romería* that the whole island attends.

Puerto del Rosario hosts a few big parties such as that of its patron saint, the Virgen del Rosario. The capital livens up with concerts, impromptu cinema screenings and, of course, the compulsory street party on October 7.

The sleepy town of Tuineje comes alive on October 13 as they re-enact an 18th-century victory against invading English troops. For something a little more relaxing, try the kite festival held annually on Playa del Burro, in the Corralejo sand dunes at the start of November.

The other important celebrations are the Fiestas del Carmen held on July 16 in the capital and throughout the island, mainly in coastal towns. As well as the maritime parade you'll witness folklore displays, demonstrations of traditional Canarian sports, handicraft markets and the all-important street party.

Food

The traditional cuisine in Fuerteventura is frugal and lacking the variety that the other islands boast, mainly due to the lack of rain and vegetation. There is one thing that the islanders do better than their neighbours: cheese. You must sample the *queso majorero*, a smooth goat's cheese and the first in the Canary Islands to be awarded a *Denominación de Origen* (and the first goat's cheese in Spain to receive one). As on all the islands, fresh fish is delightful and you should also try goat stew, though its flavour can be too strong for some people.

GETTING THERE AND AWAY
By air
Binter Canarias Tel: 902 39 13 92; www.bintercanarias.es. *Gran Canaria:* 10 flights a day. *Tenerife:* 2–3 flights a day.
Islas Airways Tel: 902 47 74 48; www.islasairways.com. *Gran Canaria:* 5 flights a day. *Tenerife:* 2 flights a day.

By sea
Fred Olsen Tel: 902 10 01 07; email: reserves@fredolsen.es; www.fredolsen.es. *Lanzarote:* 6 ferries a day (from Corralejo).
Trasmediterránea Tel: 902 45 46 45; www.trasmediterranea.es. *Gran Canaria:* 1 jetfoil a day (from Morro Jable) and 3 ferries a week (from Puerto del Rosario).
Naviera Armas Tel: 902 45 65 00; email: narmas@naviera-armas.com; www.naviera-armas.com. *Gran Canaria:* 1 a day (from Morro Jable). *Lanzarote:* 6 a day (from Corralejo).

GETTING AROUND
Public transport
There is a reasonable bus service which covers the main towns and tourist centres, though you can't really rely on it to explore smaller villages and deserted beaches. To do any great amount of bus travel, you'll need to be in the less-than-attractive capital.

Car hire
Autos Dominguez Tel: 928 85 11 57 (Puerto del Rosario); 928 86 63 20 (Corralejo); 928 54 22 96 (Morro Jable)
Betacar Tel: 928 86 07 58 (airport); 928 53 51 17 (Corralejo); 928 54 19 10 (Morro Jable)
Cicar Tel: 928 85 23 27 (airport); 928 86 64 13 (Corralejo); 928 54 16 56 (Morro Jable)
Hertz Tel: 928 86 06 28 (airport); 928 86 62 59 (Corralejo); 928 54 11 26 (Morro Jable)
Orlando Lanzarote Tel: 928 86 90 52 (Puerto del Rosario); 928 53 50 24 (Corralejo)
Union Rent Tel: 928 53 11 64 (airport); 928 54 15 49 (Morro Jable)

WHERE TO STAY
Fuerteventura is not quite ready for independent tourists yet, with the vast majority of accommodation to be found in the tourist resorts and much of it catering only to tour operators. There are a few *pensiones* around, though they tend to be overpriced compared to the other islands. There is a small but growing amount of rural accommodation. The Asociación de Turismo Rural is based in Antigua. It has a few **cottages** and two or three delightful hotels. Tel: 928 87 87 05; fax: 928 87 87 10; email: fuerteventura@ecoturismocanarias.com; wwwecoturismocanarias.com/fuerteventura. €65 for two people, €80–95 for four people.

There are around 15 **campsites**, the majority in the south of the island and one on Isla de Lobos. It's free to pitch a tent at most of them, though you do need to obtain permission from the *Cabildo* or relevant town hall. The tourist information office has an up-to-date list of campsites.

ACTIVITIES
Diving
The sea between Corralejo and Isla de Lobos provides a fascinating place for diving, as do Ajuy and Jacomer where an ancient volcano eruption created some fascinating underwater scenery. The windward sites (Corralejo to Punta de Pesebre) are accessible only from June to September because of the trade winds.

Most agree that Morro Jable is the best place to dive in Fuerteventura thanks to its sandstone wall, attracting the greatest concentration of large fish in the island.

Driving

Fuerteventura is a delight to drive around, especially if you have spent any length of time navigating the mountain curves in the more westerly isles. And if you don't want to drive yourself, take one of the island's various 4WD tours. **Norte y Solana** offer a variety of trips starting from €45 per person and promise to take you off the beaten track, reaching the parts that other tour companies don't. Tel: 928 87 03 60; email: norteysolana@jazzfree.com.

Windsurfing

This is the island's number one activity, other than catching rays. The professionals go to Jandía and specifically to the Playa del Sotavento, where the world championships have been held each year since 1985. If you're new to windsurfing, Caleta de Fuste is a good place for beginners. Less crowded areas for windsurfing are Corralejo, El Cotillo and Pozo Negro.

PUERTO DEL ROSARIO

This messy town became capital in 1860, mainly due to its growing harbour. Until 1956 it was known as Puerto de Cabras ('Port of Goats') because of the main activity of the citizens, but the powers that be decided that the name had negative connotations and re-christened it. It's unlikely that you'll fall in love with Puerto del Rosario, it being an odd place that seems to be lacking a town centre. There are a couple of squares but no parks and few interesting buildings. The only museum is rather dull and there is a dire lack of good places to eat. Its saving grace is the gradual introduction of sculptures in the streets. There are over 20 scattered around the city centre that provide an open-air gallery in the absence of any permanent art exhibitions. However, the capital is one of the only places with a reasonable amount of independent accommodation and the island's transport hub.

Getting there

There are just three buses from the airport per day, one at around 08.00, one at 15.00 and one in the late evening.

Where to stay
Mid-range

Hotel Fuerteventura Playa Blanca Calle Playa Blanca 45; tel: 928 85 11 50; fax: 928 85 11 58; email: hotelfuerteventura@cabildofuer.com; www.hotelfuerteventura.com. Not actually in the city, but only a few minutes' drive out of the capital towards the airport. This is the island's *parador*, though it lacks something of the star quality of those on other islands. Still, it's not too pricey and convenient for the city and the airport. Single €60; double: €75.
Palace Puerto del Rosario Calle Ruperto González Negrin 9; tel: 928 85 94 64; fax: 928 85 22 60; email: recepcion@hmppuertodelrosario.com; www.hmppuertodelrosario.com. Caters more to the business client than the tourist, so has an abundance of single rooms. Tastefully decorated and with all the little extras you expect in a 3-star hotel. Single €56; double €88. Buffet breakfast available for €6 per person.

Budget

Hostal Tamasite Calle León y Castillo 9; tel: 928 85 02 80; fax: 928 85 03 00. Not the smartest of the cheapies, but it is the closest to the sea. The paintwork is a trifle garish and the mattresses could stand being replaced, but it's clean and has TV. Single €27; double €36.

Hotel Valerón Calle Candelaria del Castillo 10; tel: 928 85 06 18; fax: 928 53 04 46. Not in the nicest part of town, but rooms are OK. All have TV and some have a balcony. Single €26; double €36.

Pensión Hotel Roquemar Calle Ruperto González Negrin 1; tel: 928 85 03 59; fax: 928 53 29 52; email: roquemar@tiscali.es. The only *pensión* where rooms come equipped with a minibar. Good location on the seafront and close to the city centre. Some rooms have balcony and sea view. Single €30; double €37.

Pensión Rubén Tinguaro Calle Juan XXIII 48; tel/fax: 928 85 10 88. Much better than it looks from the outside. The rooms are huge and have a lounge area and separate bedroom. They're a bit musty, but what do you want for these prices? Single €27; double €32.

Where to eat

El Potaje Near the harbour on Calle García Hernández. Good, hearty local food that won't break the bank.

La Cervecería Calle La Cruz. Has a small menu but it's apparently cooked *con cariño* ('with love'). Quite a good selection of fish, served to your liking.

Las Paraguitas Av Marítima. A limited menu of tapas fish and seafood with views of the harbour from its outdoor terrace.

Mesón A Lua Calle Patallo. Good tapas selection as well as a full menu. They also have a *menú del día* which at €10 isn't the cheapest, but there's a good choice and the food is tasty.

Pizzería Patio Opposite the Policía Local. A favourite, serving pizza, pasta and a few other dishes. They also deliver.

Tasca El Enyesque Calle García Hernández. Specialises in Canarian tapas, using products from the islands.

Tasca El Zaguan South end of Av 1 de Mayo. Typical tapas menu, with a few local dishes thrown in for good measure. It's a pretty macho place that's perhaps intimidating for a woman alone.

XX Café Av 1 de Mayo. Good coffee, light snacks and funky décor.

Nightlife

The main area for going out is Calle San Roque and along the Avenida Primero de Mayo.

Calle 54 Calle La Cruz. Has a patio, which will be very welcome in the unbearably hot summer months. It's a chilled-out bar which opens around midnight until the early hours. They sometimes have art exhibitions.

Discoteca Templo Calle Teniente Durán. The largest nightspot around. It opens late and closes in the early hours. Don't bother turning up before 02.00.

Las Escuevas Av Reyes de España. Attracts a slightly older crowd and is a perfect place for a few drinks in the open air next to the sea.

Mafasca Pub Calle La Cruz. Not really a pub at all but a late-late venue. It's a trendy place that plays mostly Spanish and international pop music.

Mama Rumba Calle San Roque. Plays Latin music and stays open till 05.00 or 06.00. They often have live music on weekends; look around town for posters announcing forthcoming gigs.

XX Café A chilled-out place to start your night.

Practicalities

Banks Banco Zaragozana, Calle Castaneyra, open Mon–Fri 08.30–14.00, Sat 08.30–13.00; Caja Rural, on the same road, open Mon–Fri 08.30–14.00, Thu 17.00–19.30; Santander Central Hispano, Av 1 de Mayo, open Mon–Fri 08.30–14.00, Sat 08.30–13.00; BBVA, near the church, open Mon–Fri 08.30–14.15, Sat 08.30–13.00.

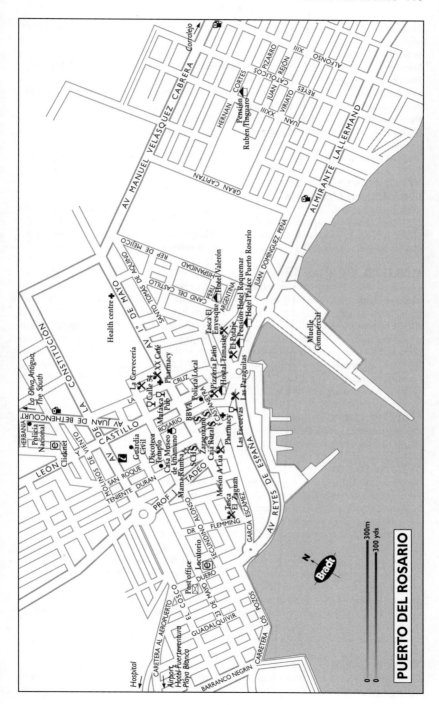

PUERTO DEL ROSARIO

N

Bradt

300m
300yds

0
0

Health The Health Centre is on Av 1 de Mayo; the hospital is just off the main road to the airport.

Internet Clicknet, Calle Gran Canaria, open every day 10.00–02.00; €2 per hour; Locutorio, opposite the post office, open Mon–Sat 10.00–15.00, 18.00–20.30; €2 per hour.

Pharmacy Next to XX Café on Av 1 de Mayo.

Police The Policía Local is on Calle Castaneyra; Policía Nacional is at the start of Av Juan de Bethencourt; the Guardia Civil is on Calle 23 de Mayo.

Post office Calle 23 de Mayo, open Mon–Fri 08.30–20.30, Sat 09.30–13.00.

Shopping The main shopping area is around the church, stretching down to the harbour.

Tourist information Av de la Constitución, open Mon–Fri 08.00–19.00, Sat 09.00–13.00.

What to see and do
Casa Museo Unamuno
This museum is dedicated to the Spanish writer Miguel Unamuno and based in the old Hotel Fuerteventura (Calle Rosario), where he stayed during his exile on the island. It's really just a collection of objects that the writer may have used during his stay as well as a few of his texts. Open Mon–Fri 09.00–14.00; entrance is free.

CALETA DE FUSTE
Caleta de Fuste is sometimes referred to as El Castillo because of the ruined 18th-century castle, San Ventura, that lies in ruins near the beach. The castle was built by military engineer Claudio de Lila in 1743 to help repel pirate attacks. It's one of the best examples of military construction on the island and reason enough to pay a visit if you're an architecture buff. However, the majority of visitors are families attracted to Caleta de Fuste by the calm waters. It has a small beach which, while it pales in comparison with the beaches of Jandía, is ideal for windsurfing beginners and small children. As tourist resorts go it isn't bad and would certainly serve if you're after a relaxing holiday.

Getting there
Buses run between Caleta de Fuste and Puerto del Rosario every half hour from 07.00 until midnight every day.

Where to stay
Aparthoteles Elba Urb El Castillo; tel: 928 16 35 00; fax: 928 16 35 01. There are three very similar complexes all in a row: Castillo de Antigua, Castillo San Jorge and Castillo Suites. All have pools, restaurants and a variety of activities on offer. An enviable position, since the grounds open out on to the promenade. Studio €78; one bedroom apartment €91.

Hotel Barceló Fuerteventura Tel: 928 54 75 17; fax: 928 54 75 25; email: fuerteventura@barcelo.com; www.barcelo.com. Large hotel with more activities on offer than you could shake a stick at, including mini-golf, archery, five-a-side football and tennis. There is also ample opportunity to relax in the spa. Single €70; double €115, including breakfast.

Hotel Elba Sara Urb Fuerteventura Golf Resort; Ctra del Sur km 11; tel: 928 16 00 20; fax: 928 16 33 24; email: elbasara@hoteleselba.com. There are plenty of amenities, such as pools, tennis, volleyball, gym, jacuzzi and a casino. There is also a free bus to the golf course and discounts on golf for hotel clients. Single €78; double €120.

Where to eat
There is no shortage of restaurants in Caleta, though recommending a few out of the multitude is rather more difficult. On Calle Juan Ramón Soto Morales you can

choose from Greek, Indian, Mexican, British, Italian, Portuguese and oh, there are a couple of 'typical' Canarian restaurants too.

Restaurante Puerto Castillo The menu is nothing to shout about but you can't argue with the location, next to the harbour. They do a bit of everything.

Nightlife
It's essentially a family resort but you will find a few places to take you into the wee hours.

Showtime Café Calle Juan Ramón Soto. The typical holiday resort bar. It hosts nightly entertainment including a range of shows and live music and karaoke once a week.
The Cavern Next to the Restaurante Puerto Castillo, this bar stays open until the early hours, playing '60s and '70s hits.

Practicalities
Banks Banca March, Calle Juan Ramón Soto Morales, open Mon–Fri 08.30–14.00, Sat 08.30–13.00; Santander Central Hispano, Av José Franchy y Roca, open Mon–Fri 08.30–14.00, Sat 08.30–13.00.
Health The Health Centre is in the Centro Comercial El Castillo.
Internet Internet Café, in the Centro Comercial El Castillo, charges €2.50 per hour; open Mon–Sat 10.00–22.00.
Pharmacy On Av del Castillo.
Police The Policía Local is next to the tourist information office.
Post office On Calle Alcalde Marcial Sánchez, open Mon–Fri 08.00–11.00, Sat 09.00–11.00.
Shopping As in all the resorts, there are various shopping centres offering pretty much whatever you're looking for. There's a 24-hour supermarket on Av José Franchy y Roca. There's also a market on Saturday mornings next to the Mahay shopping centre, selling clothes, toys and other odds and ends.
Tourist information Calle Juan Ramón Soto Morales, open Mon–Fri 09.00–15.00.

What to see and do
Boat trips
Both companies have kiosks next to the beach.

Puerto Castillo Daily catamaran excursions with possibilities of seeing turtles, dolphins and whales. Once a week they also offer the chance to go shark watching. You also get to enter their Oceanarium (like an aquarium) on your return. Adults €24; children €12.
Blue Dolphin Excursions to Pozo Negro twice a day (leaving at 10.30 and 12.30). Adults €15; children €8.

Golf
The island's only golf course is just out of the resort. It's an 18-hole, par 70 course and there is also a driving range. Green fees are €30 for nine holes and €64 for 18 holes. You can rent clubs for €15. Open every day 08.00–20.00. Tel: 928 16 00 34; email: fuerteventuragolf@grupoanjoca.com.

Diving
Deep Blue Tel: 606 27 54 68; email: info@deep-bluediving.com; www.deep-bluediving.com. Offer everything from a trial dive and theory lesson for €64 up to an open-water diver course for €330. They also rent out diving and snorkelling gear, though you need to provide a medical certificate for the former.

Windsurfing

Due to its calm sea, Caleta de Fuste is the perfect place for learners, though it doesn't hold much of interest for the more advanced. **Surf Schule** offer a two-hour taster course for €36 or a more in-depth ten-hour course for €143. They also rent out boards for €12 per hour. They have a hut next to the beach, near the San Ventura castle.

Thalassotherapy

Thalassotherapy is for those who want a less energetic water-based activity or who need to relax after a day pulling a wet sail out of the ocean. It's a relaxation treatment which uses heated sea water to ease your aches and pains. The centre is behind the beach and also offers all manner of beauty treatments. Entrance to 'The Route to Wellness' (a series of jacuzzis and water jets) is €19; open Mon–Sat 10.00–19.00; tel: 928 16 09 61; fax: 928 16 09 99; email: thalaventura@eurothermes.com.

Other activities

If it can be practised in, on or under the water, you can guarantee that it is on offer here. You can rent pedalos, jet skis, kayaks, take a boat or banana ride, try water skiing … there's even a sandcastle school on the beach every morning at 11.00. It costs €5 and by the end you could be a professional sand sculptor. You can also play mini-golf at the Barceló Club's course on the Paseo Marítimo; open daily 10.30–22.00; €3.

GRAN TARAJAL

Since it could be Fuerteventura's miles and miles of golden sand that attracted you, Gran Tarajal's 800m black beach might not appeal. If you're not bothered about the colour of the sand, it's a quiet place to catch rays and has considerably more character than some of the places further south. There's a bit of a mishmash of buildings and much of the town is under construction, giving it a slightly derelict look, but a stroll along the *paseo* is pleasant and will give you an idea of the pace of life in Gran Tarajal. If you want to see it with a bit more verve, it's worth visiting in carnival time or during the San Diego de Alcalá Fiesta. On November 13, a parade makes its way along the promenade and a raucous *romería* fills the streets of this normally sleepy fishing town. The international Deep-sea Fishing Open has been held here since 1992, mainly because of the abundance of blue marlin in these waters. You can catch it at the end of September.

Getting there

There are buses from Puerto del Rosario about every hour Mon–Sat. The bus continues to Morro Jable. There is also a bus between Gran Tarajal and Las Playitas five times a day, Mon–Sat.

Where to stay

Hostal Tamonante Calle Juan Carlos I 17; tel: 928 16 24 72. More like a hotel than a *hostal*. Rooms are bright and modern and management are constantly improving the facilities. A real bargain, considering the quality of the rooms. Make sure you call in advance as there's often no-one in reception. Single €18; double €24.

Where to eat

Avenida Italia Av Paco Hierro. Good Italian food with main dishes starting at €6.
Bar Playa Next door to Avenida Italia. A good place for a snack, a fresh juice or one of their many cocktails.
Bar Restaurante Parada Calle Princesa Tamonante, near the church. Has a *menú del día* for €7.

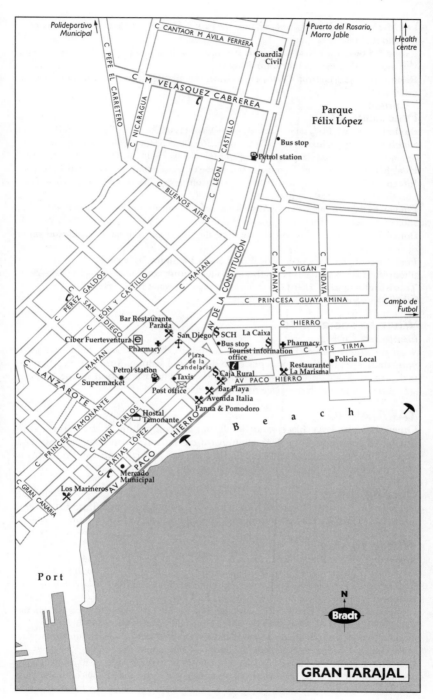

Los Marineros Calle Matias López, near the park. Decent choice of tapas and plenty of fish and seafood.

Panna & Pomodoro Next to Avenida Italia. An Argentine-run pizza and ice-cream joint. Very reasonably priced and they also deliver.

Restaurante La Marisma On the promenade. Has an OK menu with plenty of choice in meat and fish.

Practicalities

Banks Caja Rural, Plaza de Candelaria, open Mon–Fri 08.30–14.00, Thu 17.00–19.30; Santander Central Hispano, Av de la Constitución, open Mon–Fri 08.30–14.00, Sat 08.30–13.00; La Caixa, Calle Amanay, open Mon–Fri 08.15–14.00, Thu 17.00–19.15.

Health The Health Centre is out of town on the other side of the Parque Felix López.

Internet Ciber Fuerteventura, Calle San Diego, open Mon–Sat 09.00–13.00, 16.00–21.00, Sun 16.00–21.00; €2.50 per hour.

Pharmacy There's one on Calle Atis Tirma, near the tourist information kiosk and another opposite the church.

Police The Policía Local is on Calle Tindaya; the Guardia Civil is on the main road, on the way out of town.

Post office In the plaza, open Mon–Fri 08.30–14.30, Sat 09.30–13.00.

Shopping There's a large supermarket on Calle Fuerteventura, open Mon–Sat 08.30–20.30.

Tourist information There's a kiosk next to the Caja Rural Bank, open Mon–Fri 08.00–14.30, Sat 08.00–13.00.

What to see and do
Deep-sea fishing
With the International Deep-Sea Tag & Release Fishing Open held here every year, there are probably worse places to do a bit of fishing. Surprisingly, there are no companies set up to take tourists out but if you ask around in the harbour, someone's bound to have space for you on their boat.

TARAJALEJO
Other than the large black-sand beach and a small fishing harbour there's not much to recommend Tarajalejo. It surely oozed character once upon a time but has now all but been taken over by the Tofio complex. A small *pueblo* still remains, its 600 inhabitants making a living from fishing and tourism.

Getting there
Bus number 1 leaves Puerto del Rosario every hour Mon–Sat and passes through Gran Tarajal before reaching Tarajalejo and continuing to Morro Jable.

Where to stay
Apartamentos Varadero Av Marítima; tel: 928 87 20 32; fax: 928 85 10 14; www.varaderofuerteventura.com. The apartments are on the small side, but have good-sized terraces and sea views. The complex is on the seafront, near the *pueblo*. A 1-bedroom apartment is €43, but there are hefty discounts for long stays.

Camping El Brasero Ctra General, just after turning for Tarajalejo as you come from the south; tel: 928 16 11 82. Owned by the Tofio Hotel, the campsite has good facilities, including a pool, pub, children's play area and TV room. Prices vary depending on the size of the tent, but start from €3 per tent plus another €3 per adult.

Club Hotel Tofio Ctra Playa de las Palmeras; tel: 928 16 10 01; fax: 928 16 10 28. Rooms are nothing spectacular but the hotel also has swimming pools, tennis and squash courts and mini-golf. Single €36; double €53, including breakfast. There are also some studios and apartments.

Where to eat

Bar Chao Calle Bajamar. A good place for fish and seafood. Also has a fair selection of tapas. Closed on Wednesdays.

Bar Pizzería Ca'Pino Calle Cabrera Martin. Not the tastiest of pizzas, but at least it offers something different to the other restaurants around. Closed on Wednesdays.

Bar Restaurante La Barraca Calle Isidro Díaz in the *pueblo*. A friendly place with local character serving fresh fish and meat.

Restaurante El Brasero At the campsite. An uninspiring menu of Canarian and international food, though you can eat outside. Has live music on Friday nights. Main meals start at €8. Closed on Mondays.

Restaurante El Marinero Near La Barraca. Nothing special but has plenty of choice. Closed on Mondays.

Practicalities

Everything is either in La Lajita or Gran Tarajal, except for a supermarket near the Apartamentos Varadero.

What to see and do
Diving

Dive Big Blue On the beach below the Tofio apartments; tel: 928 87 21 22; email: info@dive-bigblue.com; www.dive-bigblue.com. A package of 6 dives costs €130. They also run day trips to Lanzarote for €100, which include 2 dives, breakfast and the ferry.

Sailing

Cat Company Tel: 928 16 13 76; email: info@learn-catamaran-sailing.com; www.learn-catamaran-sailing.com. They offer courses, rental and excursions in their catamarans. A taster day costs €60 and a 4-day beginners' course is €190. Rental is €75 for 4 hours (you need sailing experience!). They have a kiosk on the beach.

Horseriding

At the El Brasero campsite. Lessons are €9 for half an hour and excursions of varying lengths are also available. Same opening times as the Aquarium.

Aquarium

The aquarium at El Brasero houses over 120 species from the Fuerteventura seas. It's quite pleasant to walk through the tunnel and see the fish swimming around you. Open Tue–Sun 10.00–13.00, 16.00–20.00; €4.50, half price for children.

PLAYA DE SOTAVENTO

This is *the* windsurfers' beach and the location of the international championships. The 100% probability of wind and perfect windsurfing conditions mean that the event, held at the end of July, is firmly on the World Cup Circuit. It's also a stupendous beach for those who don't want to windsurf, with its 22km of white sand and calm salt-water lagoon that forms at low tide. Of course, it's sometimes a little windy for sunbathing, but that doesn't stop the nudists from stripping off.

Getting there

If you're using buses, you'll need to alight on the main road and either walk or hitch the 2km to the beach. There are different exits depending on whether you want to go to the hotel or further south. Both roads are signposted.

Where to stay

Hotel Sol Gorriones Tel: 928 54 70 25; fax: 928 54 70 25; email:
sol.gorriones@solmelia.com; www.solgorriones.solmelia.com. Not the most attractive
hotel and many consider it to be a bit of a blot on this otherwise unspoilt stretch of beach.
However, if you're in the hotel looking out, the view is unrivalled. Rooms are quite
modern and, if you want to splash out, the Casas del Mar are a cluster of suites away from
the hotel riff-raff. There are good windsurfing deals on offer to guests. Single €65; double
€100; suite €170, including breakfast.

What to do
Windsurfing
This is the archipelago's *numero uno* windsurfing spot. Experts will enjoy the
challenges and strong winds while beginners can learn in the calm lagoon. **Pro
Center René Egli** have two centres on the beach, one next to the Sol Gorriones
Hotel and the other two miles south. A two-hour taster session is €50, a ten-hour
beginners' course is €183, private lessons are €51 per hour and rental starts at €50
per day (for experienced windsurfers). There is a 10% discount for courses booked
from your home country. Tel: 928 54 74 83; fax: 928 54 73 88; email: info@rene-
egli.com; www.rene-egli.com.

Kiteboarding
René Egli also offer courses and rental for this newish, adrenalin-pumping sport.
An all-important ten-hour introduction course costs €300, private lessons are €80
per hour and rental for experienced 'boarders' starts at €50 per day. See above for
contact details.

MORRO JABLE
For some, Morro Jable has all the charm, while Corralejo in the north is overrun by
tourism, though for me it's completely the other way around. Morro Jable is a
funny place with two quite distinct parts, neither of them particularly appealing.
The tourist area (known as Solana Matorral) has all the artificial feel and lack of
ambience that afflicts many resorts, while the old town has character but an
unmistakably seedy feel. In fact, it's the only place in the whole archipelago where
I didn't feel 100% safe alone at night. Once a fishing village with 200 inhabitants,
these days it's home to 8,000 people, many of them foreign residents. Until 1982
there was no decent road reaching this part of the island but since then construction
work has gone crazy and there are now around 16,000 beds in Morro Jable.

Getting there
By boat
There are regular boats between Morro Jable and Las Palmas in Gran Canaria. See
Getting there and away, page 112, for details.

By bus
There are direct and indirect buses to and from Puerto del Rosario about every hour
Mon–Sat (four per day on Sunday). There is also a thrice-daily service from the
airport. Other services run to Pájara (twice a day) and Costa Calma (four times a day).

Where to stay
There are plenty of five-star hotels around and also a fair number of free
campsites. For details of the latter contact the tourist information office or the
Pájara Town Hall; tel: 928 16 17 04.

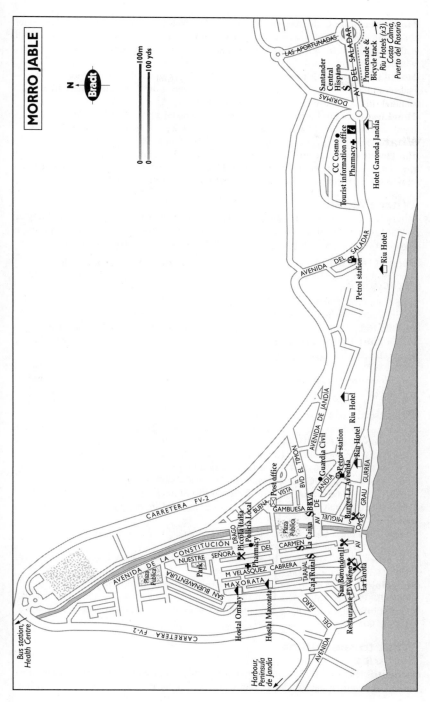

Hostal Maxorata Calle Maxorata 31; tel: 928 54 10 87. Grotty and smelly. You'd be better off up the road at Omahy. Some rooms have private bathroom, some don't (and the shared bathrooms are far from appealing). Single €18 without bathroom, €24 with; double €24 without bathroom, €28 with.

Hostal Omahy Calle Maxorata 47; tel: 928 54 12 54. Bright and clean, all rooms have bathroom and some have balcony. Definitely the better of the 2 cheapies. There are no single rooms. Double €24.

Hotel Garonda Jandía Av del Saladar 28; tel: 928 54 04 30; fax: 928 54 02 18; email: hgjr@lopesanhr.com. Low-rise beachfront hotel with 2 pools set in tropical gardens and access to the beach. Typical rooms for a 4-star hotel. Single €80; double €130.

Riu Hotels www.riu.com. As in every resort on the island, one company seems to have the monopoly and in Morro Jable it's Riu. They have 6 establishments in the resort, some of which are apartments, some hotels. Prices range from €80 to €120 for a double.

Where to eat
There is a cluster of reasonable restaurants on the coast in the old town. They all have a similar menu, offering a bit of everything. In Solana Matorral everything is based in the various shopping centres on Avenida del Saladar.

Burger La Avenida Av Tomás Grau Gurrea. It doesn't sound great, but they do a lot more than burgers. Has a great tapas menu, evident by the number of elderly *señores* that frequent the place.

La Farola Calle Chalana. Typical tourist resort menu offering a taste of everything, though it's not as pricey as many of the restaurants around.

Piccola Italia Calle Señora del Carmen. Italian food away from the main tourist area.

Restaurante El Veleno Calle Balandro. Boasts superb *ali-oli* (garlic mayonnaise) to keep you occupied while you wait and wait and wait for your meal. Good omelette selection, terrible service.

San Borondón II Calle Falua. If you want to do the tourist thing, why not go the whole hog and eat in this boat-shaped restaurant complete with portholes and anchor.

Practicalities
Banks The following are in the old part of town: Caja Rural, Calle Manuel Velázquez Cabrera, open Mon–Fri 08.30–14.00, Thu 17.00–19.30; BBVA, Av de Jandía, open Mon–Fri 08.30–14.15, Sat 08.30–13.00; La Caixa, Calle Nuestra Señora del Carmen, open Mon–Fri 08.15–14.00, Thu 16.30–19.45. Santander Central Hispano is in the shopping centre in front of the Aparthotel Palm Garden, open Mon–Fri 08.30–14.00, Sat 08.30–13.00.

Health The Health Centre is north of the old part of town.

Pharmacy One on Calle Manuel Velázquez Cabrera and another in the Centro Comercial Cosmo.

Police The Policía Local is on Calle Nuestra Señora del Carmen; the Guardia Civil is on Av de Jandía, both in the old part of town.

Post office On the corner of Calle Gambuesa and Calle Buenavista, open Mon–Fri 08.30–14.30, Sat 09.30–13.00.

Shopping There's a market on Thursday mornings from 09.00 next to the Centro Comercial Cosmo.

Tourist information In the basement of the Centro Comercial Cosmo, open Mon–Fri 08.00–15.00.

What to see and do
Boat trips
Oceano Tel: 616 91 80 55; www.oceano-sl.com. If you're feeling flush you can take a trip around the south of the island on a 16m yacht, lending the crew a hand if you want to. The

trip includes lunch, drinks and watersports. Adults €119; children €48, or you can charter the whole boat for €680 (max 10 people).

Diving

There are surprisingly few diving companies considering Morro Jable is thought to be the best place on the island for a bit of *buceo*.

U Dive Fuerteventura Based in the Occidental Grand Hotel; email: contacto@u-divefuerteventura.com; www.u-divefuerteventura.com. They are quite pricey compared with most companies around the islands, with a discovery dive costing €78 and the open-water diver course €400. There are other companies and your best bet is to wander into the large hotels and ask. Some cater for guests only but others will accept anyone's money.

WEST OF MORRO JABLE

From the map it might well look like Fuerteventura ends at the Morro Jable harbour but there is a network of well-maintained dirt tracks to lead you around one of the best parts of the island, the Península de Jandía. On the island's westernmost tip you'll find the tiny village of **Puertito de la Cruz**, a weird collection of ramshackle houses and caravans owned by a group of people who opted out of the rat race when the tourists started arriving in Morro Jable. You should try the local speciality, fish stew, served with gusto in the two restaurants. An alternative track takes you to **Cofete**, a farming village whose houses might fit better in a shantytown. For reasons unknown, this area of the island was presented to German engineer Gustav Winter by none other than General Franco. The eerie dishevelled mansion you'll see above Cofete was the fruit of the German's labours, though stories of secret Nazi bases in the area have never been substantiated. If you want to stay at the campsite on Playa de Cofete you have to get permission from the *Cabildo*, tel: 928 86 23 00. The sunsets in this part of the island are superb and there is no need for a 4WD to get about.

LA PARED

La Pared ('The Wall') takes its name from the 6km wall that once divided the early kingdoms of Maxorata and Jandía, which seemed to start in this settlement. Thanks to construction and roadworks, the wall is no longer intact, though there's enough of it left to give you a fair idea. Of course, it's little more than a pile of rocks and you probably wouldn't look twice at it if you didn't already know its importance. Barely a metre high in some places, it once stretched from coast to coast, separating the Jandía peninsula from the rest of the island. Other than the archaeological remains there's not much to see, though the coastal view is pretty impressive; follow signs to Restaurant Bahía La Pared to appreciate the wild waves crashing on the shore. The town could also be held up as a fine example of bad planning; its roads are spread out, unnamed and there is no town centre.

Getting there

There are no buses to La Pared, so you need your own wheels if you want to visit.

Where to stay

Hotel Costa Real Tel: 928 54 90 04; fax: 928 54 91 04. The hotel offers a range of activities to residents; a good thing, as there's not much else going on in La Pared. Facilities include pools, tennis courts, archery and rifle range, full-sized football pitch, gym and disco. Most rooms are 'semi-suites' with a lounge, bedroom and balcony or terrace. Single €75; double €115.

Where to eat
Restaurante Bahía Pared Definitely has the upper hand on location, with views of the ocean and the remains of the wall. Has a varied menu with the emphasis on fish and seafood.

Restaurante Camello Av Istmo. Has some tempting fish and meat dishes. The restaurant is signposted.

Practicalities
Everything is in Costa Calma or Morro Jable.

What to see and do
Golf
There's a golf school (tel: 928 54 91 03) next to the hotel for those wanting to improve their swing or just learn the basics. Prices are extremely reasonable at €25 per hour for classes and €15 for 18 holes, including clubs and balls, though you made need to study German before you learn to play golf.

Surfing
This is the best place in Fuerteventura for catching waves and surprisingly there is only one company offering classes and board hire. **Cowabunga** (tel: 619 80 44 47; email: cowabunga@infocanarias.com; www.cowabunga.de) offer a 12-hour beginners' course is €115 or an eight-hour advanced course costs €85. There are longer courses available and they also rent out boards from €9 a day. They can arrange accommodation for surfers on a nearby campsite.

PÁJARA
Although it's the capital of the municipality, there's not much action in Pájara, a sleepy place with 700 inhabitants. It has a nice church, a tranquil square and park and a reasonable restaurant, but other than that there are much better places to spend your holiday.

AJUY
This fishing hamlet is definitely worth a visit, both for the food and a trip to the impressive caves. Obviously, the local speciality is fish, though there are other dishes on offer in the three or four restaurants. Geological finds point to this being the oldest part of the island, which probably makes it the oldest part of the archipelago. Once known as Puerto de la Peña, it was the first port of call for Bethencourt and his crew of conquerors. Once you've enjoyed a fishy lunch in one of the town's restaurants, don't miss the easy paved walk to admire the weird rock formations and photogenic caves. The beach here is known as Playa de los Muertos ('Beach of the Dead'), perhaps because of its lethal currents. This is the only place in the Canary Islands from where you can view fragments of the African continental plate.

TUINEJE
The most outstanding thing about Tuineje is the architecture. There are derelict structures everywhere, many of them Berber in style and layout thanks to the Morisco slaves who settled in the area. Every year the 1740 battle of Tamasite is re-enacted here, to mark the date that 37 locals armed with farming tools fought off 50 English corsairs. The battle takes place during the fiesta de San Miguel (October 13).

In the nearby village of Tiscamanita you'll find the **Centro de Interpretaciones Los Molinos**, one of the *Cabildo*'s museums. It has a restored mill which you can see in action (if you pass on a windy day) and taste the *gofio* produced there. Staff are friendly and very knowledgeable and will explain everything you need to know about the entire process from picking the corn to eating the *gofio* in one of its many forms. There is also a tasting session when the wind has been blowing enough to grind the corn. Open Tue–Sun 09.30–17.30, closed Sat; entrance is €1.80.

ANTIGUA

Antigua is one of those one-horse towns where someone has stolen the horse, none of the streets have names and no-one looks before crossing the road as they simply don't expect a car to be coming. Still, it's got a sort of charm in spite of that, or perhaps because of it. It wasn't always like this, though: it was once the most densely populated town on the island and a bustling trading point thanks to its central location. It even held the title of capital once, albeit for just one year.

In May the town hosts an important handicrafts fare, where craftsmen from across the islands come to sell their wares. Check with the tourist office for dates.

Getting there

There are two buses a day that pass through from Puerto del Rosario to La Vega de Río Palmas, Mon–Sat only.

Where to stay

Hostal El Artesano Calle Real 4; tel: 928 87 80 39. One of life's true bargains. The rooms are small but spotless, have en-suite bathroom and even TV! It's on the main road that passes by Antigua. Single €12; double €22.

Hotel Rural Era El Corte Calle El Corte 1; tel: 928 87 87 05; fax: 928 87 87 10; email: eradelacorte@terra.es; www.eradelacorte.com. This late 19th-century house has been converted into a charming rural hotel. The rooms are all different and have character, not like a chain hotel. There's also a reading lounge, pool, tennis court and garden. Meals are available. Single €48; double €90, including breakfast.

Where to eat

The town is hardly a gastronomic awakening. There are a few places to eat but most are oozing with testosterone and boast a menu heavy on goat.

Café Bar La Noria Near the pharmacy. Doesn't look much from the outside but holds a pleasant surprise. It has excellent tapas at good prices and a relaxed atmosphere.

Restaurante Piccolo Mondo Opposite the Town Hall. At first glance it looks like a pizza joint but they also serve meat and fish dishes. It's cheap and cheerful and has a 3-course *menú del día* for €7.50.

Practicalities

Banks La Caja de Canarias is on the same road as the post office, open Mon–Fri 08.00–14.00, Thu 17.30–19.30.

Health Around the corner from the post office.

Pharmacy On the same road as the bank and post office, moving away from the church.

Police The Policía Local is in the Town Hall (next to the church).

Post office Behind the children's playground, which you can see from the main road, open Mon–Fri 08.00–11.00, Sat 09.00–11.00.

Shopping Visit the Centro de Artesanía for handicrafts from across the island (see below). There's a supermarket on the main road. In the winter months there is a market next to the church on the second Sunday of the month from 10.00–12.00. You can pick up crafts, cakes and local produce, including the famous Majorero cheese. The island's most important craft fair is held in Antigua in May. The date changes, so contact the tourist information office for more information.

Tourist information None, though you could ask in the Town Hall, open Mon–Fri 08.00–14.00.

What to see and do
Centro de Artesanía Molino de Antigua
This belongs to the *Cabildo*'s network of museums. It's a bit of a hotchpotch but an agreeable place to spend an hour. It hosts various temporary exhibitions on the history or culture of the island. You can also take a walk around its gardens, look inside an old mill and purchase a few handicrafts. The shop has a variety of crafts and does not take a cut, so what you pay goes directly to the craftsman. Open Tue–Sun 09.30–17.30, closed Sat; entrance €1.80 adults; €0.90 children.

LA AMPUYENTA
The only reason you'd stop in this little village is to visit the **Casa Museo Dr Mena**, a tribute to the area's most famous son, Dr Tomás Mena y Mesa. It's an example of a typical country house from the mid 19th century and contains a few of the doctor's belongings. Open Tue–Sun 09.30–17.30, closed Sat; entrance is free.

BETANCURIA
Betancuria was founded in 1404 during the conquest of Fuerteventura and was the first settlement on the island to be taken by the Europeans. It takes its name from its conqueror, Jean de Bethencourt, who declared it the capital of the island. It remained capital until the early 19th century, when the title went to La Oliva. These days it's home to around 700 souls. It's not difficult to see why Bethencourt decided to set up camp here; it's about the only place on the island where you'll see any substantial amount of greenery and has a superb location, surrounded by rolling hills. True, its verdure is hardly comparable to any of the western islands but it comes as a nice change having driven through the desert-like landscapes for a few days. The town itself is a delight with its well-kept buildings, tidy square and near deserted streets. Plenty of tourists pass through these days, as the ex-capital is not without its attractions.

What to see and do
You can buy one ticket to visit both the **Museo de Arte Sacro** and the 17th-century **Iglesia de Santa María** (originally built in 1593 but destroyed by Berber hordes). The museum opens on the hour for half an hour, then it closes and the church opens for half an hour (an interesting way of cutting down on staff wages). Open Mon–Fri 11.00–17.00, Sat 11.00–15.00; entrance €1.50. You can also see the ruins of the San Diego and Friary chapels, the first Franciscan monastery in the Canary Islands.

At **Casa de Santa María** you can taste various wines, jams, *mojos* and cheeses and watch the artisans at work. They still use the traditional weaving, embroidery, basketry and pottery methods and their work is on sale. There's also a 20-minute film about Betancuria and its role in the island's history. Open Mon–Sat 10.00–16.00; entrance €5 including the tasting.

Museo Arqueológico de Betancuria is on the road to La Vega de Río Palmas. It's a small but interesting museum with exhibits of aboriginal ceramics and religious idols from across the island. Open Tue–Sat 10.00–17.00, Sun 11.00–14.00; entrance €1.20.

There's a small **tourist information** kiosk behind the church open Mon–Sat 09.30–15.30.

LA VEGA DE RÍO PALMAS

This is the home of the **Iglesia de la Virgen de la Peña**, first built in 1497 and now housing the idol of Fuerteventura's patron saint. Although a sleepy hamlet for the rest of the year, La Vega hosts a wild party on the third Saturday in September in honour of the Virgen de la Peña. There is also a splendid, if slightly expensive restaurant here, Restaurante Don Antonio. As you are driving from Betancuria, you'll pass a turning for the **Zona Recreativa de Betancuria**. It's worth the 3km detour along a well-maintained dirt track to see Fuerteventura's mini pine forest. OK so it's not a patch on those of Gran Canaria or Tenerife, but somehow you'll appreciate it more as it is such a contrast to the rest of the island. It's a picnic area with a kids' playground which attracts half the island on weekends, so it's wise to visit during the week.

TEFÍA
Ecomuseo La Alcogida

This is an interesting museum consisting of seven old houses that offers a look into Canarian life at the beginning of the 20th century. There are also two houses where you can see artisans producing traditional crafts that you can later buy in the museum's shop. The only black spot of the museum is the rather sad-looking bunch of animals tethered to the floor. Open Tue–Sun 09.30–17.30, closed on Saturdays; entrance €4.20.

LA OLIVA

The capital of ancient Maxorata and one-time capital of Fuerteventura, La Oliva is a charming place and well worth a day trip. Start by visiting the **Centro de Arte Canario**, a gallery showcasing paintings and sculptures by contemporary Canarian artists including César Manrique. The centre has pleasant gardens with sculptures scattered here and there. There are also temporary exhibitions and a room with paintings by the gallery's owner, Manuel Delgado Camino. Reproductions of some of the paintings are available, while other artists have their originals on sale. Open Mon–Sat 10.00–17.00; €4.

Opposite the Centro de Arte you'll see the **Casa de los Coroneles**, a fine example of colonial architecture, although it's looking a bit dishevelled these days. You'll hear rumours that the building has 365 windows, though the truth behind this statement is debatable (and who wants to stand there and count them?) The saying comes from disgruntled poor folk who used to moan about the wealth of those who lived in the house, complaining that they 'had as many windows as there are days in the year'. It was Fuerteventura's first civic building and the residence of Bethencourt's descendants. Unfortunately, it's not open to the public, though there are talks of turning it into a museum in the future. The other place to visit in La Oliva is the **Casa Cilla Museo del Grano**. In times of old this was the building where the locals had to hand over 20% of their income to the Church. These days it houses Fuerteventura's homage to grain and agriculture. It's a small museum but worth a visit to learn a little about the history of the area. Open Tue–Sun 09.30–17.30, closed Sat; €1.20 (under 13s free).

VILLAVERDE

The only reason you're likely to stick around Villaverde is to stay in its magnificent hotel, one of the archipelago's finest. It's also not a bad place to get an idea of traditional island life or somewhere to base yourself for exploring the north of Fuerteventura.

Getting there

Buses pass through every two hours as they go from Corralejo to El Cotillo and back.

Where to stay

Hotel Rural Mahoh Tel: 928 86 80 50; fax: 928 86 86 12; email: hotelrural@mahoh.com; www.mahoh.com. Fabulous rooms decorated in rustic or antique style. The 19th-century stone building keeps you cool in the hot months (which is just about every month). The hotel has extensive gardens, a library, sports facilities and swimming pool. They also offer a horse and cart ride through the village. Single €65; double €76, including breakfast.

Where to eat

The hotel will organise meals for guests; other than that there are a couple of below par places on the main road.

Practicalities

Everything is in La Oliva or Corralejo.

What to see and do
Casa Marcos

Small shop selling crafts (some of which border on the tacky side) and local products such as cheese, wine, liquors and jam. They operate a try-before-you-buy policy. It's on the main road, open Mon–Sat 10.00–18.30.

La Rosita

This place is like a microcosm of Canarian history and society. There's a Canarian garden, palm grove, tobacco plantation, a working windmill and small museum. It's a bit cheesy but not bad for kids, who can feed the farm animals and take a ride on a camel. Open Mon–Sat 10.00–18.00; entrance is €5 for adults, €2.50 children or €11/5.50 if you want to ride a camel as well.

CORRALEJO

Although it's now one of Fuerteventura's largest and most important tourist resorts, it maintains a charm that many of them don't. You have to use your imagination a bit but you can just about see the fishing village that started it all and there is still a fair amount of local character if you venture away from the seafront. True, there are areas that are somewhat reminiscent of Blackpool and the beach isn't a patch on those in the south, but it far outshines its southern counterpart, Morro Jable. If you're looking for tranquillity it's worth getting the boat over to Isla de Lobos for the day.

Getting there
By boat

Fred Olsen and Naviera Armas operate ferries between Corralejo and Playa Blanca in Lanzarote, leaving about every hour. A one-way ticket is around €12 (slightly cheaper with Armas).

By bus
The bus station is on Avenida Juan Carlos I. There are regular buses between Corralejo and Puerto del Rosario and also a service to El Cotillo.

Where to stay
Upmarket
Hotel Atlantis Palace Av Grandes Playas 12; tel: 928 53 60 50; fax: 928 53 53 67; email: commercial@atlantishotels.com. A large complex with excellent facilities, not far from the beach. Single €80; double €110.

Hotel Oasis Village Av Fuerteventura; tel: 928 53 60 06; fax: 928 86 63 84; email: info-oasisvillage@oasisfuerteventura.com; www.oasisfuerteventura.com. A little out of the centre. It's a huge hotel though its facilities aren't as good as those at the Atlantis Palace. Single €80; double €100.

Mid-range
Hotel La Posada Calle María Santana Figueroa 1; tel: 928 86 73 44; fax: 928 53 63 52; www.hotellaposada.com. In a quiet location and offers good value. Rooms are pretty standard but bright and have satellite TV and a small fridge. The hotel also has a rooftop terrace with pool. Single €36; Double €42.

Hotel Partner Arena Calle El Muro; tel: 928 53 60 34; fax: 928 53 60 35. Quiet, low-rise place 500m from the beach. All the usual facilities plus an extensive entertainments programme. Single €50; double €70, including breakfast.

Hotel Primasol Las Dunas Calle El Muro 1; tel: 928 53 50 97; fax: 928 53 50 95. Good if you're easily bored: they have tennis courts, billiard room, kids' club and evening entertainment. Single €50; double €90 on an all-inclusive basis.

Budget
Hostal Manhattan Calle Gravina 22; tel: 928 86 66 43. The upholstery could do with being replaced and the shower is ridiculously small, meaning you flood the room whenever you wash. That said it's clean, central and reasonably priced. All rooms have a private bathroom and some have a balcony. Single €22; double €30.

Hotel Corralejo Calle Delfín 1; tel: 928 53 52 46. An ugly-looking concrete block but you can't beat the location. Single €25; double €30; triple €36.

Where to eat
Bodeguita Andaluz Calle La Ballena, near the harbour. Has a more 'special' feel than many of the restaurants around it (no plastic furniture!). The menu is limited, but offers the best in Andalucian cuisine. There is one vegetarian alternative, the rest of the menu is very meaty, with a couple of fish options.

Bombay Balti House Near the Hotel La Posada. Plenty of choice in Indian food though the restaurant itself is nothing special. Main courses are about €7.

Castaways On the seafront. One of the nicer British pubs and on the seafront but like all of them it seems to be stuck on British prices, making it rather expensive for what it is. Main meals cost around €8.

La Cabaña Asturiana Calle La Milagrosa. Tasty specials from Asturia, washed down with some excellent cider.

Los Compadres Calle La Ballena. The place to go to get a huge, tasty, cheap *bocadillo* to take to Isla de Lobos with you.

Pancho Villa On the corner of Calle La Pizarro and Calle del General Prim. Reasonable Mexican food and live music. Main courses start at €8.

Restaurante Avenida Opposite Pancho Villa. Has a typical menu incorporating Spanish and Canarian dishes and is more reasonably priced than many places around, making it the locals' choice.

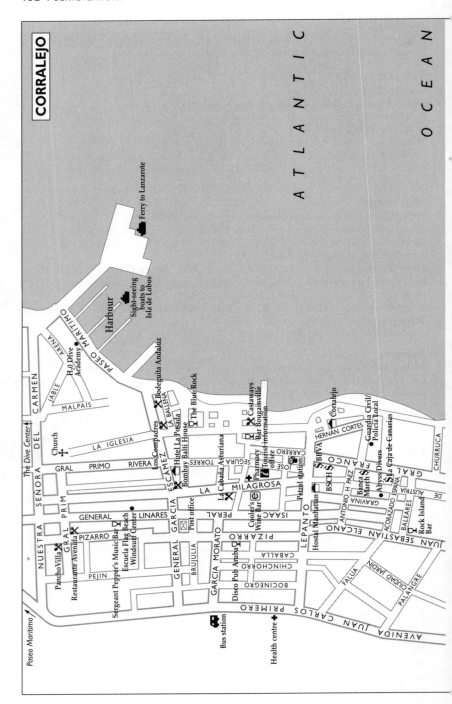

CORRALEJO

ATLANTIC OCEAN

Ferry to Lanzarote

Harbour

Sight-seeing boats to Isla de Lobos

PASEO MARITIMO

JABLE ARENA

The Dive Center

CARMEN

SENORA DEL

NUESTRA

MALPAÍS

H.0 Dive Academy

Church

LA IGLESIA

GRAL PRIMO RIVERA

Los Compadres

Bodeguita Andaluz

LA BALLENA

Hotel La Posada

Bombay Balti House

ESCAMEZ

LA

La Cabaña Asturiana

The Blue Rock

SEGURA TORRES

Pharmacy

Castaways Bar Bougainville

Tourist information office

JOSE ARREÑO

Petrol station

MILAGROSA

Cooler's Wine Bar

Corralejo

HERNAN CORTES

BSCH BBVA

Guardia Civil/ Policia Local

La Caja de Canarias

CHURRUCA

GRAL

DE AUSTRIA

Banca March

Abyss Divers

ISAAC PERAL

LEPANTO

Hostal Manhattan

BANCO

ANTONIO H PAEZ

GRAVINA

ESPAÑA

ACORAZADO

BALEARES

Rock Island Bar

JUAN SEBASTIAN ELCANO

FALUA

PALANGRE

CIUDAD JARDIN

PanchoVilla

Restaurante Avenida

GRAL PIZARRO

PEJIN

PRIM

GENERAL

LINARES

Sergeant Pepper's Music Bar

Escuela Flag Beach Windsurf Center

GENERAL

BRUJULA

GARCIA

Post office

PERAL

PIZARRO

GARCIA MORATO

Disco Pub Aruba

CHINCHORRO

BOCINEGRO

CABALLA

JUAN CARLOS PRIMERO

AVENIDA JUAN CARLOS PRIMERO

Bus station

Health centre

Paseo Maritimo

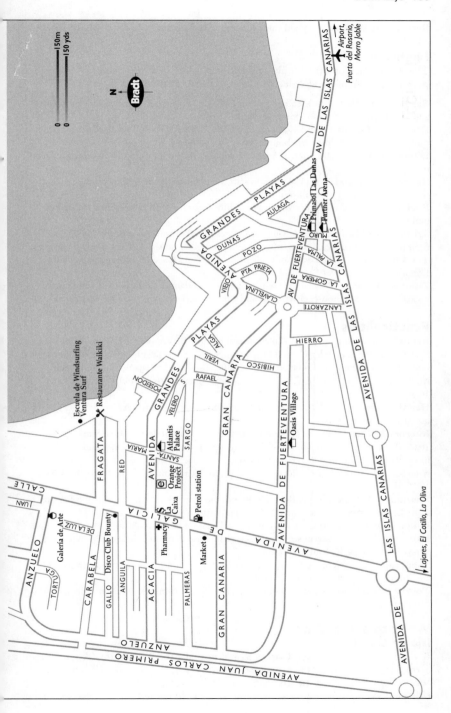

Restaurante Waikiki Has good value lunchtime specials and is on the beach (literally).

Nightlife

There is no lack of British pubs and bad live music (and the two often come as a package) but there are also decent places to paint the town red.

Bar Bougainville In a little square just off Calle de la Iglesia. Exhaustive cocktail menu and an outdoor terrace; good for early drinks.

Disco Club Bounty Centro Comercial Los Zocos. Mostly chart music with a few classics thrown in; open until the early hours.

Disco Pub Aruba Calle Pizarro. Attracts a young crowd with its loud house music. Open until 05.00.

Restaurant Waikiki Not a bad place to start the night, with a few beers on the beach as the sun goes down. Plays chill-out music.

Rock Island Bar Calle Crucero Baleares. Chilled-out bar with live acoustic music every night.

Sgt Pepper's Music Bar Calle General Linares. A rather unlikely area for a music bar, right in a residential area, but it's popular and plays good music. Attracts an older audience.

The Blue Rock On the corner of Calle de la Iglesia and Calle María Santana Figueroa. Live rock and blues every night.

Zumbar On the top floor of the Centro Comercial Atlántico. This is a late venue with varied music (R&B, house, chart, '70s) and a first-rate cocktail menu. Opens at 23.00.

Practicalities

Banks The following are all on Calle General Franco: BBVA, open Mon–Fri 08.30–14.15, Sat 08.30–13.00; Santander Central Hispano, open Mon–Fri 08.30–14.00, Sat 08.30–13.00; Banca March open Mon–Fri 08.30–14.00, Sat 08.30–13.00; La Caja de Canarias, open Mon–Fri 08.00–14.00, Thu 17.30–19.30; La Caixa, open Mon–Fri 08.15–14.00, Thu 16.30–19.45.

Health There are lots of private clinics around but the public Health Centre is next to the bus station.

Internet Av Grandes Playas. Orange Project, open Mon–Sat 08.30–01.00, Sun 10.00–01.00; €4 per hour. They give you a free drink for every hour you spend on the internet and at these prices you'd better make it a double! There's also access at Cooler's wine bar, behind the tourist information office, for €2 an hour; open daily 09.30–14.30, 19.30–late.

Pharmacy On Calle General Franco, opposite the Hoplaco apartments and another on Calle La Milagrosa near the tourist information office.

Police Both the Guardia Civil and the Policía Local are on Paseo Atlántico.

Post office On a pedestrian street between Calle Isaac Peral and Calle de Pizarro, open Mon–Fri 08.30–14.30, Sat 09.30–13.00.

Shopping If you're looking for tat, you'll be in heaven in the many *centros comerciales*. There are dozens of overpriced supermarkets too.

Tourist information The booth in the square on Calle Almirante Nelson is open Mon–Fri 08.00–15.00.

What to see and do
Isla de Lobos

It would be a crime to visit Corralejo and not take the 20-minute, 2km boat trip across to this small islet, a protected nature reserve. Isla de Lobos ('Isle of Wolves') is 5km², with its highest peak measuring 127m. Wolves are conspicuous only by their absence; the island is so named for the *lobo marino*, or

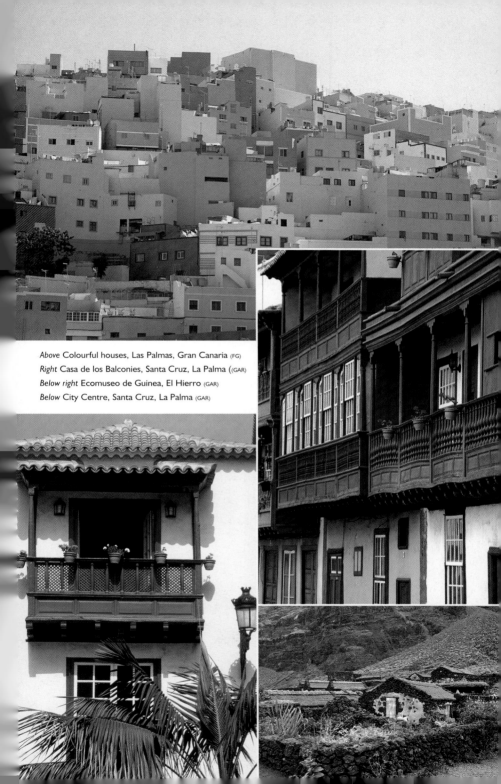

Above Colourful houses, Las Palmas, Gran Canaria (FG)

Right Casa de los Balconies, Santa Cruz, La Palma ((GAR)

Below right Ecomuseo de Guinea, El Hierro (GAR)

Below City Centre, Santa Cruz, La Palma (GAR)

Above Church, Puerto de la Cruz, Tenerife (GAR)

Below left Cathedral at night, Tenerife (GAR)

Below right Bishop Palace, Las Palmas, Gran Canaria (GAR)

Mediterranean monk seal that was abundant on the island in the 15th century. Today there are no seals to be seen, but the tiny islet racks up an impressive 130 species of flora and fauna.

To really have a good look around you need a few hours. In a little over two hours you can walk around the whole island and walk up La Caldera – worth it for the magnificent views of Lobos, Lanzarote and Fuerteventura. Officially you need permission to climb the mountain, obtainable from the *Cabildo*, though in practice there is no-one asking for permits and you can guarantee you'd be the only person who bothered. The island also has a small sheltered beach, Playa de la Caleta, with calm turquoise waters; surfers will be attracted by the big waves on the west coast. The island is a nature reserve so there are certain rules to abide by, such as sticking to the paths and not taking rocks or plants from the island. Camping is permitted on Lobos but you'll need to get a permit from the *Cabildo*, tel: 928 86 23 00. There are a couple of restaurants, which have pretty extensive menus, but they're not cheap and you might be better bringing a sandwich from Corralejo unless you're looking to splash out. Boats leave the harbour at Corralejo at 10.15, 11.45 and 15.30 and return at 10.30, 12.00 and 16.00. The return trip is €6.

Galería de Arte
There's a small art gallery, usually with exhibitions from local artists, on Calle Anzuelo. It's open Mon–Sat 09.00–14.00, 18.00–22.00; entrance is free.

Diving
Abyss Divers Calle Gravina; tel: 928 53 72 97; www.abyssdivers.com. Claim to have the best prices in town and while that may not be quite true, they are perhaps the most professional. A full-day introduction to diving costs €60, a package of 6 dives costs €135 and they do a variety of speciality dives from €100. They also run trips to Lanzarote for €100, which includes the ferry and a wreck dive.

The Dive Center Calle Nuestra Señora del Pino; tel: 928 53 59 06; fax: 928 86 62 43; email: buceodcc@divercentercorralejo.com; www.divecentercorralejo.com. An impressive choice of courses and activities for the totally bewildered up to the highly qualified. Discovery dive €45, 3-day course €300, snorkelling trip €25. They also hire equipment to experienced divers.

H2O Dive Academy Kiosk at the harbour; tel: 680 550 879; email: info@h2o-diving.com. A British-run school that visits 21 different dive sites across the island. Individual dives cost €30 and deals are available if you buy a package.

Boat trips
Catalanza Based in the harbour; tel: 609 667 246; www.catalanza.com. Run catamaran trips to the delightful Playa de Papagayo in Lanzarote. The trip includes lunch and drinks, snorkelling and a jet-ski ride. Adults €58, children €32.

There are also a few companies offering safari boat trips, with the possibility of seeing dolphins, whales, turtles and flying fish. Half-day trips generally include snorkelling, snacks and unlimited drinks. Departures in the morning and afternoon, prices are around €30 per person; shop around in the harbour.

Fishing
There are various companies offering fishing trips. They have kiosks at the harbour.

Barvik (tel: 676 407 640) take would-be fishermen out every day except Sunday. A half-day's fishing (08.30–14.00) costs €45 if you want to fish and €40 if you're watching. The price includes tackle, bait, snacks and drinks.

Windsurfing

Although not as well known as Jandía, there is excellent windsurfing to be had in Corralejo and a few companies offer lessons and hire. The beach is for intermediate to advanced surfers; there is a lagoon suitable for beginners 20 minutes away.

Escuela Flag Beach Windsurf Center Calle General Linares; tel: 928 86 63 68; email: info@flagbeach.com; www.flagbeach.com. A three-day beginner course is €120 and a 2-day intermediate course €90. If you don't want to commit to a course you can do a 2-hour taster session for €60. They also offer kiteboarding courses for beginners for €220 (2 days). You can rent the equipment and go it alone if you know what you're doing.

Escuela de Windsurfing Ventura Surf Next to Waikiki, on the beach; tel: 928 86 62 95; www.ventura-surf.com. Three-hour course for beginners €72, private lessons for €48 per hour. Also rent out windsurfing boards for €37 a day and surf boards for €12 a day.

EL COTILLO

El Cotillo is a likeable town with a maze of narrow streets, many of them deserted. There's a large golden beach, excellent for windsurfers and not bad for sunbathers either, though it has no facilities. The El Tostón Castle sits above the town and is surrounded by reasonable restaurants. Some people think that it's just a matter of time before El Cotillo becomes the next big holiday resort, though the mammoth waves and strong currents mean that it's never going to be a swimmer's beach. That said, there are a couple of enticing lagoons just south of the town that are altogether calmer places to bathe.

Getting there

There are buses every two hours from Corralejo, seven days a week. There are also occasional buses from the capital. Buses leave from in front of the hotel.

Where to stay

Hotel Mariquita Hierro Calle Mariquita; tel: 928 53 85 98; fax: 928 53 86 58; email: hotelmariquitahierro@wanadoo.es; http://usuarios.lycos.es/fuertehotels. Friendly, well-run place with rooms that are nicer than you'd expect from a 2-star hotel. Also has a rooftop pool with ocean views. Single €36; double €42, including breakfast.

There is also a **campsite** north of the town, near the lighthouse. It's free to pitch a tent and permission isn't required.

Where to eat

Café Cotillo Next to the old harbour. This is a popular place serving mainly snacks and juices.

La Marisma Calle Pedro Cabrera Saaveda, round the corner from the hotel. It's *the* place to go for fish.

Los Cabezones Next to La Marisma. It's a bakery but has a seating area so you can enjoy a coffee with your cake.

Restaurante Asiático On the corner of Calle El Aguila; serves a variety of Chinese and Japanese food. *Menú del día* €7.50.

Restaurante Casa Rustica In the upper part of town, they have a variety of salads and tapas as well as the standard fish and meat dishes.

Restaurante El Veril In a small pedestrian road near the old harbour. Probably one of the most tempting menus around. Mainly fish and seafood.

Restaurante Puerto Nuevo Not far from the castle on Calle 3 Abril 1979. Fish and seafood are their main offerings.

Practicalities

Banks The closest is in Lajares.
Health The nearest Health Centre is in La Oliva.
Pharmacy In Lajares.
Police In La Oliva.
Post office On Calle Santo Domingo; open Mon–Fri 13.30–14.30, Sat 11.30–12.30.
Shopping There are a couple of supermarkets on the main road from Lajares.

What to see and do
Castillo de El Tostón
Built in the late 18th century with the aim of preventing pirate attacks, the castle now houses temporary art exhibitions. Open Mon–Fri 08.00–15.00; entrance is free.

Windsurfing
Hardcore windsurfers swear by the board-breaking waves at El Cotillo. There is nowhere to rent a board and no-one giving classes to beginners, suggesting that this area is suitable for experts only.

DRIVES
These routes could be combined and if you're in a real rush the whole island could be seen in a day, if you didn't stop to get out of the car. Distances are long compared with the other islands but there are no mountain roads and even the dirt tracks in the south of the Jandía peninsula are sealed and won't slow you down too much.

Northern circuit
Take the FV20 out of **Puerto del Rosario** and head for **Casillas del Ángel**, a rather nondescript pueblo scattered along the main road. The only thing of note here is the series of windmills. Not long after Casillas del Ángel, take a right turn on to the FV207, signposted **Tefía**. This is the home of one of the *Cabildo*'s best museums, La Alcogida. It's definitely worth a stop to look around the typical houses and pick up some handicrafts. Continue north until you join the FV10, which soon takes you to **Tindaya**. The hamlet is dull but the mountain is the site of some pre-Hispanic rock engravings. It was a holy mountain for the island's first inhabitants and continues to be a source of legend and controversy today (see box, page 138). Not far north of Tindaya is the old capital, **La Oliva**. It's a lovely place with a few sights worth stopping for, such as the Centro de Arte Canario, a unique gallery full of work by Canarian artists. From here you can either continue along the main road to **Villaverde** or head west to the coastal town of **El Cotillo**. The latter is probably more charming, with its narrow streets and good fish restaurants, though Villaverde is quite quaint and is a good place to buy Canarian foodstuffs. If you've opted for El Cotillo, return via Lajares on a minor road and then head north to **Corralejo**. From Villaverde stick to the FV101 until you reach the same point. If you're not in a huge rush, you can take a boat across to **Isla de Lobos** from Corralejo, otherwise just wander around the older part of town. When you're done there, join the FV1 south, which takes you through the **Parque Natural de Corralejo**, an area of impressive sand dunes. There's nothing else of interest on the road back to the capital.

Central circuit
Leave **Puerto del Rosario** by the southern exit, passing the airport on your way to Caleta de Fuste. There's not much worth seeing on a day trip in this tourist

A MOUNTAIN OF LEGENDS AND MYTHS

Mount Tindaya has been the centre of debates and myths for centuries. Although its importance is unclear, the *majoreros* probably thought of it as a sacred place, though there are historians who believe it was a royal residence or perhaps the site of a rudimentary court.

In 1978 some 268 foot-shaped engravings were found around the mountain, all pointing towards Mount Teide on Tenerife, which can be seen on a clear day. Researchers believe that the carvings were meant to ward off evil spirits; and considering the native Canarians thought Teide was hell, this theory makes sense. There are masses of myths and legends associated with the mountain and any local can spout off a dozen stories telling of weird and wonderful events that happened after a visit to the mountain. Chatting to a bus driver while travelling from Corralejo to El Cotillo, I heard tales of enemies being turned into donkeys, barren women giving birth and blind men seeing once they'd passed near Mount Tindaya. There are so many tales that you can't help wondering if the locals sit at home concocting more and more unbelievable tales just to tell to tourists. Even so, it's a curious place and it's worth chatting to the villagers to see how many fables you can wrack up. The mountain itself is not much to look at, a 400m hill overlooking a less than remarkable *pueblo*. These days it's the object of a controversial plan by Basque sculptor Eduardo Chillida. He wants to hollow out the mountain and build a gigantic cube inside, filling it with information on Fuerteventura's most talked about hill. While the plan would bring tourism to the area, it has understandably been met with strong opposition from ecologists, archaeologists and other locals who feel it would damage an important part of their heritage. With so many spirits hanging around I think I'd opt for a different mountain for fear that this one might swallow me up.

resort, unless you want to look at the 18th-century castle. Not far away are **Las Salinas**, some rather unimpressive salt pans that you could easily miss without losing any sleep. The same could be said for **Pozo Negro**, a fishing hamlet a little further south. It has a certain charm and isn't a bad place for lunch, though it's a fair detour otherwise. If you opt out of visiting Pozo Negro, keep your eyes peeled for the FV50 to **Antigua**, one-time capital of Fuerteventura. Antigua is a quiet town and the site of an ethnographic museum that's perhaps worth a visit. When you're finished there, take the FV20 north to **La Ampuyenta**, a miniscule *pueblo* with a rather dull museum. Shortly after look out for a fork in the road and head southwest towards Betancuria. You'll pass through the **Llanos de la Concepción**, an area of pretty windmills, and then spot a turning for **Aguas Verdes** (Playa del Valle). It's a fine spot for a picnic, though the waters aren't suitable for swimmers and the last little stretch of road is in terrible condition. Return along the same road and head south, passing **Valle de Santa Inés** before you get to the island's trump card, **Betancuria**. Not stopping here would be a crime; it's a picturesque town with a few attractions worth visiting. The route continues south, passing the **Zona Recreativa de Betancuria**, a picnic area and mini pine forest (it's 3km off the main road but well signposted). The next stop is **La Vega de Río Palmas**, home of Fuerteventura's patron saint. There's not much else of note here or in the next town, **Pájara**, but a detour out to the coast to **Ajuy** is certainly worth the effort. It's a delightful little place with some impressive caves surviving the constant assault of the ocean. Pass through Pájara again on your return before heading to **Tuineje**, a photogenic *pueblo* but not a very exciting one. Continue south on the FV20 until you meet the FV2, then head back to the capital.

Southern circuit

If you don't mind driving on unsealed roads, this is a fine area to explore. Head south from **Morro Jable**, passing the port until you come to a dirt track. This is the route to **Puertito de la Cruz** and **Cofete**. Once you enter the Península de Jandía, the roads are signposted so it's impossible to get lost. Head to the westernmost tip first to sample some fish stew in the curious *pueblo* and then double back to visit the village and beach at Cofete. Ideally you should go to this area in the evening as the sunsets are stunning. Once you've finished exploring, head back to Morro Jable and up the coast to **Los Verodes** and **Playa de Sotavento**. You need to be on the lookout for the sign as it's not too clear. The road to the beach is in poor condition but worth it since this is one of Fuerteventura's finest and also the site of the international windsurfing championships. If you can tear yourself away, continue north on the FV2, bypassing the lifeless resort of Costa Calma. Not far after, take a westward turning towards **La Pared** and stop to admire the coast. The FV605 takes you north to **Pájara**, a town that seems to be taking a permanent siesta. Don't enter the town, instead take a left turning just before you arrive, which leads to **Ajuy**, a charming fishing village and the site of some impressive caves. Double back and pass through Pájara on your way to **Tuineje**, another pretty but uninteresting place. The FV20 becomes the FV4 as you near the coast. The more interesting *pueblo* in this area is **Las Playitas**, an attractive hamlet northeast of Gran Tarajal. The turning is just before you enter Gran Tarajal and the road continues to **La Entallada** lighthouse. When you've finished admiring the view, retrace your tracks to the FV2 and head south back to Morro Jable.

140

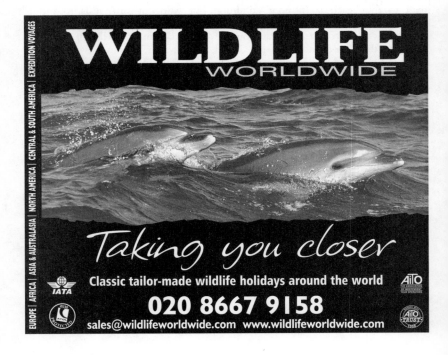

Lanzarote and Archipelago Chinijo

Lanzarote, yellow
As an African camel …

My eyes still shine
From gazing at your clear skies

Rafael Arozarena, 'Lanzarote', from
Romancero Canario, 1946

Some people dismiss Lanzarote's landscape as depressing and can't see the beauty in the stark volcanic landscape, but to me (and many others) the island is like a huge open-air art gallery. Every roundabout seems to house a César Manrique sculpture and his paintings adorn the walls of restaurants, museums and hotels. The uniform white houses with their green paintwork stand out against the arid black terrain and Mother Nature has not been unkind to the island, with the moon-like scenery providing an excellent backdrop for man's creations. Manrique's concept was to work in harmony with the island's landscape, meaning that you'll see very little in the way of garish tourist attractions of nightmarish theme parks (though there are a couple). Some Lanzaroteños go as far as to say that it's not possible to distinguish 'what was made by César and what was made by God'. It's largely thanks to Manrique's vision that the island was declared a World Biosphere Reserve in 1993 by UNESCO. These days Lanzarote's ability to develop tourism in line with the environment is recognised internationally and used as a model for sustainable tourism.

HIGHLIGHTS

No-one has done more for Lanzarote than the island's most famous export, César Manrique, and you'd be a fool to leave without visiting some of his masterpieces. The Mirador del Río offers impressive views over La Graciosa, while the Cactus Garden and the famous Jameos del Agua are perfect examples of man working in harmony with nature. A visit to the late artist's house in Tahiche is another must-do. The Timanfaya National Park is unmissable and there are various ways to see it, be it from a bus window, on foot or even on the back of a camel. The south has a few beaches to rival those in Fuerteventura, with those on the remote Punta de Papagayo the pick of the bunch. And if you can't unwind there, go for the ultimate in relaxation: a few days in La Graciosa, walking, cycling or just enjoying the islet's deserted beaches.

BACKGROUND INFORMATION
History

The island's indigenous name was Tite-roy-gatra, meaning something along the lines of 'Ruddy Mountain'. Most people agree that it took its present name from

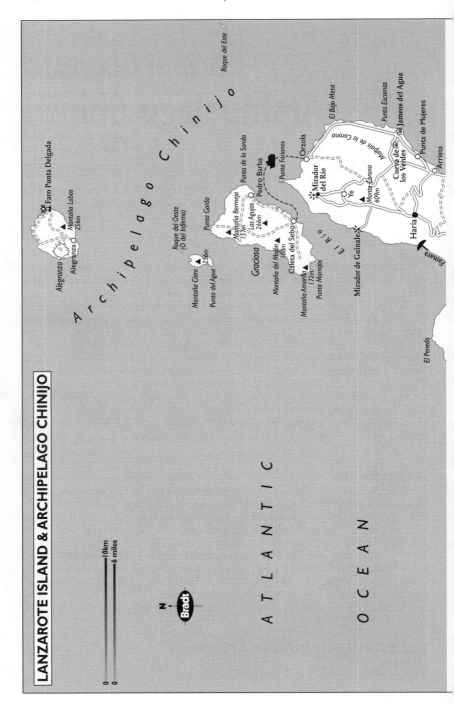

LANZAROTE ISLAND & ARCHIPELAGO CHINIJO

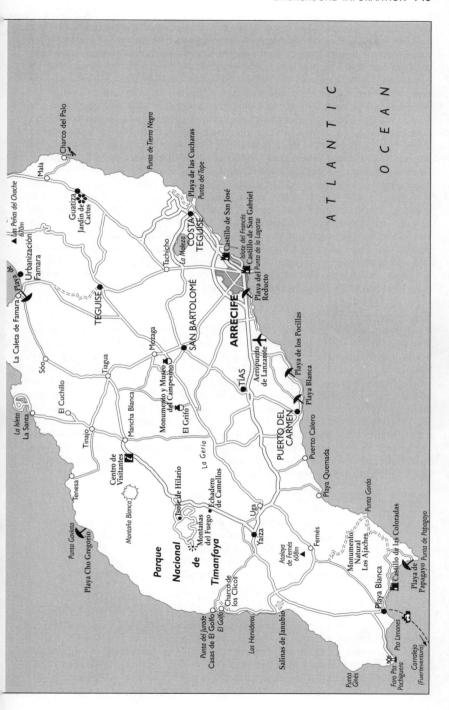

the Genovese sailor Lancelotto Malocello who passed through in the 14th century, though there are some who believe that there was a nobleman by the name of Lancelot in Jean de Bethencourt's crew. Lanzarote has suffered more than its fair share of misfortune throughout the years. The first island to be conquered by Bethencourt in 1402, it became a base for the conquering of the rest of the archipelago and although the islanders had initially welcomed the outsiders, some ended up being sold into slavery. Life plodded on, but in the 16th, 17th and 18th centuries the island suffered more than its fair share of pirate attacks, it being the first inhabited island that sailors from Europe encountered. The Lanzaroteños fled to the Cueva de los Verdes for refuge, as their aboriginal ancestors had done before them, but that didn't stop pirates from Morocco, Britain and France regularly turning up to wreak a bit of havoc and loot a few towns, taking whatever seemed valuable (including a few natives to sell as slaves if nothing better turned up). Just as the human interference seemed to be abating, nature began to work its stuff on the island with some violent volcanic eruptions in the early 18th century. The Timanfaya eruptions buried a dozen towns and seemed to pose yet more problems for the farmers, already struggling against the lack of rain. But the volcanic earth was surprisingly fertile and allowed a thriving wine industry to develop. Although the *Conejeros*, as the islanders are known, still benefit from wine production, it is the booming tourist trade that has really brought them prosperity.

Geography

Lanzarote is known as *la isla de cien volcanes* ('the island of 100 volcanoes'), though this tag is really selling it short since there are no fewer than 300 volcanic cones across its 846km^2 surface. That said, it is the least mountainous of the archipelago, with its highest point reaching only 670m (Peñas de Chache in the north). Because of the lack of high mountains, Lanzarote isn't affected by the *alisios* winds, so the climate here is hotter and drier than in the western islands. In fact, the climate more resembles that of the Sahara, which lies just 125km away. The island's landscape has been constantly changing over the centuries thanks to ongoing volcanic eruptions, leading the locals to say that the seventh day of Creation hasn't yet arrived in Lanzarote. The last eruptions were in 1824, but there are some vulcanologists who think that it will soon be Lanzarote's turn again; something that the 105,000 inhabitants surely dread.

Economy

Lanzarote only sloughed off its veil of anonymity and came into the world just 15 years ago. Before that, life was very hard and in the drought years many people had to emigrate as they had nothing to eat or drink. I remember when I was a child, people were almost ashamed of having been born on this island. Lanzarote was the Cinderella of the Canary Islands.

César Manrique, *Vale la pena vivir*

These days Lanzaroteños are more likely to brag about their island than be ashamed and the economy has received an immense boost with the increase of tourism. Of course, the lack of rain still provides problems and agriculture is limited, though wine production is quite an important earner. The harvesting of cochineal is making a low-profile comeback, but it's a slow process and not one the island could rely upon. Long gone are the days when the island was known as 'Purpuraria', due to the abundance of the natural reddish dye. Of course, revenue from tourism is as

SCARLET FEVER

Strange as it may seem, beetles were once the backbone of the Canarian economy, at least in the eastern islands. *La cochinilla* is a parasitic beetle that lives on certain species of cacti. In the mid 19th century, farmers in Lanzarote and Fuerteventura would spend hours painstakingly collecting the beetles, which would later be turned into dye (cochineal). When their bodies are crushed, they release a pigment, which was used as a red tint used in sweets, desserts and drinks – vegetarians beware! Although the industry boomed for a while, it was a slow process and all but died out in the early 20th century with the introduction of synthetic dyes. These days, cochineal is making a small-scale comeback, particularly in Guatiza (Lanzarote), a small village engulfed in cacti.

vital here as in the other islands but the leap from fewer than 200 hotel beds in 1966 to a little over 50,000 now is causing concern and the *Cabildo* is devising a limitation plan. Around a million and a half tourists a year currently descend on the island, but the authorities believe that if this rises much more, the quality tourism for which the island is famous could be in jeopardy. The other important industry is fishing, with Arrecife the second most important fishing port after Las Palmas.

Flora and fauna

The lack of rain on Lanzarote, as on neighbouring Fuerteventura, means that the flora is far less varied and abundant than on other islands. You'll spot extensive palm groves around Haría, but generally the vegetation consists of low-lying spurge, cacti and tamarisk. Virtually all of the island's endemic species are to be found around in the north where the island is highest. The most interesting animal species is the blind white crab (*Munidopsis polimorpha*), found in the Jameos del Agua, though it usually frequents much deeper waters.

Conservation

The lack of water in Lanzarote is a serious problem. With an average annual rainfall of just 157mm and highly porous surface materials, the majority of the island's water has to be desalinated – a pricey process. Please bear this in mind while you're here and respect the lack of water. Don't leave taps running and opt for showers rather than baths. Many toilets have a water-saving facility and if you press the flush button a second time it stops the flow of water.

One of the biggest problems in the national park is visitors wanting to take a memento – the park loses tons of stones each year. Park staff joke that the best place on the island to find stones is not Timanfaya, it's in the airport as they are the first things to go when the baggage is over the limit. There are 13 protected spaces on the island, counting for 41% of the total area.

There is a recovery plan for one of the archipelago's most threatened species, the Houbara bustard. The situation is critical, with just over 500 examples spread around Fuerteventura, Lanzarote and La Graciosa, but the authorities have recognised that the problem needs attention. The Houbara bustard's habitat is now protected and hunting of this endangered bird is strictly forbidden.

Festivals

The most important fiesta is that of the capital's patron saint, San Ginés. Celebrated on August 25, it is the oldest and most traditional fiesta, with the main events held in Arrecife, though the whole island tends to join in with some sort of small celebration.

The residents of the tiny hamlet Mancha Blanca thought only divine intervention could be responsible for the miraculous change of direction of the molten lava during the 18th-century Timanfaya eruptions, meaning that their village was saved. Today a cross marks the point where the rapidly advancing lava suddenly and bizarrely changed course and the locals still pay tribute to Nuestra Señora de los Volcanes. On September 15 the villagers attend a service at the Mancha Blanca hermitage and later adjourn to a popular *romería*, held in the virgin's honour. There's also a folklore festival and craft fair.

GETTING THERE AND AWAY
By air
Binter Canarias Tel: 902 39 13 92; www.bintercanarias.es. *Gran Canaria:* 8–10 a day. *Tenerife:* 5 a day to Tenerife North and 2 a week to Tenerife South.

By sea
Fred Olsen Tel: 902 10 01 07; email: reserves@fredolsen.es; www.fredolsen.es. *Fuerteventura:* 6 a day between Playa Blanca and Corralejo.
Trasmediterránea Tel: 902 45 46 54; www.trasmediterranea.es. *Gran Canaria:* 3 a week. *La Palma:* 1 a week. *Tenerife:* 1 a week. *Cádiz:* 1 a week.
Naviera Armas Tel: 902 45 65 00; email: narmas@naviera-armas.com; www.naviera-armas.com. *Fuerteventura:* 6 a day. *Gran Canaria:* 3 a week.

GETTING AROUND
Public transport
Though the bus network isn't as comprehensive as that of Gran Canaria or Tenerife, you can move around all the main towns in the *guagua* (bus). As in many of the islands, if you're planning to do much bus travel you need to be based in the capital. There are regular boats from Orzola to La Graciosa.

Car hire
Autos Cabrera Medina (Cicar) Offices island-wide; call 900 20 23 03 for reservations.
Autos Feber Tel: 928 81 08 34 (Arrecife); 928 51 73 41 (Playa Blanca); 928 51 13 08 (Puerto del Carmen)
Betacar Tel: 928 82 15 41 (airport); 928 51 75 27 (Playa Blanca); 928 51 41 84 (Puerto del Carmen)
Felycar Tel: 928 80 53 65 (Arrecife); 928 51 78 20 (Playa Blanca); 928 51 03 05 (Puerto del Carmen)
Union Rent Airport; tel: 928 82 14 38

WHERE TO STAY
More than in any other island, Lanzarote's accommodation is concentrated in the tourist resorts. The powers that be are rightly proud that they are keeping the large hotels to a minimum and confined to reduced areas but it does make things a little difficult for the independent traveller. There are a few rural hotels and a network of *casas rurales* is emerging, though there aren't nearly as many as in other islands (contact the tourist information office for the latest list). Budget accommodation is thin on the ground, with just a few *pensiones* in the capital and two or three scattered across the rest of the island. There is a campsite at Playa de Puerto Muelas in the south of the island (near the delightful Playa de Papagayo). Pitching a small tent costs €3 and a large tent or caravan €5. The site is open from Easter until the

end of September; for reservations call 928 17 37 24. There is also a campsite on La Graciosa (see page 174 for details).

ACTIVITIES
Beaches
Lanzarote has 169km of coast and while for the most part it's rocky and inhospitable, there are some delightful beaches. And contrary to popular belief, they're not all black sand; in fact there are numerous areas of golden sand that could compete with Fuerteventura's coastline. The best beaches are in the south, particularly those on the Punta del Papagayo.

Diving
The favourite diving sites are near Puerto del Carmen, where you'll find an abundance of groupers and glassfish and can also visit two wrecks. The waters around Charco del Palo are known for their high visibility, thanks to the white sand. There are also numerous caves to investigate in this area and you could spot angel sharks and electric rays.

Excursions
Lanza Travel Tel: 928 83 02 76. A full repertoire if you fancy an island tour. Some include a boat trip, others include entrance to museums. Prices range from €8 to €50 per person and they do pick-ups from the 3 main tourist resorts. Booking isn't even required for some tours – just find out the departure times and pay on the bus.

Fishing
Lanzarote Fishing Club Puerto Calero; tel: 636 47 40 00; fax: 928 51 43 78. They offer deep-sea fishing excursions for those looking to catch 'big whoppers'. Skipper Tino Garcia has 30 years' experience in local waters so you'll probably catch something good. The trip includes transfers and lunch; €60 for fishers and €30 for spectators.

Hiking
Lanzarote is not the best of the islands for a hiking holiday. It lacks the deep barrancos that characterise Gran Canaria and La Gomera and has no vegetation to compete with the forests of Tenerife or La Palma. Of course, Lanzarote has something that the others don't have and its real interest lies in its many volcanoes and lava fields. There is some walking to be done in and around the national park. Walking inside the park is forbidden unless you go with one of the park guides (highly recommended), although the coastal route is open to all.

Olita Treks Costa Teguise; tel: 928 59 21 48; email: info@olita-treks.com; www.olita-treks.com. A limited itinerary but it does include Isla Graciosa. Routes start from €30 per person.
Canary Trekking Tel: 609 537 684; email: info@canarytrekking.com; www.canarytrekking.com. They offer just 2 routes: the outskirts of the National Park and the Haría to Playa de Famara route. Tours cost €35 including transport.

Horseriding
There's a decent riding centre near Yaiza if you fancy seeing the island from horseback.

Lanzarote a Caballo Carretera Arrecife–Yaiza km 17; tel: 928 83 03 14; email: alturin@alturin.com; www.alturin.com. They offer rides from 1 to 5 hours, allowing you to see a good part of the south. Some excursions include a snack or evening barbecue. Prices range from €25–60.

Surfing

Lanzarote has the best waves in the Canary Islands and the small town of Caleta de Famara in the north is home to a small but fanatical surfer population. There are a couple of schools where you can learn how to catch a wave or improve on what you know. There are also a couple of surf schools at Costa de Teguise, though the waves around here will be of interest only to beginners.

ARRECIFE

Arrecife is a curious place. Despite having only 45,000 residents, it somehow feels like a much larger city. Many leave with a bad taste in their mouths, complaining at what an awful place it is. It's difficult to put your finger on why no-one likes the capital, though it could be to do with the strange absence of squares and parks in the city. The Calle Real (Calle León y Castillo) is a nice enough pedestrian shopping street and the Charco de San Ginés could be exploited and become a superb attraction, though at the moment it's somewhat polluted and seems to be the meeting point for the city's many down and outs. One thing Lanzarote's capital does have is a delightful and curiously empty little beach, Playa del Reducto. There is little historical interest in Arrecife due to the fact that it became capital only 150 years ago. Until then, the altogether more charming town of Teguise was capital and Arrecife was merely a port, but as maritime traffic increased and the threat of piracy diminished, the capital was established on the coast.

Getting there and around
From the airport

There are regular buses between the airport and the capital. From Arrecife you need to catch the bus from the *Cabildo* rather than the bus station. A taxi from the airport will cost around €8.

By bus

There is a bus service around the city, though you probably won't need to use it as the centre (and area of any interest to tourists) is pretty compact. Note that some bus services leave from the *Cabildo* while others leave from the bus station.

Where to stay
Mid-range

Hotel Lancelot Av Mancomunidad 9; tel: 928 80 50 99; fax: 928 80 50 39; email: hlancelot@terra.es. Essentially a business hotel but that's not to say that as a tourist you can't check in and enjoy their rooftop pool with views across the city. Rooms are standard, though the décor is quite contemporary. Live music once a week in the bar. Single €56; double €71, including breakfast.

Hotel Miramar Av Coll 2; tel: 928 81 04 38; fax: 928 80 15 33; email: reservasmiramar@ terra.es; www.hmiramar.com. Recently renovated, the hotel boasts a funky décor both in the rooms and public areas. Staff are super friendly. Single €45; double €60.

Budget

Pensión Cardona Calle 18 de Julio 11; tel: 928 81 10 08; fax: 928 81 10 12. In a much better area than the other *pensiones*, though the rooms aren't any nicer than those at the Pensión San Ginés (except that they have TV). Breakfast is available. Single €25; double €31.

Pensión España Calle Gran Canaria 4; tel: 928 81 11 90. Just opposite the Pensión San Ginés and so suffers from the same dodgy characters lingering outside. Rooms are pretty grotty and they don't have private bathrooms, though they do have a washbasin. Appears to double as a brothel. Single €12; double €17.

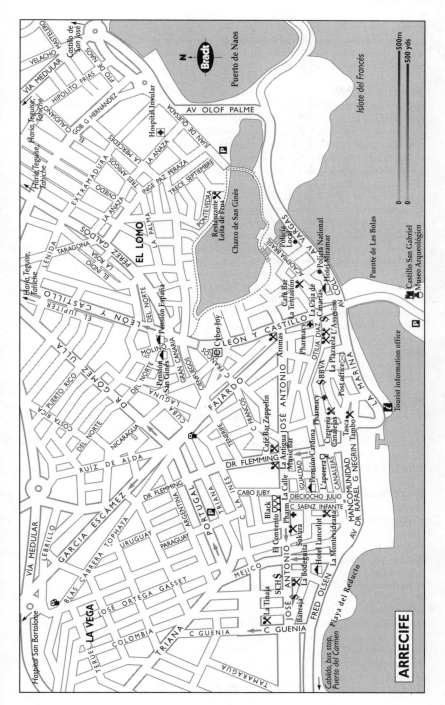

ARRECIFE

Pensión San Ginés Calle Molino 9; tel: 928 81 18 63; fax: 928 81 23 51. Despite being in a slightly unsavoury area, once you get inside it's quite pleasant and it's a stone's throw from the Charco and the Calle Real. Rooms are spacious and homely, all with private bathroom. Single €16; double €22.

Where to eat

Aromas Calle José Molina. Does an excellent cup of coffee and a tasty slice of cake.

Café Bar La Tentación Plaza de Las Palmas. Serves snackish foods with an impressive assortment of sandwiches. In a quiet square in the old part of town.

Café Bar Zeppelin Calle José Antonio. Trendy café serving metre-long sausages, and pizzas. Food served in the evenings only.

Crepería Canalejas Calle Canalejas. Does exactly what it says on the tin. A limited menu of delicious sweet or savoury crêpes.

L'Assesino Just off Calle León y Castillo. Serves pasta, tapas and sandwiches.

La Bodeguita Calle José Antonio. The house special is barbecued meat, though they also do a good line in tapas, *montaditos* (like an open sandwich) and have an impressive wine list.

La Montevideana Calle Carlos Saenz Infante. Tapas and lots of house specials. Spanish, Canarian and South American food. There's also a *Menú del día* for €9.

La Plazuela. Next door to L'Assesino. Tapas, *montaditos* and a good selection of salads. Service is friendly and they have tables outside.

La Tinaja Calle Guenia. Basque cuisine. They also have speciality weeks, such as '*la semana de setas*' ('mushroom week').

Restaurante Leita de Prua Serves mainly fish and seafood dishes. A little pricey at €10 and above for a main course but you're paying for the location as it's next to the Charco de San Ginés (but away from the weirdos).

Sakura Calle José Antonio. Average Japanese food, and there is also a Chinese take-away attached to the restaurant.

Tasca Tambo Calle Duende. Another tapas joint.

Nightlife

The *marcha* in Arrecife isn't particularly exciting and the young folk tend to head for the bright lights of Puerto del Carmen instead. However, if you do want to stay in the capital, the action is on Calle José Antonio. The bars are much of a muchness, all opening until around 03.00 or 04.00 and playing chart music. The favourites are **Black**, **El Convento**, **L'arepera**, **La Antigua Music Bar** and **La Calle**.

Practicalities

Banks La Caja de Canarias, Calle Real, open Mon–Fri 08.00–14.00, Thu 7.30–19.30; BBVA, Calle Canalejas, open Mon–Fri 08.30–14.15, Sat 08.30–13.00; Bancaja, Calle José Antonio, open Mon–Fri 08.30–14.30; Santander Central Hispano, opposite Bancaja, open Mon–Fri 08.30–14.00, Sat 08.30–13.00.

Health The Hospital General is out of the city centre, on the road to San Bartolomé, tel: 92880 16 36.

Internet Cyber Joy, Calle Hermanos Zerolo, open Mon–Fri 09.30–13.30, 16.30–21.00, Sat 09.30–13.30; €3 per hour.

Pharmacy One on the Calle Real; another nearby on Calle Canalejas.

Police The Policía Local and Policía Nacional are both on the same road though it has two names, meaning that the former is officially on Av Vargas and the latter on Av Coll.

Post office On Calle La Marina, open Mon–08.30–20.30, Sat 09.30–13.00.

Shopping The main shopping area is the Calle Real and the surrounding area. There are a few small malls in this area too.

Tourist information On the Paseo Marítimo, open Mon–Fri 08.00–15.00.

What to see and do
Museo del Arte Contemporáneo (Castillo de San José)
This is one of César Manrique's many brainchildren. He oversaw the renovation work on this 18th-century castle, which now houses sculptures and paintings from the mid 20th century. Also has temporary exhibitions and a rather nice café. Open every day 11.00–21.00; entrance is free.

Museo Arqueológico (Castillo de San Gabriel)
The city's second museum is also based in an old castle, but it was closed at the time of writing with no news of when it would reopen to the public.

SAN BARTOLOMÉ
Although the site of a few average museums and some traditional architecture, you could easily miss San Bartolomé without losing any sleep. The authorities make a big deal of the Casa del Mayor Guerra and Casa Ajei, two good examples of traditional architecture, but neither building holds anything for tourists and you can't enter them. San Bartolomé is an agricultural area, so it's only fitting that Manrique's monument to farm workers is nearby, in the village of Mozaga.

Museo Etnográfico Tanit
Based in an 18th-century mansion, the museum looks at Lanzarote life over the past couple of centuries. It's pretty dull, especially compared with some of the more interactive museums on the island. Open Mon–Fri 10.00–17.00, Sat 10.00–14.00; entrance is €6, free for kids under 14.

Around San Bartolomé
Casa Museo del Campesino (Mozaga)
Probably Manrique's most famous sculpture marks the position of this museum in the centre of the island: the Monumento al Campesino. Created in 1968, the sculpture pays tribute to Lanzarote's farmers and their endless labours on an island that doesn't make agriculture easy. There is a working museum where you can watch artisans making baskets, ceramics, leatherware and embroidered items and a good restaurant serving up hearty Canarian food. Open every day 10.00–18.00; entrance is free.

Museo del Vino El Grifo
El Grifo is the island's oldest and most prestigious wine producer. Based in the 18th-century bodega, this museum is a must for connoisseurs and those interested in the history of winemaking. You can sample five different wines from the tasting menu and a selection of local cheeses for €7.50 or choose your own tipples to taste for around €1 for half a glass. Open every day 10.30–18.00; entrance is free, tel: 928 52 49 51. Reserve in advance if you wish to visit the vineyard or wine cellar. It's on the LZ30, near the village of Masdache.

TIAGUA
Museo Agrícola El Patio
This is a privately owned museum dedicated to the success of the Lanzaroteño farmer in the face of adversity. The centre has a typical farmer's house from the mid 19th century, a small wine cellar and museum and an area dedicated to farming in Lanzarote, with crops, animals and indigenous plants. The museum is in Tiagua, a small village between San Bartolomé and Tinajo; it's well signposted. Open Mon–Fri 10.00–17.00, Sat 10.00–14.30; entrance €6.

TAHICHE
Fundación César Manrique

It's not just anyone that would look at a lava field, say 'yes, this looks like a good place to build a house', but that's just what César Manrique did when he returned from New York to settle on his native soil in 1968. As you walk around the fantasy house, designed around five lava caves (or bubbles), it's difficult to keep remembering that this was actually someone's home. But save for a few changes to make it easy for visitors to move around, the house is as it was when the artist lived there. It's now home to the César Manrique Foundation, created by the man himself in 1992 with the aim of giving modern artists a place to display their work. It also supports cultural and environmental activities in the island.

If the house itself isn't enough for you, you can admire Manrique's private Picasso collection as well as many of his own paintings and sculptures. You can also see the designs for sculptures and paintings that never made it off the drawing board. Open Mon–Sat 10.00–18.00, Sun 10.00–15.00. Entrance might seem a little steep at €6.50, but the foundation is a self-financed, non-profit organisation so your entrance fee goes straight to the foundation's activities. Free for children.

TEGUISE

Taking its name from the daughter of the island's last king, Teguise is an appealing town, with its carefully restored buildings and quiet cobbled streets. It was the capital of the island until 1852 and most agree that it's a much worthier candidate than Arrecife. Its only competitor for most charming *pueblo* is Yaiza, but Teguise has infinitely more atmosphere thanks to its decent restaurants and inviting pavement cafés.

The big drawcard is the Sunday market, which runs from 10.00–14.00 and attracts hundreds of tourists (and one or two locals). You'll find a little bit of everything, although traditional crafts and foodstuffs are a little thin on the ground. There's also some live music in the square by the church, so it's worth going as much for the atmosphere as for the shopping. If it all gets a bit much, you can take refuge in one of the town's museums. The **Palacio Spínola** was built in the mid 18th century and restored in the late 1970s under César Manrique's watchful eye in order to be opened to the public. It's now a house museum enabling you to see how the other half live (or lived in 18th-century Lanzarote). Open Mon–Fri 09.00–15.00, Sat–Sun 09.00–14.00; entrance is €3. **Convento Santo Domingo** is a 17th-century church that houses contemporary art exhibitions and is a lovely building to visit in its own right. Open Mon–Fri 10.00–15.00, Sun 10.00–14.00; entrance is free.

The marvellous Castillo de Santa Bárbara houses the **Museo del Emigrante**, a tribute to the thousands of Canarians that emigrated to the New World in search of a better life. The 16th-century castle sits atop a hill overlooking the town and while it proved rather inept at fulfilling its purpose as a watchtower for the increasing number of pirate attacks, it's a fine example of military architecture. Open Mon–Fri 10.00–16.00, Sat–Sun 10.00–15.00; entrance is €3, free for under 12s.

Bus number 7 goes from Arrecife to Teguise, continuing to Maguez six times a day (three times on weekends). There are buses from the main resorts on Sundays to take you to the market. Four buses leave from Puerto del Carmen and four from Costa Teguise between 09.00 and 11.00, returning at around midday.

COSTA TEGUISE

Costa Teguise is another place made in the Canarian tourist resort mould. There's little atmosphere and not much reason to visit unless you want to practise

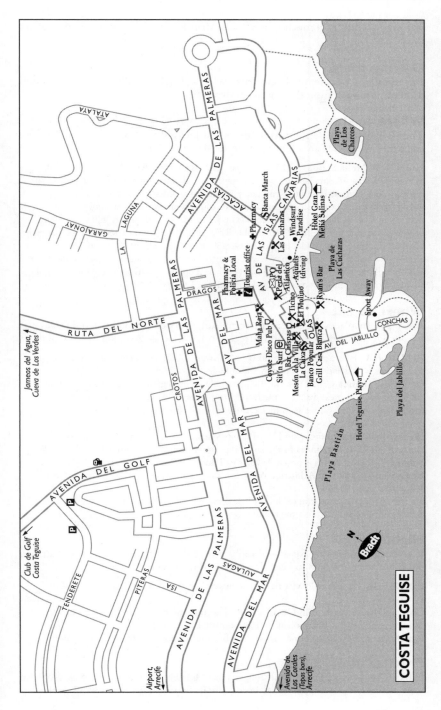

COSTA TEGUISE

watersports, but it's a much quieter place than Puerto del Carmen further down the coast.

Getting there
Bus number 1 runs regularly between the capital and Costa Teguise until around 23.00. Buses leave from the *Cabildo* in Arrecife.

Where to stay
There's precious little for anyone that's not looking for luxury accommodation, since the apartments are often reserved for tour operators.

Hotel Gran Meliá Salinas Av Islas Canarias; tel: 928 59 00 40; fax: 928 59 03 90; email: gran.melia.Salinas@solmelia.com; www.solmelia.com. If you want to splash out, this is your place. It's one of those hotels that you don't need to leave unless you really want to, with various restaurants, health spa, botanical gardens and various works of art scattered around. And if you're really feeling flush you could check into one of their private villas, each with private garden and pool. Single €260; double €350; villas range from €1,150 to €2000 per night.
Hotel Teguise Playa Av del Jabillo; tel: 928 59 06 54; fax: 928 59 09 79; email: teguise@occidental-hoteles.com; www.occidental-hoteles.com. Superb beachside location and with all the amenities you could want such as 2 pools, squash courts, gym, mini-golf, beauty salon and tennis courts. Single €96; double €120.

Where to eat
As well as the places listed here, there are some very cheap, popular and tasty tapas bars between Costa Teguise and Arrecife in Las Caletas (Avenida de los Corales).

El Molino Av Islas Canarias. For those with a sweet tooth. The menu consists of crêpes and waffles with a variety of toppings and fillings.
Grill Casa Blanca Calle Olas. A truly incredible menu which will take some reading. They specialise in meat dishes, though they have a pretty impressive choice of everything.
Maha Raja Av Islas Canarias. A nice change from all-day fry-ups, tapas and pasta. They serve Indian food.
Mesón de la Villa In the quiet Plaza Pueblo Marinero. Tapas at moderate prices.
Restaurante Las Cucharas In the shopping centre of the same name. A bit of everything, but their choice of steaks is probably what will draw you in.
Restaurante Perla del Atlántico Av Islas Canarias. Excellent fresh fish and seafood. Main meals start at €10.
Ticino Plaza Pueblo Marinero. It claims to serve typical Swiss cuisine but there seems to be a lot of pasta and tapas on the menu too.

Nightlife
If you're really looking for a wild night out you should be in Puerto del Carmen but there are a few bars to keep you occupied into the early hours.

Bar Chispas Plaza Pueblo Marinero. The place to go for cocktails; happy hour from 19.00–22.00.
Coyote Disco Pub Av Islas Canarias. Opens around midnight until very late (or very early, depending how you look at it). Plays mostly Latin music.
Ryan's Bar On the waterfront. Has nightly live music and an early evening happy hour.

Practicalities
Banks Banca March, near the Hotel Salinas, open Mon–Fri 08.30–14.00, Sat 08.30–13.00; La Caixa, at the start of Av Islas Canarias, open Mon–Fri 08.15–14.00, Thu 16.30–19.45; Banco

Popular, a little further along the same road, open Mon–Fri 08.30–14.00, Sat 08.30–13.00.
Health The Health Centre is in the precinct behind the tourist information office.
Internet Sit n Surf, Av Islas Canarias, charge €3 an hour; open every day 10.00–24.00.
Pharmacy Av Islas Canarias, opposite the Las Cucharas shopping centre.
Police The Policía Local is behind the tourist information office, the Guardia Civil is set back from the main resort, just off Calle Tenderete.
Post office Av Islas Canarias, open Mon–Fri 08.30–14.30, Sat 09.30–13.00.
Shopping Apart from the various shopping centres there are also a few nice shops on the beachfront.
Tourist information On Av Islas Canarias, open Mon–Fri 10.00–17.00, Sat 10.00–13.00.

What to see and do
Diving
Aquatis Playa de las Cucharas; tel: 928 59 04 07; fax: 928 59 25 48; email: info@diving-lanzarote.net; www.aquatis-divingcenter-lanzarote.com. All the usual packages on offer. A trial dive is €55; a PADI course €360. Dives for those already in the know are €27 but become cheaper if you book a block.

Golf
Costa Teguise has the island's only golf course, an 18-hole, par 72 course with driving range and putting greens. It's in a magnificent location, surrounded by cacti, lava and over 3,000 palm trees. Green fees are €60 and you can rent clubs for €15. It's cheaper if you play after 15.00. Tel: 928 59 05 12; email: golflanzarote@step.es.

Surfing
Windsurf Paradise offer beginners' surfing lessons. A half day costs €25 including transport, equipment and tuition. See below for contact details.

Windsurfing
Costa Teguise is the best place on the island for windsurfing and there are a couple of places where you can rent equipment or take lessons.
Windsurf Paradise Playa Las Cucharas; tel: 928 34 60 22; email: info@windsurflanzarote.com; www.windsurflanzarote.com. Offer lessons for all levels, starting from €35 for a 90-minute lesson. They also rent out boards from €50 per day.
Sport Away A little further down the beach; tel: 928 59 07 31; email: info@sportaway.com; www.sportaway-lanzarote.com.. Beginners' classes are €30 for a half day. They also rent out kayaks for €10 an hour and boards for €18 an hour.

GUATIZA
Jardín de Cactus
Located in Guatiza, where the cochineal parasite is harvested, the Jardín de Cactus showcases almost 1,500 species of cacti. Manrique's final project in Lanzarote before his death was built on an old *rofero*, a hollow left by farmers extracting the *rofe* (loose volcanic rock) to use in agriculture. There's a café and a windmill here but it's not the finest of Manrique's contributions to the island. Open daily 10.00–18.00; entrance €3. Bus number 7 passes by about six times a day (three on weekends) as it makes its way from Arrecife to Maguez.

CHARCO DEL PALO
This is the place to come if you want to let it all hang out – quite literally. Not really a naturist beach, this is pretty much a naturist town. Of course some people do wear clothes too, so you won't be gawped at for not stripping off, though you

might feel a little out of place. Expect to see naked people out walking, shopping or eating in a restaurant. And try not to stare.

Getting there
There are no buses to Charco del Palo. Drive along the LZ1 north until you reach Mala and turn right on to Calle El Rostro, just before the Restaurante Don Quijote.

Where to stay
Apartamentos Castillo de Papagayo Tel: 928 17 31 76; fax: 928 17 31 75; email: info@oboena.de. Situated on the first line of the sea and has good facilities. It's run by the German naturist tour operator Obona but accepts private customers. Don't go if you're prudish about nakedness! You have to stay for a minimum of a week. An apartment for 2 people is around €350 per week.

Where to eat
La Tunera Sometimes does a barbecue, otherwise offers a variety of meat and fish dishes. *Menú del día* €6. Closed on Tuesdays.
Peter's Pub More of a snackish place than the other eateries in town. It's in the shopping centre. Has a naturist terrace.
Restaurante Jardín Tropical Near the shopping centre. Excellent variety of Canarian and Spanish cuisine. Some dishes, such as paella, rabbit, lobster and fresh fish need to be ordered in advance.
Restaurante Romántica On the beach front; specialises in fresh fish.

Nightlife
El Pueblo Disco Pub Open until the early hours. It's next to Peter's Pub in the shopping centre.

Practicalities
Other than a small shopping centre, which has a supermarket, all amenities are in Guatiza and Mala.

What to see and do
There's only one thing to do here: whip your clothes off and take a dip in the natural pools along the rocky coast. There is an excellent dive site nearby, but as yet no diving school, so you'd need to contact one of the outfits in Costa Teguise or Puerto del Carmen.

MALPAÍS DE LA CORONA
This area of badlands was formed long before volcanic activity started in Timanfaya. Pretty it ain't, but it's a must-do, since this is the location of two superlative sights and the most magnificent volcanic tube you'll ever visit.

Cueva de los Verdes
Although the Jameos del Agua get all the fame and glory, it's the Cueva de los Verdes that is the real treasure. Named after the family who discovered it (the Greens), it's part of the same volcanic tube as the Jameos. Created around 3,000–5,000 years ago, this magnificent tunnel was formed when the lava expelled from the Volcán de la Corona made for the ocean. The upper layers of lava cooled, forming a roof over the still-moving river of lava. The islanders have always managed to find a use for the Cueva de los Verdes: first the

Guanches used it to hide from the invading Europeans, then a couple of hundred years later coastal dwellers fled there to escape pirate attacks. These days the cave is one of Lanzarote's finest tourist attractions. Although the tube stretches 6km, all the way to the sea, visitors only get to visit a portion of it since much of it is difficult to access. The tube is almost in its natural state, providing a work of art that no man could ever achieve. The minimal lighting and safety measures were installed by Jesús Soto in 1964, though for some the atmospheric music was a step too far. The superb one-hour tour takes you 2km into the cave, where you'll find a small auditorium. You then return on the upper level of the tube. Open every day 10.00–18.00 (last visit starts at 17.00); entrance is €6.60 and worth every cent.

Jameos del Agua

Jameo, in the old language of Lanzarote, was part of a volcanic tube where the roof had caved in and water had collected. Of course this is no ordinary *jameo*; it received the Manrique treatment in the 1960s and is now one of the island's top attractions and generally considered to be César Manrique's *pièce de la résistance*. A serene feeling will overcome you as you enter the dimly-lit *jameo pequeño* to the soundtrack of jingly new-age music. Although the surroundings have been given a helping hand by man, the lake is completely natural with the water level depending on the tides of the ocean. As you peer into the waters, you'll notice hundreds of white creatures and might well think that they have been painted on to the rocks. In fact, these waters are home to the blind white crab (*Munidopsis polimorpha*), a rare species normally found in deep seas. Please resist the temptation to throw coins into the water as you could damage the crabs' habitat.

Some people consider the *jameos* to be a little too commercialised but others rave about them and it's certainly worth a visit to decide for yourself. Short concerts of Canarian folk music are held in the Jameo Grande on Tuesday, Friday and Saturday evenings at 19.00. The auditorium provides stunning acoustics and seats 600. Occasional ballets and festivals are also held there. The Jameos have a café and a restaurant, the latter open 13.00–16.00; 20.00–23.00. There is also a superb information centre about volcanoes. The Jameos are open daily 09.30–18.45; entrance is €6.60.

ORZOLA

The main reason for going to Orzola is to catch the boat to La Graciosa. The town fills up for about half an hour as passengers get ready to make the short crossing and is left completely empty again once the boat departs. This sleepy fishing village is a good place to eat fish and seafood and the locals have certainly cottoned on to that fact, with an unusually high restaurant-to-house ratio! There are three buses a day from Arrecife at 08.00, 10.00 and 15.00.

What to see and do
Granja Natural Las Pardelas

This small farm is a kilometre out of the village and is really geared more towards children, allowing them to get up close to various farm animals. There's also a café, children's playground and donkey rides. Open every day 10.00–18.00; adults €3; children €2.50.

Mirador del Río

Some think it's a little unfair that you have to pay to see Lanzarote's finest view. The Mirador del Río offers a panorama of the Chinijo Archipelago, but has been designed (unsurprisingly by César Manrique) so that you can appreciate the vista only if you pay the entrance fee. The great man said that he wanted to keep the view a surprise until the very last minute, that's why you don't get any sneaky peeks as you pull up on to the car park. Cynics think it's daylight robbery. Still, it's not expensive at €3 and you can sit and have a coffee while you contemplate life on La Graciosa. The *mirador* and café are open daily 10.00–17.45. A similar view can be had for free from the Mirador de Guinate, a little further south.

HARÍA
Known as the valley of 10,000 palm trees, the municipality of Haría is an oasis in Lanzarote's otherwise arid landscape. OK, so its tag might be something of an exaggeration, but trees are worth shouting about on Lanzarote and there are certainly more palms here than anywhere else on the island. Haría resembles Teguise with its quiet squares and laid-back tapas joints and while it isn't brimming over with attractions, there is enough to occupy a morning. It's a good place to pick up some handicrafts, especially ceramics. Craftsmen stick to the traditional pottery methods in a **workshop**, open Mon–Fri 10.00–13.00, 16.00–19.00. There are other items on sale, such as embroidery and dolls made from palm leaves as well as a couple of well-stocked craft shops scattered about. On Saturday mornings (10.00–14.00) there is a **market** in the main square, where you can pick up local produce and crafts. It's not as big or renowned as the one in Teguise, but has more character and fewer tourists.

Not far away is Guinate Tropical Park, with over 1,000 species of tropical birds and a parrot show no fewer than six times a day. Open every day 10.00–17.00; entrance a rather expensive €10 for adults; €4 for children.

CALETA DE FAMARA
Caleta de Famara has Lanzarote's longest beach; a 5km stretch of golden sand flanked by the imposing Famara cliffs. The large waves make it ideal as a surfing destination, hence its tag as 'The Hawaii of Europe'. Of course, the rough seas and strong winds that attract the surfers are just what might repel sunbathers and swimmers. Caleta de Famara has a lot in common with Caleta de Sebo on La Graciosa, which lies just across the water, so it's worth a wander if you're not going to head over to the islet. The sand-filled, windswept streets seem more in line with a western film than a surfers' paradise.

Getting there
There are three buses a day from Arrecife, at 07.45, 14.00 and 20.00. Return buses leave Caleta de Famara at 07.00, 08.00, 17.00 and 20.45. There is no service on weekends or holidays.

Where to stay
Playa Famara Bungalows Tel: 928 84 51 32; fax: 928 84 51 34; email: b.famara@terra.es; www.famara.org. From a distance it looks like suburbia and indeed there are people who live in the bungalows year-round, but the majority are for holidaymakers. The bungalows come fully equipped and have small gardens. There is a communal swimming pool. You can't really miss the complex, but it's signposted just in case. Two people €55; 4 people €65; there are discounts for long stays.

Where to eat
Croissantería Av El Marinero. The place to go for breakfasts and snacks.
Restaurante Casa Ramón Av El Marinero. Comes highly recommended by locals, though its menu is pretty similar to the rest of the places around.

Restaurante El Risco Another fresh-fish joint, but boasts a seafront location so you can watch the surfers do their stuff.

Restaurante Famara Within the bungalow complex, though it's open to all. A reasonable choice of meat, though fish is what they do best.

Restaurante Sol Behind the beach. Also offers sea views and fish.

Snack Bar Las Bajas Av El Marinero. For those who don't fancy fresh fish; their menu is cheap and cheerful, with burgers and sandwiches being the main options.

Practicalities

There is a supermarket within the bungalow complex and another in the *pueblo*. Surf shop San Juan has internet access; €1 for 15 minutes. All other services are in Teguise.

What to see and do
Surfing

This is the main reason you come to Famara and there are two places offering courses and board hire.

Famara Surf Calle El Marinero 39; tel: 928 52 86 76; email: info@famarasurf.com; www.famarasurf.com. Courses start from €39 per day, though you can sign up for a week-long course. They rent out boards from €12 per day, bikes for €10 per day and can also arrange accommodation for customers for €28 per night in an apartment.

Surf Shop San Juan Behind the Gama supermarket; tel/fax: 928 52 85 48; email: surfshopsanjuan@yahoo.es. They offer surfing courses for all levels. A half day is €30; full day €45 including a picnic lunch. A full-day's board hire is €15 and you can also hire a bike for €8 a day.

Kiteboarding

Costa N-Oeste Tel: 928 52 85 97; email: info@costanoroeste.com; web:www.costanoroeste.com. If surfing doesn't get the adrenalin pumping, try this newish sport which involves being pulled around by a kite while strapped to a board. A full day (for beginners) will set you back €115, which includes lunch and a reassuring radio connection with an instructor on shore. If you want more than a taster you can take a 20-hour course over 5 days for €570. Surfing courses and combinations of the 2 sports are also available, as is equipment if you know what you're doing. They can arrange accommodation in apartments in La Santa and Famara from €260 per week (2 people).

LA SANTA

La Santa is a dull little town, with a mammoth tourist complex just outside. It's a decent place to visit if you want to practise watersports, but its appeal doesn't stretch much further than that. And having said that, for the most part you'll have to practise alone as there aren't any companies taking advantage of the good windsurfing conditions and big waves.

Getting there

Bus number 16 leaves Arrecife for La Santa eight times a day (less on weekends).

Where to stay

Club La Santa Tel: 928 59 99 99; fax: 928 59 99 90; email: clublasanta@clublasanta.com; www.clublasanta.com. This huge complex is probably bigger than many towns on the island. The daily sports and entertainments programme is quite impressive and it's definitely not a place for couch potatoes. They also have a diving school (see below). Apartment €125 for up to 3 people.

Where to eat

Garoé Tapas Bar On the main road. Has the usual tapas offerings, though it's the best place around if you don't want a full sit-down meal.

Lucy's Café & Bar On the main road. Ideal for breakfasts and healthy snacks. They have a wide selection of fresh juices, home-made ice-creams, sandwiches and salads.

Restaurante La Santa On the main road. The locals' favourite, perhaps because along with the fish and seafood choices they have a good selection of meat dishes.

Restaurante Verde Mar A little deeper into the town, on Calle Sena Encarnación. Perhaps the top option in La Santa, offering pasta, fish and meat dishes and one of the finest dessert menus on the island. Main dishes average €8.

Ristorante Pizzería Rimini Next to Lucy's Café. Pizza might come as a welcome respite from all the fish and seafood and this place has an excellent variety.

Practicalities

Ciber Touba, on the main road in the town has internet access for €3 an hour; open 17.00–23.00 every day except Friday. All other facilities are in Tinajo, although you'll find almost everything you need in the apartment complex if you're staying there.

What to see and do
Diving

La Santa Diving Email: info@lasantadiving.com; www.lasantadiving.com. Based in the La Santa complex, but lessons are open to all. A try dive in the pool is €25, a half-day baptism €75, a 3-day course €300. They also offer snorkelling trips to various sites around the island for €30.

PARQUE NACIONAL DE TIMANFAYA

> On September 1, between nine and ten o'clock, the earth suddenly opened near Timanfaya, two miles away from Yaiza. The first night an enormous mountain rose up from the depths of the earth and from its point issued flames which continued to burn for 19 days.
>
> Andrés Lorenzo Curbelo, Yaiza parish priest

Between 1730 and 1736, Lanzarote witnessed some of the most important and frightening historical volcanic eruptions ever. The violent eruptions affected around a quarter of the island and covered 11 villages, including Vega de Timanfaya. For six years the sun didn't come out at all, leading the locals to wonder what they'd done to deserve living in hell. When the ash finally dispersed, they found that their fertile fields had been converted into badlands – lava fields, devoid of vegetation. Thanks to the Yaiza parish priest, Andrés Lorenzo Curbelo, and parishioners who helped him, the eruptions were documented, allowing vulcanologists to better understand what happened. The area, declared a national park in 1974, covers 51km², just a quarter of the region affected by the 18th-century eruptions. With two million visitors a year it's the second most visited national park in Spain (after Teide). It enjoys the highest level of protection possible for a natural space, due to the fragility of land; wandering into the park can leave footprints that will be visible for years. Although to look at it you might think that the park is incapable of sustaining life, a few species thrive in this harsh environment, including lizards, birds, rabbits and over 180 types of lichen. At a glance you'd think there's no water and little in the way of food to sustain the animals, but the ground is particularly humid just below the *rofe*. The lichen provide an interesting study into the colonisation of new plantlife, but it's a slow process due to the lack of rain – the average in the park is a mere 120mm per year. A visit to the park makes for a wonderful day out, though you need to get there early to beat the tour buses.

Getting there
Bus number 16 will take you to Mancha Blanca (the village closest to the visitor centre), while line 6 goes to Yaiza. There are no buses in the park.

What to see and do
Centro de Visitantes Mancha Blanca
Before you enter the park, have a look around the visitor centre, which has heaps of information on volcanoes in general and Timanfaya in particular. There are some excellent interactive and audiovisual displays. It's just north of the park, near the village of Mancha Blanca; open daily 09.00–17.00; entrance is free.

Ruta de los Volcanes/Montañas de Fuego
There are two main ways to see the park and to get a good overall view you should really do both. The Ruta de los Volcanes is a guided half-hour bus route through the *montañas del fuego* (mountains of fire) – an area off-limits to private cars. The entrance to the route is about 4km south of the visitor centre. If you want to avoid the crowds, visit at lunchtime or in the late afternoon; the last trip of the day is generally a quiet one. At other times you might find yourself in a rather long queue just to get in. The route has been specially designed (by none other than César Manrique) so that the road cannot be seen, thus not marring your photographs (unfortunately, even the late great Manrique couldn't do anything about making the buses invisible!). Before you get on the bus you are treated to a quick demonstration of the extreme temperature just below the surface. It reaches 140 degrees just below the surface and six metres below ground rises to 400 degrees. It's also worth visiting the **Restaurante del Diablo**, where you can sample surprisingly well-priced meals cooked over the heat of the dormant volcano; open 12.00–15.30. Entrance to the park daily 09.00–17.45; the last bus tour leaves at 17.00; €6.60.

Walking
There are two walking routes within the park. The Ruta del Litoral can be walked alone or with a guide, whereas the Ruta de Termesana can be done only with a member of the park staff. The guided walks are excellent and well worth it, offering a fascinating close-up of the volcanic landscape. Walks leave the visitor centre at 10.00 on Monday, Wednesday and Friday and must be booked in advance as numbers are limited. The Ruta de Termesana is short at 3.5km but takes about two hours since the guide makes regular stops to explain the surroundings. Allow three hours in total, including transfer time.

The Ruta del Litoral follows the coast for 9km and takes about five hours. It's relatively flat but tough going as you're walking on sharp lumps of lava all the time. Many people do a short stretch and return the same way, since it's quite samey throughout. Access is via Tinajo: follow the road signposted for Tenesa but turn off on to a dirt track about 4km from Tinajo, heading towards Playa de Cho Gregorio. If you're feeling fit, you can walk all the way to El Golfo and get a taxi back to your car.

To book a place on one of the guided walks call 928 84 08 39. At busy times it's advisable to book well in advance as there are only seven places on each walk and everyone wants to have a look around this normally off-limits area of the island. You must reconfirm that you'll be going a day or two before the walk, otherwise you'll lose your place. Places on the coastal route can only be booked in person at the visitor centre and go ahead just once a week.

Echadero de los Camellos

There is a third way to see Timanfaya: on one of the park's 400 camels. The 'camel station' is a little further along the road from the entrance to the Montañas del Fuego. A ride shows you a very small part of the park and takes 20 minutes. Camels seat two and it's €5 each; you pay the camel owner directly. Open every day 09.00–16.30.

There is a small **museum** next to camel station with information panels on the national park plus an exhibition looking at the use of camels on the island. Open Mon–Fri 08.00–15.00; entrance is free.

YAIZA

There's no arguing that Yaiza is a well-kept village and one of Lanzarote's most charming. Named after a Guanche princess, it has won awards for its clean streets and is worth a look and a few photographs. Unless you're peckish and fancy a stop at the excellent Restaurante La Era, it's really just a place to stretch your legs for five minutes.

Getting there

There are plenty of buses that pass through Yaiza on their way from Arrecife to Playa Blanca.

Where to stay

Finca de las Salinas Calle La Cuesta 17; tel: 928 83 03 25; fax: 928 83 03 29; email: fsalina@santandersupernet.com; www.fincasalinas.com. Worlds apart from the tourist resorts where most of the island's accommodation is centred, this is a small hotel set in magnificent surroundings with views of the Timanfaya National Park. Rooms are a delight and the hotel also has a swimming pool. It's on the main road just before you enter Yaiza from the north. Single €100; double €150, including breakfast. They also have a couple of suites which go for €250.

Where to eat

Restaurante El Volcán On the main road. Has a few traditional dishes such as *potaje* and *puchero* but for the most part the menu echoes those in the tourist resorts, offering a little bit of everything.
Restaurante La Era Tel: 928 83 00 16. The feather in Yaiza's cap. It attracts its fair share of tourists but with good reason. Offers gourmet cuisine built on the roots of Canarian dishes. Also has a reasonable amount of choice for vegetarians. Main meals are around €10.
Restaurante Los Remedios Opposite the post office. More of a local touch to this menu and they have a good selection of Lanzaroteño wines. Menu of the day €9.

Practicalities

Banks La Caja de Canarias is on the main road, open Mon–Fri 08.00–14.00, Thu 17.30–19.30.
Health The Health Centre is out of the village, on the road to Playa Blanca.
Pharmacy On the main road.
Police The Policía Local is behind the post office.
Post office On the road that passes in front of the church, open Mon–Fri 08.30–11.00, Sat 09.00–10.00.
Shopping There's a supermarket and a shop selling handicrafts and souvenirs on the main road.

Tourist information None as such, but the staff in the Department of Culture (next to the post office) have a few leaflets and are quite knowledgeable; open Mon–Fri 08.00–15.00.

What to see and do
There are temporary art and photography exhibitions in the **Casa de la Cultura**, open Mon–Fri 09.00–13.00. It's opposite the church. There's also a private **art gallery** just outside the town on the road to Playa Blanca, open Mon–Sat 17.00–19.00.

EL GOLFO
This is the place to see the Charco de Los Clicos, better known as the Green Lagoon. A short walk leads from the car park to a *mirador* offering a stunning view of the lagoon nestled in an eroded volcanic crater. The contrast of the bright green water against the barren lava and ash is definitely worth the five-minute walk from the car. You can walk further if you want to get up close and personal. There is one place to stay in El Golfo: **El Hotelito de el Golfo** (tel/fax: 928 17 32 72). Rooms are small but all furnishings are brand new and some rooms have large balconies. Double €55; there are no single rooms. All amenities are in Yaiza, though there is no shortage of restaurants in El Golfo. As a very general rule, they tend to get better and marginally cheaper the further you venture into the *pueblo*. Remember that it's not recommended that you swim in the waters around here.

PLAYA BLANCA
Playa Blanca is Lanzarote's quietest resort but locals consider it to be well on the endangered list. The fishing village is gradually becoming engulfed in five-star hotels and international restaurants and the tranquillity is broken by the ever-increasing number of boats from Fuerteventura. Having said that, there's a long way to go until it reaches the level of Puerto del Carmen. It's a quiet resort, favoured by families and older holidaymakers and not the place to come looking for wild nightlife. The beach is tiny but if you hire a car you're within easy reach of the island's finest beaches on the Punta de Papagayo.

Getting there
There are regular buses from Arrecife, passing through Yaiza and Tías. There are several boats a day connecting Playa Blanca with Corralejo in Fuerteventura; see *Getting there and away*, page 146 for details.

Where to stay
Hotel Lanzarote Princess Calle Maciot; tel: 928 51 71 08; fax: 928 51 70 11; email: reservas.lnz@h10.es; www.h10.es. Near the beach, it has standard 4-star hotel rooms and several palm-tree-flanked swimming pools. Single €66; double €100.
Hotel Playa Dorada Urb Costa del Papagayo; tel: 928 51 71 20; fax: 928 51 74 32; email: hotel@hesperia-playadorada.com. On the beachfront in a particularly quiet area. Lots of activities on offer and has nightly entertainment. Single €80; double €110, including breakfast.
Hotel Princesa Yaiza Av de Papagayo; tel: 928 51 92 22; fax: 928 51 91 79; email: info@princesayaiza.com; www.princesayaiza.com. If you're looking for real luxury then this is your hotel. Made up of a variety of large suites, with big terraces, satellite TV and AC. Also has a gym and Health Centre, various restaurants and 2 pools with direct access to the beach, Single €130; double €200; junior and presidential suites range from €230 to €600 per night.

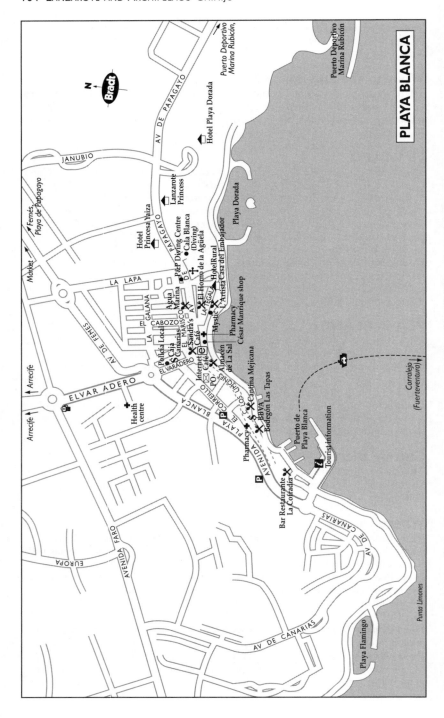

PLAYA BLANCA

Hotel Rural Casa del Embajador Calle La Tegala 30; tel: 928 51 91 91; fax: 928 51 91 92; email: reservas@casadelembajador.com; www.casadelembajador.com. Built 100 years ago and taken over by a diplomat in the middle of the 20th century, this place was accommodating fishermen and passers-by long before the first tourists arrived in Playa Blanca. It's a charming hotel with just 12 rooms and offers marvellous views across the various beaches. Single €114, double €150 including breakfast.

Where to eat
Agua Marina Av de Papagayo. The usual range of meat, fish, salads, pizzas etc but a bit cheaper than many places. They have a 2-course menu for €7 but it doesn't include drinks.
Almacén de la Sal On the promenade; tel: 928 51 78 85. Fish and seafood are the protagonists here and they don't come cheap, with main meals at around €12. Also has a more moderately priced snack menu at lunchtime.
Bar Restaurante La Cofradía In the harbour. It's generally agreed that the *cofradía* (fisherman's association) is the best place to eat fish.
Bodegón Las Tapas Calle Los Limones. An unparalleled tapas selection.
Cantina Mejicana Calle Los Limones. Tex-Mex food with a bit of tapas thrown in for good measure. Evenings only.
El Horno de la Agüela Near the Hotel Casa del Embajador. A vegetarian's nightmare. They specialise in meat and have various goat dishes and suckling pig on their menu. Also have a first-rate selection of desserts.
L'Artista Calle Tegala, but you can also enter from the promenade. An Italian restaurant that, for once, offers a lot more than pizza and pasta.
Sandra's Café Av de Papagayo. Not a bad place to start the day; they do croissants, baguettes and a good cup of coffee.

Nightlife
You'll probably find a bit of live music or karaoke in the British pubs of an evening, but other than that it's a very quiet resort. Head to Puerto del Carmen if you're looking for a night on the tiles.

Practicalities
Banks Caja Canarias, next to the Policía Local, open Mon–Fri 08.00–14.00, Thu 17.30–19.30; BBVA, Calle Los Limones, open Mon–Fri 08.30–14.15, Sat 08.30–13.00.
Health The Health Centre is just out of town on the road to Arrecife.
Internet Internet Café, Av de Papagayo, open Mon–Sat 10.00–22.00, charging a colossal €6 per hour.
Pharmacy One on Av de Papagayo, another at the end of Calle El Correillo.
Police The Policía Local is on Calle El Varadero.
Post office On Calle El Correillo, open Mon–Fri 08.30–14.30, Sat 09.30–13.00.
Shopping There are plenty of supermarkets and souvenir shops. There's also a César Manrique shop next to the Internet Café, and Mystic, a shop selling local art on the Paseo Marítimo. There's a small market on weekend mornings just off the road to Papagayo.
Tourist information Inconveniently located in the harbour, open Mon–Fri 08.30–12.30.

What to see and do
Boat trips
There are plenty of boat trips on offer if you head to the marina; some are luxury yachts which allow you to lend a hand to the crew, others are the typical glass-bottom boat excursions with drinks and a below par lunch included. A few companies offer excursions to Playa de Papagayo; shop around for prices.

Alex Sailing Tel: 610 693 644; email: alex@lanzarote.com. Not a bad option, charging from €27 per person for a 3-hour trip on an 11m yacht. Prices vary depending on the number of participants. You must reserve in advance by telephone.

Diving

Cala Blanca Centro Comercial El Papagayo; tel: 609 77 54 05; email: dive@calablancasub.com; www.calablancasub.com. A very professional outfit with all the usual options. Try dive €50, open-water diver course €350, equipment hire €40.

P & P Diving Center Av de Papagayo, opposite the church. Tel: 928 51 91 41; email: Jacobs@infocanarias.com; www.pp-diving-center.de. Discovery dive €45, courses from €150 and dives for the already qualified from €18 (the 15th dive is free).

PUNTA DE PAPAGAYO

Not far east of Playa Blanca, the paved road suddenly comes to an end, marking the entrance to this protected space (Monumento Natural de Los Ajaches). It costs €3 per car, but is worth it to reach the island's finest and most secluded beaches. Driving there is also something of a pleasure as you randomly choose which route to take in the maze of dirt tracks. The first beach you come to is, naturally, the most crowded and since there are several to choose from, it makes sense to continue if you're looking for peace and quiet (unless you're pushed for time). If you fancy stripping off, the Papagayo beaches are the place to do it; no-one bats an eyelid at nudists around here. There's also a campsite, open during the summer only. It's €3 to pitch a small tent or €5 for a large tent or caravan. You must reserve in advance, tel: 928 17 37 24. Some people rave about hiking in the Ajaches (the hills behind the beaches) but I found it to be a rather dull and monotonous landscape. If you want to explore you might find some information in Yaiza.

PUERTO DEL CARMEN

Puerto del Carmen is Lanzarote's largest tourist resort and while it's a far cry from the horrors on southern Tenerife, it has little charm. The resort stretches some 6km and for the most part the action is just on one road, the Avenida de las Playas. Evidence of its origins as a small fishing village is still visible at the southern end of the resort and this is certainly the nicest area of Puerto del Carmen, though there are still too many English pubs around for most people's liking.

Getting there

There are buses every 20 minutes from Arrecife, which continue to Puerto Calero.

Where to stay
Upmarket

Hotel Los Jameos Playa Playa de Los Pocillos; tel: 928 51 17 17; fax: 928 51 42 19; email: info@los-jameos-playa.es; www.seaside-hotels.de. Not the largest of rooms but they're bright and not as chintzy as some around here. It's a group of low buildings clustered around the swimming pools and palm trees. Single €110; double €150.

Hotel La Geria Calle Júpiter; tel: 928 51 04 41; fax: 928 51 19 19; email: lageria@hipotels.com. Lots of sporting activities and a huge pool. Single €80; double €120.

Hotel Los Fariones Tel: 928 51 01 75; fax: 928 51 02 02; email: reservas@grupofariones. Not the prettiest of hotels from the outside but it does have a good location right on the beach and close to the old part of town. Single €90; double €135; apartments range from €90 to €135.

Hotel Riu Palace Lanzarote Calle Suiza 6; tel: 928 51 24 14; fax: 928 51 35 98; www.riu.com. Low-rise 4-star hotel just behind Los Pocillos beach. Grand rooms and plenty of sports activities on offer. Single €100; double €110.

Hotel San Antonio Av de las Playas 84; tel: 928 51 42 00; fax: 928 51 30 80; email: comercial@hotelsanantonio.com; www.hotelsanantonio.com. Close to the Los Pocillos area of the resort, its gardens lead to the beach. Single €100; double €150.

Budget

Pensión Magec Calle Hierro 11; tel: 928 51 38 74. Not a bad little place in the heart of the old town. Some rooms have private bathrooms, though none of the singles do. Single €21; double without bathroom €24; with bathroom €30.

Where to eat

Puerto del Carmen suffers from the usual tourist resort affliction – an abundance of restaurants and little to recommend any of them. The problem here is that the restaurants claim to be some kind of speciality joint, like a pizzeria or Mexican restaurant, but when you get close you realise that they all have the same menu, which usually includes a large variety of meat and fish dishes, pasta, pizza, a kids' menu and very little for vegetarians. Then they have a few token dishes to back up what they are claiming to be. The best restaurants are around the old part of town, both for quality of food and ambience; seafood is the speciality. Here are a few that stand out:

Bar Restaurante Mardeleva Calle Marangalla, in the old town. Plenty of fish, seafood and tapas with a terrace overlooking the harbour.

El Ancla Av Varadero, in the old part of town. Popular with locals for its fine seafood.

Gambrinus CC Biosfera Plaza. A chain restaurant, but with a superb choice of tapas and main meals. The tapas is reasonably priced, although main courses start at €10.

La Brasería CC Tabaiba. Grilled and flambéed meats. Main courses around €10, open evenings only.

La Lonja Next to El Ancla and with a similar menu.

Plantaciones Av Las Playas, opposite CC Los Dragos. A chain café with decent coffee, cakes and snacks.

Restaurante Montmartre Calle Jameos. Atmospheric place serving French cuisine and although the menu is quite limited, the wine list should keep you choosing for a while. Open evenings only, main courses start at €10.

Tomatissimo Calle Jameos. A small restaurant serving up delicious pizza and pasta and trying to use organic ingredients where possible. Evenings only.

Nightlife

The Centros Comerciales in Puerto del Carmen are jam-packed with pubs, clubs and late, late discos and listing them would fill half of this book. Needless to say that you'll probably find something to suit, be it loud Latin rhythms, British bands doing cover versions or a quiet drink by the harbour in El Varadero. Most young people from Arrecife venture to Puerto del Carmen a couple of times a month to sample the superior nightlife.

Practicalities

Banks Banca March, in the Centro Comercial Los Pocillos, open Mon–Fri 08.30–14.00, Sat 08.30–13.00; Santander Central Hispano, Centro Comercial La Peñita, open Mon–Fri

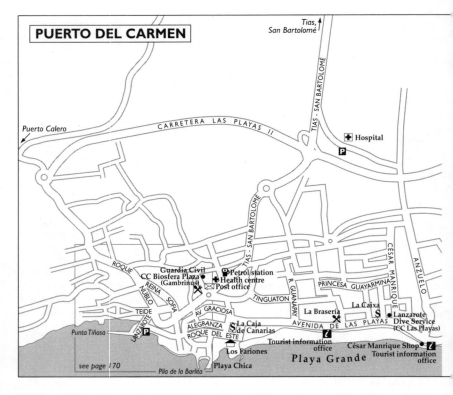

08.30–14.00, Sat 08.30–13.00; BBVA, Centro Comercial Aquarius, open Mon–Fri 08.30–14.15, Sat 08.30–13.00; La Caixa, next to McDonald's, open Mon–Fri 08.15–14.00, Thu 16.30–19.45; La Caja de Canarias, at the end of Av de las Playas, open Mon–Fri 08.00–14.00, Thu 17.30–19.30.

Health The Health Centre is opposite the post office.

Internet There's access in the amusement arcade in the Centro Comercial La Peñita, open every day 10.00–late; €1 for 30 minutes; Web room, Calle Juan Carlos I, charges €3 per hour, open Mon–Sat 12.00–15.00, 17.00–19.00.

Pharmacy There's one between the casino and the tourist information office, another next to the Hotel Jameos Playa and one on Calle Juan Carlos I.

Police The Guardia Civil is on Calle Manguia, near the post office.

Post office On Calle Juan Carlos I, just off the roundabout, open Mon–Fri 08.30–14.30, Sat 09.30–13.00.

Shopping There's no lack of shopping centres, though whether they sell anything you're looking for is another matter. The Biosfera Plaza is more like a Spanish shopping centre and has plenty of chain stores if you're looking for clothes. There's a César Manrique shop next to the tourist information office which sells reproductions and all manner of merchandise emblazoned with his art.

Tourist information There's an office near the Centro Comercial Aquarius, open Mon–Fri 10.00–17.00, and a kiosk a little further down, behind the beach, open Mon–Fri 10.00–17.00, Sat 10.00–13.00.

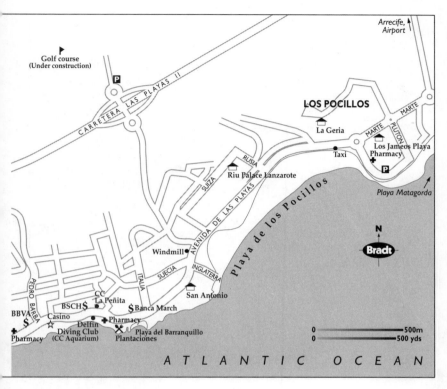

What to see and do
Diving
There are four main dive sites near Puerto del Carmen, from a shallow (10m) reef to a 30m cavern known as 'The Cathedral'. There are also two wrecks near by.

Lanzarote Dive Service CC Las Playas; tel: 928 51 08 02; fax: 928 51 69 87; email: info@lanzarotedive.com; www.lanzarotedive.com. Discovery dive €60; a series of 8 dives for qualified divers is €150. The PADI open-water diver course is €340.
Atlántica Diving Hotel Los Fariones; email: info@atlanticadiving.de; www.atlanticadiving.de. They specialise in teaching learners and promise to keep their groups small. A half-day introduction is €42 for children, €60 for adults and you can get a package of 6 dives for €100 if you're qualified.
Diving Delfin Club, also known as **RC Diving Lanzarote**, CC Aquarium; tel: 928 51 42 90; fax: 928 51 53 96; email: rcdiving@terra.es. Baptism €40; open-water diver course €320; dives for those in the know €28.

Gambling
Lanzarote's only casino is on Avenida de las Playas. The slot machines are open every day 11.00–04.00 and the big boys' gambling (roulette, poker and blackjack) 16.00–04.00; entrance is free.

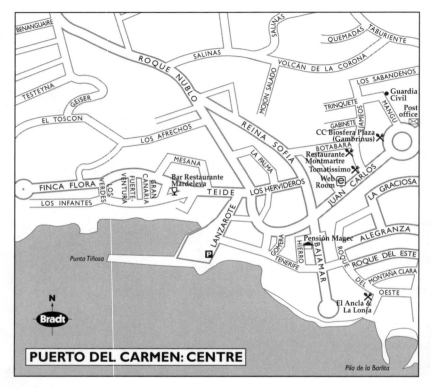

PUERTO DEL CARMEN: CENTRE

Pila de la Barlita

DRIVES
Northern circuit

Set off from **Arrecife** and head towards Tahiche to visit the **César Manrique Foundation**, based in the artist's former house – a must. From here the LZ1 takes you to **Guatiza**, where you'll see fields and fields of cacti, cultivated for the cochineal bug, once a real money-spinner for Lanzaroteños. You could also visit the **Jardín de Cactus** while you're in the area. The LZ1 continues through the nondescript village of **Mala** and on to **Arrieta**, a small beach resort and a favourite with the islanders, though it's really rather nondescript. **Punta Mujeres** is a little further up the coast and has some good fish restaurants. The road hugs the coast all the way to Orzola, passing the unmissable **Jameos del Agua** and **Cueva de los Verdes**. Next stop, **Orzola**, a small fishing town with a wealth of seafood and fish restaurants and the starting point for trips to La Graciosa. Return on the narrow inland road and rejoin the LZ1 towards **Yé**. A brief detour just before you reach this uninteresting village takes you to the **Mirador del Río**, another of Manrique's creations and one of the best places to view the Chinijo Archipelago. Returning by the other road, pass through Yé and take a right-hand turning to **Guinate**. Other than the exotic bird park, there's nothing to Guinate, but it's worth the detour for the view over the Chinijo Archipelago from the *mirador*. It's almost as good as the view than from the Mirador del Rio – and free. From here, rejoin the LZ10 towards **Haría**, an excellent place to pick up some handicrafts. This road takes you past the **Peñas del Chache**, Lanzarote's highest point at 670m. Then it winds its way down to the island's prettiest and best preserved town, **Teguise**. If you have

WINE AGAINST THE ODDS

Farmers in Lanzarote could easily have thrown in the towel after the mid 18th-century eruptions, which left a quarter of the island unsuitable for agriculture. But the superb wines from the island are testament to man's hard work and determination. Rather than let the *rofe* (volcanic earth) get them down, Lanzaroteños soon found a way to use it to their advantage. These days the vineyards not only produce one of the finest tipples in the archipelago, they also provide a unique and much-photographed landscape. The vines are planted individually in large hollows dug into the ground and then covered with a thick layer of *rofe*. During the night, the porous volcanic cinders soak up the moisture from the fertile earth below and feed the plants with the moisture they have gained the following day. A low semi-circular wall built around the vine protects it from the harsh winds, while the *rofe* acts as a screen from the fierce sun. A drive through the La Geria district will make you appreciate the hard work that goes into providing your glass of white. Recognising their toil and spirit, César Manrique created a sculpture (his most photographed) and dedicated it to the island's farm workers. The Monumento al Campesino sits outside the Casa Museo del Campesino, near San Bartolomé.

the time and inclination, it's worth driving up to **Caleta de Famara** to watch the windsurfers and kiteboarders do their stuff in the rough seas and to take a walk through the sandy streets. From here you can return along the same road or head back to Arrecife via **Soo** and **San Bartolomé**.

Southern circuit

From Arrecife, take the LZ20 towards **San Bartolomé**, where you can visit a couple of museums and brush up on Lanzaroteño culture. Not far after San Bartolomé, the LZ30 takes you through the stunning landscape of **La Geria**, the island's main winemaking area. A stop at the El Grifo wine cellar is a good way to break up the driving. Continue along the same road, skirting around Uga and heading for **Femés**, a charming little village and one of Lanzarote's highest. The road carries on to Playa Blanca but head off to the left before reaching the resort to take in the isolated **Papagayo** beaches. This is a protected area and there is an entrance charge of €3 per car. Head back along the same dirt tracks to **Playa Blanca** and then on to the **Salinas de Janubio** salt pans, a pretty sight at sunset. The road continues through some marvellous *malpaís* and past **Los Herrideros**, a rocky inlet where the waves pelt against the rocks, soaking tourists who get too close. The last port of call on this coast is the fishing village of **El Golfo**, with its emerald-green lagoon. Head inland to Yaiza, a good place to stop for lunch before the finest part of the drive – the road through the **Parque Nacional de Timanfaya**. The remaining towns of **Tinajo** and **Tiagua** are rather dull and there's not much reason to stop before heading back to **Arrecife**.

ARCHIPELAGO CHINIJO

Chinijo is a local word meaning 'small', and while it's usually used when talking about children it's been aptly adapted to refer to this mini archipelago. It consists of five islets (though two of them are little more than rocks), which form part of a nature reserve along with the Famara cliffs in Lanzarote. Only one of the islets is inhabited and the others are generally out of bounds because of their conservation status. None will argue that gazing at Chinijo invokes a desire to experience life on a desert island and César Manrique considered the view worthy of a proper lookout point. Of course, many are content with observing barren La Graciosa from the Mirador del Río on Lanzarote, though some venture the 20 minutes to visit the island and are rewarded with the warmest welcome and a few days of unrivalled R&R.

Highlights

Even if you don't fancy spending time on La Graciosa, it's still worth taking the boat across to see Lanzarote from a different point of view. If you've spent any time marvelling at the flatness of the island, you'll be surprised by the 23km of cliffs, many of them reaching 600m. If you're on a day trip to La Graciosa you won't get much further than Playa Cocina, though that's not a bad place to spend an afternoon. Those who stick around longer should hire a bike and just amble around, visiting the beaches and enjoying the local hospitality – the islanders are the friendliest bunch anywhere in the Canary Islands. There are some superlative beaches with no facilities at all, a few nice places to eat in Caleta de Sebo and a visit to the delightful *pueblo* of Pedro Barba is also worth the effort. La Graciosa is a place to come for relaxation not raving, so please stay on the larger islands if you want to go shopping, sightseeing or dancing or you could be severely disappointed.

Background information
History

When Jean de Bethencourt and his men arrived to conquer the Canary Islands in 1402, the Chinijo Archipelago was, naturally, the first land they set eyes on. Although they never stopped, Bethencourt took the time to name the islands as he passed. There's no mystery behind the name of the first islet that he sighted after a 1,000km journey that saw half his men desert the ship. He called it La Alegranza (*alegría* means 'happiness'). Nothing happened in Chinijo until the 1730s, when Lanzaroteño farmers visited La Graciosa to look for decent grazing ground for their cattle following the devastating volcanic eruptions. It wasn't populated until the mid 19th century, when a few families from Lanzarote moved in search of a better life. For a while the people lived on fish alone, until one-time Captain General Garcia allowed them to farm their land. Later on, the majority of the islanders worked in the fish salting factory and decided to stay even after the factory had closed down. A second wave of settlers moved across 'the river' in the early 20th century and set up the island's only other village, Pedro Barba. It has been a part of the Teguise municipality since 1812.

Geography

The mini archipelago of Chinijo is made up of five islets: La Graciosa is the largest at 27km², followed by Alegranza at 10km², Montaña Clara 1.25km², Roque del Este and Roque del Oeste which are little more than rocks. Roque del Oeste is also known as Roque del Infierno as it is totally incapable of sustaining life. La Graciosa, the only inhabited island, has Chinijo's highest point, Las Agujas, measuring a mere 266m.

Economy

La Graciosa is situated near one of the world's most abundant fish banks, so it comes as no surprise that its economy is based on fishing. Indeed, the wealth of fish was what brought Lanzaroteños to the island in the first place. The island also counts on a small income from tourists, most of them day trippers.

Flora and fauna

There is an abundance of sea birds in the islets, something that led them and the surrounding waters to be declared a marine reserve. There is a sizeable population of ash coloured linnets (7,500–10,000 couples), considered the largest colony in Spain. Kestrel hawk, Eleonor falcon, sparrowhawk and various species of owl can also be spotted, and the island is home to a few pairs of the Houbara bustard. This is one of the archipelago's most endangered birds and the object of a recuperation plan put into action by the Gobierno de Canarias. Over 300 species of macroalgae have been recorded in the seas around Chinijo, representing 53% of the total marine life in the Canaries.

Conservation

The five islets, along with the Famara cliffs, belong to a marine reserve, which at 70,000 hectares measures the largest in Europe. The reserve was created in 1995 with the object of guaranteeing sustainable exploitation of fishing resources, meaning that fishing in the waters around the islands is fiercely regulated. Dropping your line within a mile of Roque del Este is absolutely prohibited, with access to the rock difficult even for scientists. The mini archipelago has also been declared a special area for the protection of birds.

Food

Obviously, resources are somewhat limited to fish and seafood, but supplies are regularly brought over from Lanzarote, meaning the cuisine is more or less the same as in other islands. It would be a crime to leave without eating any fish though.

Activities

Diving

Some companies in Lanzarote run diving trips to Chinijo, taking advantage of some of the Canaries' finest dive sites. The ban on fishing around the islets means there's an abundance of fish, making it a superlative diving area. You'll find a wealth of species in El Canal, a 30m-deep channel between Alegranza and Roque del Oeste. The waters around Alegranza are superb, but you need to obtain a permit from the Gobierno de Canarias if you want to dive there, since it's part of a marine reserve. There's a 12m site near Montaña Amarilla in La Graciosa where you're likely to see dogfish, mullet and lobster.

Fishing

Although it is highly controlled, there are opportunities for fishing in the clear waters around the islets. Expect to catch marlin, tuna, David fish and possibly small sharks. There is one official fishing outfit in La Graciosa, though many of the fishermen will probably take you out with them for a small (or perhaps not so small) fee.

La Graciosa

La Graciosa is less than a kilometre from Lanzarote, separated by a choppy stretch of water known as 'The River' due to its strong currents. At 27km² it's the largest islet in the Chinijo Archipelago and the only inhabited one. Although the island has two settlements, everything you need is in Caleta de Sebo. Pedro Barba was once a town, formed by those looking for a quieter life, but these days its attractive houses are holiday homes owned by outsiders who come from the other islands or the mainland for the ultimate in a relaxing break. The island's 500 citizens all live in Caleta de Sebo.

Getting there and away

Boats leave Orzola in the north of Lanzarote three times a day to make the 20-minute crossing to La Graciosa at 10.00, 12.00 and 17.00. Boats leave the harbour at La Graciosa at 08.00, 11.00 and 16.00. A return ticket is €13. Buses to and from Orzola are timed to coincide with the boats.

Getting around

La Graciosa prides itself on being one of the few places in Europe with no paved roads and you can't bring a car across from Lanzarote, so driving is not an option. You could realistically explore the entire island on foot in a couple of days. Alternatively, you can hire bikes in Caleta de Sebo or, if you don't feel energetic, you could find a local to drive you around in his truck for around €15.

Where to stay

Accommodation is limited, so booking ahead is recommended, especially if there's a fiesta going on. There are two *pensiones*, a few apartments and a campsite on the island. It's free to pitch a tent at the campsite but you do need permission, obtainable from the Town Hall delegation in Caleto de Sebo, tel: 928 84 20 00.

Apartamentos Los Caletones Calle Los Calletones 5; tel: 928 84 21 38. The apartments have 1 bedroom and all the usual facilities. €36 per night for 2 people.

Pensión Enriqueta Calle Mar de Barlovento 6; tel: 928 84 20 51; fax: 928 84 21 29. Most rooms have shared bathroom, though a few have private bathroom. Also has a restaurant downstairs. Single/double €16 without bathroom; €19 with.

Pensión Girasol Tel: 928 84 21 18. On the seafront and recently renovated, it's perhaps the better option. Single/double with balcony €20, or €17 without. There are also a few apartments available for €36 (accommodating up to 3 people).

Where to eat

Bar La Caletilla Serves tapas and can get a bit rowdy. Good if you're looking for a bit of local atmosphere. If you walk to the end of the harbour (with the harbour on your right), turn left and you'll see the bar ahead of you.

La Pizzería Korrikkia A block behind the beach, it's a take-away pizza place (though you can also eat in). Open evenings only.

Restaurante El Italiano On the seafront. A real gem and one which you wouldn't really expect to find in a place like this. The menu changes regularly, depending on the produce available. Plenty of pizza and pasta and a couple of token meat and fish dishes. Delicious home-made desserts. Main courses start from €6.

Restaurante Terraza El Varadero The most popular choice with tourists, maybe because it's the first restaurant you come to as you get off the boat. The fresh fish and seafood are excellent. Main courses around €10.

Nightlife

If you're looking for a wild night out, you are definitely on the wrong island. There is one nightspot, **Disco Pub Las Arenas**, near the Pensión Enriqueta. It opens only on Saturday nights from midnight. The only other place with a bit of life is the **Bar El Saltadero** on the beachfront, though it closes around midnight.

Fiestas

There are two main parties on Graciosa: Carnival and the Virgen del Carmen festivities. As on other islands, carnival is a two-week celebration, culminating in a

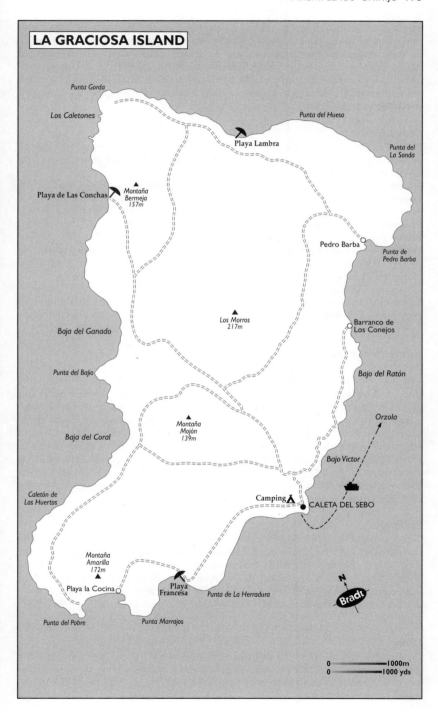

LA GRACIOSA ISLAND

Punta Gorda

Los Caletones

Punta del Hueso

Playa Lambra

Punta del
La Sonda

Playa de Las Conchas

Montaña
Bermeja
157m

Pedro Barba

Punta de
Pedro Barba

Baja del Ganado

Los Morros
217m

Barranco de
Los Conejos

Punta del Bajio

Bajo del Ratón

Baja del Coral

Montaña
Mojón
139m

Orzola

Bajo Victor

Caletón de
Las Huertos

Camping

CALETA DEL SEBO

Montaña
Amarilla
172m

Playa la Cocina

Playa
Francesa

Punta de La Herradura

N

Bradt

Punta del Pobre

Punta Marrajos

0 ————— 1000m
0 ————— 1000 yds

parade on Carnival Tuesday (the same date as Shrove Tuesday). Perhaps more important is the day devoted to Nuestra Señora del Carmen, celebrated on July 16. Fishermen decorate their boats and take the image of the virgin out in a colourful parade in the sea. Of course, there's plenty going on around the town too, with open-air theatre near the church and a party on the beach. It's undoubtedly the best time to be on the island, but accommodation is scarce so make sure you book well in advance.

Practicalities

Banks The Caja Insular de Ahorros is two 'roads' back from the beach – turn right after the Restaurante Girasol; open Mon–Fri 10.30–13.30. There's also an ATM next to Restaurante El Italiano.

Health The Health Centre is behind the church, opposite the children's playground.

Internet Rosa's Net, behind the Restaurante El Varadero, charges €3 per hour; open Mon–Sat 11.00–14.00, 17.00–24.00.

Pharmacy Opposite the church.

Police The Policía Local is on Calle García Escamez.

Post office On Calle Punta de la Sonda, near the children's playground, open Mon–Fri 10.00–12.00.

Shopping There are a couple of supermarkets and you can get souvenirs at the Restaurante El Varadero.

Tourist information None, but if you speak Spanish you'll have no problem finding out everything you need to know from any passing local. The Lanzarote tourist board publishes a nice little booklet about La Graciosa.

What to see and do
Beaches

OK, so La Graciosa can't offer good shops or wild nightlife, but if there's one thing it does well, it's beaches. The beaches here are golden, undeveloped and generally empty. The finest of them is the 400m-long Playa Las Conchas in the north, but it's considered *very* dangerous to swim here, or even to paddle if the sea is particularly rough. Caleta de Sebo has a small beach, but you'd be a fool to stay there when there are so many finer alternatives within walking distance. Playa Francesa is a couple of kilometres southwest of Caleta de Sebo and has calm waters, as does Playa Cocina, another 2km along the coast. The beach at the foot of Montaña Amarilla is quite sheltered and generally empty, other than the odd fisherman.

Cycling

There is no better place to go cycling within the Canary Islands, unless you like the challenge of a high mountain. La Graciosa is flat and you're unlikely to see a car all day. None of the roads are paved, so it can be a bit bumpy, but you can always take a rest on one of the deserted beaches. **Bike Graciosa Island** rent out mountain bikes for €8 a day. Their office is one of the first things you'll see as you arrive on the island; tel: 928 84 21 38. Open every day 10.00–13.00; 15.30–16.00.

Diving

Barcos Orzola can arrange a full diving holiday for €700 per person, including seven nights' accommodation in La Graciosa and five days' diving, with two dives per day. Minimum of four people. Tel: 928 84 25 58; fax: 928 84 25 37; email: orzola@intelmant.net.

Fishing

Juan Rafael is a local fisherman with years of experience who is happy to take tourists out for a day's fishing. A whole day of deep-sea fishing for up to four people costs €400. If you're a particularly keen angler, you can also arrange a full week's fishing. Seven nights' accommodation in an apartment plus five days of fishing costs €1,800 for up to four people. Tel: 928 84 21 16 or 669 33 56 50. **Barcos Orzola** also offer fishing trips for €150 per day for one person (prices vary depending on the number of participants). They can also arrange a full week of fishing, including accommodation on La Graciosa; seven nights' accommodation plus five days of fishing is €875 per person, with a minimum of four people required. See above for contact details.

Walking

Although you can't immerse yourself in any lush forests or verdant rolling hills, walking on La Graciosa is a pleasure. The absence of cars is a joy and at many points on the island you can turn 360 degrees and not see any signs of human life. However, it's all on the dirt tracks shared by the bikes and trucks, so it's not the most exciting hiking, but at least there's no chance of getting lost. Please stick to the paths to avoid destroying the already struggling plantlife. Note that you can cross below Montaña Amarilla only at low tide.

La Alegranza

It's possible to go to Alegranza on a day trip, though you cannot stay on the island or even wander around it. In summer months, Lineas Marítimas Romero run excursions from Caleta de Sebo to La Alegranza for €42 per person, including lunch and drinks, though you can't stray from where the boat is anchored.

It's also possible to get there from Orzola if you make prior arrangements with a fisherman. You must book in advance as the fishermen need to alert the environmental authorities and obtain a permit. Prices are negotiable, but it isn't cheap.

Tenerife

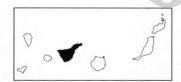

Perhaps the biggest victim of people's misconceptions, Tenerife is the archipelago's largest island at 2,036 km². It suffers more than most from its mass-tourist destination image. While the package-tourist scene undoubtedly exists and is still growing at an alarming rate, the island offers some dramatic landscapes, traditional villages and a huge variety of activities. If you fly to or between the islands in the daylight, you can't fail to be impressed by the magnificent Mount Teide poking up through the clouds and if you're like me, you'll be severely tempted to climb it. A shocking amount of tourists don't bother to leave their resort to approach the mountain, something that most locals feel should be punishable by law! Despite the year-round sun-and-fun image, Tenerife is actually lacking in good beaches but does have a stunning area of Canarian pine and two rural parks boasting laurel forest. If you get an aerial view of the southwest of the island, you'll most likely be shocked by the horrific sprawl of the tourist resorts. There were once a few distinguishable villages and towns, but these days Los Cristianos merges into the concrete tower blocks of Playa de las Américas, which is reaching ever further up the coast towards Los Gigantes. Still, it's a minute part of the island and one which can easily be avoided. Elsewhere there are some delightful little *pueblos* where traditional life is still enjoyed.

HIGHLIGHTS
Any trip to Tenerife would be incomplete without a visit to Mount Teide, the world's third largest volcano. The best way to visit the park is on foot, though taking the cable car to the top is a worthy alternative. La Laguna and La Orotava have delightful historic quarters, while Santa Cruz is the place for shopping and a stroll in the park. The natural pools at Garachico deserve a visit, as does the pine forest in the Vilaflor area. It may be rather touristy, but one of the Canary Islands' best boat trips is the tour past the imposing Los Gigantes cliffs, where there are also chances of seeing dolphins. The national parks of Teno and Anaga are any hiker's paradise and on many of the routes you won't see another walker all day. You should also try to visit a couple of typical villages to admire the architecture and sample some local produce; in the northwest you have Teno Alto and Masca, which is pretty but firmly on the tour bus route. Taganana in the northeast and Taucho and Ifonche in the south also ooze charm.

BACKGROUND INFORMATION
History
Although the term Guanche is often used to refer to the original inhabitants of all the islands, the word really means 'Sons of Tenerife' – 'guan' in their language meant descendant and 'Achinech' was the old name of the island. Their language,

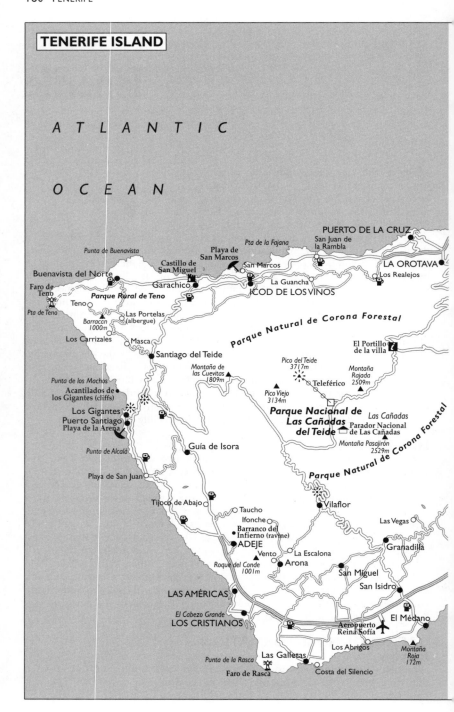

TENERIFE ISLAND

ATLANTIC

OCEAN

PUERTO DE LA CRUZ

Pta de la Fajana

Punta de Buenavista

Playa de San Marcos

San Juan de la Rambla

LA OROTAVA

Castillo de San Miguel

San Marcos

Los Realejos

Buenavista del Norte

La Guancha

Faro de Teno

Garachico

ICOD DE LOS VINOS

Pta de Teno

Parque Rural de Teno

Teno

Parque Natural de Corona Forestal

Barracán 1000m

Las Portelas (albergue)

El Portillo de la villa

Los Carrizales

Masca

Santiago del Teide

Montaña de las Cuevitas 1809m

Pico del Teide 3717m

Montaña Rajada 2509m

Punta de los Machos

Pico Viejo 3134m

Teleférico

Acantilados de los Gigantes (cliffs)

Los Gigantes

Parque Nacional de Las Cañadas del Teide

Las Cañadas

Puerto Santiago Playa de la Arena

Parador Nacional de Las Cañadas

Punta de Alcalá

Guía de Isora

Montaña Pasajirón 2529m

Parque Natural de Corona Forestal

Playa de San Juan

Tijoco de Abajo

Vilaflor

Las Vegas

Taucho

Ifonche

Barranco del Infierno (ravine)

ADEJE

Vento

La Escalona

Granadilla

Roque del Conde 1001m

Arona

San Miguel

LAS AMÉRICAS

San Isidro

LOS CRISTIANOS

El Cabezo Grande

El Médano

Aeropuerto Reina Sofía

Los Abrigos

Montaña Roja 172m

Punta de la Rasca

Las Galletas

Faro de Rasca

Costa del Silencio

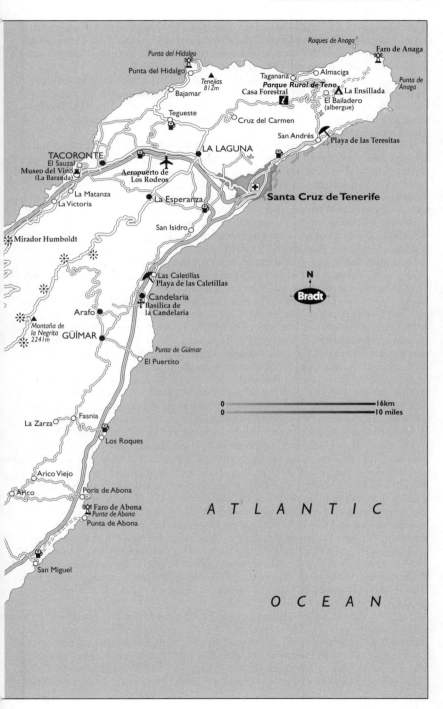

also known as Guanche, died out shortly after the Spanish conquest though it lives on in place names such as Icod, Güímar, Arona and Taganana. The natives of La Palma called the island Tenerife, which meant 'White Mountain', while on early maps it was labelled Nivaria ('Island of Snow').

Tenerife was once ruled by one leader but the united island was lost during the rule of Tinerfe. His eldest son, Bentinerfe, too impatient to wait for his father's impending death, decided to rebel against the ageing *mencey*. His eight brothers soon followed suit and they divided the island between them, creating the nine kingdoms that the Spaniards found on their arrival.

Tenerife was the last island to fall and the islanders didn't give in without a fight. In 1494 over 1,000 armed soldiers and a couple of hundred Canarios, led by Alonso de Lugo, landed on the beaches of Añazo (now Santa Cruz de Tenerife). They received a relatively friendly welcome from the peaceful *menceys* of Güímar, Adeje, Abona and Anaga, who were willing to accept the strangers' offer of friendship and even embrace the Christian faith. The leaders and their citizens united with the conquerors against the five *reinos de guerra* (warring cantons), led by *mencey* Bencomo. On meeting the newcomers, Bencomo told Lugo that if he and his men had come in peace, they would be welcomed, but if war was on their minds he should leave the island immediately or be prepared to fight. Lugo ignored this warning and fell into an ambush in the Acentejo ravine in the north of the island. It was the most crushing defeat that the Spanish suffered in the entire conquest, leaving 900 dead. Lugo survived, having swapped the cape that identified him as the leader with a soldier. The soldier was not so lucky and was chased to his death by dozens of Guanches. The site of the battle is still known as La Matanza de Acentejo (*matanza* means 'slaughter'). Lugo brought reinforcements from Spain and returned to launch a second attack on Tenerife in 1495. The Guanches, led by Bencomo, lay in wait for the Spaniards in La Laguna, but couldn't repeat their success and suffered a brutal defeat that left Bencomo dead. His son Bentor was named as *mencey* and he took the island's warriors to the canton of Taoro. Lugo attacked and despite the Guanches' battle preparations, they couldn't compete with the large Spanish army; they were beaten and many were sold as slaves. The site of this battle became known as La Victoria de Acentejo ('Victory of Acentejo').

Demoralised and suffering from illnesses brought by the Spanish, the Guanches put up little further resistance and seemed resigned to their fate as slaves, surrendering to the Spanish in 1496, though Bentor jumped into a ravine, preferring suicide to a life of slavery. The natives who had supported the Spanish had been promised freedom, while the warriors were doomed to a life of slavery. Following the general theme of treachery that had lingered throughout the conquest of the islands, Alonso de Lugo went back on his word and tried to sell both peaceful and rebellious Guanches as slaves, though the Castilian crown overruled his decision.

A large number of rebellious natives, along with a few runaway slaves, used their agility and knowledge of the landscape to their advantage and lived in freedom in the mountains for some time. The pacified Guanches, irked at having been lied to, helped these fugitives by stealing livestock from the Spanish and using the proceeds to help them.

The fate of the islanders changed in the coming years, with the introduction of various new crops from Latin America. The wine trade flourished, leading to an unbreakable bond between Tenerife and Britain, with British citizens setting up home and business in Puerto de la Cruz. The ports continued to grow and such was the economic importance of the island, it was declared capital of the archipelago in 1823. It remained capital for just over 100 years, when the islands were split into two provinces

Geography

Tenerife is in the middle of the archipelago, some 300km from the African continent. The Anaga Range crosses the island from east to west, dividing Tenerife into a moist, green north and a sunny, drier south. Tenerife counts on a considerable rainfall compared with other islands and its 425mm a year average creates some stunning areas of vegetation. There are laurel forests in the Parque Rural de Anaga and Parque Rural de Teno, while pine trees thrive in the Vilaflor area. Mount Teide is Spain's highest peak at 3,718m and for some time thought by Europeans to be the world's highest. As you'll discover at the park's visitor centre, the mountain's not dead, it just sleeps a lot, a fact confirmed by the pungent smell of sulphur at the peak. Tenerife has the archipelago's second highest population, with almost 700,000 inhabitants.

Economy

When you see the extent of the southern resorts it will come as no surprise that the island's economy is based on tourism. Agriculture is also important, with potatoes, bananas, tomatoes and wine all contributing to Tenerife's income. The CEPSA petrol refinery in Santa Cruz provides an important industry (and something for the ecologists to campaign about). The other notable industry is that of construction, though this is also a cause of concern and the uncontrolled building in the south of the island is the number one ecological problem in Tenerife.

Flora and fauna

Due to its superior size and height, Tenerife boasts more botanic diversity than the other islands, with a whopping 120 endemic plant species, mainly concentrated in Teno, Anaga and the Cañadas del Teide. Look out for the Teide violet (*Viola cheiranthifolia*) adding a flash of colour to the barren national park. Without doubt, the most emblematic tree is the Dragon (*Dracaena draco*), (see box, page 215). Tenerife's emblem is the blue chaffinch (*Fringilla leydea leydea*), which lives in the pine forest along with the endangered great spotted woodpecker (see *Conservation* below). Twenty-six cetaceans have been recorded in the seas around the Canary Islands, most of those southwest of Tenerife where a lucrative whale-watching market exists. Most, including the North Atlantic right whale (*Eubalaena glacialis*), the short-finned pilot whale (*Globicephala macrorhynchus*) and the blue whale (*Balaenopiera musculus*) are endangered.

Conservation

The Teno region is home to one of the Canary Islands' most endangered reptiles, the Canarian spotted lizard (*Gallotia intermedia*). There are 300 specimens of this endemic species in Tenerife and it's included on the national endangered species register. Breeding in captivity has not been considered necessary, though controlling numbers of wild cats and conservation of habitat has been. Higher up the endangered list is the Tenerife great spotted woodpecker (*Dendrocopos major canariensis*), rapidly disappearing as its preferred habitat, Canarian pine forest, is destroyed. Life in the sea isn't much safer and conservationists are concerned about the whales and dolphins that live off the south coast of the island. Although the ever-growing number of whale-watching tours is a boost for the economy, the often less than thoughtful attitude of the boats' operators is a threat to the magnificent mammals. Tenerife has an impressive number of protected spaces at 43, which includes Spain's most visited national park, Teide.

Festivals

Many people consider Santa Cruz's carnival second only to that of Rio de Janeiro. For two weeks the streets fill with revellers of all ages taking part in the parades, dancing competitions, watching the various carnival queens be crowned or just getting drunk in the countless makeshift bars that are set up throughout the capital. If carnival is a little rowdy, perhaps you'll enjoy the sombre *procesión de silencio*, part of La Laguna's Semana Santa (Easter) festivities. The Corpus Christi carpets, made with flower petals and volcanic stones, are particularly impressive in La Orotava, La Laguna and Tacoronte.

GETTING THERE AND AWAY
By air

Tenerife has two airports, Los Rodeos in the north and Reina Sofía in the south. The majority of inter-island flights fly to and from the North Airport, while charter flights from other countries head into the South.

Binter Canarias Tel: 902 39 13 92; www.bintercanarias.es. *Gran Canaria:* 15 a day during the week and 10 on weekends. There are also 2 daily fights from Tenerife South Airport. *Fuerteventura:* 2–3 a day. *La Palma:* 5 a day during the week and 2 on weekends. *El Hierro:* 3 a day and 6 on Saturdays. *La Gomera:* 2 a day. *Lanzarote:* 5 a day and 2 a week to Tenerife South.

Islas Airways Tel: 902 47 74 48; www.islasairways.com. *Fuerteventura:* 2 a day. *La Palma:* 6 a day. *Gran Canaria:* 1 a day.

By sea

Fred Olsen Tel: 902 10 01 07; email: reserves@fredolsen.es; www.fredolsen.es. *El Hierro:* 1 a day (from Los Cristianos). *Gran Canaria:* 6 a day (to Agaete). *La Gomera:* 4 a day (from Los Cristianos). *La Palma:* 1 a day (from Los Cristianos).

Trasmediterránea Tel: 902 45 46 54; www.trasmediterranea.es. *El Hierro:* 1 a day (from Los Cristianos). *Gran Canaria:* 3 jetfoils a day and 1 slower ferry. *La Gomera:* 2–3 a day (from Los Cristianos). *Lanzarote:* 1 a week (to Arrecife). *La Palma:* 1 a week. *Cádiz:* 1 a week.

Naviera Armas Tel: 902 45 65 00; email: narmas@naviera-armas.com; www.naviera-armas.com. *Gran Canaria:* 2 a day. *La Palma:* 1 a day.

GETTING AROUND
Public transport

The bus service is excellent, serving even the tiniest of *pueblos*, although perhaps not too frequently. If you're planning to do any amount of bus travel it's worth buying a *bono*, a pre-paid card that gets you a hefty discount on board. It also gives you half-price entrance to the *Cabildo*'s museums.

Car hire

There are scores of car-hire companies in all but the tiniest towns. Here's a small selection of what's on offer:

Autored Tel: 922 28 00 33 (Santa Cruz); 922 25 19 17 (Los Rodeos)
Auto Reisen Tel: 922 39 22 16 (Reina Sofía)
Avis Tel: 922 24 12 94 (Santa Cruz); 922 25 87 13 (Los Rodeos); 922 39 20 56 (Reina Sofía)
Cicar Tel: 922 29 24 25 (Santa Cruz); 922 63 26 42 (Los Rodeos); 922 39 02 46 (Reina Sofía)
Hertz Tel: 922 63 58 68 (Los Rodeos); 922 75 93 19 (Reina Sofía)

Bike hire

There are a few options for getting around on two wheels. If you are in the Los Gigantes area, Todo 2 Ruedas have a variety of bikes to hire from mountain bikes for €10 a day, to 50cc scooters (€24 per day) and even 250cc motorbikes for €60. Prices get cheaper if you rent the bike for longer. Tel/fax: 922 86 23 54.

WHERE TO STAY
Hotels, guesthouses and rural accommodation

It can be difficult to find cheap accommodation, especially in the large resorts where large hotels and apartment complexes rule the roost and the majority of beds belong to tour operators. Of course, there are more *pensiones* and budget hotels here than on most of the islands and only a few of them are dubious.

The network of *casas rurales* is growing and the island also boasts a few delightful rural hotels. The following companies arrange stays in rural accommodation:

ATTUR Calle Castillo 41, Santa Cruz; tel: 922 21 55 82; fax: 922 53 10 34; email: tenerife@ecoturismocanarias.com; www.ecoturismocanarias.com. Expect to pay in the region of €50–70 for 2 people and €70–100 for 4.
AECAN Av 3 de Mayo, Santa Cruz; tel: 92 59 50 19; fax: 922 59 50 83; email: aecan@cip.es; www.cip.es/aecan; €55–80 per night for 2 people.
Tenerife Sur Turismo Rural Calle La Plaza 5; tel: 922 77 03 62; fax: 922 77 03 62; email: teneriferural@navegalia.com; www.tenerifesurturismorural.com. They have properties only in the south of the island; prices range from €50 to €80 for 2 people.

There are only two places to stay in the Parque Nacional del Teide: the magnificent but pricey *parador* and the somewhat less comfortable Refugio de Altavista.

Camping and hostels

There are 20 campsites across the island, all of which are free, though you do need permission to stay and must reserve a place a minimum of three days in advance. You can stay on any campsite for a maximum of seven days and expect the most basic of conditions – many don't even have a toilet block. For information and permits call 922 23 91 99 or see the website www.cabtfe.es. There are two excellent hostels on the island, one in Teno and one in Anaga; call 922 822 056 for reservations.

ACTIVITIES
Beaches

Tenerife is not known for its wonderful beaches though there are a few that are worth a visit. Los Gigantes has a small, black-sand beach backed by the cliffs; Tejina in the south is the island's only natural golden-sand beach and has been claimed by nudists and windsurfers. Anyone can bathe there, of course, provided you can brave the strong winds and even stronger currents.

Boat trips

Tenerife is an excellent destination for whale-watching, and don't the tour companies know it! There are dozens of places offering boat trips along the western coast, though some of them operate dubious practices with regard to approaching the animals. Nashira, based in Los Gigantes, come highly recommended as a professional company who stick to the rules. Many of the boats from Los Cristianos offer on-board food, drink and entertainment, though whether this is a plus point is debatable. Prices vary depending on the length of the trip you wish to take but expect to pay around €25 for two hours, €30 for three.

Diving

There are scores of companies offering baptism dives, courses and packages for more experienced divers all across the island. The seas around Las Galletas are known for their good visibility and night dives are particularly popular here. Other divers' favourites are Los Gigantes and the Masca Bay. Expect to see trunkfish, barracuda, yellow striped bass and moray eels.

Excursions

There is no shortage of companies offering excursions in Tenerife and they all offer a similar choice.

Tenerife Excursiones Tel: 900 700 999; email: viajesteide@terra.es. A good choice, including a half-day Teide tour (€20), island tour (€25), trip to La Gomera (€50) and even a day trip to Lanzarote (€130). They are based in the south but do pick-ups from all the resorts.

The Excursion Centre Tel: 922 86 07 37; fax: 922 86 72 97. A similar choice and similar prices; they are based in Los Gigantes.

Divertour Puerto de la Cruz; tel: 922 38 69 90; email: divertour@grupoeuropa.com; www.grupoeuropa.com/divertour. Not quite such a wide range of tours but more convenient if you're based in the north of the island.

Golf

As in most of the islands, Tenerife is gaining popularity as a golfers' destination. There are currently three 18-hole courses, two 27-hole courses and a few nine-hole pitch 'n' putts. Green fees are around €50 for 18 holes. www.tenerifegolf.es.

Hiking

While not as well developed as in some of the smaller islands, there are some excellent hikes in Tenerife. You sometimes have to work at finding the best routes and obtaining the maps and route descriptions but if you stick at it you will be rewarded with some incredible landscapes and isolated walks. Obviously the main place for hiking is the Parque Nacional del Teide, where the two favourite routes are the climb to the summit and the walk through the *cañadas* (see pages 212–14 for details). Other favourite walks on the island are the Barranco del Infierno in the south of the island and the Barranco de Masca in the northwest, though these tend to get rather crowded. However, Tenerife's best-kept secrets are the two rural parks of Teno and Anaga.

Caminantes de Aguere Based in La Laguna; tel: 922 26 22 89; www.caminantesdeaguere.com. Organise trips in all 7 islands. Walks within Tenerife cost €15 and operate most Saturdays, unless the group is off to one of the other islands.

Diga Sports Tel: 922 79 30 09; fax: 922 17 68 37; www.diga-sports.de. Hiking and biking tours all across the island, prices around €40 per person.

El Cardón Tel/fax: 922 12 79 38; email: info@elcardon.com. Organise walks every weekend and also specialise in environmental education. They have the backing of the Town Hall, so their prices are lower than most but groups tend to be quite large.

Gaiatours Tel: 922 35 52 72; email: gaiatours@teleline.es. Hiking tours throughout the island, though they do pick ups only in the north.

Senderos Turisticos Gregorio Puerto de la Cruz; tel: 639 332 761; fax: 922 33 09 10; email: wanderungregorio@wanadoo.es; www.gregorio-teniffa.de. The oldest company offering hiking trips in Tenerife. They run tours to all the usual places for around €40 per person.

Terra Incognita Viajes Santa Cruz; tel: 922 29 10 25; email: terrain@arrakis.es;

www.terraincognita.es. Can organise pretty much anything that you would want to do in the open air, from walks and bike trips to diving, climbing, abseiling and *parapente*.

Shopping
Santa Cruz is a fine place to hit the shops, billed as Europe's largest open-air shopping centre. If you want to buy official *artesanía*, there are kiosks throughout the island; for details see www.artenerife.com.

Theme parks
Love 'em or loathe 'em, the island hosts more than a dozen theme parks, most of them tacky, overpriced and with no bearing on the culture or history of the island. You can choose from camel rides, waterslides, pirate fights and a series of zoos and gardens. There are a couple of places that bear some relevance to the islands, such as the 'Bananeras' and Pueblo Chico, though you shouldn't lose any sleep if you miss them.

Windsurfing
Although not as popular as the eastern islands as a windsurfing destination, there is scope for learning or practising at El Médano in the south of the island. You'll also find kiteboarding facilities there.

SANTA CRUZ DE TENERIFE
Santa Cruz took the title of capital from La Laguna in the 19th century, with the increase in traffic in the port. Most agree that it's not such a worthy candidate for the post, though it's certainly a better place for sleeps and eats than the old capital. With 230,000 inhabitants it's now the second largest city in the islands, though it somehow lacks the bustling city feel that its Gran Canarian neighbour possesses. That said, Santa Cruz outshines Las Palmas in many ways, with its marvellous parks and one of the Canary Islands' best museums, the Museo de Naturaleza y del Hombre. There's plenty of accommodation on offer, from the grottiest of guesthouses to the splendour of the five-star Hotel Mencey and you'll find some excellent, though often pricey, restaurants and lots of pavement cafés.

Getting there
From the airport
Bus number 109 leaves the Los Rodeos Airport at quarter past every hour, from 06.15 to 22.15. There is also a bus to the South Airport, which also runs every hour at ten to the hour. A taxi from the airport costs about €15. There are plenty of buses to almost everywhere from Santa Cruz, leaving from the bus station in the south of the city. Buses to La Laguna leave from the city centre.

Where to stay
Upmarket
Escuela Hotel Avenida San Sebastián 152; tel: 822 01 05 00; fax: 822 01 05 01; email: reservas.ehsc@hecansa.com. Situated in a pretty ugly area of Santa Cruz, this hotel offers experience to students on hospitality courses. It's a noisy area, what with the busy road and the football stadium opposite, but inside the hotel is calm and pleasant. Single €100; double €126; suite €190.

Hotel Atlántida Santa Cruz Avenida 3 de Mayo; tel: 922 29 45 00; fax: 922 22 44 58; email: hotelatlantida.sc@hoteles-silken.com; www.hoteles-silken.com. Located in the commercial district of the city, this hotel is definitely aimed at business people rather than tourists, though that's not to say you won't enjoy its sauna, fitness room, jacuzzi and large rooms with all mod cons. Single €107; double €119.

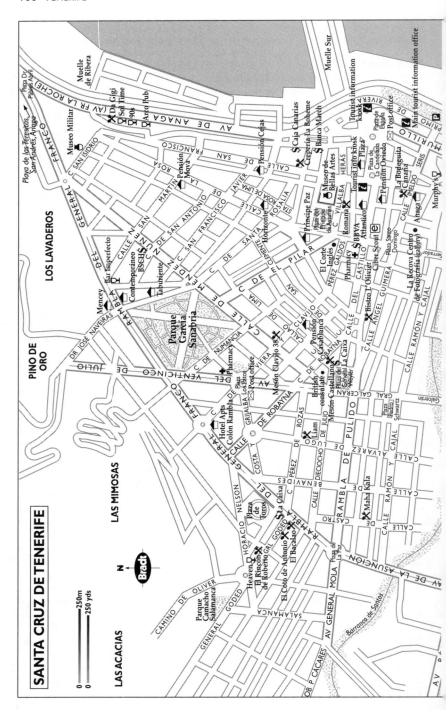

SANTA CRUZ DE TENERIFE

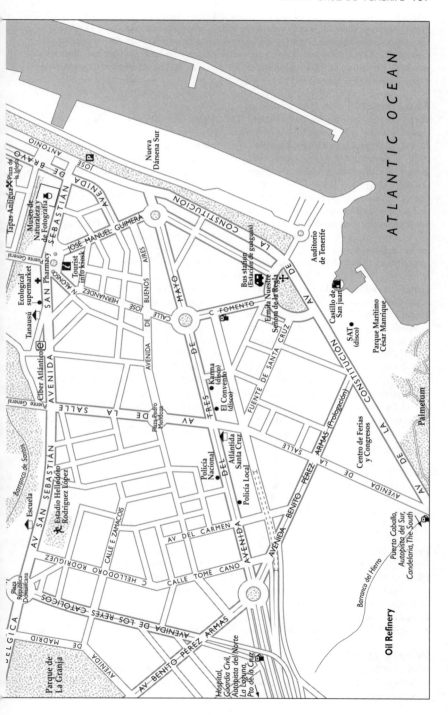

Hotel Mencey Calle Dr José Naveiras 38; tel: 922 60 99 00; fax: 922 28 00 17; email: mencey@starwoodhotels.com. The capital's *numero uno* hotel, frequented by celebrities, visiting politicians and even royalty on occasions. It has delightful gardens and some rooms overlook the courtyard. Has a pool, casino, tennis court and an excellent restaurant. Single €180; double €215; suite €350.

Mid-range

Hotel Anaga Calle Imeldo Serís 19; tel: 922 24 50 90; fax: 922 24 56 44. Basic yet comfy rooms; friendly staff. Single €32; double €53.

Hotel Apartamentos Colón Rambla Calle Viera y Clavijo 49; tel: 922 27 27 16; fax: 922 27 26 50; email: info@hotel-colonrambla.com. The apartments have a small kitchen and almost all have a terrace or balcony. They are nothing special but large and clean and there is a swimming pool. Single €65; double €75.

Hotel Atlántico Calle Castillo 12; tel: 922 24 63 75; fax: 922 24 63 78. Very basic rooms in a good central location. Single €38; double €57.

Hotel Contemporáneo Rambla General Franco 116; tel: 902 120 329; fax: 922 27 12 23; email: consultas@hotelcontemporaneo.com; www.hotelcontemporaneo.com. As the name suggests, this is a modern place which gives you a breath of fresh air after staying in oodles of chintzy hotel rooms. The pick of the mid-range bunch. Single €65; double €90.

Hotel Plaza Plaza de La Candelaria 10; tel: 922 27 24 53; fax: 922 27 51 60; email: hotelplaza@arrakis.es. Clean, but nothing special. Single €68; double €85.

Hotel Principe Paz Calle Valentín Sanz 33; tel: 922 24 99 55; fax: 922 28 10 65; email: principepaz@principepaz.com; www.principepaz.com. Some rooms have been recently redecorated, but others are rather miserable. They all have satellite TV and AC. Single €75; double €90.

Hotel Taburiente Calle Dr José Naveiras 24; tel: 922 27 60 00; fax: 922 27 05 62; email: hotabu@teleline.es; http://canaryweb.es/htabu. Good value. Nice rooms, some with a lovely view of the park. Single €53; double €63, including breakfast. Suites €120.

Hotel Tanausú Calle Padre Anchieta 8; tel: 922 21 70 00; fax: 922 21 60 29; email: hotel@tanausu.com. This hotel offers better value than many in the same price bracket in the city, with its bright, well-looked-after rooms. It's a little bit out of the centre, but within walking distance. Single €34; double €55.

Budget

Hotel Horizonte Calle Santa Rosa de Lima 11; tel: 922 27 19 36. Pretty good value, though rooms smell musty and could stand a bit of redecoration. Single €18; double €36.

Pensión Casablanca Calle Viera y Clavijo 15; tel: 922 27 85 99. Rooms are small and dark and none have private bathroom, though it's clean and not bad for the price. Single €15; double €21.

Pensión Cejas Calle San Francisco 47; tel: 922 28 18 72 . Rooms are pretty grubby and with rather unsavoury shared bathrooms, but service is friendly. Single €15; double €30.

Pensión Mova Calle San Martín 23; tel: 922 28 32 61. A little brighter than some other *pensiones* around. Single €12; double €20 without bathroom. There are a couple of doubles with bathroom that go for €24.

Pensión Oviedo Calle Dr Allart; tel: 922 24 36 43. Very clean rooms with a spotless shared bathroom. In a quiet pedestrian street near the centre. Single €15; double €20.

Where to eat

Bistro L'Olivier Calle Ángel Guimerá; tel: 922 27 58 93. French and Mediterranean cooking with a hint of the Orient thrown in for good measure. Not cheap, with main meals averaging €14. Closed on Sundays and Mondays.

Crepería La Boheme Calle Emilio Calzadilla. The largest selection of crêpes you could ever ask for, with over 50 on offer, including sweet and savoury fillings. They also have a good selection of salads.

Da Gigi Av de Anaga; tel: 922 24 20 17 or 922 24 89 71 (deliveries). Good Italian food in relaxed surroundings. Main courses range from €5 for pizza and pasta to €10 for a steak.

El Bacalao Calle General Goded; tel: 922 29 32 49. Basque cuisine with some excellent fish dishes, as the name suggests (*bacalao* means 'cod'). Main courses €10 and above. Closed on Sundays.

El Coto de Antonio Next door to El Bacalao; tel: 922 27 21 05. One for a special occasion. Their combination of Canarian and Basque dishes is legendary, so reservations are recommended. Main dishes start at €20.

La Bodeguita Canaria Calle Imeldo Serís. A typical Canarian menu, but the food is excellent, just like *mami* makes. Their *ropa vieja* is outstanding.

Liam Calle Pérez de Rozas; tel: 922 24 37 80. Super menu of creative Spanish and French cuisine and a selection of Japanese dishes. Expect to pay around €15 for a main course. Closed on Sundays and Monday lunchtimes.

Maha Kala Calle de Castro; tel: 922 27 91 36. One of a kind, serving a combination of Italian and Far Eastern dishes. They also have a good choice for vegetarians and even a macrobiotic selection. Average price for a main course €15.

Mesón Castellano Near Plaza del General Weyler. Good Spanish fare with legs of ham hanging everywhere; perhaps not ideal for vegetarians.

Mesón Clavijo 38 Calle Viera y Clavijo. This tapas bar has an excellent menu and an even better reputation. It's a little pricey, but worth the extra; expect to pay around €15 for a main course. Closed on Sundays.

Romana Calle Villalba Hervás. Serves coffee and every flavour of ice-cream going. Even has a rather unusual ice-cream sandwich on offer.

Tapas Antigua Set in a lovely, peaceful location near the Museo de la Naturaleza y del Hombre.

Nightlife

The capital isn't the liveliest place to paint the town red and many people prefer to go to La Laguna instead. Of course, there are a few places where you might see a bit of action. In the summer months a group of outdoor bars are set up near the auditorium.

90s A bar on Av de Anaga, next to Da Gigi restaurant. Things get going at around 11.00 and wrap up at 03.00.

Arco Pub On the same road. It's a music bar with varied live acts on Thursdays, Fridays and Saturdays; open 18.00–03.30.

Bar Imperfecto Calle San Martín. Plays alternative music. Open until about 03.00.

El Convento Calle 3 de Mayo. Probably the capital's favourite late-night hang-out. The music is varied and the drinks are expensive. Open from 02.00.

Heaven Calle General Goded. This place attracts a young crowd and stays open until about 04.00.

Karma Calle 3 de Mayo, next to El Convento. A good variety of music and a decent crowd. Open 01.00–07.00.

Murphy's Plaza de la Iglesia. Santa Cruz hasn't managed to escape the worldwide epidemic of Irish bars but it's a good place to get things going.

SAT Parque Marítimo César Manrique. A late, late disco playing mostly Latin and Spanish pop music. It opens at 02.00 and keeps going until 06.00 or 07.00. It's much livelier in the summer when the outdoor bars are set up around the park. You'll have to pay an entry fee of about €7 but you do get a drink for that.

Sol Time Another one in the cluster of bars on Av de Anaga. It's a place to start the night and is open until 03.00.

Practicalities

Banks Banca March, Calle La Marina, open Mon–Fri 08.30–14.00, Sat 08.30–13.00; Caja Canarias, Calle San Sebastián, open Mon–Fri 08.30–14.00, Thu 17.00–19.30; La Caixa, Plaza del General Weyler and Calle General Goded, open Mon–Fri 08.15–14.00, Thu 16.30–19.45; BBVA, Calle Valentín Sanz, open Mon–Fri 08.30–14.15, Sat 08.30–13.00; Santander Central Hispano, Calle de San Antonio, open Mon–Fri 08.30–14.00, Sat 08.30–13.00.

Health The Hospital de Nuestra Señora de la Candelaria is just off the main road as you leave Santa Cruz for La Laguna; tel: 922 60 20 00.

Internet Ciber Atlántico, Calle San Sebastian, open every day 11.00–24.00; €1.20 per hour. Ciber Scout, Calle Castillo, open Mon–Sat 08.00–23.00, Sun 14.00–23.00; €2 per hour.

Pharmacy Near Hotel Tanausú on Calle San Sebastián, opposite the post office in Plaza los Patos, on Calle Castillo in the city centre and on Calle García Morato in the north of the city.

Police The Policía Local and Policía Nacional are on Av Tres de Mayo; the Guardia Civil is south of the centre on Calle del Conde de Pallasar.

Post office In Plaza de España, open Mon–Fri 08.30–20.30, Sat 09.30–14.30. There's also one in Plaza los Patos, near Parque García Sanabria, with the same opening hours.

Shopping The best areas for shopping are in the pedestrian streets near the Plaza de la Candelaria, known as Europe's largest open-air shopping centre. There are many supermarkets around, and an ecological supermarket next to the Hotel Tanausú. There are also two branches of Spain's unrivalled department store, El Corte Inglés, where you can find absolutely anything.

Tourist information There are a few information kiosks scattered around the city; the most helpful is the one in Plaza de España. Kiosks are open Mon–Sat 09.30–17.00. There is a larger office just inside the *Cabildo* building but they seem to have more information about the rest of Spain than about Tenerife; it's open Mon–Fri 09.00–15.00, Sat 09.00–12.00.

What to see and do
Walking
The tourist information booths offer short walks around the city, taking in all the top sights and giving an informative commentary. The walks operate every morning and it's advisable to book in advance; tel: 922 23 95 29.

Museums
Museo de Naturaleza y del Hombre
An excellent museum with panels and interactive exhibits on the formation of the islands, the ancient inhabitants and their culture and way of life. There are also interesting sections on the natural history of the islands and various conservation projects. Allow plenty of time to explore the three floors. The museum is on Calle F Morales, open Tue–Sat 09.00–19.00. Entrance €3, half price for children, students and those with a *bono de guagua*. Free on Sundays.

La Recova Centro de Fotografía Isla de Tenerife
Plaza La Madera. This small centre hosts temporary photographic exhibitions, usually by Canarian artists. Exhibitions change each month. Open Mon–Sat 11.00–13.00, 18.00–21.00; entrance is free.

Museo de Bellas Artes
Calle José Murphy. There are permanent collections of 16th–20th-century paintings as well as a few on loan from the Prado Museum in Madrid. Many of the

NELSON'S ARM

While Tinerfeños like to gloat about it, it's probably a little-known fact in the UK that Admiral Horatio Nelson lost his right arm during an unsuccessful battle in the Canary Islands. In 1797 Nelson launched an attack on Tenerife's capital, Santa Cruz, with the intention of taking a shipment of gold brought from the New World, which was stowed in a boat docked in the city's harbour. The strength of the Tinerfeño army was greatly misjudged, and the battle left 150 English soldiers dead and their leader with one arm less than when he started. The remaining 700 men surrendered and only a dozen Spanish soldiers died during the battle. Legend says that he was hit in the shoulder by shrapnel from the Tigre cannon, leading to the inevitable amputation of his arm. There's a scale model of the battle and flagship *Theseus* in Santa Cruz de Tenerife's Museo Militar.

paintings are by Canarian artists and some depict the islands' history, so are definitely worth a look. There is also a room housing temporary exhibitions. Open Tue–Fri 10.00–20.00, Sat–Sun 10.00–15.00; entrance is free.

Museo Militar

Calle San Isidro. A wander through the military history of Tenerife, with a large emphasis on the fateful battle where Nelson lost his arm and Santa Cruz emerged victorious. Amongst the exhibits is a 30m² scale model of the battle. There's also some general information on the military history of the islands, a few Guanche artefacts and the archipelago's most complete collection of maps. Open Tue–Sun 10.00–14.00; entrance free.

Parks

Santa Cruz is the only city within the Canary Islands that has a decent park to visit. The **Parque García Sanabria** is in the northern part of town and is worth a wander. Manrique's contribution to Santa Cruz, the **Parque Marítimo César Manrique**, pales in comparison with the city's other park but does liven up on summer evenings when a series of open-air bars are erected and the park fills up with revellers. It's in the southern part of the city, near the auditorium. You can wander around the edge for free but if you want to enter and use the swimming pools it's €2.50; open every day 09.00–19.00.

LA LAGUNA

Founded by Alonso de Lugo in 1496 and awarded the title of city in 1531, the old capital of the island still maintains a definite charm that the current capital can't seem to acquire. Its narrow cobbled streets are a joy to amble through and the city has enough historical buildings to satisfy even the most demanding architecture buff. San Cristóbal de La Laguna, to give it its full title, was a kind of working laboratory to toy with how an 'organised city' should be laid out and the design was later adapted by many towns and cities in Latin America. It was the administrative and economical centre of the island until the early 18th century when volcanic eruptions buried the port of Garachico. This led to the development of the port at Santa Cruz and important institutions soon began to move from La Laguna to the coast. The city quickly lost economic power and the title of capital was snatched from La Laguna and handed to Santa Cruz in 1833. Designated a World Heritage

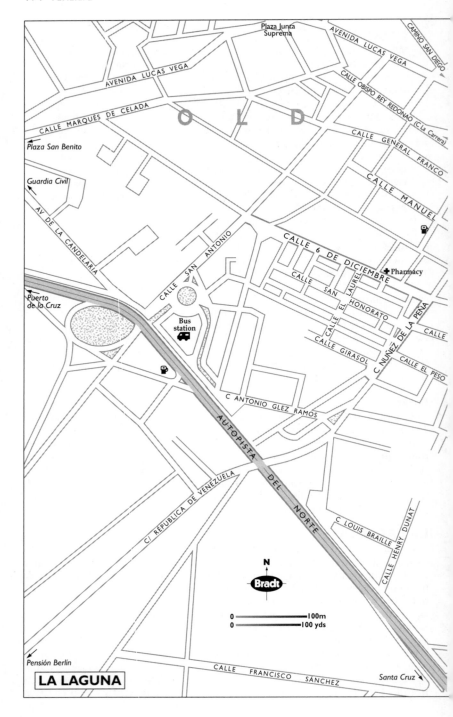

Plaza Junta Suprema · AVENIDA LUCAS VEGA · CAMINO SAN DIEGO · AVENIDA LUCAS VEGA · CALLE OBISPO REY REDONAO (C La Carrera) · O L D · CALLE MARQUÉS DE CELADA · CALLE GENERAL FRANCO · *Plaza San Benito* · CALLE MANUEL · *Guardia Civil* · AV DE LA CANDELARIA · CALLE SAN ANTONIO · CALLE 6 DE DICIEMBRE · ✚ Pharmacy · CALLE SAN LAUREL · *Puerto de la Cruz* · Bus station · CALLE EL HONORATO · C NUÑEZ DE LA PEÑA · CALLE · CALLE GIRASOL · CALLE EL PESO · C ANTONIO GLEZ RAMOS · AUTOPISTA DEL NORTE · C/ REPÚBLICA DE VENEZUELA · C LOUIS BRAILLE · CALLE HENRY DUNAT · N · **Bradt** · 0 ——— 100m · 0 ——— 100 yds · *Pensión Berlín* · CALLE FRANCISCO SÁNCHEZ · *Santa Cruz* ·

LA LAGUNA

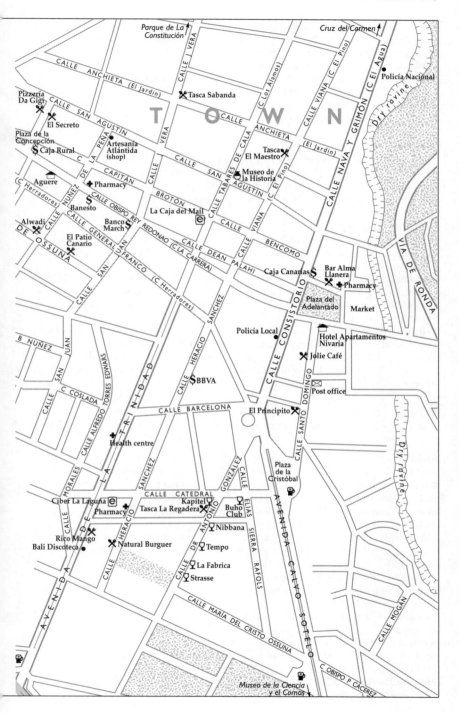

Site by UNESCO in 1999, La Laguna today has a laid-back studenty atmosphere and is certainly one of Tenerife's trump cards. La Laguna, which took its name from a long since dried-up pool in the Aguere Valley, is Tenerife's second largest settlement and the third largest in the Canaries with 113,000 citizens. Finding your way around town can be a bit confusing at times since over the years many of the street names have changed and now have two titles. Generally, locals tend to use the old names, though businesses often use the modern ones. In this book I have used the old street names, though both appear on the map.

Getting there
There are regular buses between La Laguna and the Los Rodeos Airport, though if you're coming from the South Airport you'll need to change at Santa Cruz. A taxi from the North Airport costs €6. Amongst others, bus 15 runs between La Laguna and the capital approximately every eight minutes.

Where to stay
Hotel Aguere Calle La Carrera 57; tel: 922 25 94 90; fax: 922 63 16 33. Pleasant enough rooms set around a nice patio area, though it's a trifle overpriced for a 1-star hotel. Single €48; double €63.

Hotel Apartamentos Nivaria Plaza del Adelantado 11; tel: 922 26 40 52; fax: 922 25 96 34; email: info@hotelnivaria.com; www.hotelnivaria.com. Spotless studio apartments right in the historical centre, so you can watch the goings on in the square from your balcony. Single €69; double €75.

Pensión Berlin Calle República de Venezuela 64; tel: 922 25 50 43. In a quiet, residential area, close to the bus station but a bit inconvenient for anything else in town. Most of their rooms have shared bathroom although there are a few doubles with private bathroom. Single €27; double €36 or €42, with private bathroom. Rooms are cheaper in summer months.

Where to eat
There is a cluster of *churrerías* next to the market if you're looking for a sweet way to start your day.

Alwadi On the corner of Calle Nuñez de la Peña and Calle Manuel de Ossuna. A pretty good and not too pricey Lebanese restaurant, with a few vegetarian options.

Bar Alma Llanera Plaza del Adelantado. Nothing special but it's cheap and has tables outside in the square. Serves greasy sandwiches and limited tapas.

El Patio Canario Calle Manuel de Ossuna. Best place around for traditional Canarian cuisine. Also hosts art exhibitions and occasional Canarian music recitals.

El Principito Calle Santo Domingo; tel: 922 63 39 16. Award-winning French cuisine with a menu that changes every 6 weeks, though duck is always available. Main meals are around €20.

El Secreto Calle Ascanio y Nieves; tel: 922 25 92 26. Another outstanding French restaurant with some seriously tempting dishes. Not cheap but worth splashing out; expect to pay about €15–20 for a main meal.

Jolie Café Near the Plaza del Adelantado. A chilled-out place to stop for a coffee and a slice of cake.

Natural Burguer Calle Heraclio Sánchez. If you're looking for an all-natural snack, this place is worth a look. They serve burgers and sandwiches but use all organic ingredients and have a good choice for vegetarians.

Pizzería Da Gigi Calle Ascanio Nieves, near the Plaza de la Concepción. Another branch of the small and excellent pizza chain.

Rico Mango Av de la Trinidad. Another place serving natural snacks, good vegetarian choices and a variety of natural fruit and vegetable juices.

Tasca El Maestro Calle El Pino, near the History Museum. Small and friendly tapas joint with good prices and superb service.

Tasca La Regadera Calle Dr Antonio González. A popular tapas place, particularly with the student crowd, probably due to its location in the heart of the *marcha* zone. Prices are reasonable, as is the food.

Tasca Sabanda On the corner of Calle Anchieta and Calle José Vera. A similar place, offering a range of tapas and main meals. You can eat well here for €8 if you can see your plate – it's a little on the dark side.

Nightlife

La Laguna is an excellent place for a Friday night out, with its laid-back student atmosphere and multitude of bars. The *marcha* is mainly concentrated in two streets (Calle Dr Antonio González and Calle Elías Sierra Rafols) though there are a few dissenters. The locals' pick of the bunch are **Tempo**, **La Fábrica**, **Strasse**, **Nibbana** and **Kapitel** though, since the bars all line the same two roads, the best way to sample La Laguna's nightlife is to stumble from bar to bar until you find something you like. **Buho Club**, on Calle Catedrál, is about the only place around with regular live music; it tends to be jazz, though they also have a few flamenco bands. **Bali Discoteca**, on Av de la Trinidad, fills up when all the other bars close, at around 04.00. It attracts a varied crowd and stays open until 07.00.

Fiestas

La Laguna's festivals lack the glitz of carnival in Santa Cruz but are certainly worth a look if you're after a reserved religious celebration. The Semana Santa Parade (held over Easter weekend) is the largest and most important of its kind on the island, while the Corpus Christi flower-petal carpets are undoubtedly the most impressive in the archipelago, some of them stretching for 2km. There's another large religious parade on September 14 in honour of Santísimo Cristo (Holy Christ), attended by people from across the island. The parade is followed by an enormous fireworks display.

Practicalities

Banks Caja Canarias, Plaza del Adelantado, open Mon–Fri 08.30–14.00, Thu 17.00–19.30; Caja Rural, Plaza de la Concepción, open Mon–Fri 08.30–14.00, Thu 17.00–19.30; Banesto, Calle La Carrera, open Mon–Fri 08.30–14.00, Sat 08.30–13.00; Banca March, Calle La Carrera, open Mon–Fri 08.30–14.00, Sat 08.30–13.00; BBVA, Calle Heraclio Sánchez, open Mon–Fri 08.30–14.15, Sat 08.30–13.00.

Health There's a Health Centre on Av de la Trinidad and the Hospital Universitario is south of the centre in the Urbanización Ofra; tel: 922 67 80 00.

Internet La Caja del Mail, Calle Los Álamos, open every day 11.00–23.00; €1.50 per hour. Ciber La Laguna, Calle Catedrál, open Mon–Fri 10.00–14.00, 17.00–22.00, Sun 17.00–23.00; €2.40 per hour.

Pharmacy There are plenty of pharmacies scattered around. Amongst others you'll find one in the Plaza del Adelantado, on Calle Heraclio Sánchez, on Calle 6 de Diciembre and various on Calle la Carrera.

Police The Policía Local is on Calle Consistorio, the Policía Nacional on Calle el Agua and the Guardia Civil on Camino San Lázaro (west of the city centre).

Post office Calle Santo Domingo, open Mon–Fri 08.30–20.30, Sat 09.30–14.00.

Shopping The market, in the Plaza del Adelantado, is open every day 07.00–14.00; it's mainly a food market and not a bad place to pick up a jar of *mojo* to take home. There are a couple of handicrafts shops, though Atlántida Artensanía is perhaps the best, with work from across the islands. It's on Calle San Agustín, open Mon–Fri 09.30–13.30, 17.00–20.30, Sat 10.00–14.00.

Tourist information There is an information kiosk in Plaza del Adelantado, open Mon–Sat 08.00–20.00.

What to see and do
Museo de Historia de Tenerife
Calle San Agustín.

Like all of Tenerife's museums, this is a well laid out and interesting place, explaining the island's rocky history and how society has developed since the conquest. Staff are very friendly and knowledgeable. Open Tue–Sun 09.00–20.00; entrance is €3, half price for children, students or those with a *bonobus* ticket.

Museo de la Ciencia y el Cosmos
Avenida de los Menceys, about a kilometre out of the city centre.

The idea for the museum was based on a quote from Albert Einstein: 'Most of the fundamental ideas of science are essentially simple and, generally, can be expressed in language understandable by everybody.' The bumf describes it as 'a science fairground' and it seems to have achieved its aim of making science fun with its 100 interactive experiments. There is also a planetarium and a 'cosmic tourism' room, where you can take a virtual trip around the solar system. You have to specify that you want to visit the planetarium and cosmic tourism at the main desk. They will give you a time when you should be waiting at the entrance to the attraction. If you don't have a time written on the back of your ticket, you won't be allowed to enter. Expect to wait a while as they are very popular, especially on Sundays. Open Tue–Sat 09.00–19.00; €3 for adults, €1.50 for children, students or with a *bonobus*. Free on Sundays.

Learn Spanish
The university runs various courses in Spanish for foreigners. A four-month, 75-hour course costs €270; a one-month (56 hours) summer course costs €200 and the interesting 'International Course of Spanish Language and Culture' is a 260-hour course spread over three months and costing €1,111. It includes excursions, museum visits, dance classes, cinema and of course language classes. For further information or to enrol visit www.feu.ull.es/sidiomas; email: sidiomas@ull.es; tel: 922 31 92 00; fax: 922 31 92 42.

PARQUE RURAL DE ANAGA
Tenerife's northeasternmost point is an enchanting area encompassing deep ravines, striking rock formations, a misty laurel forest and a few farming hamlets scattered here and there near the inaccessible beaches. It covers 14,418 hectares (8% of the island's surface) and was declared a rural park in 1994. It's one of the oldest regions of the island and is home to over 100 species of endemic flora and fauna (many of them exclusive to the park). As well as an abundance of birds and invertebrates you might be lucky enough to spot a few reptiles and bats or just enjoy Tenerife's largest laurel forest. The area has been inhabited since Guanche times and these days the locals make their living from agriculture, fishing and pastoral farming. It's a fine place to experience some old Tinerfeño traditions and culture, kept alive due to an isolated location and poor communications. There's even a school where you can learn the ancient art/sport *juego del palo* and you'll also

find places to see displays of the *salto del pastor*. (This is a display sport, in which participants descend ravines with the aid of a long stick. See box on page 53.) Before you explore the park you should call in to the visitor centre at Cruz del Carmen, open every day 09.00–16.00.

Getting there

To get to the hostel from La Laguna take bus 77, leaving at 10.15 and 17.00 and returning at 11.30 and 19.00. The bus will drop you off next to a hideous mint-green building, from where you'll need to walk a further five minutes along the road to reach the *albergue*. Other lines into the park from La Laguna are numbers 75 and 76. From Santa Cruz, line 247 will take you to the hostel, leaving the capital at 05.00, 15.00 and 18.00. Number 246 goes to Taganana and Almáciga.

Where to stay

Albergue Montes de Anaga El Bailadero; tel: 922 82 20 56; fax: 922 31 01 93; email: info@idecogestion.net; www.alberguestenerife.net. A *Cabildo*-run hostel aimed at those wanting to hike or bike in Anaga. It has dorm-style accommodation, though some rooms have as few as 4 beds. There's a kitchen and a TV area and the staff have an excellent knowledge of the park. €12 per person.

What to see and do
Hiking
Casa Forestal–Las Vueltas de Anaga–Taganana
Distance: 4km; time: 2 hours; difficulty: 2

This is a classic route; one of the *caminos reales* that was once the only way to get from Taganana to the mountain top and on to the capital. The walk starts behind the Casa Forestal, also a good source of information about the park. The start of the path is signposted and it's impossible to get lost. For the first five minutes you walk up to an excavated cave, from where you should take a path to the left and keep following the winding path down into the valley below. Some believe the path has as many bends as the year has days, which is perhaps an exaggeration, but who's counting? Eventually you'll emerge from the dense vegetation to a splendid view of the coast. You'll also be able to see the hamlet of Taganana. Follow the path through the terraced fields until you reach a road, turn left and then look for a steep cobbled road on your right that takes you into the Portugal *barrio*. The walk ends in Taganana, where you can catch a bus to return to the top or to get to Santa Cruz.

Zona Recreativa La Ensillada–Roque de Anambro–Cabezo del Tejo–Zona Recreativa La Ensillada
Distance: 8km; time: 2¹/₂ hours; difficulty: 2

This is a must-do walk if you are in the Anaga area. It takes you through Tenerife's finest example of laurel forest and affords splendid views of the coast. You can park at the recreation area (you can also camp here, tel: 922 23 91 99) or catch bus number 247 from Santa Cruz. From the car park (such as it is), take a wide path that leads you straight into the dense vegetation. Ignore a path off to the right which you'll see after about 20 minutes. The path is easy to follow and after a little less than an hour you'll reach Roque Anambro, the remains of a volcanic chimney left exposed to erosion for millions of years. Another half an hour's walking will take you to the lookout point at Cabezo del Tejo; not a bad place to stop for lunch. A forest track, wide enough for a car, leads back through the lower part of the forest. After about 45 minutes you'll reach the road, where you need to head up a path on your right. Quarter of an hour later, you'll be almost back where you started; turn left at the fork and head back down to the car park. If you are starting the walk from the *albergue*, you need to walk 3km along the road (in the opposite direction to El Bailadero) and add on an extra two hours overall. Bring wet-weather gear as the forest is usually enveloped in cloud if it isn't raining.

TAGANANA

If you're only going to visit one village in Anaga, it should be Taganana, a charming place with small houses and cobbled streets. Some rave about the local wine, though I found it to be a potent brew; perhaps it's an acquired taste. In the village shop you can find the famous blackberry wine, said to have medicinal properties and costing a whopping €20 per bottle. There's a restaurant in the village serving Canarian dishes like goat, rabbit, *potaje*, and fresh fish, and you should also have a mosey around the 17th-century Santa Catalina Chapel. If you're feeling particularly energetic you could attempt to walk up to the Casa Forestral, along the Vueltas de Taganana *camino real* (see *Hiking* in the Parque Rural de Anaga section), though this walk is easier and more pleasant in reverse. Nearby is Almáciga, a farming village with a small pebble beach. Bus 246 is the only one that serves these hamlets, leaving Santa Cruz every two to three hours until the evening.

SAN ANDRÉS

This fishing village is 7.5km from Santa Cruz and is home to the city's beach, Las Teresitas. The beach was created in 1975 with four million sacks of sand brought over from the Sahara and at the time it was the largest manmade beach in the world. A breakwater stops the sand from escaping and keeps the waves back, meaning it's generally safe for swimming but the water gets a bit grubby. San Andrés is a good place to eat fish, with plenty of small restaurants to choose from. You can also see the ruins of the San Andrés Castle, built in 1706 and damaged several times by floods. There are plenty of buses running between San Andrés and the capital.

BAJAMAR

This is La Laguna's summer playground, with much of the town taken up by city dwellers' weekend or summer places. There is also a German population who are mainly residents rather than tourists. It's a quiet place with not a lot to offer other than some 'natural' swimming pools. Really, there are much nicer places on the coast.

Getting there

Bus 105 leaves Santa Cruz every half an hour, passing through La Laguna and Bajamar on its way to Punta de Hidalgo.

Where to stay

Hotel Delfín Av El Sol 39; tel: 922 54 02 00; email: hoteldelfin@thsl.es. All rooms are large and bright and have either a sea view or views of the Anaga mountains. Staff are very friendly. Single €31; double €46, with breakfast. Discounts for longer stays.
Hotel Neptuno Ctra General; tel: 922 54 25 62; fax: 922 15 04 02. A pretty grotty place whose corridors might well remind you of *The Shining*. Rooms could stand a lick of paint and there is a positively anti-British attitude. Single €18; double €24.

Where to eat

Oasis Tasca Calle Gran Poder. Has all the usual choices and some German specials.

Restaurante Calabacín Behind the pools. Obviously fish and seafood feature highly on this and every menu in this area but at least this place has something to offer vegetarians.
Restaurante Casa Lourdes A good tapas menu and very reasonable prices and fresh whole fish. They also do *arepas* and other snacks.
Restaurante Los Geranios Next door to Restaurante Calabacín. Offers a bit of everything – fish, meat, seafood, pizza and a tempting dessert menu.
Restaurante Playa Casa Pepe A tapas bar with a local feel, right on the seafront.

Practicalities
Banks Both banks are on the main road from Tejina. Caja Canarias, open Mon–Fri 08.30–14.00, Thu 17.00–19.30; BBVA, open Mon–Fri 08.30–14.15, Sat 08.30–13.00.
Health The closest Health Centres are in Tejina and Punta del Hidalgo, though there is a Red Cross point by the swimming pools.
Pharmacy Next to the post office.
Police In Tejina.
Post office On the main road from Tejina, open Mon–Fri 08.30–14.30, Sat 09.30–13.00.
Shopping There is a supermarket on Calle La Luna, open Mon–Fri 08.00–13.00, 17.00–20.00, Sat 08.00–14.00.
Tourist information There's an office next to the Ermita del Gran Poder de Dios, open Mon, Wed, Fri 09.00–17.00, Tue, Thu 09.00–14.00. There are also plans to open a kiosk next to the swimming pools.

What to see and do
There are a couple of churches in the town but none of them are too spectacular and there is no historical quarter. Other than swimming in the nearly natural pools you'll be struggling to find anything to keep yourself occupied, although it's quite a convenient place to stay if you want to explore Anaga.

PUNTA DE HIDALGO
There's not much going on in Punta de Hidalgo but it's a reasonable place to relax for a couple of days if the weather holds up. There's no historical centre: the church was built in 1946 with the help of the locals who brought materials from surrounding areas. It's so new it actually looks trendy! The same can be said for the 20th-century lighthouse, a funky change from the typical Canarian lookout point.

Getting there
Bus 105 leaves the capital every hour and passes through La Laguna and Bajamar before reaching Punta de Hidalgo.

Where to stay
Apartamentos Altagay Tel: 922 15 62 37. Great location on the seafront but a seriously ugly building. Apartments are comfy but nothing special. Apartment for 2 people €35 per night, with a minimum stay of 3 nights.
Apartamentos Oceano Tel: 922 15 60 00; fax: 922 15 63 52. Expect a cool welcome, especially if you plan to stay only a couple of days; they prefer guests who stay a few weeks, if not months. Apartments are large and homely and all have sea views. Management reminiscent of *Fawlty Towers*. Studio (1 person) €85; apartment (2 people) €140 per night, including breakfast.
Atlantis Park Urb Tesesinte; tel: 922 15 64 11; fax: 922 15 61 89; email: atlapark@step.es; www.atlantis-park.com. In a very quiet area but still close to the sea. Service is friendly and the apartments are large and bright. Brush up on your German. Apartment for 2 people €70 including breakfast.

Where to eat

La Caseta On the seafront. Has a wonderfully translated menu, which includes 'loobster cocktail', 'eggs of fishes', 'advocat whit shrips' and 'troubled egg'.

Restaurante Altagay Next to the apartments of the same name. They do a good fish and seafood mixed grill and some tasty pasta dishes.

Restaurante Casa Sánchez Near the post office. Their speciality is rabbit, though they also have a tasty line in fish and seafood. Some dishes need to be booked a day before so you might want to look at the menu in advance.

Restaurante Columbus Playa A bit further around the *paseo*. Well known for their paella.

Practicalities

Banks Caja Canarias, on the main road, open Mon–Fri 08.30–14.00, Thu 17.00–19.30.

Health The Health Centre is on the main road from Bajamar.

Pharmacy Next to Caja Canarias.

Police In Tejina.

Post office On the main road, near the church, open Mon–Fri 08.30–11.00, Sat 09.00–11.00.

Shopping There are a couple of supermarkets on the main road from Bajamar.

What to see and do
Piscina Natural El Arensico

Swimming in the sea around here isn't recommended, so a dip in the pools will be welcome though it sometimes gets a bit rough even in there.

TACORONTE

The old quarter of Tacoronte is a delight and this has been recognised by the tourist information office who operate guided walks in the municipality. There are three routes to choose from: a walk around the old town, a coastal stroll, or a hike through the nearby Bosque de Agua García (cloud forest). The walks are free and leave on weekdays from 09.00–14.00. You must call in advance to book a place: 922 57 00 15. The tourist information office is on the main road from Tejina where it meets the Santa Cruz–Guía de Isora road; open Mon–Fri 09.00–14.00. The **Museo de Antropología** is on the main road from Tacoronte to Valle de Guerra. It's devoted to popular Canarian culture and houses temporary exhibitions. It closes for short periods when there is no exhibition. Tue–Sun 09.00–19.00; €3 for adults, half price for children, students and those with a valid *bonobus* ticket.

Casa del Vino La Baranda

This museum, which is on a 17th-century estate, is a splendid place to spend a few hours. After looking around the building, the art display and the small but interesting museum on the history of winemaking on the island, you get to the fun part – tasting the wines. It's the only place on the island where you can sample wines from all five of Tenerife's *Denominaciones de Origen* and they also have cheeses and dried fruits on offer. You pay per glass or half glass and of course can buy the wines after. The tasting menu changes every 15 days. Expect to pay about €1 per glass; entrance to the museum is free. Open Tue–Sat 10.00–22.00, Sun 11.00–18.00. There is also a bar and restaurant. The bar has a huge terrace with spectacular views. In summer classical concerts are staged in the courtyard. Highly recommended. It's just off the TF5; take the exit for El Sauzal.

LA OROTAVA

The Guanches knew it as Menceyato de Taoro and the Villa de la Orotava was created in the 16th century when the aristocrats were dishing out land, post conquest. It became the island's second city in the 17th century and its harbour saw plenty of traffic in the 18th century as trade with Britain and Latin America increased. These days the harbour is a bustling tourist resort (Puerto de la Cruz) and La Orotava has one of Tenerife's finest historical quarters, along with La Laguna. On a clear day Mount Teide provides a marvellous backdrop.

Getting there
There is no shortage of buses from Santa Cruz, La Laguna or Puerto de la Cruz. Bus number 348 passes through on its way to the Teide National Park, though you'll never get a seat.

Where to stay
Mid-range
Hotel Alhambra Calle Nicandro Gonzalez Borges 19; tel/fax: 922 32 34 33; email: hotel@alhambra-teneriffa.com; www.alhambra-teneriffa.com. Built in the 18th century as a 'gentleman's residence' and now converted into a 5-bedroom hotel with Arabic décor. Also has heated outdoor pool, whirlpool and sauna. Single €66; double €80.
Hotel Rural Orotava Calle Carrera 17; tel: 922 32 27 93; fax: 922 32 27 25; www.hotelruralorotava.com. Surprisingly well-priced for such a nice hotel. The rooms are set around a patio and are decorated to be in keeping with the style of the 16th-century building. Single €45; double €65, including breakfast.
Hotel Victoria Calle Hermano Apolinar 8; tel: 922 33 16 83; fax: 922 32 05 19; email: hotel.victoria@teneriffa.com; http://victoria.teneriffa.com. The décor is a little over the top but it's a lovely place to stay. Has an interior patio and rooftop sun terrace. Single €70; double €90.

Budget
Pensión Silene Calle Tomás Zerolo 9; tel/fax: 922 33 01 99. Has large and clean if a little chintzy rooms with huge terraces. All have private bathrooms. Singles €28; doubles €43 or €24/36 without terrace. Breakfast is available for €1 extra.

Where to eat
Bar Restaurante La Duquesa Plaza Casañas, near the Iglesia de la Concepción. It's a bit like a canteen with its plastic tablecloths and staff dressed like school dinner-ladies but the food is good and cheap and the building is lovely.
Los Jardines Calle Sabino Berthelot Augier. If you have a hankering for something sweet, this is your place; they have an amazing selection of cakes, biscuits and other sweet things.
Restaurante Sabor Canario Part of the Hotel Rural Orotava. La Orotava's best place to eat, with a superb choice of traditional Canarian dishes.
Tasca El Porchito Calle Sabino Berthelot Augier. Reasonable tapas menu and tables outside, albeit on a busy road.
Tasca Il Vesuvio Calle Sabino Berthelot Augier. A decent choice of pizza and pasta and some tasty fish and meat dishes too.

Practicalities
Banks Caja Canarias, Av José Antonio, open Mon–Fri 08.30–14.00, Thu 17.00–19.30; BBVA, Plaza de la Constitución, open Mon–Fri 08.30–14.15, Sat 08.30–13.00; Banca March, Calle Calvario, open Mon–Fri 08.30–14.00, Sat 08.30–13.00.
Health The Health Centre is on Calle San Isidro, near the bus station.
Internet Ciber Interbit, Calle Benitez de Lugo, open Mon–Sat 10.00–14.00, Sun 17.00–22.00; €2 per hour.
Pharmacy On Av José Antonio and in Plaza Casañas.

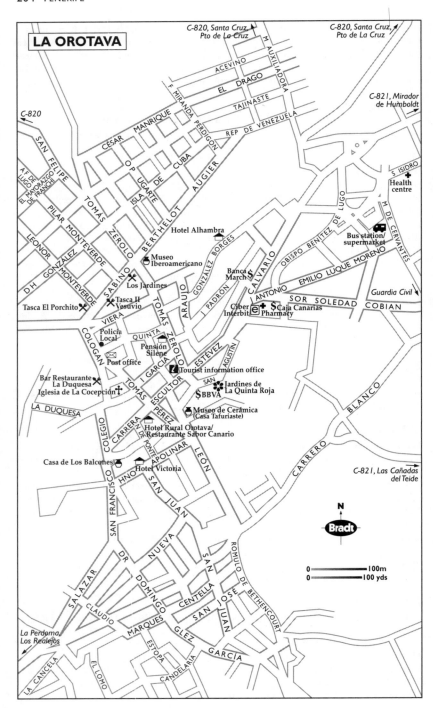

Police The Policía Local is on Calle Cólogan and the Guardia Civil on Calle Carrero Blanco.
Post office In Plaza Casañas, open Mon–Fri 08.30–14.30, Sat 09.30–13.00.
Shopping There's a shopping centre in the same building as the bus station. There is also a large supermarket here, open Mon–Fri 09.00–21.00, Sat 09.00–20.30. La Orotava is a good place to do a bit of craft shopping; the best choice is at Casa de los Balcones on Calle Colegio.
Tourist information On Calle Carrera de Escultor Estévez, open Mon–Fri 08.30–18.00.

What to see and do
Museo de Cerámica Casa Tafuriaste
Calle León.
This museum houses almost a thousand pieces of Spanish pottery and you can also watch the craftsmen at work. There is a large shop selling ceramics and other souvenirs. Open Mon–Sat 10.00–18.00, Sun 10.00–14.00; entrance €2.

Museo Iberoamericano
Calle Tomás Zerolo.
Quite a small museum but with a decent selection of Spanish and Latin American pottery, textiles and religious artefacts. It's based in the convent of the Santo Domingo Church. Open Mon–Fri 09.30–18.00, Sat 09.30–14.00; entrance €2.10.

Casa de los Balcones
Calle San Francisco.
As well as the large handicrafts shop, Casa de los Balcones has a small museum dedicated to 17th-century life on the island. Open Mon–Sat 08.30–18.30, Sun 08.30–12.30; entrance €1.50.

Jardines Marquesado de la Quinta Roja
Calle San Agustín.
This park is certainly worth a wander. There are 11,600m² of gardens, fountains and pathways to explore and it isn't a bad place for a picnic. Open every day 09.00–18.00.

Pueblo Chico
This is one of the few theme parks on the island that actually has a Canarian connection. It's basically a miniature version of the islands (though the majority of it is based on Tenerife) showing the commerce, history, tourism and nature of the islands and the aim is that you get an inkling of what you'd like to visit in person later. A nice idea, but the €11 entrance fee is a bit steep and you might well leave a little disappointed. It does have pleasant gardens with lots of endemic plants. Open 09.00–19.00 every day. The park is just off the TF5, on the way to La Orotava.

PUERTO DE LA CRUZ
This was once La Orotava's bustling harbour, but tourism arrived in a small way in the 18th century and Puerto de la Cruz has never looked back. It was Tenerife's main resort until the 1970s and isn't a bad example of mass tourism gone right. Puerto, as it is known, attracts a different class of tourist than its southern counterparts and you can still find historical buildings and a few tree-lined squares. Of course, it's not the most 'authentic' town on the island, but there are reasons to stay here.

Getting there
Bus 309 leaves North Airport every hour heading for Puerto or you can get a taxi for €25. From the capital the best route is the 103 non-stop service, though there

are other lines connecting the two cities which stop everywhere along the way. From South Airport you can catch the 340 if you're lucky; it runs at 09.45, 14.00, 20.00 and 23.30. Puerto is also connected to Playa de las Américas by the 343 with two buses in the morning and two in the afternoon.

Where to stay
Puerto de la Cruz has a huge number of hotels and apartments and what follows is a minute proportion of what is on offer.

Upmarket
Hotel Botánico Av Richard J Yeoward 1; tel: 922 38 14 00; fax: 922 38 15 04; email: hotelbotanico@hotelbotanico.com; www.hotelbotanico.com. One of Puerto's 2 5-star hotels and unquestionably the fanciest place to stay. The hotel has a full health complex, 4 restaurants offering Spanish, Canarian, Italian and Thai cuisine and everything you would expect from a hotel of this standard. Prices vary greatly from €220 for a single;

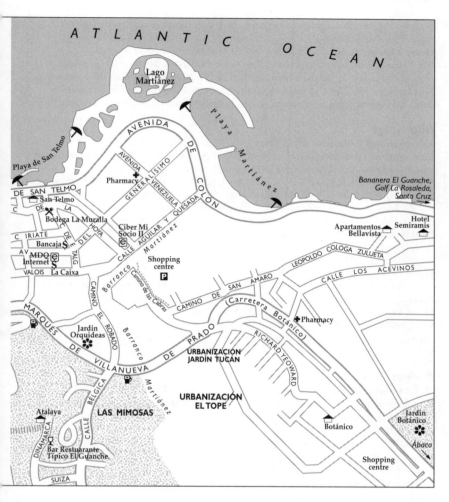

€330 double; up to €2,000 per night for the Royal Suite. Definitely one for special occasions.

Hotel Florida Tenerife Av Blas Pérez González 11; tel: 922 37 07 70; fax: 922 37 07 79; email: Puerto@floridatenerife.com; www.floridatenerife.com. Located in perhaps the least attractive part of town, although it's only 100m from Playa Jardín. Rooms have small balconies, some with views of both Teide and the sea. There are 2 pools, a restaurant and snack bar and a variety of games such as mini-golf, bowls and giant chess. Single €80; double €120.

Hotel Monopol Calle Quintana 15; tel: 922 38 46 11; fax: 922 37 03 10; email: monopol@interbook.net; www.hotelmonopoltenerife.com. One of the best locations in town, in the historic quarter next to the church. It's a lovely building and while the rooms are nothing spectacular they have all you need. Also has a typical Canarian patio. Single €60; double €90, with breakfast.

Hotel Semiramis Calle Leopoldo Cólogan Zulueta 12, Urb La Paz; tel: 922 37 32 00; fax: 922 37 31 93; email: semiramis@besthotels.es. The other 5-star place in town, though with a much more relaxed atmosphere. Semiramis is not really in the same league as Hotel

Botánico but then this is reflected in the prices. It does have top-rate views of the sea. Single €80; double €100.

Hotel Tigaiga Parque Taoro 28; tel: 922 38 35 00; fax: 922 38 40 55; email: info@tigaiga.com; www.tigaiga.com. This 4-star family-run hotel is in a quiet area, very close to the casino. It has subtropical gardens and more palm trees than the hotel has beds (apparently). There's a folklore show every Sunday morning which is tastefully done and the hotel also has demonstrations of Lucha Canaria. Single €100; double €150.

Mid-range

Apartamentos Bellavista Urb La Paz; tel: 922 38 31 11; fax: 922 38 35 18; email: info@apartamentosbellavista.com; www.apartamentosbellavista.com. Studio apartments with a small kitchen and all with sea view. €64 for an apartment sleeping 2 people.

Apartamentos Park Plaza Calle José Arroyo 4; tel: 922 38 41 12; fax: 922 37 13 38; email: parkplaza@teleline.es; www.7islas.net/parkplaza. The majority of apartments have balcony but no views. Pretty good value for somewhere so central. If you only stay one night it's €42 (for 2 people), but longer stays are €30 per night, with breakfast available for €4 extra.

Aparthotel Girasol Calle Dr Ingram; tel: 922 38 42 51; fax: 922 37 12 13; email: girasoltenerife@infonegocio.com. Large studio apartments with a kitchenette. The complex also has a pool, TV room and buffet-style restaurant. Single €30; double €40.

Hotel Atalaya Calle Dinamarca 3; tel: 922 37 60 60; fax: 922 38 70 46; email: info@hotelatalaya.com; www.hotelatalaya.com. In the quiet part of town near the casino. It has huge gardens and marvellous views. Single €55; double €80, including breakfast.

Hotel San Telmo Paseo San Telmo 18; tel: 922 38 58 53; fax: 922 38 59 91; www.hotelsantelmo.com. Slightly dated rooms but with good views. Has a swimming pool and boasts 'female kitchen staff'. What more could you ask? Single €35; double €65, with breakfast.

Budget

Hotel Puerto Azul Calle del Lomo 24; tel/fax: 922 38 32 13; email: phazul@step.es; www.puertoazul.de. Basic but good value; double rooms have balconies and there's a rooftop terrace for all to use. Single €28; double €38, including breakfast. Prices drop the longer you stay.

Hotel Régulo Calle San Felipe 6; tel: 922 38 61 61; fax: 922 37 04 20. Very nice rooms considering the prices; all have bathroom and it's close to the main square. Single €22; double €28.

Pensión Los Geranios Calle del Lomo 14; tel: 922 38 19 01; fax: 922 38 28 10. Bright, clean rooms, all with private bathroom. Single/double €24.

Pensión Rosa Mary Calle San Felipe 14; tel: 922 38 32 53. In a quiet area near the square; rooms are clean if not very spectacular and also have private bathroom. There's a TV room available. Single €18; double €30 but prices are negotiable.

Where to eat

Choosing somewhere to eat out in Puerto de la Cruz can be difficult, as the majority of restaurants offer the same thing. There is an abundance of 'typical English pubs' offering pie and chips and Sunday roasts, just as there are many 'international' restaurants offering a little bit of everything and doing it all badly.

Bar Restaurante Típico El Guanche In the quiet area opposite the Atalaya Hotel, this place gives you a good idea of Canarian cuisine and has a nice terrace

Bodega La Muralla Calle de la Hoya, near the Hotel San Telmo. A little tapas bar with a good selection; great as long as you don't mind service without a smile!

Casa Miranda Calle Santo Domingo; tel: 922 37 38 71. Good wine and ham and a few interesting dishes inspired by island specials. The restaurant is in a typical 18th-century Canarian house.

Cha' Paula Calle Blanco. Perhaps as typically Canarian as you can get without becoming tacky. They have all the local specialities such as *gofio*, goat, rabbit, *ropa vieja* and some very fattening desserts.

Manú Calle Agustín de Bethencourt. Delightful vegetarian restaurant boasting all natural ingredients, this place stands out in the ocean of international restaurants surrounding it.

La Trainera Calle San Juan; tel: 922 37 00 41. Good Canarian cuisine and some Spanish specials. Outstanding seafood and goat's cheese. Main meals start at €10.

Régulo Calle Pérez Zamora; tel: 922 38 45 06. Excellent fish dishes and out of the ordinary desserts. Has an interior patio, typical of Canarian architecture.

Nightlife

There are plenty of British pubs, karaoke bars and late, late discos in the area near Lago Martiánez and a smattering behind Playa Jardín. If you want to rub shoulders with the locals, stick to the streets around the Plaza del Charco.

Azúcar Calle Iriarte. Cuban bar serving up the best in Caribbean cocktails and salsa music. Open until 02.00.

Colors Café Plaza del Charco. Stunning décor, good cocktails and good Brazilian and African rhythms. Open until 02.00.

Elements Cocktail Bar Plaza del Charco. Another place with an extensive cocktail menu and a good location, excellent for people-watching. Open until 03.00.

Casino Taoro Even if you don't want to gamble, there's still live music, a nightly dance show and a pricey restaurant. Open 21.00–03.00; entrance €3, over 18s only.

Practicalities

Banks Banco Popular, Plaza del Charco, open Mon–Fri 08.30–14.00, Sat 08.30–13.00; Banca March next door has the same opening hours; Santander Central Hispano, Calle San Juan, open Mon–Fri 08.30–14.00, Sat 08.30–13.00; Caja Canarias, Calle San Juan, open Mon–Fri 08.30–14.00, Thu 17.00–19.30; Bancaja, Av del Generalísimo, open Mon–Fri 08.30–14.30; La Caixa, Calle de Valois, open Mon–Fri 08.15–14.00, Thu 16.30–19.45.

Health There are lots of private health clinics around where the staff probably speak either English or German. The public Health Centre is on Calle del Pozo.

Internet Ciber Mi Socio II, Calle Obispo Perez Caceres, open 09.00–02.00 every day; €3 per hour. MDQ Internet, Av del Generalísimo, open Mon–Thu 09.30–24.00, Fri–Sat 09.30 –01.30, Sun 11.00–00.00; €2 per hour.

Pharmacy There are numerous pharmacies scattered around Villanueva (near the botanical garden) and on Calle del Pozo, near the bus station.

Police The Policía Nacional is on Av de José del Campo; the Guardia Civil is on Carretera de Las Arenas, near the market. The Policía Local is in the Town Hall.

Post office Opposite the bus station; open Mon–Fri 08.30–14.30, Sat 09.30–13.00.

Shopping There's no shortage of supermarkets and tacky souvenir shops.

Tourist information The somewhat useless information office is in Plaza de Europa, near the Town Hall; open Mon–Fri 09.00–20.00, Sat 09.00–13.00.

What to see and do
Castillo de San Felipe

Built in the 17th century, this was the port's citadel, meant to ward off pirate attacks, or at least give a decent view of potential looters before they arrived. In its restored state it overlooks the beach and houses temporary art exhibitions. Contact the tourist information office for details of current exhibitions or just wander past to see if it's open. When there's an exhibition, opening times are Mon–Fri 09.00–13.00, 17.00–21.00, Sat–Sun 10.00–13.00. Entrance is usually free.

Museo Arqueológico
Calle del Lomo.
The museum is a bit of a mishmash but basically looks at the history and traditions of the archipelago and Tenerife in particular. Amongst other things, you can see aboriginal ceramics, 17th-century maps, weapons and mummified Guanche remains. Open Tue–Sat 10.00–13.00, 17.00–21.00, Sun 10.00–13.00; entrance is €3 (free on Thursdays).

Kayaking
Tenerife Kayak Tel: 922 337 065. Two-hour excursions to nearby beaches for €33; 1-hour beginners' courses for €18 and kayak hire for €5 per half-hour or €20 for a full day.

Golf
If you want to practise your swing, there's a nine-hole pitch 'n' putt golf course just outside Puerto, on the road that takes you to junction 32 of the TF5. It also has a driving range and putting green and is ideal for beginners. It costs €17 to play nine holes and an extra €5 to rent clubs and balls.

Jardín Botánico
Although it's not as complete as the Jardín Botánico in Gran Canaria, you'll certainly get a good idea of Canarian flora here. It was created in 1788 as a place to study American and Asian plantlife and currently showcases over 200 species of plants, both native to the islands and imported. Open daily 09.00–18.00; entrance €3, free for under 14s. It's in the southern part of Puerto, on the way to the TF5.

Swimming
The beaches in Puerto are far from spectacular and the sea is rough. Perhaps that's why many prefer to use the **Lago Martiánez**, a César Manrique creation. It consists of five islands surrounded by numerous salt-water pools and lush gardens. Open daily 09.30–17.00; €3.30 for adults, €1.10 for kids. **Playa Martiánez** is a black-sand beach which gets very crowded. It's a bit generous calling **Playa San Telmo** a beach at all, since it's really a concrete platform next to the sea. **Playa Jardín** is the largest beach but the sea is very rough and most swimmers emerge from the water sporting cuts and scrapes from being dragged along the stony seabed.

Bananera El Guanche
If ever there was anything you wanted to know about bananas, you'll find the answer here. There's also a large tropical garden. Open 09.00–18.00 every day. Entrance €6.75, €3.40 for children. There is a free bus to the park, leaving Puerto de la Cruz every 30 minutes; if you have your own wheels, take the Avenida de Colón in the direction of Santa Cruz.

Loro Parque
It's difficult to ignore the presence of Loro Parque, which calls itself *El 'must' de Canarias* and adorns every bin, bus, bench and hotel room in Puerto de la Cruz. Essentially it's just a zoo, though even the most adamant zoo haters admit that it's well organised and that the animals are properly cared for. It claims to have the

largest collection of parrots in the world and shows them off at regular intervals in a bizarre spectacle, which sees them riding bikes and jumping through hoops. This aside, it's not a bad day out, albeit a pricey one. Open daily 08.30–18.45; €21 for adults and €10.50 for under 12s. It's a little south of the town, on the road towards Las Arenas.

PARQUE NACIONAL DEL TEIDE

Teide was formed around 180,000 years ago but sits on the site of a much older volcano, which some experts estimate was 6,000m high. The remains of the old volcano can be seen in the 17km amphitheatre of Las Cañadas. While the origins of this massive horseshoe-shaped depression are unclear, it is generally agreed that the flanks of the ancient volcano broke off and slid towards the sea, leaving the huge *caldera* and the Icod-La Guancha Valley. Eruptions lasting several decades in the Middle Ages gave Teide its current height of 3,718m and although there haven't been any eruptions in the area since 1798, the mountain is far from extinct. Important archaeological finds have been uncovered in the park, suggesting that the Guanches took their flocks up to Las Cañadas in the summer for grazing. It's unlikely that they ever got too close, though, since they feared the volcano, believing it to be hell.

These days Teide is the Canary Islands' top tourist attraction and Spain's favourite national park, with over four million visitors a year. There are two visitor centres in the park, each with a different focus. **El Portillo**, which is in the northeast of the park, concentrates on the formation of Teide and the flora and fauna of the park. There is an amusing and informative video shown in various languages that comes highly recommended. There is also a small botanical garden, showcasing the Canarian alpine plants. The second centre, **Cañada Blanca**, looks at the relationship between mountain and man. Both are open every day from 09.00–16.00.

Getting there

There is a disgraceful lack of buses to the park, with just one each day leaving from Playa de las Américas and another from Puerto de la Cruz at 09.15. The return buses leave the visitor centre at 16.00. There are three possible approaches if you're coming by car: the TF21 from Arona if you're coming from the south, TF21 from La Orotava or the TF24 from La Laguna. The last is the least used and the most beautiful.

Where to stay

Parador Nacional del Turismo Tel: 922 37 48 41; fax: 922 38 23 52; email: canadas@parador.es; www.parador.es. If you're going to splash out anywhere in Tenerife, it might as well be at 2,200m in 4-star luxury. Views from hotel rooms don't get much better than this, especially if you visit when Teide is snow-capped. Single €80; double €100.
Refugio de Altavista For serious hikers only. The refuge is 3,270m above sea level and a 5-hour walk from El Portillo, though climbing to it is not as difficult as arranging a stay in it! You have to call 922 23 98 11 to make a reservation and will be given a bank account number. Once you've paid at a bank, you need to fax proof of payment to 922 23 98 12. And don't forget to take your receipt to the refuge with you or you could end up paying again. Beds are dormitory style and cost €12 per person; don't expect clean sheets or hot water. There is a toilet and a gas burner where you can heat food. Be prepared for the cold and a possible lack of water. You can stay only one night, though why you'd want to stay longer is a mystery. It's often closed in winter.
Camping There are no campsites in the park. The closest is San Juan de la Rambla, which

is on the road from La Orotava. There are no facilities and it's almost 2,000m above sea level, meaning that you'll need some warm gear to sleep in. It's free to stay there but you need a permit (see page 185).

Where to eat
There are a few overpriced and very touristy restaurants about a kilometre from the El Portillo visitor centre.

What to see and do
Hiking
Without doubt the best way to get to know Teide is on foot and there are numerous well-marked paths in the national park enabling you to do so. In total there are ten hikes of varying lengths and levels. Staff in the two visitor centres are helpful and will be able to advise on suitable routes. You can also take part in an interesting guided walk, free of charge. Contact the park office for details and bookings: 922 29 01 29. Walks leave from the El Portillo visitor centre.

El Portillo–Refugio de Altavista
Distance: 12km; time: 5 hours; difficulty: 3–4
This is one of the favourite walks for avid hikers. It's long, but not too difficult until the final ascent to the refuge. Setting off from behind the visitor centre, follow route number six, which has only a gentle slope. After a couple of hours, change to route seven (it's clearly marked) which is a little tougher and will lead you up to the refuge.

Refugio de Altavista–Pico del Teide
Distance: 3km; time: 2 hours; difficulty: 4–5
Most people who spend the night at the refuge do so in order to climb to the summit the following day. The typical way is to get up when it's still dark and walk to the top in time for sunrise. Don't forget your torch! The walk itself isn't too difficult until you get to La Rambleta, but the altitude, darkness and possible bad weather can impede you somewhat.

Siete Cañadas
Distance: 15km; time: 5 hours; difficulty: 2
This walk is ideal for those who want to see a bit of the park on foot but don't feel up to hiking to the summit. It's a long walk, but all flat, leading you through the stark *malpaís* of Las Cañadas. It starts from El Portillo and ends at the Parador, from where you can later catch the bus. The route is never going to win any awards for the prettiest hike in the islands but it's fascinating and unique.

Cable car
The cable car takes you from the road to La Rambleta at 3,500m above sea level. It takes eight minutes to transport you 1,250m up and costs €10 each way. The cable car doesn't run in bad weather, which includes wind at the top of the mountain, so be prepared for possible disappointment.

Conquering Teide
For conservation reasons only 50 people are allowed at the summit at any one time, which is a good idea, but they could make it easier for you. Unless you plan to be up there before 09.00, you need to make a trip to the Teide office in Santa Cruz

REACHING THE PEAK – IT WASN'T MEANT TO BE

Visible from almost every island, you'll see a lot of Mount Teide during your stay in the Canaries and understandably might want to climb it. The first time I tried to reach the summit the experience turned into a nightmarish combination of poor planning and sheer bad luck. Fooled by the 'eternal spring' climate, I was embarrassingly badly prepared, with no gloves, hat, or even a coat. After a couple of hours' walking, the long trousers and jumpers went on, but an hour later when the rain started I had nothing else to wear. Much to my dismay it soon began to snow and a hellish two hours later I arrived at the Refugio de Altavista sporting a sleeping bag holder as a hat and sweaty socks for gloves. It was with mixed feelings that I awoke the following day to find that heavy snow and strong winds prevented me from reaching the peak. While I was disappointed in not achieving my goal, all I really wanted to do was get back to the road and sup a cup of hot chocolate, preferably laced with something highly alcoholic.

So two years on, fit and with a bag brimming over with waterproofs and winter woollies, I set out again with plans to reach the summit and take some fine photographs of all seven islands from the top. On reaching the freezing cold mountain hut it hadn't started to snow and there wasn't so much as a drop of rain in the air so I went to bed like a child on Christmas Eve, excited to finally be achieving my goal of conquering Spain's highest mountain. Setting off at 05.00 I quickly realised I wasn't as well prepared as I'd thought. For some reason I never thought to pack a torch and found myself clinging to the man in front, gasping to keep up and stepping only where he stepped. After an hour I began to wonder why it wasn't getting any lighter and if I'd make it to the top without being blown off the side of the mountain. As the clouds thickened and I felt the first few drops of rain, my hopes of snapping the perfect picture were fading fast but I soldiered on, determined at least to make it to the summit. In retrospect I wonder why I refused to turn back with the majority, since when we got to the top we could barely see our own feet. Having waited half an hour and realised that the sun was unlikely to make an appearance that day, dejectedly we began the descent. Of course by the time we dragged ourselves down to road level, the peak was clearly visible and there was not a cloud in the sky. Once again I had been beaten by the mighty Teide. I think next time I'll join the rest and take the cable car.

(Calle Emilio Calzadilla 5, open Mon–Fri 09.00–14.00) with a photocopy of your passport, and specify the date and time you'll be reaching the peak. Early risers (those who stay in the refugio and get up to watch the sunrise) don't need a permit. From the cable car it's about 15 minutes' walk up to the summit and it's not an easy walk, especially if it's windy.

ICOD DE LOS VINOS

Icod is one of the place names that survive from pre-Hispanic times, though the 'de los Vinos' part was added in the 16th century in homage to the area's superior wines. While it's a pleasant enough place, there isn't really much to keep you here for more than a few hours. The town's main drawcard is the

Drago Milenario, an excellent example of a dragon tree and probably the world's oldest. Scientists argue about the age of the tree and while locals and tourist boards will tell you it's 2,000–3,000 years old, latest views suggest that the tree is closer to its 800th birthday. You can view it from the square, but if you do want to get up close and personal you have to pay €4, which includes a guided tour of the gardens surrounding it. The park is open every day 09.30–18.30. Near to El Drago and taking advantage of the tourism the tree brings is the **Mariposario del Drago**, a small butterfly zoo. Though it's a pretty place, it really isn't worth the €6.50 entrance fee (€4 for children); open Mon–Sat 09.00–19.00, Sun 09.30–19.00. **Casa Museo Los Cáceres** is a doll and teddy museum and has a few exhibits that are sure to give you nightmares. It's another expensive one at €6 for adults and €2.50 for children, and it seems to have nothing to do with Icod at all. The plaza is a lively place and is dominated by the **Iglesia de San Marcos**, which asks an entry fee of €0.60. Finally, there are several places around town that offer wine tasting and surprisingly don't charge for it (though they do expect you to buy a bottle). The tourist information office is on Calle San Antonio, near the square. It's open Mon–Fri 09.00–17.00.

There is also a decent beach near Icod: **Playa San Marcos**. It's a locals' favourite and one of the finest places to practise potholing, since it boasts the longest volcanic tube in the archipelago at 1,820m. Some hiking companies organise walks through the tube (see *Hiking*, page 186).

GARACHICO
Garachico was founded in 1496 and was the island's premier port in the 16th and 17th centuries. Then in 1706 the Arenas Negras eruption changed its fortunes, destroying a good part of the town. As is so often the case, Garachico managed to find something positive from its misfortune and one of its main attractions are the natural pools created by the 1706 lava flows. Its curious circular layout and deserted cobbled streets make it one of the island's jewels and although it's got a couple of splendid places to stay, it's infamous for its terrible restaurants.

Getting there
Bus 107 leaves Santa Cruz every two hours from 07.15 to 19.15. From Puerto de la Cruz you can catch the 363 which leaves every half-hour.

Where to stay
Upmarket
Casa Ida Calle La Oliva 8, Genovés; tel: 922 13 32 97; email: ida@ruralida.com; www.ruralida.com. This mini complex of gorgeous rural houses is about halfway between Garachico and Icod, in Genovés. The houses are fully equipped and have fabulous views of the coast and Teide. Has extensive gardens and communal terraces. Houses sleep 4 and are €60 per night.
Hotel La Quinta Roja Glorieta de San Francisco; tel: 922 13 33 77; fax: 922 13 33 60; email: hotelquintaroja@quintaroja.com; www.quintaroja.com. Set in a historical building in the town square, it's a great little place with each room differently decorated. Single €85; double €100.
Hotel Rural El Patio Finca Malpaís; El Guincho; tel: 922 13 32 80; fax: 922 83 00 89; email: reservas@hotelpatio.com; www.hotelpatio.com. Just outside Garachico on the way to Icod. Impressive hotel in the middle of a banana plantation; it has a small wine cellar, heated pool and lovely gardens. Single €72; double €90, including breakfast.
Hotel San Roque Calle Esteban de Ponte 32; tel: 922 13 34 35; fax: 922 13 34 06;

DRAGON'S BLOOD

A place shrouded in so much legend and myth needs a worthy emblem, so it's only fitting that the dragon tree (*Dracaena draco*) serves as a symbol of the Canary Islands. Although the tree is found throughout Macronesia, it's most abundant in the Canaries where it prefers precarious locations such as ravines, slopes and cliffs. The legend says that Hercules had to collect three golden apples from the Garden of Hesperides and to do so he had to defeat Landon, the 100-headed dragon. He achieved his task and left the dragon bleeding on the ground. The blood soaked into the earth and on that spot the first dragon tree grew. Many people liken the tree to a dragon, claiming that the tight clusters of leaves clinging to the end of the numerous spiky branches represent Landon's 100 heads.

Throughout the years the dragon tree has certainly proved useful to the islanders. Before the conquest, the Guanches used the sturdy bark to make shields, coffins, pots and musical instruments and the leaves to feed their livestock. However it's the sap that has really been of interest throughout history.

The scarlet sap, known as dragon's blood, was thought to have magical or medicinal properties and the demand for it in medieval times led to the destruction of many trees in the archipelago. It was used to help with anything from haemorrhages and internal bleeding to cleaning teeth and sealing letters. It was even tested as a wood stain, in the belief that Stradivarius applied dragon's blood to his violins.

The dragon tree can grow to a height of 20m and sprouts small off-white flowers and orangey-red fruit, though it doesn't flower often. Putting an age on the tree is difficult and controversial, though many believe that they can live for thousands of years. It's a source of much debate in Icod de los Vinos, where the finest example is to be found. Impartial observers reckon the tree to be no more than 300 years old, though locals insist that it's pushing 3,000. Extracting and selling the sap is no longer allowed, but the trees continue to attract attention, though these days they are more of a tourist attraction than a one-stop pharmacy.

www.hotelsanroque.com. Designer rooms in an 18th-century mansion provide what is, for me, the Canary Islands' finest hotel. There are some lovely touches such as a video recorder and hi-fi in your room. And the jacuzzi in the bedroom isn't bad either! Single €150; double €180; suite €270.

Budget

Pensión Jardín Calle Esteban de Ponte 8; tel: 922 83 02 45. From one extreme to the other; Pensión Jardín has basic rooms with shared bathroom and a reasonable little restaurant. Single €18; double €30.

Where to eat

Garachico has a bit of a reputation for bad restaurants, so it's best to ask around before you sit down.

Asadero Daute Calle Conde de Palmar. A place for meat eaters, offering barbecued meat and good wine at reasonable prices.

Bar Restaurante La Perla Calle Rolo de Armas. Does a *menú del día* for €7.50.

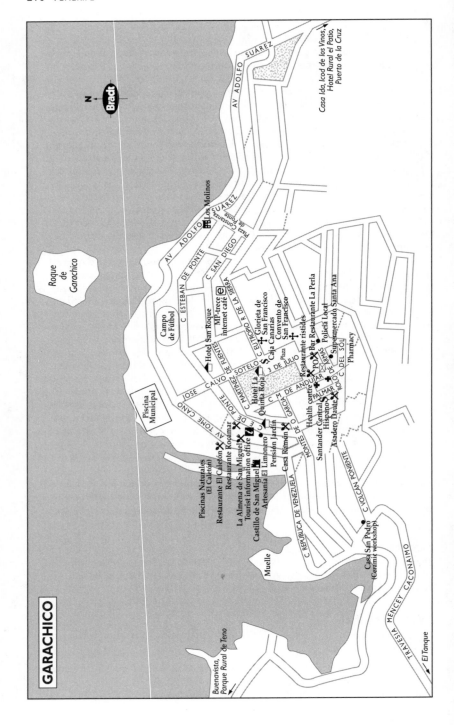

GARACHICO

Casa Ramón Calle Martínez de Fuentes. A limited menu but what they do they do quite well. Serves typical Canarian options, such as *ropa vieja, potaje* and *arroz con leche*.
La Almena de San Miguel and **Restaurante El Caletón** On the seafront. Both specialise in fish and seafood and of course have good views.
Restaurante Aristides Just off the main square. It offers typical Canarian food, with a reasonable choice of fresh fish and seafood.
Restaurante Rocamar Calle Esteban de Ponte. Another place specialising in fish and seafood. It has a nice patio area.

Practicalities

Banks Caja Canarias, in the plaza, open Mon–Fri 08.30–14.00, Thu 17.00–19.30; Santander Central Hispano, Calle Conde de Palmar, open Mon–Fri 08.30–14.00, Sat 08.30–13.00.
Health The Health Centre is on Calle Martín de Andújar, near the plaza.
Internet MP-trece, Calle Eutropio Rodríguez de la Sierra, open every day 09.00–late; €1.50 per hour (€1 on weekends).
Pharmacy Next to the Health Centre.
Police The Policía Local is at the side of the Town Hall.
Post office Opposite the pharmacy, open Mon–Fri 08.30–14.30, Sat 09.30–13.00.
Shopping There is a supermarket on Calle Rolo de Armas. You can buy handicrafts at Artesanía El Limonero, next to the tourist information office. Garachico is also a good place to pick up some pottery; at Casa San Pedro they make pots to order, though it's on the wheel rather than using aboriginal methods. It's on Calle Volcán Poniente.
Tourist information Opposite Pensión Jardín, open Mon–Fri 10.00–14.00, 15.00–18.00, Sat 10.00–15.00.

What to see and do

There are a few historical buildings to visit in Garachico. Starting at the natural pools, you'll see the **Castillo de San Miguel** ahead of you. It's a 16th-century construction, built to ward off pirate attacks. These days it has a rather more humble use: it's a somewhat dull museum devoted to all things nautical (though most of the exhibits are shells and various relics rescued from the sea). It's open every day 10.00–18.00; entrance is €0.60. In the centre of town there's a charming square, lined with magnificent 16th- and 17th-century buildings. The former **Convento de San Francisco** now houses the library, exhibition hall and a small natural history museum, open Mon–Sat 10.00–18.00, Sun 10.00–14.00; entrance €0.60. Heading east of the centre you'll reach **Los Molinos**, two watermills which have been kept in mint condition, open Mon–Fri 10.00–15.00; entrance is free. Garachico's star attraction is the set of natural pools, known as **El Caletón**. These really are as nature intended, unlike many of the so-called natural swimming pools on the other islands. They were formed in the 1706 eruption, so at least something good came from it. This is the perfect place to cool off without risking the unpredictable tides of the north coast. Local youngsters fancy themselves as La Quebrada divers as they leap from the rocks into the sea, though the rocks here are somewhat lower than those in Acapulco!

PARQUE RURAL DE TENO

Arguably the prettiest spot in Tenerife, Teno was declared a natural park in 1987 and was reclassified as a rural park in 1994. The park measures 8,063 hectares and has just a few hamlets dotted here and there, with the total population of the park being 1,400. Situated in the most northwestern section of Tenerife, it offers a similar array of activities as Agana in the northeast: hiking, seeing a bit of rural island-life, or just escaping and chilling out for a few days.

Getting there

This is the least connected area of the island, with just two services penetrating the park from Buenavista. The 355 leaves at 06.15, 09.30, 14.15 and 15.45 and passes through Masca on its way to Valle Santiago. Return buses leave Masca at 06.45, 10.55, 15.00 and 17.15. Bus number 366 runs between Buenavista and Las Portelas approximately every two hours and is the bus to catch if you're heading to the hostel. There are buses from Santa Cruz to Buenavista. The road to Punta de Teno is considered dangerous as it's prone to falling rocks. It's not officially closed but if the large warning signs don't put you off, perhaps the thought of giving your hire car back with a dented bonnet will. If you do brave it, the views are stunning.

Where to stay

The best place to stay is the **Albergue Bolico**, a kilometre off the main road in Las Portelas. It's bright and modern with friendly, knowledgeable staff. Rooms are dormitory style and cost €12 per person. Meals are available or you can take your own food and make use of their kitchen. Reservations are not always necessary but recommended; tel: 922 822 056 or 922 127 334; email: teno.parque@cabtfe.es.

There are also a couple of rural houses dotted around and in Masca everyone seems to have a room to rent.

Where to eat

El Mesón del Norte Las Portelas. A fine place to sample some local cuisine. They specialise in meat cooked over a wood fire. Closed on Mondays.

Restaurante La Fuente Masca. Although rather touristy, there are some delicious local offerings such as fresh juice made from cactus fruits, goat's yoghurt with palm honey, lots of Masca-made jams and some tasty cakes, all using locally grown products.

What to see and do

Hiking

This is the main reason you'd want to come to the park. Exploring the deep barrancos or immersing yourself in the laurel forest is a treat, especially if you're seeking a spot of solitude. Not all routes are well marked, though, so you'd do well to ask for a bit of local advice before setting off. If you're staying at the *albergue*, staff are more than happy to explain routes or lend you a detailed walking book (in Spanish). They also offer guided walks at weekends for €6 per person.

Albergue Bolico–Monte del Agua–Albergue Bolico

Distance: 12km: time: 3¹/₂ hours; difficulty: 2 (the only tough section is the initial 45-minute climb)

From the back of the hostel, follow the 'camino real' signs that take you up a relatively steep climb and on to a forest track. On reaching this track, turn right and walk for no more than five minutes, all the time looking for a path leading in amongst the trees on the left. The path is opposite some derelict barns, though they can be difficult to spot as they are somewhat overgrown. The path initially takes you through fruit trees before reaching the laurel forest (about 20 minutes from the barn). This path is a downhill one and along the way you will see various paths leading off to the left. Ignore them until you notice that your way is not clear (after about half an hour); at this point you need to look for a clear path off to the right. Eventually you'll reach a partially cobbled forest track next to a stream. Turn left on to this track and continue for about an hour until you reach Las Portelas. Once there, head for the bus shelter on your right and then turn left on to a road that serves as a shortcut back to the hostel.

Barranco de Masca
Distance: 8km; time: 3 hours; difficulty: 3
This is one of Tenerife's top walks and while there are some who dismiss it as touristy and commercial, there is no denying the ravine's beauty or the pleasure in catching the boat at the bottom. The walk leaves from the village of Masca (ask any local to point you in the direction of the starting point) and is easy to follow as it descends the ravine to the coast. Once at the bottom, you'll need to catch the boat to Los Gigantes, passing the cliffs en route. You should buy a ticket for the boat in Masca; the fare is €10 and boats leave at 13.45 and 15.30. Touristy it may be but it provides a great day out.

Carrizal Alto–Tierras de Abache–Carrizal Alto
Distance: 4km; time: 2 hours; difficulty: 2
Drive to Carrizal and leave the car in the village (or catch the bus and get dropped off on the main road running past Carrizal). The walk starts about 100m before the village itself (after one solitary house on a sharp bend). Look for the footpath between two large rocks, which leads to a palm tree – the most difficult part of the walk is finding the starting point! Passing the tree, the path starts to climb and after about ten minutes you'll come to a fork in the path. Take the lower, right-hand path – the other leads to Masca. A couple of minutes later you'll be at the Asomada de Juan Lopez, a good place to stop and take a few photos. A further 15 minutes along a gently sloping path and you'll have reached La Barbita – a rock with a John Travolta chin. Soon the path becomes more difficult to follow as you reach the old irrigated terraces of Abache. Look out for red blobs and arrows painted on the rocks and keep heading for a pyramid-shaped rock on the horizon. This area used to be used for cultivating cereals, lentils, chick-peas and beans but the natural vegetation has grown back since farmers stopped using the area in the 1960s. The path takes you to a ruined barn, which is really where the walk ends unless you're feeling adventurous. A few more minutes on, you get a stunning view of the cliffs plummeting down to the coast, but there is no path, meaning you'll have to clamber over rocks to see it – and don't get too close to the edge! The walk is an out-and-back one, though the scenery is so stunning that you won't mind seeing the same thing twice.

Villages
Masca
Once a farming village, Masca is now very firmly on the tourist trail, with almost every building housing a restaurant or souvenir shop. Nevertheless, you can still see the village's charm, its few stone houses clinging precariously to the hillside 600m above sea level, and it's easy to see why the tour companies chose Masca for their 'typical Canarian village' excursion. Many people pass through on an island tour, spending just enough time there to sample some papaya juice and take a few snapshots of the stunning scenery. There is more to explore though and it's worth parking up and visiting the small museum, open Mon–Sat 11.00–17.00. It's also a fine place to have lunch and is the starting point for the walk down to the beach (see *Hiking*, above). There is one official *casa rural* in the village but if you ask around there are a few people with a room to let out. Expect to pay about €35 for a double room.

Teno

If you want to know what Masca was like before the tour buses arrived 30 years ago, Teno (or Teno Alto to give it its full title) is the place to go. It's a tiny village seven kilometres from El Palmar, along one of those roads that make driving in the islands tiresome. Perhaps that's why it remains relatively untouched, though there is one shop aimed at tourists and selling, amongst other things, the goat's cheese that the village is famed for. There is also a small church, a couple of bars and some very quaint stone houses.

Diving
Club de Buceo Punta de Teno Tel: 657 567 902; email: puntadeteno@hotmail.com. Run short diving courses for €100.

Other activities
Staff at the *albergue* are happy to organise a variety of activities, though for most there is a minimum requirement of four participants. Amongst others, they offer canyoning for €35 per person, kayaking for €10 per person and also give talks on the local environment and way of life in the villages.

LOS GIGANTES, PUERTO DE SANTIAGO AND PLAYA DE LA ARENA

These three resorts are now joined together to form one and while they're artificial and there's little of cultural interest, at least they aren't yet as hideous as their southern counterparts. Puerto de Santiago still retains something of its original fishing village identity, though you have to squint and search for it. The main reason to visit is to see the 500m cliffs that provide a backdrop for the small black-sand beach in Los Gigantes. To get a good view you need to take a boat trip, which unfortunately are all rather too geared towards the package holidaymaker and include all-you-can-drink lunches.

Getting there
The 325 makes frequent trips from Puerto de la Cruz to Playa de la Arena. There are regular departures from Las Galletas, passing all the tourist resorts en route. This bus (473) also serves as a regular shuttle between Los Gigantes, Puerto de Santiago and Playa de la Arena.

Where to stay
Apartamentos The Harbour Club Av González Forte 26; tel: 922 86 22 73; fax: 922 86 08 58. One of the only places on Los Gigantes that isn't completely taken up by a tour operator, though the majority of its apartments belong to timesharers so booking is essential. A 1-bedroom apartment is €85 per night, with special offers for stays of longer than a week.
Hotel Apartamentos Los Dragos del Sur Av Marítima, Puerto de Santiago; tel: 922 86 25 50; fax: 922 86 04 13. Another run-of-the-mill 3-star place with pool, sauna, massage parlour etc. Good location close to Playa de la Arena. Single €75; double €90.
Hotel Barceló Santiago Calle La Hondura 8, Puerto de Santiago; tel: 922 86 09 12; fax: 922 86 18 08; email: Santiago@barcelo.com. Just what you'd expect from a hotel of this standard: large, bright rooms, nicely furnished, most with sea views and some with views of the cliffs. Single €85; double €140, including breakfast.
Hotel Lagos de César Calle José González González, Puerto de Santiago; tel: 922 86 21 58; fax: 922 86 72 09; email: lagocesares@hotasa.es; www.hotasa.es. Close to the beach and in a slightly less touristy area. All rooms are suites, with large terraces and either a sea or

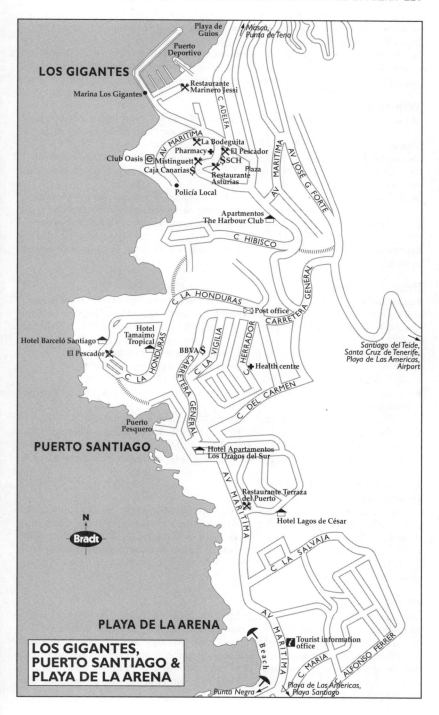

mountain view. Staff can be a little brusque. Also has nightly entertainment. Single €78; double €120, including breakfast.

Hotel Tamaimo Tropical Calle La Hondura, Urb Puerto de Santiago; tel: 922 86 06 38; fax: 922 86 07 61; email: subdirector.tamaimo@hotetur.com. Large apartments with a separate bedroom. Set around the pool area. €75 for 2 people.

Where to eat
El Pescador Calle Flor de Pascua. This fish and seafood joint comes highly recommended by locals. There is a sister restaurant, El Pescador II near the Hotel Barceló in Puerto de Santiago.

Restaurante Marinero Jessi Near the harbour. Good for breakfasts and seafood lunches.

Restaurante Asturias Plaza de la Iglesia. Excellent northern Spanish food with some good meat dishes.

Mistinguett In a precinct off Calle Flor de Pascua. Offers something a bit more special than burgers and chips, such as original pasta dishes and wonderfully sweet desserts.

La Bodeguita In the same precinct as Mistinguett. Large selection of salads and savoury crêpes if you fancy something a bit healthier.

Restaurante Terraza del Puerto Av Marítima, Playa de la Arena. The best place around to sample Canarian specials.

Practicalities
Banks Santander Central Hispano, Calle Flor de Pascua, open Mon–Fri 08.30–14.00, Sat 08.30–13.00; Caja Canarias, next to the Hotel Los Gigantes, open Mon–Fri 08.30–14.00, Thu 17.00–19.30; BBVA, Ctra General in Puerto de Santiago, open Mon–Fri 08.30–14.15, Sat 08.30–13.00.

Health The Health Centre is on Calle Herrador in Puerto de Santiago.

Internet Access at the Club Oasis pool complex, on Av Marítima, open every day 10.00–18.00; €3.50 per hour.

Pharmacy On Calle Flor de Pascua near the Los Gigantes Hotel and on the Ctra General in Puerto de Santiago.

Police The Policía Local is at the end of the Av Marítima in Los Gigantes.

Post office On the junction of Calle La Hondura and the Ctra General in Puerto de Santiago, open Mon–Fri 08.30–14.30, Sat 09.30–13.00.

Tourist information Just off the main road in Playa de la Arena, open Mon–Fri 09.00–14.30.

What to see and do
Boat trips
There are plenty of companies offering trips past the cliffs, so shop around for prices. While the majority of the whale-watching trips leave from Los Cristianos, there are a few leaving from the harbour in Los Gigantes. Nashira (tel: 922 86 19 18) is, by many, considered to be the best and most environmentally friendly boat. Trips start at €15 for a one-hour trip. They also operate the boat from Playa de Masca to Los Gigantes, which costs €10.

Hiking
Due to its location close to Teno and not too far from Teide, Los Gigantes isn't a bad place to base yourself for a few days of hiking. **Hans's Wander-Club** specialise in hiking for the older generation (though anyone can participate), meaning they take it quite slowly and stick to easyish routes. Prices are negotiable but are around €20 per person. Tours can be booked at Rent-a-car Las Rosas in Playa de la Arena or by telephone: 922 862 187. Sun Holidays also offer hiking trips around the islands; tel: 609 166 850.

Fishing

There's some good fishing to be done in this area, although not many companies offer trips. Punta Umbria V will take you out for half a day for €60 (full-day trips available), tel: 922 86 19 18.

Diving

Marina Los Gigantes In the harbour; tel: 922 86 80 95; email: gigantes@tenerifeafondo.org; www.tenerifeafondo.org. Cater more for already qualified divers, with a package of 6 immersions costing €120. They also run whale- and dolphin-watching excursions.

PLAYA DE SAN JUAN

If you're looking for a tourist-friendly town, but one that has some personality and no all-you-can-drink beer offers, Playa de San Juan is a good bet. A few British holidaymakers and residents rub shoulders with the Spanish *señoras* in the market, while the men play dominoes in the square, but so far it's undiscovered by the tour operators. Of course, the town is on the endangered list, since Los Gigantes is expanding from the north and Playa de las Américas from the south and cynics believe it's only a matter of time before San Juan gets swallowed up by mass tourism. All the more reason to rush and enjoy its lazy charm before the worst happens.

Getting there

Bus 473 passes through regularly on its way from Las Galletas to Los Gigantes. There is also a service to Guía de Isora every two hours.

Where to stay

Apartamentos Carlomar Calle Isla del Hierro 55; tel: 922 13 88 00; fax: 922 13 89 31. Very nice apartments, some with sea view and enormous balconies. 1 bedroom €39; 2 bedrooms €45; special offers for longer stays.

Apartamentos Don Marcos Calle Isla de Gran Canaria; tel: 669 681 848/686 520 777. These apartments are huge and with brand-new furnishings. They are generally let on a long-term basis, hence the homely feel, but they are available for shorter stays as long as it's for a minimum of three nights. 1-bedroom apartment €45 per night; special prices for stays of more than a week.

Pensión Palmero Calle Isla Bonita 11; tel: 922 86 54 21. One of the Canary Islands' true bargains, the rooms are basic but bright and clean. All have private bathroom (hot water slightly temperamental) and most have a small balcony overlooking the street. Single €13; double €19.

Where to eat

Restaurants are all on the Avenida del Emigrante unless otherwise specified.

Bar Restaurante Puesta del Sol Doesn't really serve anything spectacular but it is the best place to watch the sun set behind La Gomera.
Bar Star Specialises in food from the Americas, namely Tex-Mex, Caribbean and a few Argentine dishes.
Chino Sur A fairly average Chinese restaurant, though the service is very friendly.
Euro Dulce The place to go if you have a hankering for something sweet. They make delicious handmade chocolates and cakes which you can take away or eat in their tearoom.
Peppers Wine Bar A British-run place and definitely more of a pub than a wine bar. Still, it offers something a little different with its selection of stuffed pitta breads. Also serves old English favourites if you fancy fish and chips or roast beef.

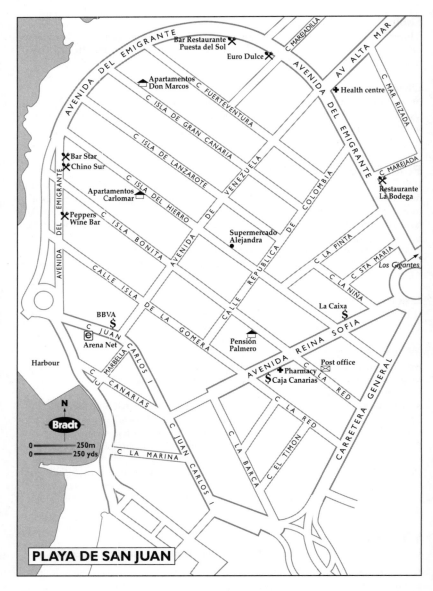

PLAYA DE SAN JUAN

Restaurante La Bodega Calle Marejada. The classiest place in town, offering a varied menu with good fish dishes. They also serve delicious crêpes in the early evening.

Practicalities
Banks BBVA, Av Juan Carlos I, open Mon–Fri 08.30–14.15, Sat 08.30–13.00; Caja Canarias, Av Reina Sofia, open Mon–Fri 08.30–14.00, Thu 17.00–19.30; La Caixa, Av Reina Sofia, open Mon–Fri 08.15–14.00, Thu 16.30–19.45.
Health The Health Centre is on Av del Emigrante.

Internet Arena Net, Av Juan Carlos I, open Mon–Sat 10.00–13.30, 17.00–00.00, Sun 17.00–00.00; €2.50 per hour.
Pharmacy On Av Reina Sofia.
Police In Guía de Isora.
Post office Just off the Av Reina Sofia, open Mon–Fri 08.30–11.00, Sat 09.00–11.00.
Shopping Supermarket Alejandra, Calle Isla del Hierra, open Mon–Sat 08.00–13.00, 17.00–21.00. There's a food and handicrafts market every Wednesday and Sunday morning in the church square.
Tourist information None, though the travel agencies can be quite helpful.

What to see and do
Boat trips
There is just one boat that leaves from the tiny harbour at San Juan, the *Nostramo*. It's essentially a dolphin safari, though naturally you take in the Los Gigantes cliffs as well. A five-hour excursion costs a whopping €45 for adults or €22.50 for children and includes lunch and drinks; tours leave the harbour daily at 10.00.

Diving
Guido's Bubble Club Calle Isla Bonita; tel: 922 86 65 51; email: info@guidos-bubble-club.de; www.guidos-bubble-club.de. Cater only for qualified divers and offer immersions for €25 with equipment. A package of 10 dives costs €200.
Solo Buceo Calle Canarias 10; tel: 922 86 59 00; email: solobuceo@terra.es; www.solobuceo.es.vg. A discovery dive is €42, or for qualified divers €30 per immersion, including the rental of equipment.

PLAYA DE LAS AMÉRICAS AND LOS CRISTIANOS
Although in recent years these two resorts have been trying to smarten up their acts, with the gradual closure of troublesome nightspots and opening of classier hotels, it is still a mass-tourism destination with little to offer in the way of culture. The two resorts have virtually united, making it almost impossible to see where one ends and the other begins, although they belong to separate municipalities (the majority of Playa de las Américas to Adeje and Los Cristianos to Arona). There is a huge British community here, who, far from emigrating to learn a little about the culture and life of Canarians, have managed to recreate a bit of Britain in the sun. English pubs serving roast beef and all-day breakfasts abound, though good restaurants are hiding in there if you can be bothered to look. The resorts took hold in the 1970s and since then a building frenzy has engulfed the area, which now stretches up the coast to La Caleta (the resorts have different names to try to escape Las Américas' reputation, though there is no huge difference between them). If you're looking for late, late nightlife, bad cabaret, English pub quizzes and buckets of sangria, this is definitely the place for you.

Getting there
The good news here is that the resorts are very well connected, so should you find yourself here on a package deal there is a means of escape. Regular buses run between Santa Cruz, Puerto de la Cruz, Granadilla and Icod de los Vinos. There is also a daily service to the Teide National Park and a line that runs from the South Airport. There are ample buses to shuttle you around the immediate area.

Where to stay
With over 300 hotels and apartment complexes in the resorts, it's impossible to list them all and would be, in many cases, pointless, as the majority of beds are given

over to tour operators. Most of the accommodation on offer is in three- or four-star hotels or two- or three-key apartments, though there are a few extremes. Los Cristianos has a couple of *pensiones* and there are some five-star hotels around that could put you in the red for the next couple of years.

If you are bent on staying around here, try contacting an accommodation agency.

Anyka Sur Edificio Ocean Azahara, Av Suecia; tel: 922 79 13 77; fax: 922 75 19 57; email: anykasursl@interbook.net; www.anykasur.com. Apartments and studios in the Los Cristianos area ranging from €40–70 per night.

Canary's World Centro Comericial Bahía de los Cristianos; tel: 922 78 85 36; fax: 922 78 85 37; email: info@canarysworld.es; www.canarysworld.es. Arrange accommodation across the archipelago in hotels, apartments and *casas rurales*.

There is also a **campsite** on the road to Arona; prices are from €4 per night per person, plus €4 per tent. The site is fully equipped with restaurants, supermarket, sports facilities and pool. It's on the Ctra 6225, km 1.5; tel: 922 78 51 18.

Where to eat

It can be a little taxing to find a good restaurant amongst the endless British pubs and all-you-can-eat Chinese restaurants. There are a few OK tapas bars frequented by locals on Av Juan Carlos I and Av Antonio Dominguez. Other decent places include:

La Rana Parque Santiago IV, Av Litoral, Playa de las Américas; tel: 922 75 22 22. Expensive and rather fancy but one of the best restaurants around. Main meals from €15.

Mama Rossa Under the Colon II apartments in Playa de las Américas; tel: 922 79 48 19. A good Italian/international place with a few unusual choices and excellent service. Main meals around €15.

Mantra CC San Telmo, Av de la Habana, Los Cristianos; tel: 922 79 71 34. Bright and funky oriental restaurant with some good vegetarian options. Main meals from €8.

Molino Blanco Av Austria 5, San Eugenio Alto; tel: 922 79 62 82. A tasty menu offering a few specialities like ostrich and wild boar. It's based in a lovely building and has nightly live music, which although a little random (Mariachi, Peruvian, classical and a singing chef) is very good. Main meals from €15. Reservations recommended.

Tiziano Av Rafael Puig, Playa de las Américas; tel: 922 75 77 00. Charming restaurant and at these prices you want somewhere pleasant to eat your dinner. Elaborate Italian cuisine, with main meals around €20. Open evenings only.

Nightlife

There is certainly no shortage of nightlife here. Although many of the bars and clubs in the **Veronicas** complex have closed in recent years due to drug-related problems, there are still numerous options, all of them similar and none of them too appealing. Close to Veronicas is the **Metropolis**, a large club open until very late. If you're looking for a different night out, **Joe's Piano & Sax** is a laid-back joint with a dress code to keep the riff-raff out! They have nightly music which feels more like you've stumbled on a jamming session than a practised repertoire. Easily the best place around; you'll find it on the Avenida Rafael Puig near the Palm Beach Hotel.

Many of the shows in the area entail buckets of alcohol and audience participation, though there is one that stands out above the rest: **Carmen Mota's Danza y Fuego**. Performed Mon–Fri in the Pirámide de Arona, the show starts with various Spanish dances and continues with a modern version of Bizet's opera *Carmen*. Frequented by Spaniards as well as tourists and well worth the €35 per ticket.

Practicalities

There are countless numbers of everything you'll need here, and far too many to mention. There is a helpful tourist information office on Avenida Rafael Puig opposite Parque Santiago II, open Mon–Sat 09.00–17.00. The island's biggest market is held every Sunday morning next to the Gran Arona Hotel in Los Cristianos. There's an awful lot of tat and very little in the way of traditional foods or handicrafts.

What to see and do
Golf

The south of the island is not a bad place to be if you want to get in a couple of rounds of golf. There are five courses in the area: Golf del Sur, between Las Galletas and Los Abrigos; Amarilla Golf and Country Club; Golf las Américas, at the back of the resort; and Golf Costa Adeje, a little further up the coast towards San Juan. For beginners, children or those who want lessons, the nine-hole pitch 'n' putt Los Palos, between Los Cristianos and Las Galletas, is probably the best bet. It's cheaper than the others and you need about an hour to finish a round. Expect to pay around €50 for 18 holes, with an extra charge for club hire.

Theme parks

There is no shortage of theme parks in this area, though whether you'll want to visit them or not is another matter! Choose from numerous Aquaparks, the Camel Park, Tenerife Zoo, Parque Ecológico (an eagle park), Centro de Las Orquideas, Bananera… the list goes on. In the resort you can also go up in a balloon, try bungee rocketing, take a ride in a horse-drawn cart or go to any of a number of tawdry night-time shows.

Boat trips and fishing

There are dozens of companies in the Port at Los Cristianos offering whale- and dolphin-watching tours for around €40 per person, including lunch and drinks. A few companies offer deep-sea fishing trips for about €70 for a full day.

Other things to do
La Finca del Arte

About five minutes' drive from Los Cristianos, off the road to Arona, is the Finca del Arte, a small gallery showcasing art from local artists. You can admire the work and enjoy a snack in the café, or buy a painting or sculpture. They also have barbecues, Canarian music and craft workshops on weekends. See their website: www.finca-del-arte.com.

Hiking
Arona–Vento–Roque del Conde
Distance: 4km; time: 3¹/₂ hours; difficulty: 3

The walk really begins in the languid hamlet of Vento, east of Arona, though if you haven't got your own wheels you'll need to catch a bus to Arona and walk the extra 20 minutes to Vento (passing the petrol station on the main road and then turning left up a narrow lane). The walk starts from an alleyway between two houses in Vento (ask locally if you're not sure, but the alley is usually recognisable from the cars parked in the vicinity). The path immediately descends and crosses the small Barranco de la Arena. The path is easy to follow as it zigzags across the far larger Barranco del Rey. From here the path ascends steeply. Watch out for a turning off to the left which takes you past a derelict stone house. From here the path widens and begins to wind gradually to the top of Roque del Conde at 1,020m above sea level. The panorama from the top offers the best and worst of Tenerife, with the ever-growing tourist resorts to the south and on a clear day Mount Teide just visible to the north. The return is done the same way.

Barranco del Infierno
Distance: 8km; time: 3 hours; difficulty: 2
Emily Kingston
The Barranco del Infierno is undoubtedly one of the most popular hikes in the Canary Islands. Its proximity to the tourist resorts of southern Tenerife and the relatively easy walking means it appeals to hikers and less experienced walkers alike. Due to the popularity of the walk, the *Cabildo* has recently introduced an entrance charge of €3 and declared that a maximum of 80 people can enter the ravine at any one time. This is a great measure for protecting the environment but it does result in long queues, so arrive early to beat the crowds. Another of the *Cabildo*'s projects is the installation of experienced guides who can explain the origins of the ravine and its complex ecosystem. Access to the ravine is from the picturesque village of Adeje. Head up Calle Los Molinos, from where the walk is signposted. The entrance to the barranco is just behind a large restaurant on the right. The route is obvious throughout, so ignore all other paths that lead off the main track. The vegetation changes dramatically along the length of the ravine. It starts out dry and sparse, since the water in Tenerife's only year-round natural running water source has been piped off for irrigation further down the barranco. After 30 minutes you'll reach the first viewpoint, Acequía Larga, from where there are great views over Adeje and the coast. A further 30 minutes' walking along the floor of the ravine brings you to a stream; at this point the vegetation becomes more verdant and lush. Criss-crossing the stream and various pools, you might be lucky enough to encounter some birdlife. The last five minutes are the most difficult as you navigate mossy rock faces, but you're rewarded with the 80m waterfall, hidden on three sides by the steep 1,000m ravine walls. The perfect spot for a picnic before returning to Adeje the same way.

LOS ABRIGOS
Los Abrigos is a small fishing village between Las Galletas and El Médano. It's an excellent place to eat fish and there is a selection of restaurants, most with good views of the harbour. It also hosts the island's only evening market, a rather unimpressive affair held on Tuesdays from about 19.00.

EL MÉDANO
El Médano is a small town whose main clientele are here for the excellent windsurfing. Things have changed a little since the 1857 census, which registered the town as having 'five neighbours and 25 inhabitants', but it's still a quiet place and retains the local feel that other resorts along this coast are so lacking. The only problem is the strong wind that blows relentlessly, though of course for many this is El Médano's appeal.

Getting there
Bus 116 leaves Santa Cruz every two hours, passing through El Médano and then heading to Granadilla. The town is also linked to Playa de las Américas by regular buses.

Where to stay
Apartamentos Marazul Calle Evaristo Gómez; tel: 922 17 71 59; fax: 922 17 72 77. Good-sized, clean apartments, some with balconies. 2 people €50; 4 people €60.

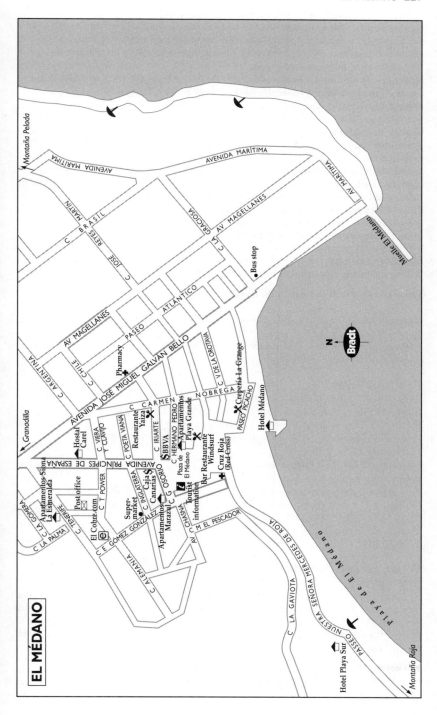

EL MÉDANO

Apartamentos Playa Grande Calle Hermano Pedro 2; tel: 922 17 63 06; fax: 922 17 61 68. Tastefully decorated and with absolutely everything you'll need, including washing machine and satellite TV. From €45 for 2 people, though they offer good deals for those who plan to stay for more than a week.

Apartamentos Siona La Esmeralda Calle Tenerife 10; tel: 922 17 69 46. Huge and homely apartments with a reasonable kitchen. 2 people €45; 4 people €65.

Hostal Carel Av Príncipe de España 22; tel: 922 17 60 66; fax: 922 17 68 28; email: info@residencecarel.com; www.residencecarel.com. This place is currently awaiting its upgrade to hotel status as it is far too smart to be considered a *hostal* or *pensión*. It has both apartments and rooms and all are clean and bright. Single €36; double €55; apartment (2 people) €68.

Hotel Médano La Playa de El Médano; tel: 922 17 70 00; fax: 922 17 60 48; email: reservas@medano.es; www.medano.es. Medano's best hotel, with its large rooms, all with balcony and most with sea views. Staff are very friendly. Single €50; double €70.

Hotel Playa Sur La Playa de El Médano; tel: 922 17 61 20; fax: 922 17 63 37; www.htci.com. The best location, right on the beachfront. Rooms are nice and quite large. Lots of sports on offer. Single €64; double €106.

Where to eat
There is a string of tasty fish restaurants on the Paseo Marcial García.

Bar Restaurante Windsurf In the square. Has tables outside and a *menú del día* for €6.50.

Crepería La Grange Behind the Hotel El Médano. Has a mouth-watering menu of over 50 crêpes, both sweet and savoury.

Restaurante Yaiza Calle Iriarte. Offers a respite from fish, specialising in meat dishes from northern Europe and France.

Practicalities
Banks Caja Canarias, Calle García Osorio, open Mon–Fri 08.30–14.00, Thu 17.00–19.30; BBVA, Av Príncipes de España, open Mon–Fri 08.30–14.15, Sat 08.30–13.00.

Health The closest Health Centre is in San Isidro.

Internet El Cobre.com, Paseo Marcial García, open Tue–Sat 10.00–23.00, Sun 10.00–21.00; €2.50 per hour.

Pharmacy On Av José Miguel Galván Bello.

Police In Granadilla.

Post office On Pasaje el Guardia, open Mon–Fri 08.30–14.30, Sat 09.30–13.00.

Shopping There's a supermarket on Calle Evaristo Gómez González, open Mon–Sat 09.00–13.30, Sun 17.00–20.30.

Tourist information Just out of the main square, open Mon–Fri 09.00–14.00, Sat 09.00–12.00.

What to see and do
Kiteboarding
This new sport is really taking off (boom boom!). Basically, you are attached to a board and a kind of parachute, meaning you get pulled around the water and occasionally take off, giving the ultimate thrill. El Médano is an ideal place for it due to the strong winds. You have to have a land lesson first to learn how to control the kite.

Kitecenter Playa Sur Tel: 922 176 688; email: medano@kitecenter.info; www.kitecenter.info. They offer introductory lessons for €45 and practical lessons from €38 an hour.

Above Haría, Lanzarote (GAR)

Right Dromedaries in Parque Nacional de Timanfaya, Lanzarote (GAR)

Below Montañas de Fuego, Parque Nacional de Timanfaya, Lanzarote (JN)

Above Parque Nacional del Teide (GAR)

Below right Mount Teide above the clouds (taken from Gran Canaria) (FG)

Bottom right El Teide landscape (LC)

Below Peak of Mount Teide, Tenerife (PC)

Windsurfing

El Médano is also an excellent place for windsurfing, be it learning or practising what you already know.

Surf Center Playa Sur Tel: 922 17 66 88; email: surfcenter@medano.com; www.surfcenter.info. Lessons from €35 an hour, board rental for €50 per day or €185 per week.

Hiking
Montaña Roja
Distance: 2.5km; time: 1¹/₂ hours; difficulty: 2
Walking to the top of Montaña Roja is easy and rewards you with a good view of the coast. You can start from the beach at El Médano and head for the mountain, following the path that hugs the back of the beach until you reach the track that leads you to the top. The mountain has been declared a special nature reserve due to the vast amount of bird species found there – more than a hundred have been sighted. There are also over 130 species of plants, some of which are threatened, so please stick to the paths and stay out of the breeding areas at the southern end of the beach. And keep an eye out for UFOs; there have been several sightings of curiously shaped objects hovering around Montaña Roja in the past 30 years...

GRANADILLA

Although the town itself isn't brimming over with attractions, Granadilla is a good base for exploring the surrounding area and offers a few charming accommodation options. It's one of the best places to stay in the south of the island, if you don't want to be on the coast.

Getting there

Granadilla is well connected to Santa Cruz and Playa de las Américas. There are also a few buses to Vilaflor and one a day from the South Airport, at 14.50.

Where to stay

Casa Rural El Traspatio Calle Arquitecto Marrero 9; tel: 922 63 05 96; fax: 922 39 24 69; email: eltraspatio@terra.es. Next to the museum, it's a charming *casa rural* divided into 3 well-equipped apartments. €48 per apartment (sleeping up to 3 people).
Casa Rural Anton Piche Calle El Draguito 38; tel: 922 77 28 38; fax: 922 77 01 48; email: antonpichesur@msn.com; www.antonpiche.com. Kind of a cross between a hotel and a rural cottage. It's a beautiful, well-run place with large terraces, shared kitchen and access to the gardens. A delicious breakfast is also available. It's a couple of kilometres south of the town centre but the owners will ferry you back and forth if you haven't got wheels. Double €53 including breakfast.
Hotel Rural Senderos de Abona Calle de la Iglesia; tel: 922 77 02 00; fax: 922 77 03. A lovely place with pleasant courtyards and gardens to relax in after a hard day's hiking. Single €36; double €60, including breakfast.

Where to eat

Arepera Venezuela Near the Town Hall. OK if you want only a snack. There are tables outside.
Casa Tagoro On the road of the same name, a little above the town. The menu has a Bavarian slant and offers nightly specials from different regions of Germany and Austria.
La Tasca Calle Fundador Gonzalo González. A nice place to stop for a beer, though their tapas choice is a bit pitiful.

Tasca Pablo's A lovely little place on Calle Pino (the road which runs down from the Hotel Rural), which has an excellent tapas menu and good prices. I would even go so far as to say the best tapas bar on the island.

Practicalities

Banks Santander Central Hispano, Calle El Calvario, open Mon–Fri 08.30–14.00, Sat 08.30–13.00; Caja Canarias, Calle Pedro González Gomez, open Mon–Fri 08.30–14.00, Thu 17.00–19.30.

Health The Health Centre is on Calle Fundador Gonzalo González, on the way to San Isidro.

Internet Fussion Cyber, Calle Fundador Gonzalo González, open Mon–Sat 10.00–23.00, Sun 14.00–23.00; €2.50 per hour. Oasis, Calle El Calvario, open Mon–Fri 07.00–21.00, Sat 08.00–20.00; €2 per hour.

Pharmacy On Calle Pedro González Gomez.

Police The Policía Local is in the Town Hall, the Guardia Civil is on Calle Santo Domingo de Guzman, out of the centre.

Post office On Calle Fundador Gonzalo González, open Mon–Fri 08.30–20.30, Sat 08.30–14.00.

Shopping The farmers' market in nearby San Isidro is open every Sat and Sun from 08.00–14.00 and is an excellent place to pick up some local fruit, cheese, home-made desserts and wine, amongst other things. In Granadilla there is an art and handicrafts shop on Calle San Francisco, opposite the library.

Tourist information There is a small office based in the Hotel Senderos de Abona which has information concerning rural tourism; open Mon–Fri 09.00–14.00, 16.00–18.00. The main tourist office is in El Médano.

What to see and do
Museo de la Historia

Calle Arquitecto Marrero. An interesting enough little place, with exhibits on the history and culture of Granadilla. All information is in Spanish only. Open Mon–Fri 10.00–14.00, 16.00–20.00; entrance is free.

VILAFLOR

Vilafor is the highest municipality in Spain at 1,500m and perhaps one of its prettiest too. It's an agricultural town with a pleasant square and old quarter and some tranquil hotels, though the main attraction is the surrounding scenery. The nearby pine forest is a wonderful place to go walking and Vilaflor is conveniently close to the Parque Nacional del Teide.

Getting there

There are buses between Vilaflor and Granadilla, and a service connecting Vilaflor with the southern resorts, that leaves Los Cristianos at 06.00, 11.00 and 17.00. The bus heading for Teide passes through too, though whether or not you'd get a seat is another matter.

Where to stay

Casa Chico Calle Santa Catalina; tel/fax: 922 70 90 52. A family-run place which also has a restaurant serving local specials and a rather odd museum. Rooms are basic but clean and have heating – necessary in the winter months! Single €25/30, without/with breakfast; double €45/55.

Hotel Alta Montaña Camino Morro El Cano 1; tel: 922 70 90 00; fax: 922 70 92 93. A very quiet place above the town. It has a swimming pool and stunning views. A good place to relax for a few days. Single €84; double €128.

Pensión Germán Calle Santo Domingo 1; tel/fax: 922 70 90 28. Bright, clean rooms, all with private bathroom and some with balcony. Single €20; double €35.

Where to eat

Don't miss sampling some of the town's typical *dulces* (cakes and biscuits); they are renowned across the island. **Dulcería Vilaflor** is a good place to start; it's on Calle Castaños.

Bar Restaurante La Fuente In the main square. While it's nothing spectacular, it's nice to sit out and breathe the wonderful Vilaflor air.

El Sombrerito Calle Santa Catalina (part of the Casa Chico Hotel). Good Canarian food and a warm welcome. Diners get free entry to the museum.

Tasca El Rincón de Roberto Av Hermano Pedro. Has a reasonable tapas menu, nice décor and a welcoming atmosphere.

Practicalities

Banks Caja Canarias, Calle Santa Catalina, open Mon–Fri 08.30–14.00, Thu 17.00–19.30.

Health The Health Centre is on Av Hermano Pedro.

Pharmacy Opposite Casa Chico on Calle Santa Catalina.

Police The Policía Local is in the Town Hall.

Post office On Calle El Calvario, open Mon–Fri 08.30–11.00, Sat 09.00–10.30.

Shopping There are a few craft shops scattered around the town; the local specialities are embroidery and crochet-work. There's a supermarket on Calle Dolores; open Mon–Sat 08.00–13.00, 17.00–20.00.

Tourist information In the Town Hall, which is at the opposite end of the square to the church; Mon–Fri 09.00–14.00.

What to see and do
Hiking

The Town Hall has information on 11 routes in the municipality. The walks are generally well marked and it's a fabulous area to do some hiking. The following walk is actually in the *municipio* or Granadilla, but access is through Vilaflor.

El Paisaje Lunar
Distance: 5km; time: 2 hours; difficulty: 2

Driving along the road from Vilaflor to Las Cañadas look out for a dirt track on the right, just after kilometre 66. After almost 7km of track, look out for a sign marking the start of the walk and park your car (you need to get here early if you hope to find a spot for it). Follow the path for about 300m, then take the turning off to the right (there is a sign painted on a rock). From here the walk is easy to follow and there is little danger of getting lost. After about an hour you'll reach the weird 'lunar landscape', an area of pumice stone which has been affected by erosion. The path leads you right under the rocks and then down through the pine forest (Tenerife's finest) to the Madre del Agua campsite. Once there, turn right on to the dirt track back to the car. This is one of the island's nicest walks as it is easy, circular and takes you through a beautiful, varied landscape.

SOUTHEAST

There really isn't much to see between Granadilla and Güímar and you'd do well to drive it along the motorway, saving time and petrol. However, if you really want to explore every corner of the island there are minor points of interest. **Las Vegas**, a couple of kilometres off the main road, is a pleasant little village with a small church and a restaurant offering good local food. **Villa de Arico** has nothing for the visitor, but **Arico Nuevo** (which, curiously, is the old part of the municipality, **Arico Viejo** being the new part) is a pleasant place to stop for a little wander. It consists of one road running off the main road with a few good examples of typical houses. There is a rural hotel here, **Hotel Viña Vieja** (tel/fax: 922 16 11 31) but it's pretty run-down. Double €70 with breakfast, single room prices negotiable. From here to Güímar there is nothing but ugly towns and seemingly endless mountain roads.

GÜÍMAR

Güímar is similar to Icod de los Vinos, in that it has one large tourist attraction to bring you here but little else to keep you once you've arrived. The tree-lined square is pleasant enough and has a lovely church (Iglesia de San Pedro) and a wander round the narrow streets near the square is a nice way to kill 20 minutes. The best thing about Güímar is the impressive backdrop and the two delightful rural hotels, though you should also visit the star attraction, the **Pirámides de Güímar**. Various theories exist as to the origin and age of the pyramids. Some think that they are related to relatively recent agriculture, while others believe that they relate to pre-Hispanic beliefs. Historians think that any link to the Guanches is highly doubtful but this is the line that the theme park has decided to take, adding exhibits on other mysterious ancient cultures, such as Easter Island (one of world's largest photographic exhibitions on the Pacific island). Aboriginal finds have been located near the pyramids along with a cave dating back to between AD680 and 1020. The park also has an area devoted to experimental voyages and a large section of endemic plants. It is just out of the town centre, but is well signposted. Open every day 09.30–18.00; adults €9.25, children (9–12yrs) €4.50.

Where to stay

Finca La Raya Calle La Raya; tel: 922 51 38 38; fax: 92 51 48 57; email: casalaraya@hotmail.com; www.casalaraya.com. A delightful 16th-century hotel, about a kilometre above Güímar, with impressive views of the town and the mountains behind. They also have information on walks that start from the hotel's grounds. Double €108; suite €150, including breakfast. There are no singles but a price can be negotiated.
Hotel Rural Finca Salamanca Ctra Güímar–El Puertito km 1.5; tel: 922 51 45 30; fax: 922 51 40 61; email: info@hotel-fincasalamanca.com; www.hotel-fincasalamanca.com. An old manor house converted into a fabulous rural hotel with 50,000m² of land. Definitely worth splashing out on. Single €80, double €130, with breakfast.

CANDELARIA AND LAS CALETILLAS

The Virgin of Candelaria might be defined as 'the spiritual ambassadress of the Franciscan missionaries'. It was after her appearance on the beaches of the menceyato of Güímar that the Guanches began to receive the evangelical message with enthusiasm.

Rumeu de Armas

The basilica in Candelaria holds the image of the Virgen Morenita, the patron saint of the Canary Islands. The figure appeared on Playa de Chimisay at the end of the 14th century and was taken to the cave of the *mencey* of Chingaro, where Guanches from across the island flocked to see it. They called the virgin Chaxiraxi, though since the conquest she has been known as Candelaria. After the conquest, the first festival of purification (or Fiesta de las Candelas) was celebrated in the cave where the statue was kept. Many of the natives were baptised and the town of Candelaria was formed. These days there are essentially two parts to the town; the historical quarter and Las Caletillas. The former has an impressive square dominated by the basilica while the latter is a mini resort used by Spaniards from the mainland and Tinerfeños coming to take advantage of the extensive black-sand beach. Although it attracts a fair number of tourists and holidaying locals year-round, the town really fills up on February 2 and August 15 as the locals celebrate in honour of the virgin.

Getting there
There are regular buses from Santa Cruz and Güímar and no shortage of lines that run from the old town to Las Caletillas.

Where to stay
Both the area's hotels are in Las Caletillas.

Hotel Punta del Rey Av del Generalísimo 165; tel: 922 50 18 99; fax: 922 50 00 91. Built in classic '70s tower-block style, it's not the prettiest place and could do with a lick of paint in the rooms too. Has swimming pools, tennis, squash, rifle-shooting and mini-golf available, amongst other activities. Single €55; double €63.
Hotel Tenerife Tour Tel: 922 50 02 00; fax: 922 50 23 63; email: tenerifetour@tenerifetour.com; www.tenerifetour.com. Standard rooms with TV and a fan, which is most welcome. Almost all rooms have good sea views and good-sized balconies. Single €41; double €52, including breakfast.

Where to eat
Bar Restaurante Candelaria Perhaps has the best location, with its tables out in the square giving you a view of the magnificent church. Seafood is the protagonist of their menu.
Casa Gladys On the main *avenida* between the old town and Las Caletillas. The home-cooked Canarian specialities make it popular with locals.
Casa Valentina Up in the narrow streets of the old part of town. A lovely restaurant, offering creative cuisine based on Spanish favourites.
El Guanche Next to the post office. A popular bakery, good for a sweet snack.
El Rey de la Gamba Next to the plaza. Smart place with a good fish and seafood menu.
La Piccola Opposite the Mercadona supermarket. Offers all the usual Italian dishes with a few tasty seafood ones thrown in as well.
Restaurante La Barraca Near the Hotel Tenerife Tour. Definitely the best restaurant in Las Caletillas. The cuisine is Valencian, with rice dishes their speciality. Main courses average €10.
Yogen Früz Av del Generalísimo, about halfway between the old town and Las Caletillas. They claim to have 1,000 combinations of frozen yoghurt and fresh fruit; nice in the midday heat.

Practicalities
Banks Caja Canarias, Calle Obispo Pérez Caceres, open Mon–Fri 08.30–14.00, Thu 17.00–19.30; Santander Central Hispano, opposite the tourist information kiosk, open Mon–Fri 08.30–14.00, Sat 08.30–13.00; La Caixa, next to the supermarket, open Mon–Fri 08.15–14.00, Thu 16.30–19.45; BBVA, on Av del Generalísimo, open Mon–Fri 08.30–14.15, Sat 08.30–13.00.
Health The Health Centre is on Calle Periodista E Salcedo in the old town.
Internet Cyber Dream near the post office has access for €1.80 per hour; open Mon–Sat 10.30–14.00, 17.00–00.00, Sundays afternoons only.

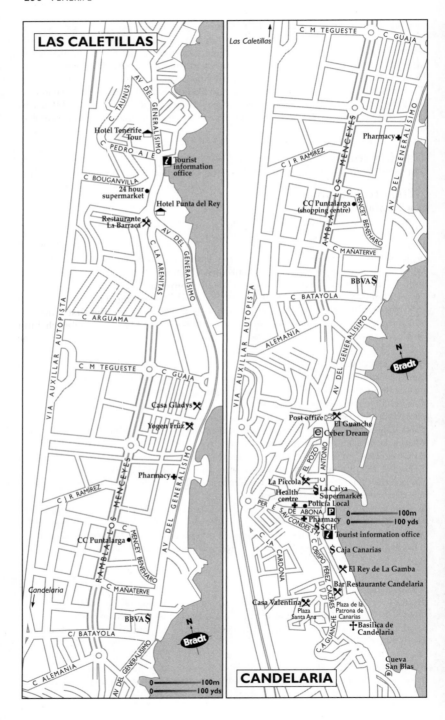

LAS CALETILLAS

Las Caletillas

C M TEGUESTE
C GUAJA
AV DEL GENERALISIMO

Pharmacy +

C TAUNUS
AV DEL GENERALISIMO
C R RAMIREZ

Hotel Tenerife Tour

C PEDRO AJE

Tourist information office

RAMBLA LOS MENCEYES

C BOUGANVILLA

24 hour supermarket

Hotel Punta del Rey

CC Puntalarga (shopping centre)

MENCEY BENEHARO

Restaurante La Barraca

AV DEL GENERALISIMO

C LA ARENITAS

C MAÑATERVE

BBVA $

C ARGUAMA

C BATAYOLA

VIA AUXILIAR AUTOPISTA

ALEMANIA

AV DEL GENERALISIMO

C M TEGUESTE
C GUAJA

N
Bradt

Casa Gladys

Yogen Früz

Post office

El Guanche

Cyber Dream

Pharmacy +

C EL POZO
C ANTONIO

La Piccola
La Caixa
Supermarket
Health centre

C R RAMIREZ

Policia Local

PER E SAV CONDES SM

DE ABONA

RAMBLA LOS MENCEYES

Pharmacy

P

0 ——— 100m
0 ——— 100 yds

CC Puntalarga

SCH

MENCEY BENEHARO

Tourist information office

C MAÑATERVE

$ Caja Canarias

Candelaria

C LA CARDONA

El Rey de La Gamba

Bar Restaurante Candelaria

BBVA $

C/ BATAYOLA

OBISPO PEREZ CACERES

Casa Valentina

Plaza Santa Ana

Plaza de la Patrona de Canarias

C ALEMANIA

AV DEL GENERALISIMO

C A GUANCHE

+ Basilica de Candelaria

N
Bradt

0 ——— 100m
0 ——— 100 yds

Cueva San Blas

CANDELARIA

Pharmacy One on Av Condes, another on Av del Generalísimo near BBVA and another opposite the Hotel Tenerife Tour.

Police Next to the Health Centre.

Post office At the start of Av del Generalísimo, open Mon–Fri 08.30–14.30, Sat 09.30–13.00.

Shopping There are a few so-called handicraft shops on Calle Obispo Pérez Caceres but they are really little more than tacky souvenir shops. The large supermarket on Calle José Antonio opens every day 09.00–21.30 and there's a 24-hour shop next to the Hotel Punta del Rey. There's also a shopping centre between Candelaria and Caletillas: Centro Comercial Puntalarga. Candelaria hosts a market on Wednesday mornings in the main square.

Tourist information The kiosk at the end of Calle Obispo Pérez Caceres is open Mon–Fri 09.00–16.30. The other kiosk is in Las Caletillas, near the Hotel Punta del Rey, open Mon–Fri 09.00–14.00, 16.30–18.30.

What to see and do
Swimming
If you don't want to dip in the sea, you can use the pools at the Hotel Tenerife Tour, open 10.00–18.00 every day. Entrance is €3 for adults, €1.50 for children.

Cueva de San Blas
Known in pre-Hispanic times as Achbinico Cave, this is where the image of the virgin was sheltered when it was moved from the *menceyato* de Chinguero (Güímar). The virgin was then known as Chaxiraxi, meaning 'The Mother of the Keeper of Lands and Skies'. The figure remained in the cave, the first Christian place of worship in Tenerife, until 1526 when it was moved to a church built where today the cathedral stands. When the church was destroyed by fire, the image was returned to the cave and now resides in the basilica. In February 1497 the cave was officially declared a church. You'll meet many a girl called Candelaria in the Canary Islands, though there are also people who prefer to honour the Guanches and name their daughter Chaxiraxi.

Basilica de Candelaria
The basilica was built in the mid-20th century, as a new resting place for the Virgin de la Candelaria. It's a stunning church, which overlooks the Canary Islands' finest square. The nine bronze statues lining the promenade are of the island's *menceys*. The church is open Mon–Fri 07.30–13.00, 15.00–19.30, Sat–Sun 07.30–19.30. Please don't enter if a service is in progress.

La Gomera

La Gomera is round, even, beautiful and the most pleasing of all the islands since in addition to its mildness of climate and bright skies, it is full of gentle rolling hills and densely forested valleys which, in the eternal summer, never lose their leaves.

Leonardo Torriani, 16th century

From the sky, La Gomera is an impressive sight, the deep ravines carving wedges out of the island at random intervals. The locals liken the island to a cake with a few slices missing and, presumably, the green layer of the Garajonay National Park is the icing on the cake; true in more senses than one. Agriculture has always played an important part in the island's economy despite the unhelpful landscape and you'll soon appreciate the hardships that Gomeran farmers have had to overcome. La Gomera is the island that has best preserved its culture, partly through choice and partly due to its bad roads and lack of transport, which slowed down the island's progress somewhat. The tiny airport was built in 1999 but the majority of visitors still arrive by boat.

HIGHLIGHTS

A walk through the laurel forest in the Garajonay National Park is unmissable, especially after a rainy spell when you can see that unusual phenomenon in the Canaries: running water. Driving can be a bit tiresome, so break it up by stopping at the *miradors* to admire the island's striking landscape. One of the finest lookout points is the Alto de Garajonay, where on a clear day you'll see El Hierro, La Palma and Tenerife (and occasionally even Gran Canaria). The other way to admire the cliffs and ravines is from the sea. The typical boat trip is past Los Órganos in the north of the island, though a trip on the passenger boat from Valle Gran Rey to San Sebastián is a cheaper, shorter alternative. Finally, don't miss a demonstration of the *silbo*, La Gomera's unique whistling language, which allows conversation on any topic. Awe inspiring.

BACKGROUND INFORMATION
History

Origins of the island's name are sketchy, though there is a Berber village in North Africa called Ghomera, providing another clue to suggest that the Canary Islands' culture is linked to that of their neighbours on the continent. Unlike the other islands, there are no fixed dates or details of the conquest of La Gomera. It's almost as if they saw that their neighbours were fighting and losing bloody battles and just gave in before they were attacked, though that's not to say that they made life easy for the Europeans once they arrived. At the time, La Gomera was divided into four

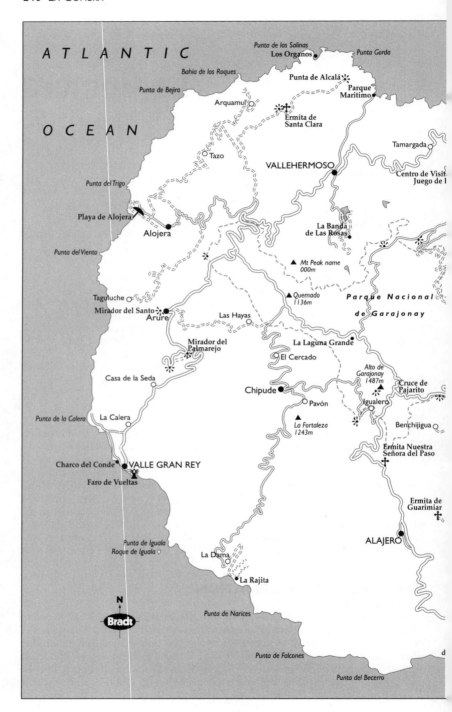

cantons: Ipalán, Mulagua, Orone and Agana, each one governed by a *mencey*. La Gomera suffered years of repression under the rule of the Peraza-Herrera family and experienced some of the bloodiest battles that the archipelago had ever seen (see box opposite). The natives staged a few uprisings themselves in protest at the despotic way in which they were ruled and although they achieved short-term victories, they ended up suffering terribly. Their misery came to an end in 1837 when the island finally became a part of the Castilian crown along with El Hierro, Fuerteventura and Lanzarote.

In 1492 a visitor arrived who would put the island on the map once and for all: Christopher Columbus. He stopped in the San Sebastián harbour on three of his four journeys across the Atlantic, perhaps because of a love affair with Beatriz de Bobadilla or perhaps simply for his love of the island. Other explorers such as Hernán Cortes, Francisco Pizarro and Vasco Nuñez de Balboa followed his lead, bringing a small amount of prosperity to the island as port traffic increased. Of course, once La Gomera became well known it also suffered its fair share of misfortune. In the 16th century a series of pirate attacks devastated San Sebastián and the city was razed to the ground in 1618 by Berbers. La Gomera suffered mass emigration in the mid 20th century as those sick of the isolation, economic problems and poor communications left to start a new life in Latin America. Today the island has the second lowest population in the archipelago, with 22,000 residents.

Geography

> A knowledge of the Gomeran landscape is essential to the understanding of the history of its inhabitants. The steep rugged terrain has left its mark on the society and is one of the keys to unlocking the mystery of the island's past.
>
> Alberto Darias, *La Gomera – Space and Time.*

La Gomera is often labelled a mini Gran Canaria on account of its near-round shape and the striking ravines that characterise the landscape. It's the second smallest island at 378km², measuring just 17km at its widest point and 26km at its longest. The highest point, the Alto de Garajonay, reaches 1,487m and offers first-rate views of the other islands. The last eruptions on La Gomera were around two million years ago, making it the only island that hasn't suffered volcanic activity in recent times. Because of this you won't see volcanic cones or areas of *malpaís*, but during this time erosion has worked its magic, giving La Gomera a different but no less spectacular terrain. It's most emblematic rock formation is that of the Los Órganos cliffs. Thanks to the constant assault of the ocean, the cliff resembles an organ (if you use your imagination) with its curious columns rising up 80m from the ocean. Water has played a no less impressive part within the island and it's normal to see streams throughout the year, La Gomera being the island with the most natural springs. The average annual rainfall is 370mm, not inconsiderable for the Canary Islands. As well as boasting the archipelago's most abundant laurel forest, the Garajonay National Park also contains over 20 types of trees, 18 species of ferns and over 120 herbaceous plants and bushes. Along with the ravines, the terraced farmland is a striking feature of the landscape and testament to man's struggle.

Economy

Despite the tough terrain they've been dealt, Gomeros have always survived on agriculture and evidence of their toil can be seen on the carefully terraced hillsides.

LA GOMERA'S BLOODY PAST

The post-conquest years turned out to be much worse than the invasion itself for the inhabitants of La Gomera. True, they didn't experience the violent battles that other islands did during the conquest, due to their indifference to the European soldiers. Although there are no records of the island being conquered, it was overcome in the first wave of attacks and became a part of the *señorio*. La Gomera's darkest period began when the Herrera-Peraza family started to govern the island in the mid 15th century. Hernán Peraza the Younger was a tyrannical ruler, which led to a number of uprisings and eventually his murder in the Guadehum Cave in 1488. He had been having a secret affair with a native woman, Iballa, and the islanders felt this was a step too far. One day while visiting his mistress he was ambushed and killed in a manner suiting the brutal way he had lived. His death sparked another rebellion which was to be suppressed in a manner that the islanders could never have imagined. During previous revolts, Peraza and his wife Beatriz de Bobadilla had shut themselves in the Torre del Conde and awaited help from Gran Canaria's governor, Pedro de Vera, so Bobadilla wasted no time in raising the alarm again. Showing a malevolence rarely matched, de Vera set about murdering every islander over the age of 15. Some were hanged, others had their hands and feet lopped off and some had weights attached to them and were offloaded into the sea. De Vera made gifts of the youngsters, condemning them to a life of slavery. Beatriz de Bobadilla later married another repressive Spaniard, Alonso Fernández de Lugo, and was rumoured to be Christopher Columbus's bit on the side whenever he was in town. She died in Madrid in 1504.

The island's main export was once cochineal, which was taken over by the tomato and then the banana. These days the islanders make a living from their bananas, potatoes, wine and the unique date-palm sap (*guarapo*), which is made into *miel de palma* (palm honey). Fishing could be exploited to create a larger income but fishermen lack resources and tend to stick to traditional and less productive methods. There are reminders of better times such as the abandoned davits and the tuna canning factory at La Rajita. Rural tourism has been developing slowly since the 1980s, although most visitors tend to come on day trips from Tenerife and little of their money goes into the local economy.

Flora and fauna

The Canary Islands' most important laurel forest is in the Garajonay National park, where there are also 40 endemic species. Vallehermoso has a sizeable area of juniper trees, though they've been all but wiped out in other areas as the land has been cultivated. The island is relatively rich in fauna with around 40 species of nesting birds, three types of bat, three types of reptile and 2,000 insects. Expect to see woodcock, Canary laurel pigeons, sparrowhawks and buzzards.

Conservation

The most endangered species in La Gomera is the *silbo*. The ability to whistle your thoughts to a friend a couple of barrancos away seems a bit too much like hard work for many these days, when you can send a text message in seconds. The *Cabildo* has wisely devised a project where the whistling experts visit schools to give demonstrations and optional classes in mastering this peculiar language, which is so much a part of the island culture. The classes have so far been a surprising success...

Also on the endangered list is the Gomeran giant lizard (*Gallotia simonyi gomerana*), a species found only on this island. The biggest threat comes from predators introduced from abroad, mainly the wild cat. The Canarian government, along with European Project Life has started a breeding programme and set up the 'Lizard Haven' in Valle Gran Rey, close to their natural habitat to facilitate reintroduction. The first year of the recovery plan was a success, with seven lizards born in captivity, and conservationists are now searching for females amongst existing colonies in order to enhance the breeding programme.

There are 16 protected spaces on La Gomera, counting for almost a third of the island. Amongst them are the Garajonay National Park, Los Órganos Natural Monument and the Valle Gran Rey Rural Park.

Festivals

Without a doubt the island's most important festival is that of its patron saint, Nuestra Señora del Guadalupe, held every five years. The festivities begin at the hermitage in Puntallana, near San Sebastián, from where fishermen take the image of the virgin to the capital by boat. What follows is a month of non-stop parties, concerts and events across the island as the virgin visits each town. The party starts on the Monday after the first Sunday in October but won't be celebrated again until 2008.

As on other islands, the fiestas de San Marcos are important and Agulo is the place to be if you want to witness the locals jumping over bonfires on June 24.

Every year a large handicrafts fair is held in San Sebastián, with craftsmen from across the islands coming to sell their wares. It's usually held in September but it's wise to check with the tourist information office if you particularly want to visit.

Food

La Gomera has plenty of speciality foods that you won't find even in the other islands. As well as numerous goat's cheeses you'll find *almogrote* on many menus. It's a tasty paste, made of goat's cheese, oil and garlic. There are plenty of *dulces tipicos* (traditional cakes and biscuits), most of which contain almonds, dried fruit and honey. Another favourite is *leche asada*, a milk pudding usually doused, as most desserts are here, in the delicious *miel de palma*, made from the sap of palm trees. The Gomeros are also fond of a tipple and at some point you should sample *parra*, a lethal liquor, *mistel*, a sickly sweet and often strong wine and Gomerón, a mix of *parra* and *miel de palma*.

TAPPING THE DATE PALM
One of La Gomera's tastiest exports is the fruit of a drawn-out procedure. Canary Island date palms (*Phoenix canariensis*) are a key feature of the Gomeran landscape, with over 100,000 across the island. Their appeal stretches further than their simple visual pleasure though; they are the source of an important element in Gomeran cooking. The trees are tapped for palm sap or *guarapo*, which is used to make palm syrup, unique to the island. The leaves are pruned in winter and then the top of the tree is cut and the sap gradually oozes into a bucket. The buckets must be collected every day and the tree checked to stop it from drying out. The sap is then boiled to turn it into the *miel de palma*, important in many Gomeran recipes.

GETTING THERE AND AWAY
By air
Flights are operated by NAYSA, though you still book through Binter. They use 20-seater planes so it's worth flying if you can afford it, to experience the tiny plane and the stunning views.

Binter Canarias Tel: 902 39 13 92; www.bintercanarias.es. *Gran Canaria:* 2 a day. *Tenerife North:* 2 a day.

By sea
Fred Olsen Tel: 902 10 01 07; email: reservas@fredolsen.es; www.fredolsen.es. *La Palma:* 1 a day. *Tenerife:* 4 a day (from Los Cristianos).
Trasmediterránea Tel: 902 45 46 54; www.trasmediterranea.es. *El Hierro:* 1 a day. *Tenerife:* 2–3 a day (from Los Cristianos).

GETTING AROUND
Public transport
Although better than the service on El Hierro, La Gomera's public transport is far from comprehensive. San Sebastián has a bus station but in other towns you'll have to ask around to find out where the bus stops. The main routes leave San Sebastián for Alajeró, Valle Gran Rey, Vallehermoso and the airport. Fares are pretty steep considering the distances involved but necessary considering the tiny number of people that use the buses. There are no *bono* tickets to make travel cheaper but using buses is not a stressful business; when I missed the last bus of the day from San Sebastián to Playa Santiago, staff at the bus station radioed the driver and asked him to wait at a convenient point while I made my way up on another bus!

By boat
La Gomera is the only island with a passenger-boat service running between its towns, a great idea that other islands' *Cabildos* would be wise to steal. The Garajonay Exprés leaves Valle Gran Rey and then stops at Playa Santiago and San Sebastián before continuing on to Tenerife. It's well worth the trip, both for the coastal views and to avoid another nauseating drive or bus ride around La Gomera's winding roads. Boats leave San Sebastián at 09.45, 14.55 and 20.35, returning from Valle Gran Rey at 06.45, 10.35 and 17.30. The trip takes just under an hour and costs €3.50, or €2.50 if you're going only to Playa Santiago. Tickets are on sale in all harbours.

Car hire
The following have offices in San Sebastián, Playa Santiago and Valle Gran Rey.

Cicar Tel: 922 14 11 46
Garajonay Tel: 922 87 16 40
Gomera Safari Tel: 922 87 10 10
Hertz Tel: 922 87 04 61

WHERE TO STAY
La Gomera has an incredible number of *casas rurales*, meaning that you really should stay in one for at least a couple of nights and the chances are you won't want to leave once you're there, since they nestle in some of the island's finest spots. The easiest way to book is through the rural tourism association; tel: 922 14 41 01; fax: 922 88 10 38; email: gomera@ecoturismocanarias.com; www.ecoturismocanarias.com/

gomera. Prices vary but you can expect to pay around €50 for two people and €70 for four people. The island has its fair share of *pensiones*, though none are hugely cheap. There is just one campsite on La Gomera – in El Cedro – and camping is prohibited anywhere else. There are a fair number of apartments in Playa Santiago and Valle Gran Rey and three luxury hotels on the island – Jardín Tecina in Playa Santiago, El Paso in Alajeró and the Parador in San Sebastián.

ACTIVITIES
Boat trips
As well as the useful Garajonay Exprés that shuttles islanders and tourists around La Gomera (see *Getting around*, page 245), there is another excellent maritime excursion on offer. Boats leave Playa Santiago and Valle Gran Rey most mornings to take in the awesome Los Órganos cliffs. The boats usually stop at a secluded beach for lunch and sometimes do a full circuit around the island, weather permitting. While on board you can also try your hand at fishing.

Diving
Opportunities for diving off the shores of La Gomera are fewer than in other islands. This is a shame since the impressive underwater rock formations and abundance of large fish make it a super place to dive. There is only one official diving school, based in the Hotel Jardín Tecina in Playa Santiago.

Golf
There's one 18-hole golf course on the island, next to the Hotel Jardín Tecina.

Hiking
The Canary Islands' finest hike is in La Gomera, taking you through the magnificent national park (see page 264). Other spots worth a wander include the area north of Vallehermoso and the ravines surrounding Valle Gran Rey. Hikes in the south are tough, due to the deep barrancos, but worth it for the dramatic scenery. There aren't many companies offering hiking tours but the few that exist have a comprehensive choice.

Piloto Tours Based in Hermigua; tel: 922 88 18 15; email: pilototour@terra.es; www.nordwestreisenmagazin.de. There are 13 different tours on offer, for €22 per person per walk. They also arrange 10-day hiking holidays on the island, from €600 per person, which includes 6 hikes, a boat trip around the island, 9 nights in an apartment and picnic lunches.
Timah Valle Gran Rey; tel: 922 80 70 37; email: info@timah.net; www.timah.net. A decent range of tours for around €25–30 per person.
Vivotrek Tel: 922 80 71 56; fax: 922 80 59 04; email: info@vivotrek.com; www.vivotrek.com. Walking tours across the island for €28 per person. They also organise climbing and canyoning trips from €40 per person. Their office is in Valle Gran Rey but will do pick-ups from other towns.

SAN SEBASTIÁN
Founded in 1440 and serving as the island's capital ever since, San Sebastián is currently home to a mere 6,000 inhabitants. This gives it the ambience of a quaint seaside town rather than a bustling capital city but don't let the locals hear you call it a *pueblo*. The delightful harbour was once a favourite stop-off for Christopher Columbus and plenty of modern-day sailors are keen to follow in his footsteps. Although the city was ransacked numerous times by pirates, examples of

architecture from throughout the centuries can still be seen, such as the early 16th-century Ermita de San Sebastián and the 15th-century Torre del Conde, built to protect the island's governor from unhappy natives. The main street, as it has always been, is the Calle del Medio (also called the Calle Real), though parallel Calle Ruíz de Padrón has its fair share of shops and restaurants these days. The capital has two small beaches, with Playa de la Cueva being much cleaner and quieter than Playa de San Sebastián. The former is a five-minute walk past the harbour, passing under the hilltop where the *parador* sits.

Getting there
There are buses from the airport at 10.10 and 17.30, but you don't need to worry about the times – the buses wait for plane passengers. Buses back to the airport leave the bus station at 07.00 and 13.00 daily. A taxi from the airport will cost around €15.

Where to stay
Upmarket
Parador Nacional de Gomera Tel: 922 87 11 00; fax: 922 87 11 16; email: gomera@parador.es; www.parador.es. La Gomera's *parador* is a 16th-century Canarian mansion on the cliff above San Sebastián, affording superb views over the capital, the port and Tenerife. It has a pool, tropical gardens and an excellent restaurant serving local specialities. Single €98; double €122, breakfast extra.

Mid-range
Apartamentos Quintero Plaza de las Américas 6; tel: 922 14 17 44; fax: 922 87 09 22; email: apquintero@teleline.es. Good-sized apartments with separate bedroom; most have sea view. 2 people €47; 4 people €53.
Apartamentos San Sebastián Calle del Medio 20; tel: 922 14 14 75; fax: 922 87 13 54. The apartments are quite small but very clean and have everything you'll need. 2 people €40; 3 people €42.
Hotel Garajonay Calle Ruiz de Padrón 15; tel: 922 87 05 50; fax: 922 87 05 54. Some rooms have a balcony, some a terrace and some neither, though prices are the same for all. There are also some with a bath and some with just shower, so be specific when you book. Single €38; double €45, breakfast extra.
Hotel Torre del Conde Calle Ruiz de Padrón 19; tel: 922 87 00 00; fax: 922 87 13 14; email: hoteltorreconde@iespana.es. Other than the *parador*, this is the smartest place in town and with pretty reasonable prices. Some rooms look on to the street, others on to the park. There is also a good restaurant serving Canarian specials. Single €48; double €64.
Hotel Villa Gomera Calle Ruiz de Padrón 68; tel: 922 87 00 20; fax: 922 87 02 35. Friendly management. The large if somewhat sparse rooms could do with a bit of brightening up, but are OK. Single €35; double €4,7 including breakfast.

Budget
Apartamentos Canarias Calle Ruiz de Padrón 3; tel/fax: 922 14 14 53. Studio or 1-bedroom apartments either with street views or views of the Torre del Conde and the park. Studio €35; 1-bedroom apartment €38.
Pensión Colombina Calle Ruiz de Padrón 81; tel: 922 87 12 57. Good value compared with its competitors. All rooms have private bathrooms and are very bright and clean. Single €20; double €35, with reductions if you stay for a number of days.
Pensión Colón Calle del Medio 59; tel: 922 87 02 35. Very basic rooms but in a lovely old building opposite Casa de Colón. All have shared bathroom. Single €18; double €25 with street view or €22 for rooms at the back.

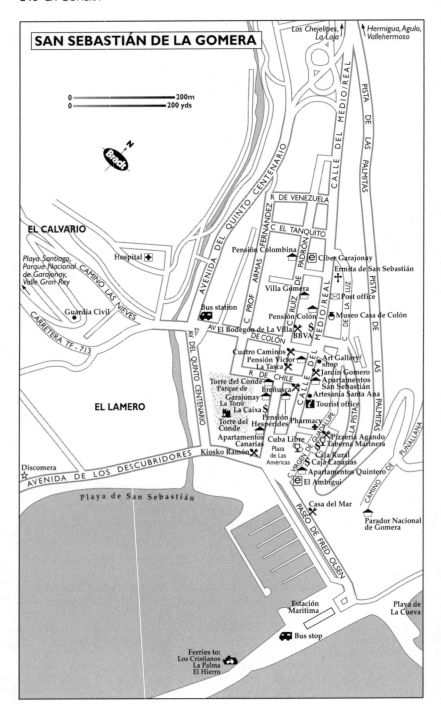

SAN SEBASTIÁN DE LA GOMERA

Los Chejelipes,
La Laja

Hermigua, Agulo,
Vallehermoso

0 ——————— 200m
0 ——————— 200 yds

N

EL CALVARIO

Playa Santiago,
Parque Nacional
de Garajonay,
Valle Gran Rey

Hospital

Guardia Civil

CARRETERA TF - 713

EL LAMERO

Discomera

AVENIDA DE LOS DESCUBRIDORES

Playa de San Sebastián

CAMINO LAS NIEVES

AVENIDA DEL QUINTO CENTENARIO

AV DEL QUINTO CENTENARIO

C PROF ARMAS

C FERNÁNDEZ

RUIZ DE PADRÓN

CALLE DEL MEDIO/REAL

PISTA DE LAS PALMITAS

R DE VENEZUELA

C EL TANQUITO

Pensión Colombina

Cíber Garajonay

Ermita de San Sebastián

Villa Gomera

C DE LA LUZ

Post office

Museo Casa de Colón

Bus station

Pensión Colón

AV El Bodegón de La Villa
DE COLÓN

BBVA

Cuatro Caminos
Pensión Victor
La Tasca

R DE CHILE

Art Gallery/
shop

Jardín Gomero
Apartamentos
San Sebastián

Torre del Conde
Parque de
Garajonay
La Torre
La Caixa
Torre del
Conde
Apartamentos
Canarias
Kiosko Ramón

Breñusca

Artesanía Santa Ana

Tourist office

Pensión
Hespérides

Pharmacy

Cuba Libre

Plaza
de Las
Américas

Pizzería Agando
Taberna Marinera

C VIRGEN DE GUADALUPE

Caja Rural
Caja Canarias
Apartamentos Quintero

El Ambigui

PISTA DE LAS PALMITAS

PUNALLANA

CAMINO DE

Casa del Mar

Parador Nacional
de Gomera

PASEO DE FRED OLSEN

Estación
Marítima

Playa de
La Cueva

Bus stop

Ferries to:
Los Cristianos
La Palma
El Hierro

Pensión Hespérides Calle Ruiz de Padrón 42; tel: 922 87 13 05. Not the brightest option in town but it's cheap and some rooms have private bathroom. Single €17; double without bathroom €27; with bathroom €30.

Pensión Victor Calle del Medio 23; tel: 922 87 00 20/607 51 75 65; fax: 922 87 13 35. Another lovely old building converted into a small guesthouse. Some rooms are a little musty but spotless and there's a nice patio. No private bathrooms. Single €18; double €24.

Where to eat

Casa del Mar Paseo de Fred Olsen; tel: 922 87 12 19. This is *the* place to go for fresh fish.

El Bodegón de la Villa Calle Ruiz de Padrón. Smarter than most of the restaurants in San Sebastián. Lots of steaks on the menu and a variety of home-made sauces. There are also a few vegetarian options.

Kiosko Ramón Near the harbour in the Plaza de las Américas. A cheap and cheerful place with a limited menu but the food is tasty, the service is fast and the prices are very reasonable. Closed on Mondays.

Pizzería Agando Opposite the pharmacy, just out of Plaza de la Constitución. They mainly do pizzas but dabble in a bit of everything.

Restaurante Cuatro Caminos Calle Ruiz de Padrón; tel: 922 14 12 60. Like the rest, it specialises in Gomeran cuisine, though it has a bit more choice than most and an excellent fish menu.

Restaurante Breñusca Calle del Medio. Specialises in local cuisine and is a favourite with Gomeros. Closed on Sundays.

Restaurante Jardín Gomero Calle del Medio. The tree-filled patio in the middle draws the punters in, though you should stick to the fish if you don't want to be disappointed with your meal. Good local wine on offer.

Restaurante La Tasca Next to Restaurante Cuatro Caminos. Good choice of starters and pizzas at excellent prices.

Nightlife

It's hardly a wild night out, though you'll certainly find a bit of life on a weekend evening. The party usually starts around the Plaza de la Américas, with the favourite haunts being **Taberna Marinera**, **El Ambigui** and **Cuba Libre** for a few Cuban cocktails and rhythms. The action then moves to **Kiosko Ramón** before ending the night in the city's only disco, the wonderfully named **Discomera**, at the far end of the Avenida de los Descubridores.

Practicalities

Banks Caja Canarias, Plaza de las Américas, open Mon–Fri 08.30–14.00, Thu 17.00–19.30; Caja Rural, Plaza de las Américas, open Mon–Fri 08.30–14.00, Thu 17.00–19.30; BBVA, Calle del Medio, open Mon–Fri 08.30–14.15, Sat 08.30–13.00; La Caixa, Calle Ruíz de Padrón, open Mon–Fri 08.15–14.00; Thu 16.30–19.45.

Health The hospital is just out of the centre, in the El Calvario district, tel: 922 14 02 00.

Internet You can check your mails over a coffee at El Ambigui for a whopping €5 per hour, open every day 08.00–00.00. Ciber Garajonay, Calle Ruiz de Padrón, has a connection for €2 an hour; open Mon–Sat 11.00–14.00, 17.00–23.00, Sun 17.00–23.00.

Pharmacy There's one just out of the Plaza de la Constitución and another next to Casa Colón.

Police The Guardia Civil is in the El Calvario district of town and the Policía Local is based in the Town Hall.

Post office Calle del Medio, open Mon–Fri 08.30–14.30, Sat 09.30–13.00.

Shopping Artesanía Santa Ana has offerings from across the island, including pottery and food. There is also an art gallery/shop on Calle del Medio with work by local artists. Every

Wednesday and Saturday morning there is a small but excellent food market in the Plaza de la Constitución.

Tourist information The office on Calle del Medio is open Mon–Sat 09.00–13.00, 16.00–18.00, Sun 10.00–13.00. There is also a kiosk in Plaza de las Américas, open Mon–Fri 09.00–14.00.

What to see and do
Museo Casa de Colón
Calle del Medio.
Whether or not Columbus stayed here is somewhat debatable, but locals will tell you that this is the only building that fits the description of where he resided when he docked in San Sebastián. The museum has little to do with the great explorer though, with the ground floor dedicated to pre-Hispanic pottery from Mexico and Peru and the upper floor used for temporary art exhibitions. Mon–Fri 10.00–13.00, 16.00–18.30, Sat 10.00–13.00; entrance is free.

Torre del Conde
Unlike other military constructions in the archipelago, this 15th-century tower was not built to ward off pirate attacks. In fact, Hernán Peraza the Elder, the first lord of La Gomera, had it built to provide a sanctuary from internal attacks and it certainly came in useful. It's a pleasure to wander inside and think of the despotic Peraza the Younger hiding here with Beatriz de Bobadilla as the natives revolted outside. Since the Gomeros seem quite a peaceful lot these days, the tower is used as a home for old maps of La Gomera, San Sebastián and a few of the archipelago. Mon–Fri 10.00–13.00, 16.00–18.30; entrance is free.

PLAYA SANTIAGO
This small fishing village experienced something of a boom in the 1930s when the Rodríguez López company chose it as the site for their tuna canning factory. The factory closed in the mid 1970s when the company's owner died, although it remained standing until 1996. These days, the residents of Playa Santiago make their living through fishing, agriculture and tourism. It's a quiet town which has stayed true to its roots, save for the five-star hotel and golf course built on the outskirts. Women travelling alone might initially find it a little intimidating since there are large groups of men hanging around everywhere, but a brief chat will probably reveal that you make them much more nervous than they make you.

Getting there
By bus
Bus number 5 passes through on its way from the airport to San Sebastián. There is also a bus from San Sebastián at 10.10, 14.30, 18.30 and 21.30 (10.10 and 18.30 only on weekends). This bus continues to Alajeró.

By boat
The Garajonay Exprés leaves for San Sebastián and Valle Gran Rey three times a day. The one-way fare to either place is €2.50. You can also carry on to Los Cristianos in Tenerife for €17. Tel: 902 34 34 50.

Where to stay
Upmarket
Hotel Jardín Tecina Tel: 922 62 83 84; fax: 922 62 83 85; www.jardin-tecina.com. This impressive complex is just above Playa Santiago, on the road to San Sebastián. Its gardens

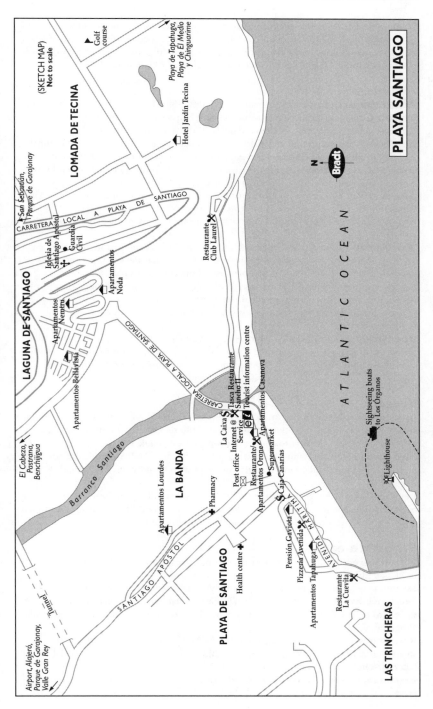

PLAYA SANTIAGO

Airport, Alajeró,
Parque de Garajonay,
Valle Gran Rey

Tunnel

El Cabezo,
Pastrana,
Benchijigua

San Sebastián,
Parque de Garajonay

(SKETCH MAP)
Not to scale

Golf
course

Playa de Tapahuga,
Playa de El Medio
y Chinguarime

Hotel Jardín Tecina

LOMADA DE TECINA

CARRETERA LOCAL A PLAYA DE SANTIAGO

LAGUNA DE SANTIAGO

Iglesia de
Santiago Apóstol

Guardia
Civil

Apartamentos
Nemtru

Apartamentos
Noda

Apartamentos Bellavista

CARRETERA LOCAL A PLAYA DE SANTIAGO

Barranco Santiago

Apartamentos Lourdes

LA BANDA

Pharmacy

PLAYA DE SANTIAGO

Apartamentos
Casanova

Tourist information centre

Tasca Restaurante
Sancho II

Restaurante
La Caixa
Internet @
Service

Restaurante/
Apartamentos Orone

Supermarket

Post office

Apartamentos Casanova

Caja Canarias

Health centre

Pensión Gaviota

Pizzería Avenida

AVENIDA MARÍTIMA

Apartamentos Tapahuga

Restaurante
La Cuevita

LAS TRINCHERAS

Restaurante
Club Laurel

ATLANTIC OCEAN

N

Bradt

Sightseeing boats
to Los Órganos

Lighthouse

boast over 50 different varieties of plants from around the world and the hotel runs a guided botanical walk once a week for guests. You can also take scuba or tennis lessons, play golf, swim in one of the five pools, play squash, indulge in the spa or eat in one of the five restaurants (some open to non guests). Single €120; double €190.

Mid-range

Apartamentos Bellavista Calle Santa Ana; tel: 922 89 55 70; fax: 922 89 52 08; email: info@casascanarias.com; www.casascanarias.com/bellavista. Based in the Laguna de Santiago, about 5 minutes' walk from the beach, the apartments are British-run. A friendly welcome awaits and the apartments have good amenities such as a communal washing machine, internet access and good information about the island. They also arrange stays in *casas rurales* across the island. Prices vary from €45 to €55 depending on whether you want a balcony, terrace or neither.

Apartamentos Casanova Av Marítima; tel: 922 89 50 02. Some apartments have sea views and some have balconies but not all and there's just one price, so it's first come first served. It's €42 per night but there are significant reductions for stays of more than a few days.

Apartamentos Lourdes La Banda; tel/fax: 922 89 54 65; email: haslousara@terra.es; www.apartamentoslourdes.com. Up a hill above the town, these large apartments have good-sized terraces and vistas of the town. Apartments for 2 people €40.

Apartamentos Orone Av Marítima 14; tel: 922 89 56 10; email: orone@arrakis.es; www.orone.arrakis.es. Bright studio apartments, most with sea view, but you'll pay extra for it. Service is very friendly. Apartments for 2 with sea view €45, or €35 without the view.

Apartamentos Tapahuga Av Marítima; tel: 922 89 51 59; fax: 922 89 51 27; email: info@tapahuga.com; www.tapahuga.com. Homely apartments on the seafront with a swimming pool. Apartments €50 per night with discounts for stays of more than 5 nights.

Budget

Apartamentos Nemtru Laguna de Santiago; tel: 922 89 51 38. Could do with a bit of smartening up and the reception is a little cool. Still, they're cheap and all apartments have sea views and TV. Apartments for 2 people €25; 4 people €30.

Apartamentos Noda Laguna de Santiago 73; tel: 922 89 50 87. Somewhat in need of a refit but very cheap and clean. A family-run place with friendly service. 2 people €24; 4 people €30.

Pensión Gaviota Av Marítima; tel: 922 89 51 35. Cheerful, nicely furnished rooms with balconies. The *pensión* is on the first row, meaning some rooms have sea views and even sea noise. All have private bathroom. Single €21; double €24.

Where to eat

Pizzería Avenida Cheap and cheerful and on the seafront – useful if you fancy a slice of pizza with a sea view.

Restaurante Club Laurel Extension of the Av Marítima, below the Hotel Jardín Tecina; tel: 922 14 58 50. Pricey local and international food in perfect surroundings on the seafront. The restaurant belongs to the hotel but is open to all. Open evenings only, closed on Sundays.

Restaurante La Cuevita At the end of the Av Marítima; tel: 922 89 55 68. The town's smartest restaurant if you don't count those in the Hotel Jardín Tecina. It specialises in fish and seafood and is based in a cave on the seafront. Main courses start at €8.

Restaurante Orone Av Marítima. A pretty mixed menu with a reasonable choice of pizzas and a large covered terrace.

Tasca Restaurante Sancho II The last building before you cross the bridge to Laguna de Santiago. It specialises in fish and rice dishes and has a good selection of local desserts. Also does a *menú del día* for €7.50.

Practicalities

Banks La Caixa, next to Restaurante Sancho II, open Mon–Fri 08.15–14.00, Thu 16.30–19.45; Caja Canarias is in the square, open Mon–Fri 08.30–14.00, Thu 17.00–19.30.
Health The Health Centre is about 100m behind the *pensión*.
Internet Internet @ Service, Av Marítima charges €2 per hour; open every day 10.00–13.30, 16.00–19.00.
Pharmacy On Calle Santiago Apostól.
Police The Guardia Civil is behind the church in the Laguna district.
Post office Calle Santiago Apostól, open Mon–Fri 08.30–13.00, Sat 10.00–12.00.
Shopping Supermarket El Paso II has more choice than the others. It's on Av Marítima and is open Mon–Sat 08.00–14.00, 16.00–20.00, Sun 09.00–13.00. There are a few souvenir/handicrafts shops around.
Tourist information On Av Marítima; open Mon–Fri 09.00–13.00, 16.00–19.00, Sat 09.00–13.00.

What to see and do
Boat trips
Boats leave the harbour for a trip around the island, taking in Los Órganos cliffs and maybe a spot of fishing or whale-watching. Excursions with **Siron** leave at 09.00 on Tuesday, Thursday and Sunday, picking up passengers in Valle Gran Rey before heading north. Call 922 80 54 80 to book or ask around in town where you can buy tickets, which cost €36. Count on a full day out. **Tina Excursiones** run the same tour on the same days, also leaving Santiago at 09.00 and heading straight around the island without stopping at Valle Gran Rey. Adults €36; children €18; tel: 922 80 58 85; www.excursiones-tina.com. All excursions include lunch and drinks.

GIVE A LITTLE WHISTLE
Long before mobile telephones or walkie-talkies, Gomeros had to find a way to communicate across their rugged landscape. Imagine: you've descended a barranco with the goats only to realise when you get to the bottom that you've left your sandwiches on the kitchen table. You can't go back for them and don't want to go hungry and you know that your neighbour will be joining you shortly with his herd, so you need to contact him quickly. It's along these vague lines that the *silbo gomero* was thought up. It's a way of whistling your thoughts to a friend up to 4km away and considerably pre-dates the conquest. You might think that the possibilities are limited to a few essential phrases like 'a storm is approaching', or 'put the kettle on, I'm on my way home' but it's actually possible to convey any thought by changing the position of your fingers. If it ever existed in the other islands, it died out long ago and there is a rational fear that the same could happen in La Gomera. That's why the *Cabildo* is attempting to maintain the tradition by offering *silbo* to schoolchildren as an extracurricular activity. You can see demonstrations at Las Rosas, La Zula in Agulo and at the *parador* in the capital. If you're particularly lucky you could see the *silbo* in its natural state, though Chipude is one of the few places where it's still practised.

Golf

Playa Santiago is home to the island's only golf course (tel: 922 14 59 50; www.tecinagolf.com), set in the grounds of the Hotel Jardín Tecina (but open to all). Eighteen holes on this par 71 course will set you back €95, including clubs and balls. They also offer lessons for €36 per hour. Open 08.00–21.00 in summer, 07.30–19.00 in winter.

Diving

Playa Santiago has the island's only official diving school too (tel: 922 89 59 02; fax: 922 89 59 99; email: gomera@arrakis.es), also at the Jardín Tecina. A one-day discovery course costs €108, while a four-day open-water diver course costs €355.

ALAJERÓ

Alajeró is the capital of the municipality but unless you have a particular hankering to see a town hall, there is little reason to come. It does offer super views of the coast and El Hierro on a clear day. There is a magnificent hotel and a few below-par restaurants.

Getting there

Line 3 leaves San Sebastián four times a day (twice on weekends); see Playa Santiago section for times. The return bus leaves the Alajeró Town Hall at 05.30, 08.00, 14.00 and 16.30 (08.00 and 16.30 only on weekends).

Where to stay

El Paso Hotel Suite Lomo Los Cardos; tel: 922 89 54 44; fax: 922 89 53 20; email: info@elpasohs.com; www.elpasohs.com. The ideal place to relax, if you can afford it. In a spectacular and quiet location with views of El Hierro. As the name would suggest, there are no standard rooms, only suites. There is also a pool, gym, beauty salon and two restaurants. Single €130; double €170.

Where to eat

Bar La Alegría On the main road as you enter the town. It emits the aromas of *gofio* and goat's cheese and has a reasonable choice of Gomeran goodies.

WHEREFORE ART THOU JONAY?

Never was a story of more woe than this of Gara and her Jonay. Yes, La Gomera was relating the most romantic story ever told before Shakespeare had even bought his first parchment. It all started at a harvest festival, where Princess Gara of La Gomera got chatting to the handsome son of a Tenerife *mencey*, Jonay. The youngsters soon fell in love and wanted to spend all their time together. Nothing wrong with that I hear you say, but their families thought the union would spell disaster for Canarian life as they knew it. You see, Gara was the princess of Agulo, a place of water, while Jonay was a fire child, born on Tenerife, the island of hell. Ignoring his elders' warnings, Jonay returned to La Gomera to see his love. The story tells how he swam the 47km between the two islands aided by some inflated pigs' bladders. Once together the lovers realised that they could not continue their relationship and so, rather than be apart, they fled to La Gomera's highest point and flung themselves from the peak. The point where they died still bears their names today – Alto de Garajonay.

Bar Restaurante Columbá On the main road from Playa Santiago, just before you enter Alajeró. Offers the usual range of tapas, sandwiches and local dishes.

Flor de Venezuela Opposite the square. A friendly place offering snackish things like *arepas*, sandwiches and the odd bit of tapas.

Restaurante Las Palmeras On the main road; tel: 922 89 54 71. The best and most expensive choice. If you can't find the Gomeran special you're looking for here, it doesn't exist. Main courses are around €10. Closed on Mondays.

Practicalities

Banks There's an ATM below the Town Hall.
Health The Health Centre is behind the Town Hall.
Pharmacy In Playa Santiago.
Police The Policía Local is in the Town Hall.
Post office In Playa Santiago.
Shopping There's a shop on the road to the hotel, open Mon–Fri 08.30–13.30, 17.00–20.00, Sat 09.00–13.00. At time of writing there were plans to open a cheese shop in the town.

What to see and do

From the El Paso Hotel you can take a pleasant 45-minute walk to the Ermita de San Isidro. Further down the road towards the airport you'll find La Roseta, a cultural centre with an art gallery showcasing work by local artists, music and dance shows and displays of *lucha canaria* and *juego de palo*. Opening times vary; call 639 83 79 44 for more information. There is also a market at La Roseta every Saturday where you can buy local products.

CHIPUDE

There's little reason to stay in Chipude, unless you're looking for somewhere that's seriously off the beaten track. However, it is conveniently close to the Garajonay National Park and has a certain character but you definitely need to bring your own entertainment.

Getting there

Line 1 passes through four times a day on its way from San Sebastián to Valle Gran Rey. There is also a bus to and from the airport. It's best to ask a local what time the buses usually pass through the village and where they stop.

Where to stay

Pensión Sonia Plaza de Chipude; tel: 922 80 41 58; fax: 922 80 43 10. All rooms have bathroom and some have balcony. Single €17; double €26.

Where to eat

There are a couple of bars that serve the usual choice of tapas and Canarian cuisine. Your best bet is the restaurant under the *pensión,* since there's not so much testosterone in the air although, frankly, a trip into Las Hayas for lunch is infinitely preferable.

Practicalities

Banks Caja Canarias, on the main road opposite Pensión Sonia.
Health The Health Centre is on the main road.
Pharmacy Near the square.
Police The closest police station is in Alajeró.
Shopping There's a supermarket next to Pensión Sonia.

What to see and do

Other than sit in the square and admire the 16th-century Templo de Candelaria with the locals, you'll be stuck for anything to do in Chipude. If you're staying here you definitely need a car so that you can visit the surrounding villages of El Cercado, Las Hayas and Pavón and, of course, the Garajonay National Park.

EL CERCADO

This hamlet attracts more tourists a day than it has residents. The allure of El Cercado is its pottery, made using traditional methods (no potter's wheel). There are three workshops where you can pick up ceramics and other crafts. It's also a good place to pick up some local food products such as *almogrote* and *miel de palma*.

LAS HAYAS

Due to its altitude Las Hayas is often shrouded in mist, so what better place to fill up with a warming lunch? Casa Efigenia (also known as Restaurante La Montaña) is one of La Gomera's culinary treats if you want to try local cuisine. Efigenia prepares a large salad, followed by vegetable stew, served with *gofio* and some seriously spicy *mojo*. It's washed down with home-brewed wine, spring water and followed by the dessert of the day, Efigenia's own creation. Everything she prepares is organic and home-grown (or home-made) and it's all suitable for vegetarians. The full meal costs €10, there is no menu and allow plenty of time (minimum two hours) as it can get pretty busy and the emphasis is on well-prepared dishes, not fast food. It's on the right-hand side of the road as you enter from Arure; tel: 922 80 08 02.

PARQUE NACIONAL DE GARAJONAY

Taking its name from two tragic lovers (see box, page 254), this magnificent area became a National Park in 1981 and was declared a World Heritage Site by UNESCO in 1986. The park occupies a tenth of the island's surface area and contains the archipelago's most abundant laurel forest. The sea of clouds that envelopes the park ensures the survival of over 150 different plant species as well as year-round running water. Animal life is not so rich, though you might see the two endemic doves and any of the hundreds of insects. The park is superbly set up for tourists, with countless lookout points scattered around and a few well-equipped picnic areas. It would be an absolute crime not to visit if you're on the island and it's a reason in itself to take a day trip from Tenerife.

Getting there

Bus number 1 passes Cruce de Pajaritos, leaving San Sebastián at 10.10, 14.30, 18.30 and 21.30 or Valle Gran Rey at 05.30, 08.00, 14.00 and 16.30.

What to see and do

Before you visit you should have a look around the visitor centre which is located inconveniently far from the park itself (see *Las Rosas*, page 262). Next, you can drive around and stop to admire the view at every *mirador* or have a picnic at one of the recreation areas. Of course, the best way to see the park is on foot and there is a good network of well-signposted paths. You can also take advantage of the guided-walk service offered free of charge by the park authorities on Wednesday and Saturday mornings. You must book a place a couple of days in advance, tel: 922 80 09 93. For details of a superlative walk in the park, see *Hikes*, page 264.

EL CEDRO

This hamlet is on the outskirts of the national park and is *the* place to stay if you want to escape the rat race and get up close with nature. There are a few rural cottages which can be booked through the rural tourism association (see *Where to stay*, page 245). There is also a bar/restaurant just outside the village with good traditional food on offer. This is the home of La Gomera's only campsite, La Vista; tel: 922 88 09 49. Staff at the restaurant will arrange horseriding excursions, but only for experienced riders.

ARURE

The village has a couple of restaurants with good local specialities. **Bar Restaurante El Jape** also sells local produce, such as *miel de palma*, *almogrote* and a variety of cakes and biscuits and they allow you to taste the wine before you buy. Next door, **Bodega Vino Tinto** has some pretty strong home-brewed wine on offer. Both are on the main road as you leave Arure heading for Valle Gran Rey.

VALLE GRAN REY

Once home to the island's greatest kings, Valle Gran Rey is now the main tourist centre and for many Gomeros a worrying sign of things to come and a place to be avoided. The black-sand beach lies at the bottom of a fertile valley, dotted with villages and farming terraces. Most people think of it as a pleasant resort, not a place ruined by mass tourism, but when compared with the rest of the island you can understand why the locals are concerned. Valle Gran Rey is split into five districts, each a small village desperately trying to maintain its character. La Calera's steep roads are lined with small guesthouses and decent restaurants, while La Playa has the larger apartment complexes and international restaurants. La Puntilla has the least charm and the most expensive places to eat and drink while Borbalán is pretty much lacking in everything. Along with La Calera, Las Vueltas is the most enticing area with its curious backpacker feel. There is budget accommodation to be found in Las Vueltas, though for the most part you need to knock on doors and ask if anyone has a room going. There are also a few decent bistros and some funky shops hidden in its labyrinth of cobbled alleys.

Getting there
By boat
The Garajonay Exprés leaves for San Sebastián three times a day stopping at Playa Santiago on the way and you can continue all the way to Los Cristianos in Tenerife; tel: 902 34 34 50.

By bus
There are four buses a day from San Sebastián (see the Garajonay section for times). There is also a service to and from the airport. Buses leave Valle Gran Rey (near Pensión Las Jornadas) at 06.30 and 13.00.

Where to stay
Upmarket
Hotel Gran Rey La Puntilla; tel: 922 80 58 59; fax: 922 80 56 51; email: webmaster@hotel-granrey.com; www.hotel-granrey.com. Another of La Gomera's top-notch hotels, though not in the league of the Jardín Tecina. Very close to the sea but also has a pool on the roof, in case you're feeling particularly lazy. Single €80; double €120.

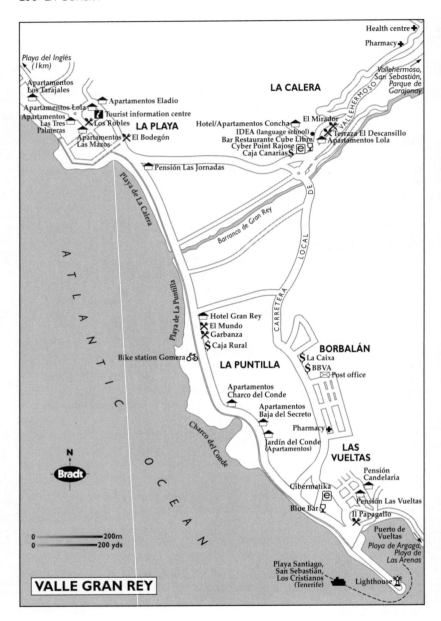

Health centre
Pharmacy

Playa del Inglés
(1km)

Apartamentos
Los Tarajales

LA CALERA

Vallehermoso,
San Sebastián,
Parque de
Garajonay

Apartamentos Eladio

Apartamentos Lola
Apartamentos
Las Tres
Palmeras

Tourist information centre
Los Robles

El Mirador

LA PLAYA

Hotel/Apartamentos Concha
IDEA (language school)

Terraza El Descansillo
Apartamentos Lola

Apartamentos
Las Mazos

El Bodegón

Bar Restaurante Cube Libre
Cyber Point Rajose
Caja Canarias

Pensión Las Jornadas

Playa de La Calera

Barranco de Gran Rey

ATLANTIC

Playa de La Puntilla

Hotel Gran Rey
El Mundo
Garbanza
Caja Rural

BORBALÁN

Bike station Gomera

LA PUNTILLA

La Caixa
BBVA
Post office

Apartamentos
Charco del Conde

Charco del Conde

Apartamentos
Baja del Secreto

Pharmacy

OCEAN

N

Bradt

Jardín del Conde
(Apartamentos)

LAS
VUELTAS

Pensión
Candelaria

Cibermatika

Pensión Las Vueltas

Blue Bar

Il Papagallo

0   200m
0   200 yds

Puerto de
Vueltas
Playa de Argaga,
Playa de
Las Arenas

VALLE GRAN REY

Playa Santiago,
San Sebastián,
Los Cristianos
(Tenerife)

Lighthouse

Mid-range

Apartamentos Baja del Secreto Av Marítima, Charco del Conde; tel: 922 80 57 09; fax: 922 80 59 29; email: bajadelsecreto@navegalia.com. Small apartment complex with all the usual amenities. 1-bedroom apartment €49; 2 bedrooms €68.

Apartamentos Charco del Conde Av Marítima, Charco del Conde; tel: 922 80 55 97; fax: 922 80 55 02; email: info@charcodelconde.com; www.charcodelconde.com. Low-rise apartments set around the swimming pool, most with excellent views. Also has mini-golf. Studio €44; 1-bedroom apartment €50.

Apartamentos Las Mozas Ctra Playa del Inglés; tel: 922 80 61 01; fax: 922 80 71 41. Bright modern rooms, some with balcony and a sea view, others with neither, and there is no distinction in price so it's just luck of the draw. Apartments for 2 people €50.

Apartamentos Las Tres Palmeras Camino Playa del Inglés; tel: 922 80 57 93; fax: 922 80 58 88; www.trespalmeras.com. Modern complex with large apartments. Most have sea view. Apartment for 2 €60.

Apartamentos Los Tarajales Callao Las Mozas; tel: 922 80 53 25; fax: 922 80 56 53. The majority of apartments have superlative views, since it's situated on the seafront. Pretty good facilities. Studio €44, 1-bedroom apartment €50.

Jardín del Conde Av Marítima; tel: 922 80 60 08; fax: 922 80 53 85; email: info@jardindelconde.com; www.jardindelconde.com. Living up to its name (*jardín* means garden), the grounds are chock-a-block with plants as are the rooms and balconies. Apartments for 2 people €60.

Hotel/Apartamentos Concha La Calera; tel: 922 80 60 63; fax: 922 80 60 64; email: hotelconcha@telefonica.net; www.hotelconcha.com. This was Valle Gran Rey's first *pensión* but these days it's a pleasant little hotel. The rooms and basic apartments are surrounded by gardens, have large terraces and good views of the sea or mountains. Single €30; double €42; apartment €48. They also have a decent *pensión* next door: single €30; double €36.

Budget

Apartamentos Eladio La Playa; tel: 922 80 51 24. A small, family-run place with reasonable apartments. Studio apartment €30.

Apartamentos Lola La Calera; tel: 922 80 51 45. In a charming, quiet area about 10 minutes' walk from the beach. Apartments have a small kitchen and separate bedroom; all have either balcony or terrace. Apartment for 2 €36.

Apartamentos Lola La Playa; tel: 922 80 57 77; fax: 922 80 54 00; email: lola@ap-lola.com; www.ap-lola.com. There are no decent views but you do get a TV. 1-bedroom apartment €36.

Pensión Candelaria Las Vueltas; tel: 922 80 54 02. Not a bad little place, hidden away in the narrow back streets of Las Vueltas. Rooms are bright and most have balconies. There is also a tiny kitchenette in each room. Single/double €30.

Pensión Las Jornadas La Playa; tel: 922 80 50 47; fax: 922 80 52 54. Not the smartest of rooms but it is right on the seafront. Some have shower, some don't, but none have a toilet. A couple of rooms have a balcony, and there is a large rooftop terrace for all to share if you can't manage the 20m walk to the beach. Single €18; double €28 (cheaper if you stay for more than 3 nights).

Pensión Las Vueltas In the upper part of Las Vueltas; tel: 922 80 52 16. Some rooms have private bathroom or there are others with a bathroom shared between two rooms. Single €20; double €25 (€20 with shared bathroom).

Where to eat

As well as the places listed here, there are a few bistros in Las Vueltas, most of which have vegetarian options.

Bar Restaurante Cuba Libre Behind the Centro Cultural in La Calera. Has a small but well-done selection, mainly seafood and salad.

El Bodegón Right next to the main beach, tel: 922 80 54 75. There's a friendly, relaxed atmosphere and it's a bit smarter than a few other places nearby. It has a very meaty menu, with few other alternatives. There are tables outside.

Garbanza Next to Restaurante El Mundo. Excellent choice of Middle Eastern cuisine. Main courses are around €10.

Il Papagallo Next to the harbour in Las Vueltas. An incredible pasta selection.

Los Robles Near the Apartamentos Las Tres Palmeras. It's an Argentine-run restaurant, so obviously aimed more at the carnivores amongst us. They also serve home-made pasta and have some tempting salads.

Restaurante El Mirador La Calera; tel: 922 80 50 56. Their speciality is rabbit, though they have a good selection of fish and it's not a bad place to have breakfast either. Closed on Sundays.

Restaurante El Mundo Next to the Hotel Gran Rey. Decent Indian food with a few vegetarian options.

Restaurante Terraza El Descansillo La Calera. A family-run establishment offering only the earthiest Gomeran cooking, with *gofio*, goat's cheese and fresh fish featuring heavily on their menu.

Nightlife

Valle Gran Rey is basically a quiet resort, but you might find a bit of late night entertainment in Las Vueltas. **Blue Bar**, on the Avenida Marítima, is a chilled-out place, attracting the young hippy crowd. If you delve into the side streets you'll find numerous bistros, some with live music.

Practicalities

Banks Caja Canarias, La Calera, open Mon–Fri 08.30–14.00, Thu 17.00–19.30; BBVA, in Borbalán, open Mon–Fri 08.30–14.15, Sat 08.30–13.00; La Caixa, next to BBVA, open Mon–Fri 08.15–14.00, Thu 16.30–19.45; Caja Rural, near the Hotel Gran Rey, open Mon–Fri 08.30–14.00, Thu 17.00–19.30.

Health The Health Centre is signposted from the main road to Arure; it's just outside La Calera.

Internet Cyber Point Rajose, La Calera, open Mon–Fri 09.00–13.30, 16.30–20.00, Sun 10.00–13.00; €2 per hour; Cibermatika, in Las Vueltas, open Mon–Fri 10.00–14.00, 16.00–21.00, Sat 10.00–13.00; €3.50 per hour.

Pharmacy There's one on the Borbalán–Vueltas road and another next to the Health Centre.

Police The Guardia Civil is a couple of kilometres out of the centre, on the main road to Arure.

Post office In Borbalán, open Mon–Fri 08.30–14.30, Sat 09.30–13.00.

Shopping There are plenty of supermarkets and souvenir shops scattered around.

Tourist information In La Playa, open Mon–Sat 09.00–13.30, 16.00–18.30, Sun 10.00–13.00.

What to see and do

Beaches

The main beach, Playa de la Calera, is a large black-sand beach; take care when swimming. There's a nudist beach, Playa del Inglés, 1km north of La Playa. The safest place for swimming is the Charco del Conde.

Boat trips

Boats heading for Los Órganos leave the harbour at 10.30 daily except Friday. A full-day excursion, which includes lunch, drinks, a spot of fishing and a stop at one of the southern beaches, costs €30; tel: 922 80 54 80 or head to the harbour to buy tickets.

Cycling

If you feel energetic you can rent a bike from **Bike Station Gomera**, near the Charco del Conde. A mountain bike costs €7 per day and you can also rent all manner of scooters and motorbikes. Tel: 922 80 58 02.

Hiking

There are a couple of hiking and adventure sports companies based in Valle Gran Rey, though they operate tours throughout the island.

Learn Spanish

There is a language school in La Calera, IDEA (tel: 922 80 57 03; email: idea@spanish-course.com; www.spanish-course.com.), offering short courses in Spanish for all levels. A 20-hour per week course costs €170 for one week or €290 for two weeks. A 30-hour per week course is €250 for one week or €420 for two weeks. The school has basic, *pensión*-style accommodation available or will arrange accommodation in nearby apartments. They also operate excursions at weekends.

VALLEHERMOSO

This is the largest municipality, stretching from coast to coast, though the town itself is compact with almost everything in or near the square. There's nothing to do in Vallehermoso, but if you have transport a drive past La Presa de la Encantadora and on to La Banda de las Rosas is well worth it.

Getting there

Buses leave San Sebastián for Vallehermoso four times per day during the week and twice a day on weekends. There is also a bus to La Dama, passing through El Cercado and Chipude, leaving Vallehermoso Mon–Sat at 14.00.

Where to stay

Casa Bernardo Calle Triana; tel: 922 20 08 49; www.geocities.com/casas_bernardo. Run by Bernardo, who wants you to join his anti-capitalist world and enjoy his gardens! Rooms are spotless and a good size. Bathrooms are shared and you also have access to a kitchen and huge terrace. Single €15; double €27 and there is one apartment for 4 people for €55, with a minimum stay of 3 days.
Hotel Rural Tamahuche La Hoya 20; tel/fax: 922 80 11 76; email: hoteltamahuche@ecoturismocanarias.com; www.ecoturismocanarias.com/hoteltamahuche. Just 5 minutes' walk from the square towards the beach. It's a lovely rural hotel in a mid 19th-century building. Most rooms have a large terrace and those that don't have window seats. Single €50; double €72.
Pensión Amaya Plaza de la Constitución; tel: 922 80 00 73; fax: 922 80 11 38. In the square, in an unmarked building, but for information on prices and booking go to Bar Restaurante Amaya. Rooms are comfortable and all have private bathroom. Single €18; double €30.
Pensión Central Plaza de la Constitución; tel: 922 80 00 23. Basic rooms, though all with own bathroom. Home-made food downstairs in the bar. Single €10; double €20.

Where to eat

Restaurante Tamahuche In the hotel of the same name. The restaurant prides itself on using organic products and where possible locally grown ones. International cuisine but with a Gomeran influence. Main courses are around €10.

Practicalities

Banks Caja Canarias, in the square, open Mon–Fri 08.30–14.00, Thu 17.00–19.30. There's also a cash point outside Yayo's.
Health The Health Centre is in a yellow building in the square.

Pharmacy Just out of the centre, on the road to the coast.

Police The Policía Local is in the Town Hall.

Post office On Calle Triana, open Mon–Fri 08.30–12.00, Sat 09.00–11.30.

Shopping There's a tiny farmers' market next to the Town Hall, generally open Mon–Sat in the morning, though there's no fixed timetable. Next to Bar Central is Tienda de Rafael Cordero, a family-run place that has been selling everything typically Gomeran for the past 70 years. You can pick up foodstuffs, craftwork and some potent alcoholic brews. No fixed opening hours. There are also a couple of supermarkets on Calle Triana.

Tourist information None, though the staff in the Local Development Agency next to the farmers' market are helpful and knowledgeable; open Mon–Fri 08.15–15.00.

What to see and do

At the time of writing there was nothing to see in the *pueblo* itself, although the Town Hall had a few projects in the pipeline, amongst them a botanical garden, a large handicrafts centre and the reopening of the Parque Marítimo César Manrique.

LAS ROSAS

One thing that you simply must do while you're in La Gomera is see a demonstration of the famous *silbo*. Unfortunately it is a dying art and there aren't many opportunities to see this curious whistling language in action. **Restaurante Las Rosas** is yet another Fred Olsen initiative and while it may be very touristy (the car park is always full of Tenerife day-tripper buses) it doesn't stop the demonstration being amazing. The restaurant is a good place to try local dishes and is surprisingly cheap (starting from €5 per main dish). The demonstration takes place at around 14.30; the restaurant is open only at lunchtimes; tel: 922 80 09 16.

Not far away is the **Juego de Bolas** visitor centre. This is actually the information centre for the national park, though it's located an inconvenient distance from the park itself. The centre is well set out and has information on the formation of La Gomera, models of the island, endemic gardens, a small ethnographic museum and craft workshops. Open daily 09.30–16.30; entrance is free.

AGULO

Three *barrios*, La Montañeta, Las Casas and El Charco, make up this agreeable town, known as *el bombón de La Gomera*. There's absolutely nothing to do but it's a photogenic little place. In theory you should be able to see a demonstration of the *silbo* at the Café Zula, but it's generally reserved for groups only and management is amongst the rudest I've ever come across, so whether you'll be able to arrange it is another matter.

Getting there

Line 2 from the capital passes through before heading to Vallehermoso. It's best to ask locally what time the bus usually arrives.

Where to stay

Apartamentos Bajip Tel: 922 14 61 29. A family-run place; clean if a little rough around the edges. Rooms are pleasant enough and have private bathroom. Single €20; double €30. As the name suggests, there are also apartments up for grabs, though no prices were available at time of writing.

Apartamentos Escuela Calle Pinto Aguiar 10; tel: 922 14 61 94; fax: 922 14 61 77. Clean and homely, with a decent kitchen and TV. Apartment for 2 people €30.

Where to eat
Bar Restaurante Alameda is a very average place, with a small tapas menu and sour-faced service. It's next to the football pitch.
Café Bar Bertermann On the roundabout as you enter Agulo. Rather limited menu of tapas and a few Gomeran dishes such as *almogrote*.
Café La Zula Tel: 922 14 61 09. This place is for pre-arranged groups only, though how you arrange anything is beyond me since the manager refuses to give information over the telephone. There is a chance of seeing a display of the *silbo* here but frankly you'd be infinitely better off at Las Rosas Restaurant.
Tasca la Vieja Escuela In the upper part of town on Calle del Poeta. This tapas bar is the most stylish place in Agulo. It combines Gomeran specialities with traditional Spanish dishes to offer something a little bit different. Closed on Sundays.

Practicalities
Banks Caja Canarias, Calle Pintor Aguiar, open Mon–Fri 08.30–14.00, Thu 17.00–19.30.
Health The Health Centre is next to the football ground.
Pharmacy On the main road.
Police The Policía Local is next to the post office.
Post office On the main Hermigua–Vallehermoso road; open Mon–Fri 08.30–12.00, Sat 08.30–11.30.
Shopping There's a supermarket next to Apartamentos Escuela; Mon–Fri 08.00–13.30, 17.00–20.00, weekends 08.00–13.00.
Tourist information Round the side of the post office; open Mon–Fri 10.00–14.30, Sat 10.00–13.30.

HERMIGUA
Hermigua is a funny little place – you're never quite sure when you've arrived there as it and its surrounding *barrios* are spread out along the main road for a couple of kilometres. Hermigua starts in El Convento, a *barrio* that takes its name from a group of Dominican monks that settled here in the 17th century and built a monastery. The monastery was confiscated and closed in 1821 and the monks' dwellings sold and converted into private houses. Today only the church remains. The Hermigua Valley is La Gomera's main banana producing area and a pretty place to spend an afternoon.

Getting there
Line 2 leaves San Sebastián at 10.10, 14.30, 18.30 and 21.30 (10.10 and 18.30 only on weekends). Return buses leave Vallehermoso at 05.30, 08.00, 14.00 and 16.30 (08.00 and 16.30 on weekends).

Where to stay
Apartamentos Los Telares El Convento; tel: 922 88 07 81; fax: 922 14 41 07; email: telares@canary-islands.com; www.canary-islands.com/gomera/telares. Large studio apartments with mountain views. Most are for 2 people and are €36, though there are a couple of larger ones for 4 people at €48. They can also arrange accommodation in *casas rurales*.
Hotel Rural Ibo Alfaro Tel: 922 88 01 68; fax: 922 88 10 19; email: iboalfaro@terra.es; www.ecoturismocanarias.com/iboalfaro. A 19th-century manor house which has recently been restored and is now a delightful rural hotel. It's just off the main Hermigua road and is well signposted. Single €56; double €75, including breakfast.
Hotel Rural Villa de Hermigua Tel: 922 88 02 46; fax: 922 88 07 77; email: gomeraturismo@wanadoo.es; www.gomeraturismo.com. Another 19th-century house, restored and made into a nice little hotel. There's a kitchen available for communal use. Double €55, including breakfast.

Where to eat
Café Don Juan About halfway between El Convento and the church; it's another typical tapas bar.

La Casa Creativa Near the Iglesia de la Encarnación. Offers something a bit more special, has stunning views and vegetarian options. Main courses start at €10.

Los Telares (see page 263) Has a small restaurant serving local food. It's mainly for guests but if you are passing and they have a spare table, they will feed you.

Restaurante Iratxe Specialises in Basque cuisine, which could come as a lovely change after several days eating *gofio* and goat!

Practicalities
Banks Both banks are on the main road: Caja Canarias, open Mon–Fri 08.30–14.00, Thu 17.00–19.30; BBVA, open Mon–Fri 08.30–14.15, Sat 08.30–13.00.

Health On the main road.

Pharmacy On the main road near the Hotel Villa de Hermigua.

Police The Guardia Civil is near the Town Hall, between El Convento and the Iglesia de la Encarnación; the Policía Local is in the Town Hall.

Post office Next door to the Town Hall, open Mon–Fri 08.30–14.30, Sat 09.30–13.00.

Shopping There's a variety of craftwork for sale at Los Telares, open Mon–Fri 09.30–17.30, Sat 09.00–13.00. The supermarket is open every day 08.30–13.30, 16.00–21.00; it's about halfway between El Convento and the Iglesia de la Encarnación. Further down the road, past the church, Domingo Febles has a workshop where he makes woodcrafts; open Mon–Fri 08.15–13.00, 15.30–19.00, Sat 08.00–13.00.

Tourist information The island's rural tourism office is based in Hermigua, next to the BBVA bank; open Mon–Fri 09.00–13.00, 16.30–19.30, Sat 09.00–12.00.

What to see and do
There's a small museum at Los Telares (opposite the apartments) with exhibits reflecting traditional Gomeran life. Opening times are the same as for the shop (see above). Entrance is free. At the time of writing there were also plans to open a larger ethnographic museum in the town.

HIKES
Cruce de Pajarito–Alto de Garajonay–El Cedro–Hermigua
Distance: 12¹/₂km; time: 4 hours; difficulty: 2

The most delightful walk on the island and I might venture to say the best of the archipelago. The walk starts at Cruce de Pajarito, reachable by bus from San Sebastián and Valle Gran Rey (you could also leave your car here but that provides the problem of collecting it later). Take the right-hand path leading to the Alto de Garajonay where, on a clear day, you'll get views of El Hierro, La Palma, Tenerife and sometimes even Gran Canaria. This is the only uphill stretch of the walk (about 15 minutes). From here, follow signs to Contadero, which will soon lead you into a clearing with a dirt track running alongside. Turn right on the dirt track and when you reach the road, cross it and take the path for El Cedro. This downhill path takes you through the Canary Islands' largest laurel forest and past some *miradors* offering postcard views of Tenerife. Not long after reaching a small stream, which runs throughout the year, you'll come to a fork in the path where you should opt for Arroyo de El Cedro. Cross the stream and then follow it to Arroyo, from where it is just 0.5km to Ermita de Nuestra Señora de Lourdes. Follow the sign for Caserío de El Cedro, a picturesque village set in a valley. On reaching the hamlet, take the path that leads around the valley to the right, pass the houses (which are *casas rurales* available to rent), descend the cobbled steps and follow the dirt track to the right. You'll soon start to see signs for the bar, an excellent place to stop for a traditional lunch. Or, if you've brought a picnic, the first waterfall isn't far away. A path in front of the bar leads you to the waterfall, which you can see from above. From here steep stone steps take you all the way down to the valley of Hermigua and if you look back you'll see the 175m waterfall. The tourist board describes it as 'spectacular' though in truth it's not much more than a trickle, albeit a very long one. This part is tough on the knees (though preferable to walking up!). When you eventually reach the road, cross it and turn right. Almost immediately you'll see some steps on the left. These take you to another road where you should turn left, through the houses and continue for about 200m until you come to another set of steps on the left. These steps take you down to El Convento, where you can catch the bus back to San Sebastián.

Arure–Llanos de la Mérica–La Calera (Valle Gran Rey)
Distance: 7¹/₂km; time: 3 hours; difficulty: 3
As you leave the village of Arure behind you, you'll soon see a sign for the Mirador El Santo. You could make the five-minute detour to admire the view but it's hardly worth it since the views you'll get on the walk far surpass this one. The paved road becomes a dirt track once you pass a few houses. Stick to this track, keeping your eye on a row of trees on the horizon. You are heading for the top tree, so look out for a path to the right about 200m before reaching the trees. There is a path that takes you between the trees lower down – do not take it: there is a sheer drop on the other side! Once you pass the trees you'll encounter herds of goats and a cave, often used as a shelter for the goats. After around an hour you'll reach the plains (Llanos de la Mérica) and here the descent begins. You zigzag down through the Picacho Canyon for around an hour, eventually reaching the La Calera *barrio* of Valle Gran Rey.

Vallehermoso–Ermita de Santa Clara–Vallehermoso
Distance: 9km; time: 3¹/₂ hours; difficulty: 3
Emily Kingston
From the Calle Mayor in Vallehermoso, look for a narrow alley on your left which takes you up some steps and joins the road to the cemetery. Follow the path to the right of the cemetery that descends to the valley floor. Cross the bridge and follow the path which passes under a cluster of hillside houses overshadowed by the enormous Roque El Cano. On reaching the houses, keep to the left and head up into the Barranco de la Era Nueva. Carry on along the path, ignoring any secondary paths leading to the left, for a gentle ascent which lasts about an hour. You'll eventually enter the evergreen forest where the real climb starts. Dark and damp, the path may become slippery in wet weather. On a clear day, however, your efforts will be rewarded with a magnificent view of the many barrancos visible from the ridge. Continuing through the heather, the path eventually flattens out. After 15 minutes you should see the Ermita de Santa Clara, an eerie sight emerging from the mists that often settle here. If you're lucky you'll find an elderly señor on duty to unlock the chapel, if not you'll have to settle for views as far as La Palma (weather permitting). Return the same way, though if you're feeling brave a path that passes the chapel takes you on a somewhat treacherous walk down to the Vallehermoso beach (another two hours' walking).

DRIVES
Driving is a tiring business in La Gomera and circular drives are difficult, since most of the roads lead from the centre of the island out to the coast. When I last

visited, a 3km stretch of road in the north was closed temporarily, which meant a 35km detour around the island. However, if you're short on time, the following drives will allow you to see all of the main sights in a couple of days. You could feasibly drive around the whole island in one day but you'd have no time to stop at any *miradors* or even have a bite for lunch.

Northern circuit

From **San Sebastián**, follow signs for Valle Gran Rey, along the TF713. Approximately half an hour's driving will bring you to the island's most impressive rock, **Roque de Agando**, a good place to stop and admire the view. Continuing along the same road it's only a further ten minutes to the **Alto de Garajonay**. There are parking places here if you want to take the 15-minute walk up to the highest point on La Gomera (well worth the effort). Back on the TF713, head for Vallehermoso. If you're interested in typical Gomeran villages and don't mind a particularly nasty stretch of road, you can take a detour to **Alojera** and/or **Tagaluche**, though neither is recommendable in bad weather. There's no reason to stop in **Vallehermoso** but it is worth heading up to **Presa de la Encantadora**, a large dam and the minuscule hamlet **La Banda de las Rosas** (turn right off Calle Triana, behind the square). While this road isn't much fun, it takes you through one of the most picturesque parts of the island and La Banda is an excellent place to buy some wickerwork. Once back in Vallehermoso, rejoin the TF711 to **Las Rosas**, the site of a reasonable restaurant with daily *silbo* displays. A minor road takes you to the **Juego de Bolas** visitor centre, full of information on the national park and the island in general. Continue until you come to an even narrower road and turn right. This road cuts straight through the **Garajonay National Park**, giving you a reasonable taste of the park if you're short on time. Eventually you'll rejoin the TF713, heading towards San Sebastián. If you're not tired of the infinite mountain bends, opt for a minor road on the left (before you reach Roque de Agando) which borders the national park and goes past **El Cedro**, a stunningly located hamlet. This road joins the TF711, where you can turn right and head back to the capital or turn left to **Hermigua** and **Agulo**, later retracing your steps back to **San Sebastián**.

Southern circuit

While the northern route might have greater beauty, with its lush green valleys, banana plantations and palm groves, the south is of higher cultural and historical interest. Starting from **Valle Gran Rey**, take the only road out of town, stopping at the **Mirador de Palmarejo**, a César Manrique creation with stunning views of the valley and a decent restaurant. The road goes to Arure, but don't enter the town itself, take the road on the right, signposted **Las Hayas**. This is an excellent place to stop for a hearty lunch, but only if you've got plenty of time. From Las Hayas, the road leads to **El Cercado**, famous for its pottery, and later to **Chipude**, a nondescript little place. Not far after Chipude you come to a junction, where you should turn right. The impressive rock formation known as **La Fortaleza** provides a backdrop for the hamlet of **Pavón**. An hour's walk will take you to the top, affording incomparable views over the south of the island (not recommended in wet weather). Once you've passed through Pavón, the road continues to **La Dama**, closed in by banana plantations. The paved road ends here and you can contemplate the bizarre ghost town, **La Rajita**, at the foot of a kamikaze dirt track. This was once the site of a tuna canning factory and a whole complex was built there in the 1920s including homes, a small church and even a football pitch. The factory closed in the mid 1970s and nowadays the whole place is deserted, although the buildings still stand. I found it strangely enticing but didn't brave the terrible road to go and wander around (you could walk down in less than half an hour). Once you've dragged yourself away from La Rajita, head back the way you came and turn right just after you pass through Pavón. This road takes you through **Igualero** (a good place to buy cheese), past the **Nuestra Señora del Buen Paso** hermitage to **Alajeró**. There's little of interest here, so keep going until you reach the coast and **Playa Santiago**. Finally, head north to join the TF713 and turn left, passing **Roque de Agando** and stopping to admire the view from the **Alto de Garajonay** (a 15-minute walk from the road). Keep to the main roads all the way back to **Valle Gran Rey**.

La Palma

The first thing you'll notice as you land at La Palma's airport is the abundance of banana trees surrounding the runway and stretching to the ocean. The island's most important crop hugs the east and west coasts, contributing to the island's moniker, *la isla verde* ('the green island'). It's more commonly referred to as *la isla bonita* ('the pretty island'), a tag that few would dispute, since the relatively high rainfall creates a fertile layer of vegetation over the volcanic landscape. When people ask me my favourite island I struggle to answer, since each has its own charm, but if pushed I'd have to say La Palma. The lush central mountains contrast with the stark *malpaís* in the south, while the people are welcoming and proud of their history and well-preserved culture. Although there are no golden beaches, there are some charming black-sand coves, hidden away from the increasing number of tourists who visit the island. It's the fourth most populous island with a little over 80,000 inhabitants, though you're unlikely to feel crowded at any point.

HIGHLIGHTS

Hiking is the main activity in La Palma and the Ruta de los Volcanes is the best of the best. The impressive Caldera de Taburiente is unmissable and can be seen on foot or in a 4WD taxi. La Palma is superb star-gazing country and houses the astrophysics observatory at Roque de los Muchachos, one of the northern hemisphere's most important and open to the public just one day a year. The little-visited north is a well-kept secret, especially some of the typical villages between Santo Domingo and Barlovento. In the northeast relax in the impeccable San Andrés on the coast and make day trips to the laurel forest at Los Tilos. Another of the island's best hikes takes you to the Marcos and Cordero springs, passing through 13 tunnels on your way. There are also a few sites with aborigine markings where you can learn a bit more about the elusive Benahoaritas, the first inhabitants of the island.

BACKGROUND INFORMATION
History

Before the Spanish arrived, the island was known as Benahoare, which meant 'My Homeland', and was divided into 12 cantons, each governed by a chief (*mencey*). The first settlers were called the Benahoaritas and are thought to have arrived around 2000BC, though from where no-one is sure. At the time of the conquest there were reckoned to be around 4,000–6,000 inhabitants on the island. They have been described as the tallest men in all the islands and it was even said that giants lived amongst them, though studies of skeletons found that the average height was 1.7m for men and 1.65m for women. The women were noted as being 'Amazonian' and

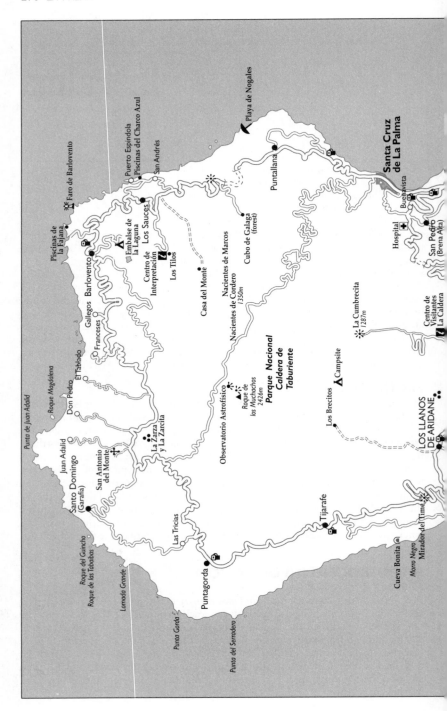

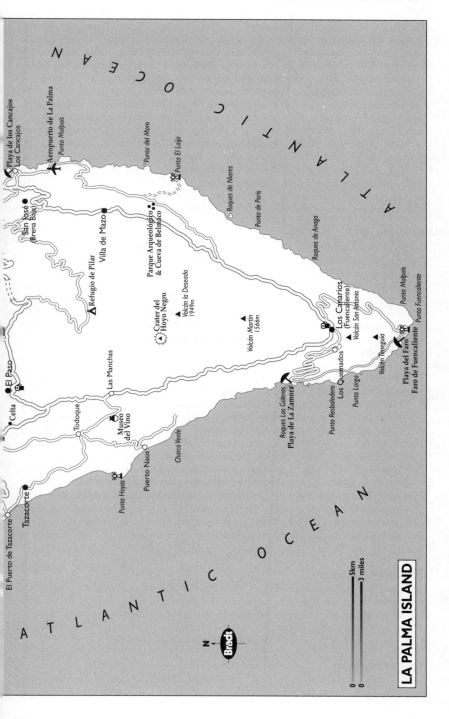

LA PALMA ISLAND

fearless, as Leonardo Torriani recorded: 'They went in front of the men during combat and fought with virility.' La Palma was one of the last islands to fall to the Spanish and was a walkover other than the opposition offered by Tanausú, the *mencey* of Taburiente. But his resistance proved futile when he was betrayed by his relative, Juan de Palma. Tanausú and his subjects fell into an ambush in 1493, marking the end of Alonso Fernández de Lugo's assault on *la isla bonita*. The capital was founded on May 3 of that year. La Palma became quite rich in the 16th century, with revenue brought in from the export of sugar, honey and wine. Their economy grew as the traffic between Europe and America increased, strengthening the port of Santa Cruz. Alas, this new-found prosperity was not without its drawbacks and Santa Cruz frequently fell foul of pirates including the notorious Frenchman François Le Clerc (Peg Leg). He and his men razed the capital to the ground in 1533, destroying many important monuments. The 19th century brought new prosperity to the island with the cultivation of cochineal, the first electric light system in the Canaries and the growth of the shipbuilding industry.

Geography
Heart-shaped La Palma is 708km^2 and is the second highest island, with Roque de los Muchachos reaching 2,426m. The landscape in the extreme south of the island is reminiscent of Lanzarote: moon-like and with little vegetation due to the eruptions in the 1970s, the most recent in the Canary Islands. The central part of the island is dominated by the massive Caldera de Taburiente. Although the *caldera* was long thought to be an immense volcanic crater, most geologists these days agree that it's the result of erosion and formed by numerous old craters forced together over time. La Palma is the most humid island and has an annual rainfall of about 700mm.

Economy
Agriculture is the main source of income on the island and it won't take you long to work out that the number one export is the banana, with an annual production of 140,000 tons. The wines of La Palma are also famous and account for a small portion of the island's income, though nothing compared with the wine trade that once existed here. Another minor industry is tobacco, with cigars from La Palma considered second only to *Cubanos*. Embroidery, basketry and woodwork provide a minimal handicraft industry and one that is generally linked to the newest earner – tourism. Although rural tourism has been providing a steady income for some years, the tour operators are showing an interest in *la isla bonita*. In the '90s British airline JMC started its charter service to Santa Cruz de La Palma, to the dismay of many islanders who look at the south of Tenerife and fear the worst. But for the moment the tourist who visits *la isla bonita* comes for the surroundings and to enjoy some hiking. Nightlife is limited and there are no golden beaches (nor plans to build any).

Flora and fauna
La Palma boasts 700 species of flora and some 50 of them are found exclusively on the island. Some, such as the magnificent Pininana (*Echium pininana*), found only in the northeast, are in danger of extinction as they are used for feeding animals. There are impressive laurel forests in the north of the island, namely Los Tilos and Cubo de Galga, and an extensive area of pine south of El Paso.

Conservation
Lack of water is not such a problem on La Palma, although forest fires are and large areas of Canary pine are charred each summer. The Barbary sheep (*Ammotragus*

lervia), which was introduced to the island after the conquest, is a problem in the Caldera de Taburiente. Its eating habits put uneven pressure on the park's flora and although hunting is permitted, the animal thrives. About 35% of La Palma falls under some level of environmental protection.

Festivals

Carnival is a crazy affair, as in the rest of the archipelago. On the Monday before Mardi Gras the citizens of Santa Cruz honour their ancestors by dressing as emigrants returning from the Americas. For reasons unknown, the revellers spend the evening throwing talc at each other, while salsa music and cigar smoke fill the air.

Since 2002, La Palma has been the location for the International Digital Film Festival, better known as *El Festivalito*. The whole island is converted into a film set as directors rush around to record their videos in a week. It takes place at the start of July; for more information see www.elfestivalito.com. Directors who fancy an even greater challenge can participate in Videosub, an underwater film festival. It's held in September and lasts about five days.

However, these new festivals can't compare to the centuries-old celebration of the Bajada de la Virgen de las Nieves. In 1676, Bishop Bartolomé García Ximénez ordered that the Madonna be brought down from her sanctuary to the capital to prevent the island being devastated by a drought. His plan worked and the custom has been continued every five years since that date, with the whole island flocking to the capital for a six-week party. From late June until early August lavish street parties are held with traditional dances such as the entertaining dance of the dwarves. The Madonna is returned to her sanctuary on August 5.

There are lots of local festivals throughout the island with the best partying months being August and September.

Food

As on the other islands, goat, rabbit, cheese and of course the ubiquitous *papas arrugadas* with *mojo* reign supreme; and beware: Palmeran *mojo* has a kick.

La Palma prides itself on its good wine, particularly the Malvasía variety, but the real delight in La Palma comes after the meal in the form of sickly *postres*, unique liqueurs, and of course a famous *palmero* (cigar). La Palma is the island for those with a sweet tooth, offering some of the most syrupy cakes and desserts you'll ever find. The most common is *bienmesabe*, a gooey cake made with sponge, eggs, almonds, sugar and honey. Less sickly are the *almendrados*, biscuits made of almonds, sugar and eggs. *Rapaduras* are probably the most well known of the Palmeran desserts. To look at, you'd wonder if they are a food at all since they more resemble an ornament. They're made from honey, *gofio*, cinnamon, lemon sugar and almonds fashioned into a hard cone-shaped sweet that you'll struggle to eat in one sitting. Los Sauces is a good place to sample sugar-cane rum, while Tazacorte is well known for its coffee liqueurs.

A great place to try it all is the Mercadillo in Mazo, where local producers get together to sell their goods, and happily allow you to sample everything on offer before making your decision.

GETTING THERE AND AWAY
By air

Binter Canarias Tel: 902 39 13 92; www.bintercanarias.es. *El Hierro:* 2 a week. *Gran Canaria:* 2 a day. *Tenerife North:* 5 a day during the week, 2 on weekends.
Islas Airways Tel: 902 47 74 48; www.islasairways.com. *Gran Canaria:* 2 a day. *Tenerife North:* 6 a day.

By sea

Fred Olsen Tel: 902 10 01 07; email: reserves@fredolsen.es; www.fredolsen.es. *La Gomera:* 1 a day. *Tenerife:* 1 a day (from Los Cristianos).
Trasmediterránea Tel: 902 45 46 54; www.trasmediterranea.es. *Gran Canaria:* 1 a week. *Tenerife:* 1 a week. *Lanzarote:* 1 a week (to Arrecife). *Cádiz:* 1 a week.
Naviera Armas Tel: 902 45 65 00; email: narmas@naviera-armas.com; www.naviera-armas.com. *Tenerife:* 4 a week.

GETTING AROUND
Public transport
The bus system is reasonable, serving the majority of the main destinations, though often you need to return to Santa Cruz or Los Llanos to catch another bus. Timetables are available at the tourist information offices at the airport and in Santa Cruz. Buy a *bono* if you intend to do much bus travel as it'll save you a fair amount.

Car hire
Most companies can arrange for your car to be delivered to and collected from your hotel.

Autos Magui Tel: 922 41 28 83 (Santa Cruz)
Betacar Tel: 922 42 80 42 (airport); 922 40 80 13 (Puerto Naos)
Buen Viaje Tel: 922 41 14 05 (Santa Cruz); 922 43 47 56 (Los Cancajos)
Cicar Tel: 922 42 80 48 (airport)
Hertz Tel: 922 42 85 94 (airport)

WHERE TO STAY
The island has a good range of accommodation with 7,500 beds scattered around hotels, *pensiones*, apartments, *casas rurales* and a few camping grounds. The **Asociación de Turismo Rural Isla Bonita** has almost 100 rural houses across the island and they are some of the best in the archipelago. The minimum stay is a week. Expect to pay around €250 for two people, €300 for four people per week. Their office is in Casa Luján in Putallana (tel: 922 43 06 25; fax: 922 43 03 08; email: islabonita@infolapalma.com; www.islabonita.com). There are six **camping** grounds on the island, some under management of the Town Hall or *Cabildo* while others are privately owned. Facilities vary as do prices. The tourist information office has details of the campsites.

ACTIVITIES
Diving
Although it's not as well developed as on other islands, there is scope for diving around La Palma. The seas at the south of the island are of particular interest, since the recent volcanic eruptions have created some fascinating underwater sights. Submarine fauna is not abundant but the waters are particularly clear.

Hiking
This is the number one activity in La Palma, and rightly so. With a good network of footpaths offering some spectacular views, it really is hikers' heaven. There are some companies offering guided hikes, which is a good option as ramblers have been known to get lost in the Caldera de Taburiente (and I managed to get lost in various other places on the island too). Going it alone is perfectly feasible and the tourist information office has a useful guide to hiking, but double check if there are any routes that haven't been checked recently (overgrowing plants can cause

havoc). As in every island, transport to and from the walks is a problem and sometimes a taxi is the only option. The two finest hikes are the Barranco de las Angustias in the Caldera and the long, tough and superb Ruta de los Volcanes.

Natour On the main road in Los Cancajos; tel: 922 43 30 01; fax: 922 43 30 11; email: natour-trekking@infonegocio.com; www.natour-trekking.com. Operate walks for all levels and rent out boots, backpacks and walking sticks. They have multi-lingual guides and always try to form groups of people with a common language. Prices range from €24 to €44.

Jean Luis Cerckel Tel: 922 44 03 47. An independent guide who's been wandering around the islands for the past six years. He offers tailored tours from around €15 per person, depending on the location and the number of people.

North Trekking Tel: 922 42 08 93. Offer all the usual routes, average price €35, pick-ups from Santa Cruz, Los Cancajos and Puerto Naos.

Shopping

La Palma is known for its quality embroidery, woodwork and basketry and there's also some excellent pottery to be had. One of the best places to purchase handicrafts is in Mazo, where you have the choice of buying from the Escuela de Artesanía (Handicrafts School), the weekend market or from the El Molino pottery workshop. There are also food and handicrafts markets in Garafía, Puntagorda and Los Llanos. The other handmade speciality is cigars. You can see them being rolled by Señor Vargas in the capital or at the craft shop in the airport.

Star-gazing

With some of the clearest sky in the northern hemisphere, La Palma is a fine spot to look at the stars. Roque de los Muchachos is a fascinating place, though you have to time your trip well if you want to visit – the observatory is open to the public just one day a year. It's usually in mid August, though you should check with the tourist office for the exact details. The rest of the year you'll have to be content with taking a few snaps of the space-age observatory above the clouds. Note that the gate is locked at 20.00, so make sure you get there with enough time to take pictures and leave while you still can.

Swimming

Some of La Palma's beaches have lethal tides and swimming is unwise in places. Playa de Nogales is particularly dangerous and more than a couple of tourists a year drown there. You're better off sticking to the natural pools of La Fajana and Charco Azul in the north and Charco Verde in the south. Generally, if there are lifeguards and other people swimming you should be OK, but take great care on deserted beaches. While they're very picturesque, the sea might not be so welcoming.

Wine tasting

Mentioned on more than one occasion by Shakespeare, Canarians make a fine drop of wine and there are various bodegas you can visit on La Palma. All will let you sample their vintages before you buy. A good place to get an overall view (and taste) of La Palma's wines is the Museo del Vino in Las Manchas.

SANTA CRUZ DE LA PALMA

It's a picky person who can't find something to like about the island's capital. Walking through the narrow, steep cobbled streets and admiring the traditional Canarian architecture that greets you at every turn is a pleasure (although

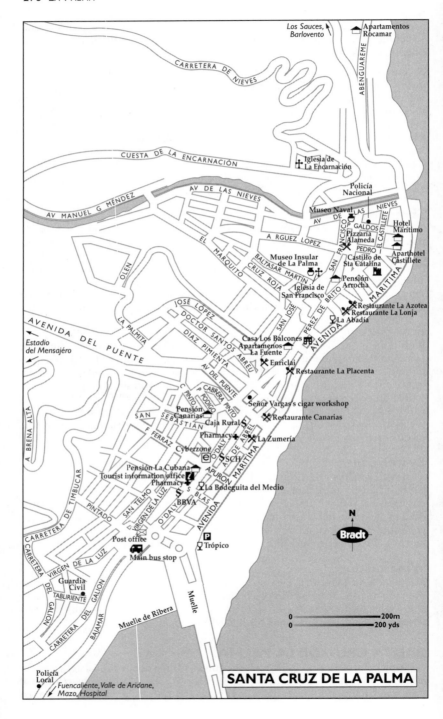

SANTA CRUZ DE LA PALMA

sometimes hard work). The capital has a totally irregular layout and its steep streets might have you gasping for breath, but don't let that put you off. Don't miss Casa de los Balcones on the Avenida Marítima – probably the finest example of typical Canarian architecture in the archipelago. Charming pavement cafés are tucked away in every square and the majority of shops are based around the Calle Real (Calle O'Daly and Calle Pérez de Brito). The capital was founded in 1493, once the island had fallen to the Castilian crown. It is currently home to a little over 17,000 inhabitants, so it manages to maintain an intimate air without feeling like a *pueblo*.

Getting there
By bus
A bus from the airport to the capital is €0.90 and takes about 15 minutes. They leave every half an hour in the morning and afternoon and every hour in the evening from the bus stop outside the terminal (leave by the doors to the right). There's no bus station as such in Santa Cruz but buses leave from in front of the post office.

By taxi
A taxi from the airport will cost around €10.

Where to stay
Mid-range
Apartamentos la Fuente Calle Pérez de Brito 49; tel: 922 41 56 36; fax: 922 41 23 03; email: lafuente@cajacanarias.net; www.la-fuente.com. A variety of accommodation, ranging from the tiny and dark to enormous apartments with balcony and sea views. All have kitchen, bathroom, radio and satellite TV. Prices range from €32 to €52, with a charge of €8 per extra bed.

Apartamentos Rocamar Calle Abenguareme 10; tel: 922 41 19 46. They don't look much from the outside and are not in the nicest part of town, but inside they are clean and comfortable. Try to get one with a sea view as the others overlook the busy main road. Prices are €30 for 1 person; €36 for 2; €52 for 4 and €75 for 6 people.

Aparthotel Castillete Av Marítima 75; tel: 922 42 08 40; fax: 922 42 00 67. Probably the best place in the mid-range bracket, with a choice of rooms, studios or apartments, some with sea view. There is a rooftop swimming pool and restaurant. Single €41; double €47; studio €53; apartment €60 for 2 people.

Hotel Marítimo Av Marítima 75; tel: 922 42 02 22; fax: 922 41 43 02; email: info@hotelmaritimo.com; www.hotelmaritimo.com. Large rooms with television and balcony, some with sea view, others have a vista of the mountains. The hotel also has a cafeteria, restaurant and rooftop sun terrace. Single €52; double €67, including breakfast.

Budget
Pensión Arrocha Calle Pérez de Brito 27; tel: 922 41 11 17. A basic place with simple, clean rooms and shared bathrooms. Single €15; double €21.

Pensión Canarias Calle Cabrera Pinto 27; tel/fax: 922 41 31 82. Located in very quiet streets behind the main pedestrian area, Pensión Canarias offers the best value of the budget options and is very clean. Most rooms have TV. Single €21; double €28. There's one single room without bathroom which goes for €17.

Pensión La Cubana Calle O'Daly; tel: 922 41 13 54. Located in a marvellous old Palmeran building, this place has basic, pretty clean rooms, all with shared bathrooms. Rooms at the back are quieter, though a little dark. Slightly overpriced at €20 for a single; €26 for a double.

Where to eat

Enriclai Near to the Teatro Chico; tel: 699 27 05 14. This place boasts the title of La Palma's smallest restaurant with just 4 tables. As you watch your food being cooked you'll feel more like you're at a friend's house for dinner than in a restaurant. The food is good, with some tasty vegetarian specials and mainly organic ingredients.

La Zumería Av Marítima. Every juice you could ever think to order, plus fast food and metre-long sausages.

Pizzería Alameda The pizzas aren't great but the location is good, with tables outside in the Alameda.

Restaurante Canarias Av Marítima. Has a tapas menu, a full menu and a *menú del día*: three courses and a drink for €7.50.

Restaurante La Azotea Av Marítima. A good place to sit and admire the traditional balconies while sampling some fresh fish and delightful desserts; their fish platter for 2 is excellent. Tables outside or on the roof.

Restaurante La Lonja Av Marítima. An excellent menu with plenty of choice in fish and meat, plus the sweetest of La Palma puds. Later on it becomes a night-time hang-out and stays open until the early hours. Closed on Sundays.

Restaurante La Placeta Placeta Borrero; tel: 922 41 52 73. Has tables outside in an attractive square. They have a variety of dishes including some vegetarian options and some Palmeran specials. Closed on Sundays.

Nightlife

Although not as lively as other island capitals, Santa Cruz has some laid-back late bars and at least you're not faced with tough choices as to where to go.

La Abadía Av Marítima. Stays open until 02.00 or 03.00, a lively place with inexpensive drinks.

La Azotea A restaurant by day but fills up on weekend nights from midnight onwards.

La Bodeguita del Medio Calle Alvarez de Abreu. A popular place to start the night with a few *mojitos*, the house special. It gets so busy that people spill out into the pedestrian street. There are a few other bars in this area whose popularity comes and goes.

La Lonja Pretty much the same as La Azotea, though the atmosphere is friendlier.

Trópico The place for late-night owls. It a curious-looking bar at the port end of the Avenida Marítima, looking like a cross between a circus tent and a children's playground, but everyone goes there until daybreak, probably because it's the only place still open!

Practicalities

Banks On Calle O'Daly: Santander Central Hispano, open Mon–Fri 08.30–14.00, Sat 08.30–13.00; BBVA, open Mon–Fri 08.30–14.15, Sat 08.30–14.00; Caja Rural, open Mon–Fri 08.30–14.00, Thu 17.00–19.30.

Health The hospital is to the west of the town, tel: 922 18 50 00.

Internet Ciberzone on Calle O'Daly is open 10.00–13.00 and 17.00–22.00; connection €2.25 an hour.

Pharmacy There are numerous pharmacies on Calle O'Daly.

Police The Guardia Civil is on Calle Taburiente in the upper part of town near the Ermita de La Luz; the Policía Nacional is on Calle Pérez Galdós; the Policía Local is on Av Bajamar as you leave the city.

Post office At the south end of town, open Mon–Fri 08.30–14.00, Sat 09.30–13.00.

Shopping For handmade cigars head to Calle Volcán, where Señor Vargas rolls the finest smoking material. The Calle Real is the main shopping street.

Tourist information On Calle O'Daly, open Mon–Fri 09.00–19.30, Sat 09.00–15.00, Sun 09.00–14.00. By far the most helpful and informative office in the Canary Islands.

Above Isla Graciosa from the air, Archipiélago Chinijo (GAR)

Left Drying fish, Orzola, Lanzarote (GAR)

Below Puerto de La Restinga, El Hierro (GAR)

Next page Isla de Lobos, Fuerteventura (GAR)

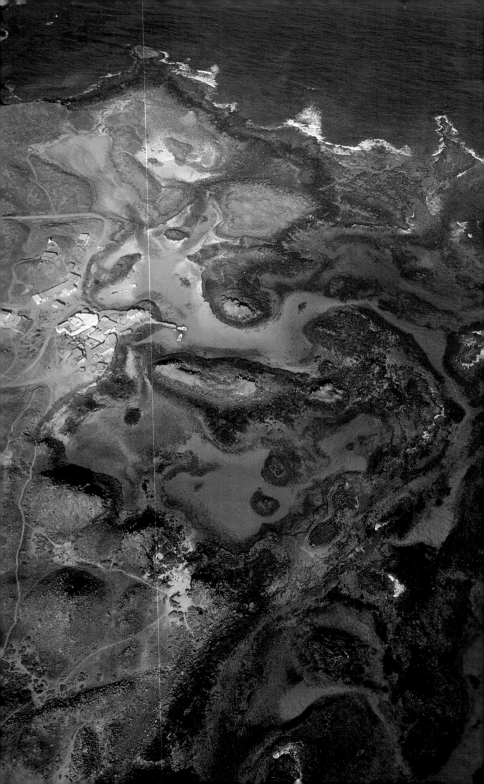

What to see and do
Although there aren't many museums, there's no lack of churches, each with its own information panel. Churches are more likely to be open in the morning. The castle at the end of the Avenida Marítima is open only on special occasions.

Museo Insular de La Palma
Housed in a 16th-century convent in the Plaza de San Francisco, the museum has exhibits on the history, flora and fauna of La Palma and a collection of 16th- and 20th-century paintings. It also has an ethnographic section explaining the customs and way of life of Palmeros. It's quite an old fashioned museum, though the section on the Benahoaritas is interesting. Mon–Fri 09.30–13.30, 16.00–18.00; entrance is €1.80.

Museo Naval
Based in the Alameda, this naval museum has some excellent old maps of the islands. The boat is a replica of the Santa María, a ship in Columbus's fleet – an odd idea since he never actually set foot on La Palma. In winter it's open Mon–Thu 09.30–14.00, 16.00–19.00, closed Friday afternoons; in summer it's open Mon–Fri 09.30–14.30; €1.30 for adults, free for children.

LOS CANCAJOS
The residents of La Palma were probably shaking in their boots when the first charter flight arrived in the mid 1980s. Since then, Los Cancajos has continued to grow but generally attracts quality tourism and is worlds apart from the likes of Playa de las Américas in Tenerife. It's 3km south of Santa Cruz and so the main summer playground for the capital's residents. It also attracts a fair amount of foreign tourists and has the unmistakably fake feel of a resort and little charm. There are no street names yet but it's a small place and everything is easy to find. At the time of research there were considerable building works being carried out at the south end of the resort, suggesting that many more hotels are on the way. Boot-quaking remains firm amongst the locals.

Getting there
The number 8 bus stops on its way to and from the airport every half-hour on weekdays or every hour on weekends.

Where to stay
Upmarket
Apartamentos H10 Costa Salinas Tel: 922 43 43 48; fax: 922 43 45 10; email: costa.salinas@h10.es. The complex has excellent facilities which it shares with the Hotel Taburiente next door: 3 pools, gym, mini-golf, satellite TV in all apartments and a choice of places to eat. One bedroom apartment €70; 2 bedrooms €82.
Hotel H10 Taburiente Playa Tel: 922 18 12 77; fax: 922 18 12 85; email: taburiente@ h10.es. Large rooms with balconies, many of which have a sea view. Shares facilities with the Costa Salinas apartments next door. Single €70; double €100, including breakfast.

Mid-range
Apartamentos Centrocancajos Centro Comercial Centrocancajos; tel: 922 18 13 00; fax: 922 43 44 03; email: centrocancajos@wanadoo.es. Apartments are on the small side, but have everything you need. There's a swimming pool and TVs are available to rent. Apartments are €42 for 1 person; €50 for 2 people and €54 for 4.
Apartamentos Lago Azul Urb San Antonio del Mar; tel: 922 43 43 05; fax: 922 43 46 62; email: lagoazul-recepcion@telefonica.net. The apartments are clean and the service is

friendly. There's a good-sized swimming pool and a restaurant. Good value at €42 per apartment for 2 to 4 people.

Apartamentos La Cascada Urb San Antonio del Mar; tel: 922 43 42 80; fax: 922 18 12 59. New apartments with well-equipped kitchens. All have balconies, some with sea view. Also has a swimming pool and TVs are available to rent. Apartments for 2 people €53; 4 people €60.

Where to eat

Backería In front of Apartamentos La Cascada. German bakery with a good line in snacks and breakfasts.

Bar Restaurante El Pulpo Right on the beach and *the* hang-out of the locals. Excellent fish and seafood. Closed on Wednesdays.

Restaurante El Coral At the front of the Centro Comercial. A few Canarian specials but mainly serves international food.

Restaurante Montmartre In the Centro Comercial; tel: 670 81 62 55. French cuisine in a restaurant that's a cut above most in the resort. It has some delicious choices including a few very tasty salads. Main courses start at €12; open evenings only.

Restaurante Nosotros Next to Apartamentos La Cascada; tel: 922 43 43 29. A friendly place with good food and daily specials. Good for pasta and fish and some fiendish home-made desserts. Also has a menu of the day for €14. Closed Sundays and Mondays.

Restaurante Tiuna Next door to El Coral, an Italian joint with a good choice of pizzas and pastas.

Snack Bar El Típico II Outside the Centro Comercial. Cheap and cheerful, specialising in burgers, hotdogs and sandwiches.

Nightlife

Although it's generally a quiet resort, there are various places behind the Centro Comercial that can entertain you until the early hours. Start off at the **Lambada Beach Bar**, then sample some home-made sangria at **Guantanamera** before moving on to **Pepe's Disco Pub** for a bit of dancing.

Practicalities

Banks There's an ATM next to the Spar in the Centrocancajos shopping centre.

Health In Santa Cruz, though the hotels and apartments will call a doctor if required.

Internet La Palma Diving has internet access for €2.50 per hour; open Mon–Sat 08.30–13.00, 17.00–20.00. Yenet Cibercafe charges €3 an hour and is open Mon–Fri 09.00–14.00, 18.30–late, Sat–Sun evenings only.

Pharmacy There's one in the Centro Comercial and one on the main road.

Post office The closest is in Santa Cruz.

Police In Santa Cruz.

Shopping There are numerous souvenir shops in the Centro Comercial.

Tourist information At the time of writing there were plans to open an information booth next to the beach.

What to see and do
Sunbathing

The main reason to come is for the *playa*, a pretty black-sand beach with very calm waters: ideal for children or wave-phobic adults.

Diving

Buceo Sub Next to the Apartamentos Costa Salinas; tel: 922 18 11 13; email: buceosub@gmx.net; www.buceos-sub.com. Baptism dives €52 and a variety of courses for

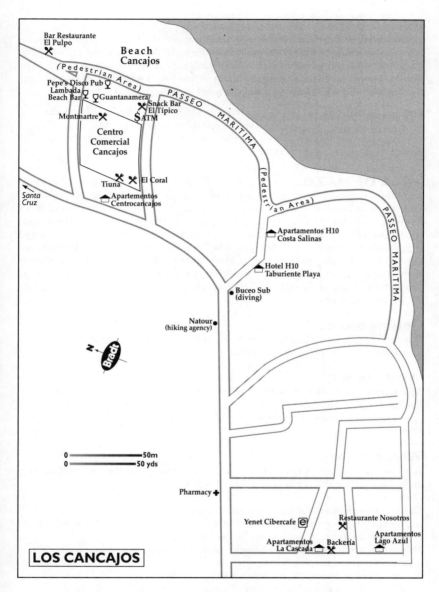

LOS CANCAJOS

anyone aged 10 and over. They also rent out snorkelling gear for €9 an hour.
La Palma Diving Centro Comercial Los Cancajos. Discovery dives €62; a series of 5 dives
costs €219.

Other activities

Several agencies offer walking trips, boat trips and island excursions. Viajes Tanausú
near to the Cibercafe has quite a good choice. Natour, the island's biggest walking
agency, has its office on the main road near to the Costa Salinas apartments.

BREÑA BAJA

There isn't much to this tiny province, a narrow stretch of land crammed between the municipalities of Breña Alta and Mazo. Its main drawcard is the resort of Los Cancajos. It is also home to the island's *parador* (a government-run hotel). The hotel is just off the road from San Antonio to San José. From the LP1 follow signs for San José and when you get close the hotel is signposted.

Parador de la Palma Tel: 922 435 828; fax: 922 435 999; email: lapalma@parador.es; www.parador.es. It's everything you'd expect, with a gym, sauna, swimming pool and plenty of excursions on offer. Some rooms have impressive views overlooking the coast. Single €90; double €115, meals extra.

VILLA DE MAZO

At 500m above sea level and flanked by volcanic cones, Mazo is one of La Palma's most charming *pueblos* and there's a surprising amount to see and do in a town so small. It's like a one-stop glimpse into Palmeran culture. Mazo hosts the island's finest farmers' market on weekends, while you can gain an insight into aboriginal pottery at El Molino. The local Corpus Christi celebrations are famous island-wide, though if you can't attend and see the colourful flower carpets in the flesh, visiting the exhibition at Casa Roja is a worthy alternative. While in Mazo, you should try the local wine which holds one of the island's *denominaciones de origen*.

Getting there

Bus number 3 leaves Santa Cruz about every two hours, passing through Mazo on its way to Fuencaliente and Los Llanos.

Where to stay

Apartamentos Alisios Calle María del Carmen Martínez Jerez; tel: 922 42 83 60. Excellent value and well looked after, the apartments have a nice garden area. A basic apartment (with kitchen and bathroom) for 2 people is €20. Ask in Bar Restaurante San Blas.

Where to eat

Bar Los Faroles On the main road from San Pedro. Join the locals for a beer and a game of dominoes on the terrace outside. Certainly has plenty of local character – and local characters.

Bar Restaurante San Blas Calle María del Carmen Martínez Jerez. Combines Canarian and international food with a little Mazo touch. Good local wines, stews, soups and grilled meats. *Menú del día* €11. Closed on Sunday evenings and Mondays.

Diber Next to the post office. The place for burgers and ice-cream, when you just can't manage any more tapas.

Restaurante Las Toscas On the main road, opposite the bus stop. An extensive and original menu, heavy on red meat. They also have a *menú del día* for €8.50. Closed on Sundays.

Practicalities

Banks Caja Canarias, on the main road, open Mon–Fri 08.30–14.00, Thu 17.00–19.30; Santander Central Hispano, Calle Calvo Sotelo, open Mon–Fri 08.30–14.00, Sat 08.30–13.00.

Health The Health Centre is on Calle Maximiliano Pérez Díaz.

Pharmacy On the main road next to Caja Canarias.

Police The Policía Local is behind the Town Hall on a pedestrian street.
Post office On the main road, open Mon–Fri 08.30–13.00, Sat 09.00–10.00.
Shopping Mazo is handicrafts heaven, with the weekend market, El Molino and the Escuela de Artesanía. There's a supermarket on Calle Calvo Sotelo.
Tourist information In the Escuela de Artesanía, open Mon–Fri 09.00–13.00, 15.00–18.00.

What to see and do
Mercadillo

The main attraction is the market held on weekends. Local farmers get together to sell their wares to the public, meaning you can try some of the finest *mojos* (and there are more than you ever could have imagined), the sweetest cakes, the tastiest cheeses and the strongest wines on offer. And you know that your money is going straight to the producer. Upstairs is the handicrafts section, which mainly sells embroidered goods. Open Sat 15.00–20.00, Sun 09.00–13.00. The market is on Calle Enlace Dr Morera, a little further along from the Escuela de Artesanía.

Casa Roja

This magnificent early 20th-century building now houses the Corpus Christi Information Centre and the Embroidery Museum. Corpus Christi is celebrated in a big way in Mazo; flower-petal carpets and impressive arches are displayed in the streets during the festival. On the ground floor of Casa Roja you can see examples of these decorations and learn about the origins of the celebration. The upper floor pays homage to one of the most popular handicrafts of La Palma: embroidery. Its origins and importance in Palmeran culture are bizarrely explained through the eyes of an embroidery stitch. Entrance to the museum is €2 for adults and €0.75

for children under 12. Open Mon–Fri 10.00–14.00, 15.00–18.00, Sat 11.00–18.00, Sun 10.00–14.00.

Escuela de Artesanía

You can watch the handicrafts students at work and later buy the fruits of their labour in the shop. If you have a real hankering to learn one of the local crafts, and plan to be on the island a while, you can enrol on one of their courses. The shortest course they offer lasts two months. For further information call 922 44 00 52. The school and shop are open Mon–Fri 09.00–13.00, 15.00–18.00.

El Molino

Follow the steep road to the left of the church for about 800m and you'll be rewarded with the chance to see and buy some almost authentic Benahoarita pottery (well, as authentic as you're gonna get). El Molino is a converted mill where craftsman Ramón Barreto and his wife Vina Cabrera work, making reproductions of aboriginal ceramics. There is a small museum with artefacts from the original mill, which was built in 1867 and restored in 1995. There is also a shop where, alongside the usual souvenirs, you can buy the reproductions – the only place on the island (or indeed in the world) where they are sold. Open Mon–Sat 09.00–13.00, 15.00–19.00.

Around Mazo

Parque Arqueológico de Belmaco

A small but interesting centre that showcases the first stone engravings to be found in the Canary Islands along with ten cave dwellings. It's well laid out and has useful information panels. Also has a small multimedia centre. It's on the main road between Hoyo de Mazo and Fuencaliente. Open Mon–Sat 10.00–18.00, Sun 10.00–15.00; entrance €2 or €0.75 for the under 12s. There is an unrelated and well-stocked handicrafts shop opposite.

LOS CANARIOS (FUENCALIENTE)

Spain's most recently created village has two interchangeable names. The maps and signs call it Los Canarios, while locals insist it's called Fuencaliente and the person who wrote the road signs was from out of town... Anyway, it isn't the most exciting place on the island and perhaps the main reason you'd find yourself here is because it's at the end of the Ruta de los Volcanes (unless you opt for the hardcore walk to the coast, and still you might want a beer and an *almendrado* as you pass through the town). There are a few bodegas around if you fancy a bit of wine tasting and it's not a bad place to base yourself if you want to see the beaches and volcanoes in the south, which you certainly should see.

Getting there

Bus number 3 leaves Santa Cruz about every two hours daily on its way to Los Llanos.

Where to stay

Pensión/Apartamentos Central Calle Yaiza 4; tel: 922 44 40 18. At the back of the town in a quiet area. Rooms in the *pensión* have private bathrooms and some of the doubles have a balcony for a couple of euros extra. There are also some 1-bedroom apartments. For information and keys go to Bar Imperial on Calle San Antonio. Single €16; double €21; apartment for 2 people €25.

Pensión/Apartamentos Los Volcanes Ctra General del Sur 84; tel: 922 44 41 64; fax: 922 44 40 62. Their studio apartments are pretty spacious and have balconies and sea views.

The *pensión* rooms all have bathroom and a couple have a balcony. It's a well-looked-after place with friendly staff. Apartments for 1 person €20, 2 people €24, 3 or more €27; single €17; double €20.

Where to eat

The restaurants in Fuencaliente are pretty humdrum and you might be better off moving a little out of town for something to eat.

Bar Parada On the main road. It's an excellent place to familiarise yourself with the Palmeran sweet tooth. They specialise in *almendrados* and *rapaduras* and if you're lucky you could get some straight from the oven.

Restaurante El Patio del Vino Tel: 922 44 46 23. Just out of the town centre and definitely the best place for a spot of lunch. Naturally, being a part of the bodega, the wine list is more important than the menu. Closed on Sunday evenings and Mondays.

Tasca la Era Signposted from the town; tel: 922 44 44 75. You'll find it just off the road from Fuencaliente to Las Indias. It's a good place for a bit of local cuisine, particularly pork cooked on the grill. Closed on Wednesdays.

Practicalities

Banks On the main road: Caja Canarias, open Mon–Fri 08.30–14.00, Thu 17.00–19.30; Caja Rural, open Mon–Fri 08.30–14.00, Thu 17.00–19.30; Banesto, open Mon–Fri 08.30–14.00, Sat 08.30–13.00.

Health The Health Centre is on Calle Emilio Quintana Sánchez, a block south of the main road.

Pharmacy Opposite Pensión Los Volcanes.

Police In the Town Hall, at the back of the Plaza del Ayuntamiento.

Shopping The Centro de Artesanía Fuencaliente is open 10.00–19.30; watch the craftsmen at work and then buy their wares.

What to see and do
Diving
The Fuencaliente coast is considered the best place in La Palma for diving due to the unusual underwater scenery created by the 1971 eruption of Teneguía. **Atlantic 28** on the main road offer baptisms for €45, though they really cater more for experienced divers. They charge €30 per dive, with every sixth dive free.

Wine tasting
One of the island's favourite wines has its base in Fuencaliente. Bodegas Teneguía is open 09.00–14.00 and 15.00–18.00. You're welcome to try the wines before you buy, though there isn't a facility for learning about wine appreciation. You can also sample the wines at the restaurant, El Patio del Vino, which specialises in meat grills and Canarian cuisine with flair. Bodegas Carballo is not far away if you want to sample another vineyard's produce. It's on the road from Los Canarios to Las Indias and is open Mon–Fri 08.00–20.00.

Volcanoes
Fuencaliente is the municipality with the highest number of recorded volcanic eruptions on the island, including the Canary Island's most recent, Volcán Teneguía (1971). The most spectacular is Volcán San Antonio, which now has a good visitor centre. There's a rather odd film to watch, recommended for its comedy value since it concentrates more on promoting the island than informing about the volcanoes. Once you've read up on the San Antonio and Teneguía eruptions, you can take a short walk to admire the craters up close. The visitor centre is a little south of Los Canarios, on the road to Los Quemados. Open every day 09.30–20.00; entrance is €3, kids under 12 go free.

Beaches
There are some wonderful beaches in the south, all well off the beaten track – the bad roads keep the masses away. **Playa Zamora** is a lovely secluded beach, surrounded as everything is around here by banana plantations. A little further south you come to **Punta Larga**, which has a pebble beach and a few more visitors, almost all of them Palmeros on holiday. The bar here is ideal for those who have problems choosing what to order – they serve fish, salad and *papas arrugadas*. Continuing south and east through the bananas, you'll come to **Playa del Faro** and if you're looking for some real peace and pure untouched beauty, **Playa de Cabras**. You have to take a badly signposted turn-off on your left before you reach the lighthouse and the road to the beach is in terrible condition, which adds to its isolation, since no-one wants to ruin their suspension to get there. Swimming here isn't recommended in high tide.

EL PASO
There are much nicer places in La Palma than El Paso, and you might be better off staying on the outskirts if you're here to explore the national parks near the town. The town is ugly and charmless, except for the narrow streets around the church. There's precious little to see or do and an incredible lack of nice places to eat.

Getting there

Bus number 1A leaves Los Llanos every half-hour on weekdays and around once an hour on weekends. Number 1 passes through every hour or so from Santa Cruz on its way to Los Llanos.

Where to stay

Hotel Monterrey Calle Antonio Pino 7; tel: 922 48 51 75; fax: 922 48 51 76. It's pretty run-down which is a real pity because you can see that it was once glorious, with its large courtyard, bar and even a small theatre. Rooms are in need of redecoration but the service is friendly. Rooms are €18 per person.

Refugio del Pilar Tel: 922 41 15 83. This campsite is in the pine forest south of El Paso and marks the start of the Ruta de los Volcanes walk. It's free to stay there but you must book a place at least a week in advance. There are showers, toilets, a children's playground and a picnic/barbecue area.

Where to eat

El Paso has more than its fair share of your typical bar-cafés serving the same old stuff.

Restaurante Pizzería Adagio On the main road from El Paso to Santa Cruz. Worth the 5-minute drive for a tasty lunch.

Tasca Barbanera At the far end of Calle José Antonio. It's the pick of the bunch if you must stay in the town. They have a good tapas menu and tables outside.

Practicalities

Banks All on Av José Antonio: Caja Rural, open Mon–Fri 08.30–14.00, Thu 17.00–19.30; Santander Central Hispano, open Mon–Fri 08.30–14.00, Sat 08.30–13.00; La Caixa, open Mon–Fri 08.15–14.00, Thu 16.30–19.45.

Health The Health Centre is at the end of Av José Antonio.

Pharmacy One on Av José Antonio and one on Calle Tanausú.

Police The Guardia Civil is on Calle Paso de Abajo, the Policía Local is on Calle Fermin Sosa Pino.

Post office Next to Las Hilanderas on Calle Manuel Taño, open Mon–Fri 08.30–14.30, Sat 09.30–13.00.

Shopping Everything you'll ever want is in the Hipermarket. There are a few souvenir shops and don't forget the handmade silk goods at Las Hilanderas.

Tourist information Try in the travel agencies, though you may have to brush up on your German first!

What to see and do
Las Hilanderas
Calle Manuel Taño.

A working museum where you can see silk garments made using traditional methods. There are also a few items on sale, though never many since demand is high and the process is a time-consuming one. Be warned: workmanship this good doesn't come cheap – many garments are around the €200 mark. The museum is open Mon–Fri 10.00–13.00 and also on Tuesday and Thursday evenings 17.00–19.00. Entrance is €2.50 and under 14s go free.

Around El Paso
Palmex
Signposted from the main Los Llanos–El Paso road, this is a small privately owned cactus garden, with over 70 varieties on show, though how many of them are indigenous is another matter. There's no entrance fee as such, though you have to buy a packet of seeds for a whopping €4. One for real cactus enthusiasts only. Open Tue–Thu 10.00–18.00.

Parque Paraíso de las Aves
Another privately owned park, this time for bird fans. The park houses birds from all over the world and runs a programme to help preserve endangered species. There is also a restaurant specialising in mushroom dishes. Entrance is €6 for adults and €3 for children, and if you have your ticket stamped you can return an unlimited number of times. It's on Calle Panadero 16, though you'll find it easily enough from the signposts.

PARQUE NACIONAL CALDERA DE TABURIENTE
In truth, this huge horseshoe-shaped mass of rock is not a *caldera* – a large crater caused by a violent eruption – but a product of erosion. While some believe it was an immense volcano that erupted with such venom that it flung its heart into the air, creating the island of Tenerife, the more accepted theory is that it's composed of various volcanic cones united by erosion. Whatever its origins, there is no denying its scientific importance or stunning beauty and it was declared a national park in 1954. The main part of the park is the Barranco de las Angustias, a horseshoe-shaped rock formation 8km in diameter and 2,000m high. About halfway up the cliffs you'll find natural springs that produce waterfalls as they navigate the steep drops (there are some 100 springs within the park). Most of the waterfalls are crystalline, except those

originating in Las Rivancers ravine which have been turned a ruddy orange colour by dissolved ferrous salts. There's a waterfall here, known as the Cascada de dos Colores ('Two-Colour Cascade'). So the park is of huge interest to geologists, vulcanologists and nature lovers, but that's not where its appeal ends: it is also of substantial cultural and historical interest. Although the area was never permanently inhabited by the Benahoaritas, it was used as pastoral land during the summer and important archaeological finds have been made here. There are numerous rock carvings in the *caldera* and artefacts such as tools, weapons and ceramics have been found within the stone walls. These days the park sees more birdlife than grazing animals, although imported species such as goat, rabbit and Barbary sheep roam the land, threatening the fauna. There are 25 recorded species of birds in the park, three types of bat and numerous invertebrates. The Canary Island pine dominates the landscape and you'll also see large numbers of rock plants along with crops that man has planted, such as cereals, vines, tobacco and fruit trees.

Getting there
Bus number 1 will take you as far as the visitor centre. Really you need your own wheels to get to the car park at the end of the Barranco de las Angustias although a few taxi drivers are willing to damage their suspension and dirty their car on the rough dirt track for around €20 (from Los Llanos). From here you can walk through the ravine, heading for the campsite or you can catch a 4WD taxi to Los Brecitos. It's €10 per person and takes about an hour to reach the *mirador*, from where you start the walk down to the campsite and through the ravine back to the car park.

What to see and do
Centro de Visitantes La Caldera
Before you decide how to explore the park, pop in to the visitor centre. The staff are enthusiastic and helpful and will try to show you the best way to see the *caldera* depending on your priorities, mobility, desire to walk etc. They also provide maps and information about the flora and fauna of the park. It's on the main El Paso–Santa Cruz road, open every day 09.00–14.00, 16.00–18.30.

Hiking
There is a free guided walk service which operates from the information point at La Cumbrecita (in the south of the park). For information on the hikes or to book a place, call 922 48 60 00. It's perfectly feasible to walk without a guide and staff at the visitor centre will be happy to explain the possible routes to you. The most popular walk starts at Los Brecitos and takes you through the pine forest, past the campsite and information centre and down into the Barranco de las Angustias. As you make your way to the car park you'll pass the Cascada de dos Colores and the powerful Cascada de dos Aguas, where you can bathe if you wish. The walk is easy to follow as it is well signposted and there is no lack of other hikers en route. It's not difficult and is almost all flat or downhill, though it can get slippery and isn't advisable in wet weather. From Los Brecitos to the campsite it's 5½km and takes about 1½ hours. From the campsite to the car park in the Barranco de Las Angustias it's another 8km and takes three to four hours. For other hikes contact the visitor centre. See *Getting there*, above, for information on how to get to the start of the walk.

Miradors
For those who can't or don't want to hike through the *caldera*, there are some spectacular vistas to be seen from the *miradors*. La Cumbrecita offers stunning

views of the southern part of the park; you can drive there from the visitor centre. The finest lookout point on the island (if not the world!) is Roque de los Muchachos, where you can peer into the *caldera* and make out the ocean through the sea of clouds below you.

Camping
There is one campsite within the national park and another just outside its border. Both are free and have limited facilities, though they do have toilets and somewhere to have a wash. El Riachuelo is reachable by car: it's on the road from the visitor centre to the La Cumbrecita viewing point and information centre. The other campsite (tel: 922 49 72 77; email: caldera@mma.es) is in the heart of the park, reachable on foot only (either by walking the length of the Barranco de las Angustias or by catching the 4WD taxi and descending from Los Brecitos through the pine woods; see *Hiking*, above). You need to book in advance and provide passport details.

LOS LLANOS DE ARIDANE
It's difficult to choose the nicest town on La Palma, but Los Llanos is certainly in the running. It's long been the main economic centre on the island and one reason for its prosperity was the use of water from the Caldera de Taburiente to irrigate the sugar plantations. It's also one of the most important banana-growing regions in the Canary Islands, with over 1,500 hectares of banana plantations. Nowadays it has a kind of student-hippy ambience and is one of the best places in the archipelago to eat out, with an amazing number of vegetarian-friendly restaurants and some delightful tapas bars boasting original menus. Exploring the narrow streets lined with higgledy-piggledy colourful houses is a pleasure, as is sitting out in the church square for an early evening beer.

Getting there
Bus number 1 leaves Santa Cruz for Los Llanos every hour during the week or every two hours on weekends. You could also get there from the capital on number 3, though it's a long drive going via Fuencaliente. From Los Llanos there are buses to Santo Domingo, El Paso and Puerto Naos. The bus station is on Calle Ramón Pol.

Where to stay
Upmarket
Hotel Amberes Av General Franco 13; tel: 922 40 10 40; fax: 922 40 24 41; email: hotel_amberes@vodafone.es. Easily the jewel in Los Llanos' crown. It has the air of a honeymoon hotel, with its romantic garden in the courtyard and fantastic large rooms. Also has a restaurant with Canarian and vegetarian specials. Single €65; double €100.

Mid-range
Apartamentos Doña Paquita Calle Teniente General González del Yerro 8; tel/fax: 922 40 20 00; email: paquita@lapalma.com. Large, homely apartments with TV, balcony and plants. There is also a beauty salon and restaurant. Apartments for 2 people €48; 4 people €62.
Hotel Valle Aridane Calle Glorieta Castillo Olivares 3; tel: 922 46 26 00; fax: 922 40 10 19; www.hotelvallearidane.com. A very friendly welcome awaits you from owner Ramón, who loves to practise speaking English. Rooms are very clean, if a bit old-fashioned. All have private bathroom, TV and telephone. Breakfast is available at an extra cost. Single €33; double €40.

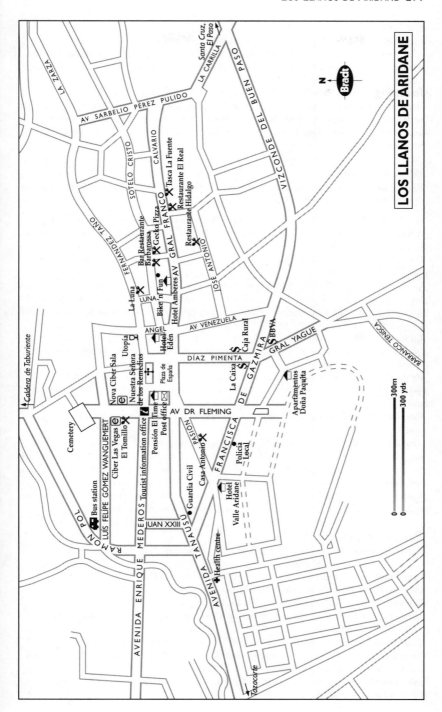

LOS LLANOS DE ARIDANE

Budget

Hotel Edén Plaza de España; tel: 922 46 01 04; fax: 922 46 01 83; email: eden@edenlapalma.com; www.edenlapalma. Friendly and in a great location, right on the square. Rooms are bright and all have balconies. There's a bar and TV room. Single €31 (or €21 with shared bathroom); double €36.

Pensión El Time Calle Iglesia 3; tel: 922 460 907. Housed in a magnificent old building in the town square, this is definitely a place with character. Family-run and very well looked after, if a little pricey. No rooms have private bathroom and all have beds reminiscent of a hospital ward. A bit overpriced at €19 for a single; double €32; triple €46.

Where to eat

Eating out in Los Llanos is a treat, with lots of small restaurants in the narrow streets around the central plaza.

Bar Restaurante Barbarossa Calle Aridane. A quiet place in a peaceful street. They have a fantastic menu with good meat, fish and seafood choices – a welcome respite from all the bars serving typical Canarian food.

Casa Antonio Calle Pasión. A popular place, always busy at lunchtimes when they have a *menú del día* for €6.60.

El Tomillo Av Dr Fleming. A quiet place specialising in wine and cheese.

Gecko Pizza Calle Aridane. You can smell it a couple of streets before you reach it: the wonderful aroma of a *leña* (wood-burning) oven. It's a small place with just half a dozen pizzas on the menu. You have to order at the counter.

La Luna Calle Fernández Taõ. Music café with a courtyard in the middle allowing you to admire the clear La Palma night sky. Their speciality is lentil omelette, though their hors d'oeuvres are excellent. There is varied live music on Thursdays.

Restaurante El Hidalgo Calle José Antonio; tel: 922 46 31 24. A good place for vegetarians or those who want a change from meat and fish. They do a good line in salads and pasta dishes and also offer children's portions. Closed on Wednesdays.

Restaurante El Real Calle Calvario. Another place with a tempting menu and an excellent choice of starters.

Tasca la Fuente Calle Calvario. 'Tapas, tapas y más tapas' is what their menu states and they offer some original choices rather than the same dishes you'll find everywhere else: try the dates wrapped in Serrano ham and stuffed with almonds. They also have some salads, a few main meals and some naughty but nice desserts. Closed on Sundays.

Utopia Behind the main square. They serve breakfasts and snacks until 14.30, then reopen at 22.00 as a cocktail bar with a menu that would impress even Tom Cruise.

Practicalities

Banks BBVA, Calle Francisca de Gazmira, open Mon–Fri 08.30–14.15, Sat 08.30–13.00; La Caixa, Calle Francisca de Gazmira, open Mon–Fri 08.15–14.00, Thu 16.30–19.45; Caja Rural, Calle Díaz Pimienta, open Mon–Fri 08.30–14.00, Thu 17.00–19.30.

Health The Health Centre is on Calle Princesa Dacil.

Internet Nova Ciber Sala on Av Doctor Fleming, open every day 09.30–13.30, 16.00–19.30; €2 per hour. Almost opposite is Ciber Las Vegas, open Mon–Sat 09.30–13.00, 17.00–21.30; €2.25 per hour.

Pharmacy One on Av General Franco, just out of the square.

Police Guardia Civil is on Av Tanausú, near the Hotel Valle de Aridane; the Policía Local is on Calle Francisca de Gazmira.

Post office In the square, next to Pensión el Time, open Mon–Fri 08.30–20.30, Sat 09.30–13.00.

Shopping It's surprisingly dull to go shopping in Los Llanos, though there are plenty of supermarkets and some chain stores if you're looking for clothes.

Tourist information On Av Doctor Fleming, in the centre of the avenue, open Mon–Fri 10.00–14.00, 15.30–18.30, Sat 10.00–14.00.

What to see and do

Oddly enough there are no museums or art galleries in Los Llanos. Activities are limited to ambling around the streets or sipping some *malvasía* in a pavement café, although there are a few attractions not too far away. Los Llanos is also the closest town to the *caldera* if you plan to go walking in the Barranco de las Angustias.

Cycling

Bike 'n' Fun Calle Calvo Sotelo; tel: 922 40 19 27; email: bike_fun@teleline.es; www.lp-b.com/bikenfun. A huge range of mountain-biking excursions at all levels for €40. The price includes helmet, gloves, transport to the starting points and a guide. An excellent way to see the island, if you're up to it! They also rent out bikes for €12 a day.

Around Los Llanos
Pueblo Parque

This is a curious tourist attraction, selling itself as a museum about the island. In reality it's a weird mishmash of endemic and foreign plants, caged birds, a few farm animals, a small handicrafts display and some scary aborigine dummies. They also sell cosmetics and remedies made from medicinal plants. Entrance is daylight robbery at €7, which includes a sample of local wine, though children can enter for free. Open Mon–Sat 10.30–15.00.

Casa Museo del Vino

Located in the tiny village of Las Manchas, this museum is a good place to learn a bit about the island's wine and taste some of it too. The bonus here is that, for a couple of euros, you can sample various wines from different vineyards rather than having to visit each one individually to decide what you like. They also have craftwork and photography exhibitions and a very small vineyard. Entrance is €1.50; open Mon–Fri 10.00–18.00, Sat 11.30–14.00. To get there take Camino el Callejón, a small turning off the Los Canarios to Los Llanos road in San Nicolás, and follow this narrow road all the way to the bottom.

CELTA

Celta is a curious little place: a leafy suburb of Los Llanos which now attracts a fair number of German package tourists. It's a very quiet spot with relatively upmarket accommodation.

Getting there

It's signposted from the LP1, about 2km south of Los Llanos. There are no buses to Celta, though bus number 3 will take you as far as the main road (only a five- or ten-minute walk).

Where to stay

Apartamentos El Castaño Tel: 922 40 12 01. The apartments are usually reserved for German and Dutch tour operators but you might get lucky in less busy months. It's a nice place with a pool set amongst the gardens. Reserving at least a couple of weeks in advance is recommended. Apartments for 2 people €45.

Apartamentos Tamara Tel: 922 46 36 36. Well-equipped apartments and friendly service. They don't take bookings too far in advance but you'd be wise to call before you turn up. Apartment for 2 people €36.

Where to eat
Restaurante Carmen Tel: 922 40 26 18. An excellent menu, with a good choice of fish, rice and pasta dishes and a huge wine list, and much of what they serve is Palmeran produce. Closed on Sunday.

Practicalities
There's a supermarket near the La Palma Jardín apartments; Mon–Fri 08.00–13.30, 16.30–19.30, Sat 08.00–13.30. There is also a launderette next door. All other facilities are in Los Llanos.

What to see and do
Other than relax around the pool, there's nothing to occupy you in Celta. If you need to relax even more, **Tara** offer all manner of beauty treatments including full days of pampering. Tel: 922 40 26 88; www.la-palma.de/tara.

PUERTO NAOS
Puerto Naos is a small resort on the west coast of the island. Although it's a far cry from the tourist resorts in other larger islands, it lacks something of the charm that the rest of La Palma offers. It's difficult to put your finger on why, since Puerto Naos existed as a fishing village long before the tourists discovered its pleasant black-sand beach. There's only one large hotel and a few locally run apartments on offer, but the whiff of mass tourism is in the air as the fish restaurants are replaced with all-you-can-eat Chinese buffets and tacky souvenirs take over from quality handicrafts. The beach is fine for sunbathing (as long as you don't actually touch the scorching sand) but the seas can get very rough. Stick to the spots that the locals choose for a dip. A little further along the coast you can swim in the natural pools at Charco Verde. The bus that comes from Los Llanos continues to Charco Verde, or it's about half an hour on foot.

Getting there
Buses from Los Llanos run every hour into the late evening.

Where to stay
The majority of places don't have a reception, making booking ahead necessary.

Upmarket
Hotel/Apartamentos Sol La Palma Tel: 922 40 80 00; fax: 922 40 80 14. Depending on your point of view this is either the only accommodation in Puerto Naos worth staying in, or the only blot on its landscape. It's a typical holiday complex with numerous pools, sports facilities and an entertainments programme. Single: €90; double €130; studio €80; 1-bedroom apartment €95.

Mid-range
Apartamentos Abel Calle Mauricio Duque Camacho 9; tel: 922 46 10 87. Next door to the Atlántida País apartments and offering a similar level of comfort. Large apartments with 2 bedrooms are €30 per night for up to 4 people (though you'd be more comfortable with just 3).

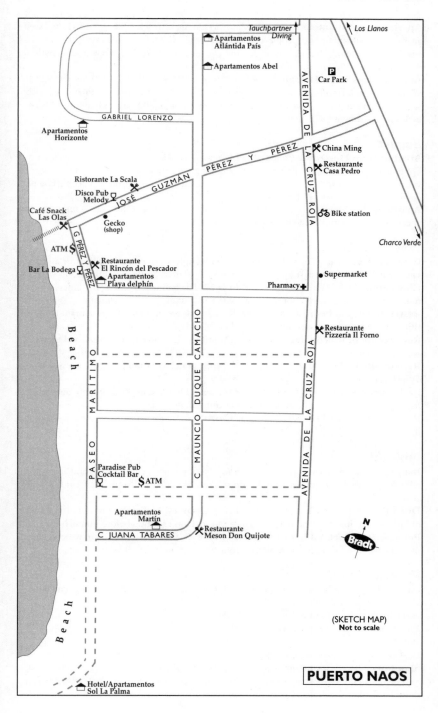

PUERTO NAOS

(SKETCH MAP)
Not to scale

Apartamentos Atlántida País Calle Mauricio Duque Camacho; tel: 922 46 41 26. Basic apartments sleeping up to 3 people and with the hugest balconies you'll ever see. An odd smell lingers around, though, and make sure you agree on a price before you sign anything. €45 per night, with discounts for stays of more than 3 nights.

Apartamentos Playa Delphín Calle José Guzmán Pérez 1; tel: 922 40 81 94; fax: 922 46 12 00; www.lp-b.com/playa-delphin. Modern studios and 1-bedroom apartments, all with sea and mountain views. One of the best accommodation options around. Studio €38; 1-bedroom apartment €47.

Budget
Apartamentos Horizonte Calle Gabriel Lorenzo; tel: 922 40 81 47; www.tamanca.com. Quiet location in the upper part of town, offering good views over the resort. Far better value than the apartments in the mid-range section. Apartments for up to 3 people €35 per day with a minimum stay of 3 days.

Apartamentos Martín Calle Juana Tabares 1; tel: 922 40 80 46. Not exactly luxurious but cheap and the service is friendly. Studio apartment €30.

Where to eat
Café Snack Las Olas The food is nothing special unless you're after a burger or a sandwich, but it has the best location in Puerto Naos, right on the beachfront.

China Ming Av de la Cruz Roja; tel: 922 40 83 52. The typical tourist-resort Chinese restaurant. They also do take-aways, in case you fancy eating in your apartment.

Restaurante Casa Pedro Av de la Cruz Roja. Locals recommend this restaurant for fresh fish and a few Canarian specialities. Closed on Mondays.

Restaurante El Rincón del Pescador Av Marítima. Extensive fish and seafood menu and has a rooftop terrace with sea views.

Restaurante La Scala Calle José Guzmán Pérez. Good pasta and pizza and a few fish dishes. Has a lunchtime *menú del día* for €8.50.

Restaurante Mesón Don Quijote Calle Mauricio Duque Camacho. Superb tapas and fish dishes, disappointing desserts and rather unfriendly service.

Restaurante Pizzería Il Forno Av de la Cruz Roja. Another reasonable pizza joint and they also have a take-away service.

Nightlife
Bar La Bodega Av Marítima. Small bar with a young crowd, cheap drinks and an owner with the strongest anti-tourist attitude you're likely to find anywhere in the islands. Closes at around 01.00.

Disco Pub Melody Calle José Guzmán Pérez. Opens on weekends only and plays a mix of Spanish and international pop and dance music. Don't turn up before midnight.

Paradise Pub Cocktail Bar Av Marítima. Laid-back atmosphere and a pretty good choice of cocktails. Also has a terrace on the seafront. Stays open until you leave.

Practicalities
Banks There's a cashpoint by the supermarket on Calle Mauricio Duque Camacho and another near Bar La Bodega.

Health The closest Health Centre is in Todoque.

Pharmacy On Av de la Cruz Roja.

Police In Todoque.

Post office The closest is in Todoque.

Shopping There is a supermarket on Av de la Cruz Roja, open Mon–Sat 08.00–21.00, Sun 08.00–14.00. Gecko, on Calle José Guzmán Pérez, has some interesting handicrafts, though whether they're very typical of the islands is another matter.

Tourist information As yet there isn't a tourist info point, though you could try asking in the Sol Hotel.

What to see and do
Cycling
Bike Station do trips all over the island from €35, which includes a guide and transport to and from the start of the ride. You can also rent a bike for €15 per day. The office is on Av de la Cruz Roja.

Diving
Tauchpartner Just off Av de la Cruz Roja, on the way out of town; tel/fax: 922 40 81 39; email: tauchpartner@la-palma.de; www.tauchpartner-lapalma.de. Package of 5 dives €100; discovery dive €48; also arrange boat trips for €22 per person and rent out snorkelling gear for €5 per day.

TAZACORTE
The town centre isn't particularly attractive, but the narrow streets in the old part of town are certainly worth exploring for half an hour. Tazacorte is home to the island's first religious building, the Ermita de San Miguel Arcángel.

Getting there
Bus number 2 leaves Los Llanos once an hour until 20.30. It passes through Tazacorte on its way to the harbour. The service runs daily.

Where to stay
Apartamentos Casher Av Felipe Lorenzo 7; tel: 922 48 05 88. As basic as you can get but clean and relatively cheerful. For information or to pick up keys you need to go to the office above Bar Tropico, on Calle Primero de Mayo. Apartment for 2 is €24 and there are reductions of 50% if you stay for a month.
Apartamentos Isa II Calle Progreso 14; tel: 922 48 00 52; fax: 922 48 00 66; www.apartamentosisa.com. Probably the most attractive option in Tazacorte, it has largish apartments, some with balcony, and a swimming pool on the roof. They also arrange car hire. Prices vary from €34–52 for 2 people, an extra €7 per person for extra people. They also have the slightly less appealing Isa I on the same street.
Apartamentos Morro Sol II Av Felipe Lorenzo; tel: 922 48 04 03; fax: 922 48 01 89. A grotty-looking building just out of town. Large balconies but a rather depressing place to spend your holiday. Information on Av de la Constitución 3. Apartments for 2 people €28; or for 4 people €30 with a minimum stay of 3 days.

Where to eat
Restaurante Bagañete Calle Lomo Blanco. Worth a visit, if only for the hilarious and slightly off-putting menu translations. They have a good selection of meat and fish dishes and a friendlier atmosphere than some other places in town.
Restaurante Bar Oveja Negra Calle Nueva; tel: 922 40 61 33. Head and shoulders above the rest. Recognisable by the sheep on the sign that looks scarily like Michael Jackson. Its lamb specialities come as a breath of fresh air after constant offerings of goat, rabbit and pork. They also have a good line in vegetarian food. Evenings only, closed on Sundays.

Practicalities
Banks BBVA, on the corner of Av de la Constitución and Calle Nueva, open Mon–Fri 08.30–14.15, Sat 08.30–13.00; Caja Canarias, Av de la Constitución, open Mon–Fri 08.30–14.00, Thu 17.00–19.30; Banesto, Calle General Serrador, open Mon–Fri 08.30–14.00, Sat 08.30–13.00.

Health The Health Centre is in Puerto de Tazacorte.
Pharmacy On Calle Nueva, near the Restaurante Oveja Negra.
Police The Policía Local is in the Town Hall.
Post office Behind the Town Hall, open Mon–Fri 08.30–14.30, Sat 09.30–13.00.
Tourist information Try the Town Hall, open Mon–Fri 08.30–14.00.

What to see and do

There are worse ways to spend a day than to get lost in the narrow side streets of Tazacorte, although there's not much more to do here than that. The church was the first religious building built on the island after the conquest, so it's worth a visit for its historical value. Other than that, it's only a five-minute drive to the beach at Puerto de Tazacorte.

PUERTO DE TAZACORTE

Alonso Fernández de Lugo began his La Palma offensive on these very shores in 1492 and the court of Tazo, as it was then known, soon fell to the Spanish despite brave efforts by their *mencey*. These days it's a small fishing town which doubles as a holiday resort for the islanders. It has more atmosphere than Puerto Naos and Los Cancajos, and is the place to come to eat fish, lie on the beach or watch the boats come and go. There are a couple of decent boat trips leaving from the harbour.

Getting there

Buses run from Los Llanos every hour until the late evening.

Where to stay

Apartamentos Orion Tel: 922 41 56 36; fax: 922 41 23 03. Owned by the same people as Apartamentos La Fuente in Santa Cruz. All apartments have 2 bedrooms and are fully equipped. Balconies are sea facing, affording good sunset vistas. Also have satellite TV. Minimum stay is one week. 2 people €37; 4 people €53.

Where to eat

Bar La Marina A good choice of pizzas, and of course seafood and fish. It also has tables outside with wonderful sea views. Closed on Mondays.
Cervecería La Cabaña La Explanada. A nice line in tapas and wine, with a fair range of local cuisine as well. Closed on Mondays.
Restaurante Taberna del Puerto Tel: 922 48 09 07. Probably the best place in town, mainly specialising in fish and seafood dishes, though they also offer some good dishes for carnivores. They also have kids' portions. Closed on Tuesdays.

Practicalities

The Health Centre is next to the Orion Apartments and there is a pharmacy on the road from the town to the harbour. Other than that everything is in the *pueblo* of Tazacorte.

What to see and do
Boat trips

Puerto de Tazacorte is a good place to take a boat trip, with the sunset voyage to Cueva Bonita (Pretty Cave) perhaps the best on offer. Cueva Bonita is so named because at sunset the light enters from a small crevice, spectacularly illuminating the interior. Lanzaroteño artist César Manrique dubbed it the 'Sistine Chapel of modern art'.

There are also regular 'safari' boats to take you dolphin- and whale-spotting. **Fancy II** have a good choice of excursions from €20 per person. You can reserve a space by telephone: 922 406 057 – recommended at peak times – or take your chances and turn up at the port. **Agamenon** offer similar excursions for a similar price: bookings tel: 650 77 77 48.

Fishing

Fancy II do deep-sea fishing trips, from €100 per person. See above for contact details.

TIJARAFE

Tijarafe is one of those places that you see on a map and drive through, only realising that you were in it once you reach the next town. Almost everything is based on the main road, although you could park and take a quick wander around its cobbled side streets if you're really stuck for something to do. There is a very small museum with a few pieces of reproduced aboriginal pottery and panels explaining the town's big festival, El Día del Diablo. There is also a centre where you can taste and buy local foodstuffs. It is worth stopping by on September 8, when the square is full of revellers waiting for the devil to appear. Each year the Madonna defeats the devil and he explodes in a frenzy of fireworks, which are actually getting a little dangerous as the festival grows in popularity and the tiny town gets overcrowded.

PUNTAGORDA

If there's one thing that will strike you about Puntagorda, it's the incredible number of signposts. Shops, bars, restaurants and public buildings are all indicated at intervals of 100m. There are a couple of decent restaurants here, a recreation area which is good for picnics and barbecues and a weekly farmers' market. There are no hotels although there are a fair amount of *casas rurales* in the area and one campsite.

Getting there

Puntagorda is one of the least well-served towns on the island, with just one bus line reaching it. Number 5 passes though from Los Llanos on its way to Santo Domingo seven times a day, though on weekends there are only two buses, leaving Los Llanos at 10.30 and 19.30.

Where to stay

Camping La Rosa Tel: 922 49 33 06. Located in a pine forest, the campsite has showers, toilets, a picnic area and a children's playground. You can stay in a hut for €10 or pitch your tent for €5 per day. Tents are also available to hire for an extra €4 per day. As with everything, the campsite is well signposted from the town.

Where to eat

Bar Parrilla Pino de la Virgen Calle Pino de la Virgen; tel: 922 49 32 28. A real carnivore's place, with barbecued meat the recommended dish. It's well signposted as you enter the town.

Pizzería Spelonchi Usual range of pizzas and pastas in a nice setting. You'll find it on the road to the picnic area and market.

Restaurante Jardín de las Naranjas On the way to the picnic area; tel: 922 49 33 82. If the town's other best restaurant is a meat-eater's dream, then this is the place for vegetarians. Plenty of choice for all and using largely organic produce. Open weekdays from 17.00 and weekends from 12.00.

Practicalities
All amenities are on or around the main road near the Town Hall. There's a farmers' market 2km north of the town on weekends, open Sat 15.00–19.00, Sun 11.00–15.00.

SANTO DOMINGO
The main town in the Garafía district is perhaps one of the best preserved on the island. The local economy is still based on farming and the production of cheese with few tourists venturing this far north. Santo Domingo is a very quiet town that seems to be taking a permanent siesta, so it's not the place to go if you're looking for a wild night out. It is, however, an excellent base for exploring Garafía, an often overlooked and underrated area of the island. It has a spectacular coastline and there are some charming villages nearby.

Getting there
If approaching from the south, opt for the LP114 unless you're a real fan of mountain bends. The LP1 will make even the sturdiest traveller car sick.

Buses from Santa Cruz leave for Santo Domingo at 07.10 and 14.10 daily. The journey takes almost three hours. There are also regular buses from Los Llanos.

Where to stay
There are no hotels or apartments in Santo Domingo, but there are some beautiful *casas rurales* around. For information and bookings contact Isla Bonita (see *Where to stay*, page 274 for contact details).

Where to eat
Café Plaza At the far end of the square. A good place to meet some locals over a plate of tapas. There are no strict opening times.

Restaurante Santo Domingo Next to the post office. A meat-eater's paradise, with pork, rabbit and of course, goat dishes on the menu. They also have a good selection of Palmeran desserts and wines. Closed on Tuesdays.

Taberna Santi Next to the Spar. A typical tapas menu, with a covered patio area. Open weekday evenings and all day on weekends.

Practicalities
Banks Caja Canarias, on the main road, open Mon–Fri 08.00–14.00.

Health On Calle Josefa Argote, at the back of the town.

Internet Limited free access is available in the Centro de Interpretación.

Pharmacy At the end of the square.

Police Policía Local office is next to the post office.

Post office Next to the Town Hall, open Mon-Fri 10.00–13.00, Sat 11.00–13.00.

Shopping There's a Spar and a handicrafts shop on the main road. Other than that the farmers' market is worth visiting (see below for details). You can also get some nice craftwork from the La Tahona Centro Artesanal in Las Tricias.

Tourist information Staff in the Centro de Interpretación are very helpful and have maps and pamphlets. You might find some info at the Town Hall too. There's a board at the far end of the plaza with information on local walks.

What to see and do
Centro de Interpretación Etnográfico de Garafía
This small information centre gives an insight into the local community through its history, industry, crafts and festivals. It also has a small exhibition on the astrophysics observatory, located at Roque de los Muchachos. Staff are passionate

about the area and more than happy to point you in the direction of the local beauty spots. Open Mon–Fri 09.00–13.00,15.00–18.00; entrance is free.

Market
The municipality has one of the most important farmers' markets on the island. It's held in the square in Santo Domingo on the first Sunday of every month. As well as local foodstuffs you can pick up some good craftwork. The market moves to the San Antonio recreation area on the second Sunday of the month and south to the village of Las Tricias on the third Sunday. In winter months there is also a gastronomic season which gives you the chance to sample some local specialities. Open 11.00–17.00.

Hiking
The north of the island is a generally unexplored and spectacular place to go walking. There are plenty of routes to choose from, from short wanders, to mammoth treks around the island. There is an information panel near the church which gives various routes near the town. Most walking companies don't get this far north, though Jean Louis Cerckel is happy to take hikers to his favourite spot on the island (see *Hiking* in the activities section for contact details).

The walk down to the port is well worth it for the views of the impressive northern cliffs. From the town centre, take the road towards Cueva de Agua then follow the footpath signs; the walk will take about two hours there and back. You can drive part of the way and walk the last 20 minutes. Beware: the road is in a bad way and if you don't want to drive your hire car on the rough road, leave it at the point where the paved road ends. Hiking from here will take about an hour for the round trip. Swimming is possible in low tide and there are a couple of gorgeous natural pools. The houses down here are holiday homes and if any of the Palmeros spot you, they're sure to invite you for a glass of wine and some typical *dulces*.

Around Santo Domingo
San Antonio del Monte
There is a camping area near to the hermitage, with picnic and barbecuing facilities and a hostel-like hut where you can stay for €10 per person, or €25 if you want full-board accommodation. You must book in advance; tel: 922 40 04 44. It's also a good place to do some hiking; ask at the hut for advice on where to walk.

La Zarza and La Zarcita
If you visit only one set of aboriginal markings on La Palma, make it La Zarza. These are the island's most important *grabados* and certainly the most remarkable. There is an information centre with interesting multimedia displays on the hows and whys of the markings in various languages. Once you know the theories, you can take a walk around the park and admire the engravings. They are not the most impressive sight but when you think of the trouble it took to make them, you can appreciate their importance. Entrance to the park is €1.80 for adults and €0.90 for children; open every day 11.00–17.00, 11.00–19.00 in summer.

Hike
La Zarza–San Antonio–La Zarza
Distance: 7km; time: 2 hours; difficulty: 2.
Leaving the La Zarza visitor centre, follow signs for Caldera del Agua. You'll soon find yourself on a dry riverbed in jungle-like surroundings that you probably wouldn't associate with the Canary Islands. Cross a wooden bridge,

following the markings painted on rocks and trees. These are few and far between, though the path is generally easy to follow. After crossing a third bridge, take the right-hand path which leads you steeply up on some stone steps carved into the rock. You enter a clearing and if you look back on a clear day you'll see the astrophysics observatory behind you. Continue climbing for a few more minutes until you come to a clearing and a road. Turn left and at the next turning take the right-hand path past a small house. After crossing the tarred road, look for a clearing to the right. Here you'll see a post with no sign and next to it a path leading through the forest. This path will lead you to the valley floor and out of the forest on to a dirt track. Turn left on to the track which will take you to the church of San Antonio del Monte. The path back to La Zarza is marked from the far right of the church.

BARLOVENTO
The town of Barlovento is wholly unremarkable, scattered as it is along a relatively busy main road. The only things of note in the area are the natural swimming pools on the coast, a few quaint villages on the north coast and La Laguna recreation area.

Getting there
Bus number 11 passes through Barlovento on its way to Santo Domingo, leaving Santa Cruz at 07.10 and 14.10 daily.

Where to stay
Hotel La Palma Romántica Tel: 922 18 62 21; fax: 922 18 64 00; email: reservas@hotellapalmaromantica.com; www.hotellapalmaromantica.com. This marvellous hotel is a little outside the town on the road to La Laguna. It has excellent facilities including tennis courts, swimming pool, jacuzzi and an observatory. Rooms are large and beautifully decorated. Singles €80; doubles €110; suites from €140. Breakfast and dinner are available at an extra cost.
Campsite La Laguna Tel: 922 69 60 23. The campsite is run by the Barlovento Town Hall and has good facilities including electricity, showers, a bar, picnic area, children's playground and barbecue area. It costs €4.50 per tent or caravan during the week and €9 on weekends. From the town, take the LP111, following signs for the Embalse de La Laguna. The campsite is next to the reservoir.

Where to eat
Bar La Terraza On the main road. A menu that you may have seen before, including local dishes like goat, pork and rabbit. It has a pleasant terrace.
Bar with no name The yellow building next to the bus stop. This is the most popular choice in town, and seemingly with good reason. They have a good selection of hams and other meats and do a fine cup of coffee.
Hamburguesería Bocata el Drago On the main road. A friendly place to grab a quick burger and a beer.
Restaurante La Palma Romántica In the hotel of the same name; tel: 922 18 64 11. They serve traditional Canarian food with a few international dishes thrown in. There are also a few vegetarian options on the menu. Main dishes start at €12.

Practicalities
Banks Caja Rural, on the main road, open Mon–Fri 08.00–14.00, Thu 17.00–19.30; Caja Canarias, Calle del Drago, open Mon–Fri 08.00–14.00, Thu 17.00–19.30.
Health The Health Centre is on the corner of the main road and Calle Carmen Hernández Paz.

Pharmacy On the main road.

Police The Policía Local is in the Town Hall, in Plaza del Rosario (just off the main road).

Post office Just off the main road on the road to Las Cazadebas, open Mon–Fri 08.30–10.30, Sat 11.00–13.00.

Shopping There's a Spar on the main road, open Mon–Sat 08.00–14.00, 17.00–20.00.

Tourist information At the La Laguna recreation area, open Mon–Sat 09.00–15.00.

What to see and do
La Laguna
The island's largest reservoir, although not an overly pretty sight, is in a magnificent setting which is also home to the campsite and recreation area. There's a very small market on Saturday afternoons, 12.00–18.00, with the best local produce on offer. There's also a small handicrafts shop.

La Fajana
These natural swimming pools are considered by many to be the best on the island, though they might be a disappointment to those expecting naturally *formed* pools. There are showers, toilets and a restaurant here. You'll find the pools 1.5km from the road between Los Sauces and Barlovento; the turn-off is signposted.

SAN BORONDÓN

If you're standing on the west coast of El Hierro or La Palma and you think you sight land in the distance, don't worry – you wouldn't be the first. For centuries there have been many mariners who swear to have seen San Borondón, though none could provide much in the way of evidence. Some sailors even claimed to have landed on the mythical island and it made its debut on a map in the 15th century. In times gone by, fishermen maintained that San Borondón was inhabited by cannibals who would raise the island from the seabed when they got hungry, swim over to the Canary Islands and snatch a few children for a late night snack. Historian Abreu Galindo ventured to give San Borondón's co-ordinates: 10° 10' longitude, 29° 30' latitude, that is to say northwest of El Hierro, though it has been sighted at various locations over the years – some even claim to have seen it off the coasts of Gran Canaria and Tenerife.

The legendary island takes its name from an Irish Benedictine monk, St Brendan, who in AD480 was searching the Atlantic for heathen lands to which he could take Christianity. After several terrifying days spent adrift in the ocean, he and his crew spotted an island on the horizon and happily dropped anchor. While the other sailors were asleep, Brendan stayed up to pray and soon became aware that the island was moving steadily eastwards. In fact this huge mass was a whale, gradually taking them towards unknown lands. The trip continued for another 40 days, when the sailors landed on a lush island inhabited by unfamiliar birds. They spent seven years there, enjoying its pristine black-sand beaches, eating the rich and abundant fruits and strange-looking sheep. The myth of St Brendan, or San Borondón, has been immortalised in poems throughout the centuries and remains the legend closest to most Canarians' hearts. Scotland has the Loch Ness Monster, the Canaries have St Borondón.

Villages

Not far from Barlovento you'll encounter two typical villages *par excellence*: Gallegos and Franceses. Both are tiny, cut off from civilization and oozing with personality. There's some good local food to be had and some of the finest Palmero hospitality. Beware: the roads to the villages are not in good condition and you could have problems manoeuvring the tight bends in a big car.

LOS SAUCES

It wouldn't be unfair to say that Los Sauces is the least charismatic town on the island. Much of it is based around the busy main road, making it a noisy place. There's one dingy place to stay and a seemingly infinite number of dingy places to eat. Its only saving graces are the huge Iglesia de Nuestra Señora de Montserrat and the relatively interesting *gofio* museum.

Getting there

Bus number 11 passes by on its way to Santo Domingo, leaving the capital every two hours on weekdays and every four hours on weekends.

Where to stay

Residencia El Drago Tel: 922 45 03 50. The only place to stay in town, its rooms are large but gloomy and it's a noisy place since it's on the main road and above a rowdy bar. All rooms have bathroom. Singles/doubles €28.

Where to eat

It's impossible to single out any restaurants here since they all offer the same staid menu and grotty surroundings. Suffice it to say that your taste buds won't be tantalised in Los Sauces.

Practicalities

Banks Santander Central Hispano, Plaza Antonio Herrera, open Mon–Fri 08.30–14.00, Sat 08.30–13.00; BBVA, next door, open Mon–Fri 08.30–14.15, Sat 08.30–13.00; Caja Rural is on the main road, open Mon–Fri 08.00–14.00, Thu 17.00–19.30.
Health The Health Centre is on the road to Barlovento.
Pharmacy On the main road, next to Caja Canarias.
Police The Policía Local is in the Town Hall, in Plaza Antonio Herrera.
Post office On Calle José Antonio Primo de Rivera, open Mon–Fri 08.30–14.30, Sat 09.30–13.00.
Shopping There's a supermarket behind the Caja Rural Bank, open Mon–Sat 09.00–21.00. You can taste and purchase wines and rum in Sanlupe, in the Plaza Antonio Herrera.
Tourist information In the Town Hall, open Mon–Fri 08.30–14.00.

What to see and do
Museo El Regente
If you ever wanted to know anything about *gofio*, you'll surely find the answer here. Built in 1873, El Regente was a functioning watermill, producing *gofio* for the residents of Los Sauces and around. These days it's an ethnographic museum dedicated to that most Canarian of carbohydrates. It's on the same road as the Town Hall (Calle Los Milonos) but you need to walk (or drive) a kilometre up the hill. Open Mon–Fri 11.00–17.00; adults €2, children €0.75.

SAN ANDRÉS

I fell in love with San Andrés within minutes of arriving. It's one of the Canary Islands' most delightful *pueblos*, whether you're stopping for lunch in the square or a few days of local hospitality and relaxation. Surrounded on all four sides by banana plantations (yes, they even managed to get a few in between the village and the ocean) and only five minutes from the natural pools of Charco Azul, it is the ultimate destination for getting away from the rat race. After a few days here, even the calmness of the capital will seem like scary hustle and bustle.

Getting there
Buses run to and from Los Sauces about every two hours during the day but they stop in the early evening, so if you plan to get out a bit while staying in San Andrés, a car is necessary.

Where to stay
Pensión Las Lonjas Calle San Sebastián 16; tel: 922 45 07 36. Probably the better option although you won't receive nearly such a friendly welcome as in the town's other guesthouse. All rooms have private bathroom. Single €18; double €24.

Pensión Martín Calle San Sebastián 4; tel: 922 45 05 39. You couldn't wish for a warmer welcome than you receive here and you do feel as though you're staying in someone's home rather than a guesthouse. Rooms have probably seen better days and could do with a bit of redecorating. Still, it's clean, friendly and the cheaper of the 2 places in town. Bathrooms are shared. Single €15; double €21. There is also an apartment available for €30.

Where to eat
Bar Miami Opposite Pensión Martín. A typical menu of varied tapas and local dishes with tables outside.

El Montadito In the upper part of the square. A breath of fresh air with its chilled-out atmosphere, friendly staff and excellent Italian food. If nothing else you must try one of their home-made desserts (though the pasta and vegetarian dishes also come highly recommended).

Restaurante San Andrés Also in the square, this popular place does a good line in meat and fish dishes and has tables outside.

Practicalities
All amenities are in Los Sauces, although there is a shop on the road below the square. It's the yellow building with green woodwork and it sells a little bit of everything. Open Mon–Sat 09.00–13.00.

What to see and do
Other than take a walk around the town to see its two contrasting churches (one huge, the other with just six pews) there's nothing to do. The joy of this place is appreciating some quiet time in the square. It's a real recharge-your-batteries place. Nearby you can swim in the *almost* natural pools of Charco Azul. The water is 100% natural, but man has lent a helping hand with the construction of a kids' pool, terrace and a couple of restaurants. Nearby Puerto Espíndola has a good fish restaurant. Charco Azul is a 20-minute walk from San Andrés, through the banana plantations; Puerto Espíndola is another five minutes along the road, but it lacks San Andrés' charm.

LOS TILOS
When someone bestowed the title of 'la isla bonita' upon La Palma, it's possible that they had Los Tilos in mind, with its verdant laurel forest. Flora fans will be in heaven, with a high number of endemic and native plants growing in this region, and non-enthusiasts will just be awed by the beauty of the forest. Bird lovers are also well served and can expect to see chaffinch, blackbirds and various species of

pigeon, some exclusive to the area. La Palma's most important springs are at the end of the ravine. They used to fall freely, creating an impressive waterfall, but since the 1950s have been re-routed to produce hydro-electricity. The electricity created here accounts for 7% of the island's total consumption. It's a fascinating area to explore on foot, with one of the island's finest hikes starting from near the visitor centre – the Marcos y Cordero springs. This long walk takes you through 13 tunnels to a stunning set of waterfalls and is particularly slippery underfoot. The tourist information office recommends that you don't undertake the walk alone, but join a hiking group (see *Hiking*, page 274, for contact details). If you do go it alone, a torch is imperative and some people even advise that you wear a helmet. The walk is more than 20km long and takes around four to five hours.

Access to Los Tilos is on the LP107. At the end of this paved road there is a **Centro de Interpretación**, with plenty of information about the ravine and its vegetation, including a 12-minute video in various languages. There's also a restaurant and play area here. Open every day 08.30–14.00, 14.30–18.00.

SAN JUAN DE PUNTALLANA

Just north of Santa Cruz, San Juan de Puntallana is an OK place to spend an hour or so, though you'd struggle to find things to occupy yourself for any longer. It's the centre of the municipality and usually referred to as just Puntallana. There's a nice church and square and a few rather average bar-restaurants. Casa Lujan, on the road below the church, has information on rural tourism and is the reservation centre for the island's rural cottages. Bus number 11 passes through, leaving Santa Cruz every two hours on weekdays and every four hours on weekends.

HIKES
La Ruta de los Volcanes
Distance: 20km as far as Fuencaliente, 28km to the lighthouse; time: 6 hours to Fuencaliente, 8 hours to the lighthouse; difficulty: 4.

The most complicated part of this hike is getting to the start. There are no buses and you wouldn't want to walk up from the main road as this would add another few hours to the total hiking time. Unless you want to pay and join a hiking group, you have three options: you could hitchhike to the start of the walk, but there's not much traffic along this road and you could end up walking it all. Or you could leave your car at the campsite and hope to find a friendly passer-by to take you to collect it. The more realistic option is getting a taxi from El Paso, which will cost around €20, and later get the bus back from Fuencaliente. Once you're at the Refugio del Pilar recreation area (you can camp here – see El Paso section for details), the route is superbly signposted and there is no possibility of getting lost. It's a stunning but difficult hike that first takes you through a pine forest and later over the stark landscape created by recent volcanic activity. Walking on the volcanic earth is tough going and there are plenty of uphill sections, so you do need to be in shape. Most people walk as far as Fuencaliente, though some opt for the full-on route to the coast (which poses the further problem of how to get back again, since no buses go that far south).

El Hierro

El Hierro is by far the least developed of the islands. Tourism hasn't really arrived and is unlikely ever to do so, since there are no golden beaches or crazy nightlife. Thanks to its preservation and environmental value, the island was declared a biosphere reserve by

UNESCO following a unanimous vote by the International Biosphere Reserve Committee in 2000. It is also part of the 'Island Biosphere Reserve' chain along with Lanzarote, Menorca, Guadeloupe and the Galápagos Islands. El Hierro is the smallest of the Canary Islands at 278km^2 and it's not only its size that makes it the baby of the family: it's also the archipelago's youngest island. At the southwestern edge of the archipelago, it was long thought to be the end of the world until explorers ventured across the Atlantic to the Americas. In the 1st century AD, Greek astronomer and cartographer Ptolemy decided that since El Hierro marked the end of the world, the zero meridian should be placed there and there it remained until 1883 when it was moved to its present position in Greenwich.

Despite the size, it's the island with the lowest population density at 35 people per km^2. The pace of life is slow and you'll receive a warm welcome, soon feeling like you're on first-name terms with half of the islanders (not an impossible feat in a place with only 9,000 inhabitants). It is the least developed of the islands, maintaining a charm perhaps enjoyed by its original inhabitants, the Bimbaches.

HIGHLIGHTS
El Hierro is the place to go if you want to relax and breathe a bit of fresh air. Don't go expecting to find nightlife, big resorts or large hotels. Enjoy a walk along some of the *caminos reales*, sample some *queso herreño* and a glass of *vino de Frontera*. Enjoy fishing and diving in the unspoilt waters off the La Restinga shore and retire to your *casa rural* to relax in the evening. El Hierro has no golden beaches, but its few black-sand ones are undeveloped and uncrowded.

BACKGROUND INFORMATION
History
As with all the islands, the origin of El Hierro's first inhabitants, the Bimbaches, is uncertain, though it is agreed that they were a peaceful people who relied on farming, fishing and gathering food for their survival. When the Spanish invaded in 1405, they employed a treacherous tactic, characteristic of the Canarian conquest. Bethencourt conned the island's *mencey*, Armiche, into surrender, promising a peaceful takeover. The Bimbaches offered no resistance and many were captured and sold as slaves, decimating the population.

The most important historical site on the island is El Júlan, with its undeciphered petroglyphs dating back to the neolithic period. Also found in this

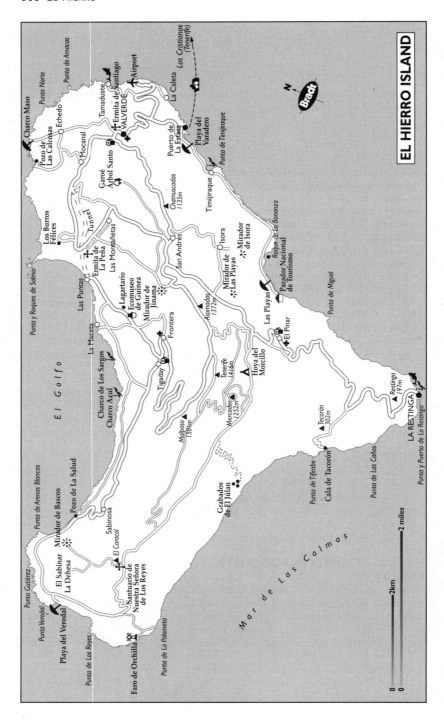

EL HIERRO ISLAND

TREE WORSHIP

The years following the El Hierro conquest were not easy for the newcomers, who suffered in the long drought that hit the island. They were shocked at the absence of rivers, streams and waterfalls and were concerned about their long-term future on El Hierro. Their curiosity and anger were roused on seeing that the Bimbaches didn't seem to be affected by the lack of water, not knowing that they were surviving thanks to their holy tree, the Garoé. The natives hid the tree and claimed that their survival depended on collecting rainwater, thinking that the outsiders would leave if they couldn't find enough water to survive.

The 15m Garoé tree was a true miracle for the Bimbaches, who worshipped its water-giving properties. Taking moisture from the dense clouds that often linger around El Hierro's highlands, the tree never failed to fill the wells surrounding it. The humidity condensed on the leaves and dripped into the manmade wells, and for many years provided a constant source of drinking water. According to a legend, the future of the tree became unstable once the Europeans learnt of its existence. The legend says that Teseida, a direct descendant of the former Guanche king, fell in love with one of the soldiers and revealed the whereabouts of the tree to him. Naturally they took control of it, banning the natives from going near. The Bimbaches in turn banished Teseida. The tale says that the revered tree was ripped out of the ground by an angry god soon after, though perhaps a more dependable explanation of its disappearance is the 1610 hurricane that hit El Hierro. A replacement tree measuring 10m was planted in 1949.

Today, the substitute tree is something of a tourist attraction, though it's probably rather less impressive than the original. It's in the north of the island, near San Andrés, and is open to the public Tue–Sat 10.30–14.30, 17.00–19.00, Sun 11.00–14.00.

area were human remains and artefacts such as tools and cooking utensils. The engravings are known as ideograms; symbols which express ideas, although they don't correspond to sounds. The symbols are mainly oval and circular with lines dissecting them, and they draw many parallels with rock engravings discovered in the Atlas Mountains in northwest Africa, suggesting a link between the inhabitants of these two areas. Like the lineage of its inhabitants, the island's name also remains a mystery. It is widely agreed that there is no metallic connection (*hierro* means 'iron') and many believe that the name comes from the ancient Canarian word *hero*, meaning 'milk'.

Geography

Somewhere between one and five million years ago, movements in the earth's crust caused the ocean bed to rise until it broke the surface of the ocean and created El Hierro's three-pointed-star formation. The volcanic activity continued and successive eruptions formed a pyramid crowned by a 2,000m volcano. Lava flowed through the cracks in the island's surface, eventually solidifying and forming three mountain ranges and the vertical basalt cliffs that today characterise El Hierro's landscape. The island continued to grow until 50,000 years ago when disaster struck. A huge landslide caused 300km² of land to break off and slip into the sea, creating the region today known as El Golfo. The tsunami caused by this landslide is estimated to have measured 100m and would probably have been felt on the American coasts. There has not been any volcanic activity in El Hierro for 200 years but it still has the highest density of volcanic cones of any of the Canary Islands, with 500 on the surface and another 300 covered by later lava flows.

Although the climate is mild, the island is often shrouded in a gloomy fog. Average annual rainfall is 350mm and water is at times scarce due to the porous land and lack of natural springs.

Economy
In times gone by the cochineal trade was El Hierro's biggest earner and it is currently enjoying something of a comeback, although it is hardly the base of the economy. The four main pillars of the Herreño economy are agriculture, fishing, livestock farming and tourism, although revenue is also won from the sale of craftwork. Small-scale tourism is developing on the island and while it doesn't bring in the kind of money that it does on other islands, in the absence of large hotel chains and tour operators taking their cut a higher percentage of the revenue goes straight to the islanders.

Flora and fauna
The most notable animal species is the endangered El Hierro giant lizard (see *Conservation*, below). El Hierro has minor laurel and beech forests but the most emblematic tree on the island is the juniper tree, which is found in the southwest of the island. Strong winds have twisted the trees grossly out of shape and you might find yourself wondering if the tree you're looking at is actually alive. An extensive pine forest lies just below El Hierro's highest point, Malpaso, at 1,501m.

Conservation
The El Hierro giant lizard (*Gallotia simonyi machadoi*) was thought to be an extinct species until 1975 when it was rediscovered and a breeding programme started. It produced good results and the lizards were reintroduced into their natural habitat. There are now over 300 examples roaming free in the Fuga de la Gorreta area of the island. However, the lizard remains firmly on the endangered list. Tourists can see the lizards, which can grow to lengths of 75cm, at the recuperation centre in Las Puntas. See box, page 323.

Festivals
On January 6 (Kings' Day) 1546, a group of sailors landed on the La Orchilla coast, desperately seeking provisions to take with them to the Americas. Some local shepherds helped them out and in return received the image of a virgin. Since then she has been worshipped and was named in honour of the day she was left on the island. El Hierro's main event, the Bajada de la Virgen de los Reyes, takes place only every four years, so some planning is necessary if you want to enjoy the party. The virgin is carried from the Ermita de los Reyes along 42km of footpaths to the capital, and the whole island parties along the way. There's plenty of traditional music, dancing and of course food and drink. The festival begins on the first Saturday in July, although the virgin then visits every *pueblo* on the island so the party continues for the whole month. It will next be celebrated in 2005. Accommodation gets booked very early throughout the festival so it's wise to book far in advance if you want to join in.

The Madonna has another festival in her honour, the Fiesta de los Pastores (Shepherd's Festival), held in La Dehesa on April 25.

El Hierro's oddest festival has to be the Fiesta del Carnero, held during the carnival period. The fiesta almost disappeared after the civil war but was rescued by a Frontera citizen, Benito Padrón, and is now a popular annual event. The young men of the town are the stars of the festival, dressing in smelly dried sheepskins and running after townsfolk, dousing them in black dye. One lucky citizen gets to dress as the madman, a masked shepherd who charges at the spectators. This one certainly gains a place in the weird Canarian fiestas hall of fame (see box, page 22). If you want to see the islands' most traditional sport being practised, there are plenty of opportunities to watch some *Lucha Canaria* in El Hierro; ask at the tourist office for details of fights.

Food
The island's culinary treats are wine and cheese, both locally produced. Fresh fish, kid's meat, rabbit and the various Canarian stews are all widely available and very tasty. You should also try *quesadillas*, small cakes made with local cheese, which are widely available in shops and bars, though they are something of an acquired taste.

GETTING THERE AND AWAY
By air
Binter Canarias Tel: 902 39 13 92; www.bintercanarias.es. *Gran Canaria:* 4 a week. *La Palma:* 2 a week. *Tenerife North:* 5 a day during the week and 2 on weekends.

By sea
Fred Olsen Tel: 902 10 01 07; email: reservas@fredolsen.es; www.fredolsen.es. *Tenerife:* 1 a day (to Los Cristianos).
Trasmediterránea Tel: 902 45 46 54; www.trasmediterranea.es. *Tenerife:* 1 a day (to Los Cristianos).

GETTING AROUND
Public transport
The bus service is very limited and very limiting. From Monday to Saturday buses leave Valverde at noon for most of the *pueblos,* or leave the villages heading for the capital at around 06.30–07.00. There are other services, some of them running once a week, but planning a stay on the island and relying entirely on the public transport would mean that you would miss some of the highlights or else have to stay for a few months.

Car hire
Due to the lack of buses, hiring a car, at least for a few days, is essential. The majority of offices are in Valverde, though most companies will arrange for you to collect your car at the port or airport. It is highly recommended to book a car in advance, especially in peak season.

Autos Bamir Tel: 922 55 12 45 (airport); 922 55 01 83 (Valverde); 922 55 90 77 (Frontera)
Autos Cooperativa Tel: 922 55 07 29 (Valverde)
Autos Cruz Alta Tel: 922 55 00 04 (Valverde)
Cicar Tel: 922 55 13 95 (airport)
Rosamar Rent A Car Tel: 922 55 04 22 (Valverde)

There are only three petrol stations on the island, in Valverde, Frontera and El Pinar.

Hitchhiking

If you're not hiring a car and you don't want to be mooching around small towns all day waiting for the next bus, a bit of hitchhiking will be necessary. It's pretty easy to get a lift and don't be surprised if someone goes 20km out of their way to take you where you want to go – there are very few people in a rush on El Hierro. Although it's never 100% safe to get in a car with a stranger, Herreños will laugh at the suggestion that hitchhiking is a risky business – for them it's a necessary part of life.

WHERE TO STAY

Accommodation is not in abundance (there are 800 beds island-wide), so booking ahead is highly recommended, especially in peak seasons. One thing you won't find (and probably won't miss) is a high-rise hotel. In fact, the authorities are rightly proud of the fact that there isn't a single lift on the island. The majority of the beds are to be found in *casas rurales* or self-catering apartments, though there are also a few hotels and some budget options. Meridiano Cero has **cottages** across the island, all in beautiful locations. Their office is in Mocanal, but everything can be arranged by email or telephone; tel: 922 55 18 24; fax: 922 55 05 75; email: hierro@ecoturismocanarias.com; www.ecoturismocanarias.com/hierro. You'll pay about €55 per night for two people and €65 for four. The tourist information office has an up-to-date list of privately owned rural houses on the island.

There is only one **campsite** on El Hierro, at Hoya del Morcillo. To stay you must get a permit from the department of environment of the island council (*Cabildo*); tel: 922 55 00 17; fax: 922 55 02 71. Once at the campsite there is a charge of €4.50 per person.

ACTIVITIES
Diving

El Hierro is fast becoming known as a diving destination and there are various companies offering baptism dives, courses or diving for the already qualified. The main divers' destination is La Restinga, where several companies offer courses and equipment hire. There is also a diving school in Timijiraque. The water temperatures are marginally higher than in other islands, giving you the chance to see tropical species that you won't find around the other islands such as porcupine fish and golden tailed moray. Diving has been heavily controlled around La Restinga since the waters were declared a marine reserve.

Driving

There are some thrilling drives around the island and many of the tourist attractions can be seen in a couple of days if you have your own wheels. The roads are well signposted and there is usually only one road to take, meaning the chances of getting lost are slim. Some of the roads are unpaved and there is a fair amount of mountain driving, so start training your nerves of steel for those sharp bends and sheer drops. If you're not up to it, La Sanjora offer tours around the island: €108 for up to three people; €140 for four to eight people. For contact details see *Hiking*, below.

Fishing

The best place for fishing is La Restinga, though you can join the locals in many of the coastal villages, such as Tamaduste, La Caleta and Punta Grande. There's nowhere to hire equipment, though, so you'll have to take your own.

Hiking

Walking on the island is a pleasure, thanks to a few well-signposted and well-maintained routes. The only drawbacks are the lack of public transport, meaning that car hire is obligatory for hikers, and that almost all trails are out-and-back walks rather than circular routes. The tourist information offices have a useful map with the various routes marked and descriptions of the walks (in Spanish only). **La Sanjora** operate hiking tours for €26 per person, which includes transport and a picnic. They can also organise *parapente*, canyoning, mountain-bike hire, diving and fishing. Their office is on Avenida Dacio Darias 65, Valverde; tel: 922551840; fax: 922 551 463; email: lasanjora@hotmail.com; www.lasanjora.com.

VALVERDE

Once a Bimbache settlement, Valverde is now home to around 1,800 Herreños, making it by far the least populous of the Canarian capitals. It is also the only capital not on the coast and the highest, at 600m above sea level. It has a completely irregular layout, making orientation a little difficult, and the steep, narrow streets could have you gasping for breath. There are prettier places on the island but if you want to use public transport (such as it is) you really need to hang around in Valverde. While you're there you can visit the museum, church and hang around in the square, watching the world go by as the locals do. You'll also find the island's only discos here, though whether they'll be open is another matter. Valverde gets chilly at night, even in the summer months, so do remember a jumper or light jacket and some closed shoes, or you could live to regret it.

Getting there and away

If you're not going to have your own wheels to get from the airport (see page 311), try to arrive on the morning flight as a bus leaves for Valverde at 08.55 Mon–Sat. Otherwise, a taxi will cost around €10 but get out of the terminal quickly as there will be only two or three cars waiting! If you've missed the boat, call 922 55 07 29 and a taxi will be dispatched from Valverde. There is a bus from Valverde to the airport at 08.15 Mon–Sat. There are also buses to Puerto de Estaca at 13.30 and 23.00, though none from the port to the capital. A taxi from the port will cost about €15. Other buses leave from the bus station at 12.00 most days for the majority of the *pueblos* and tend to return at around 07.00.

Where to stay

There are only three places to stay in Valverde, other than a few *casas rurales*.
Hostal Residencia Casañas Calle San Francisco 9; tel/fax: 922 55 02 54. Large spotlessly clean rooms with TV and view. Single/double/triple €25/32/38.
Hotel Boomerang Calle Doctor Gost 1; tel: 922 55 02 00; fax: 922 55 02 53. The town's slightly more upmarket option. The hotel also has a bar and restaurant serving mainly seafood and tapas. Single €37; double €50.
Pension San Fleit Calle Santiago 18; tel: 922 550 857. Basic but clean rooms, some with TV. Rooms at the back are quieter. Single €18/€23 without/with bathroom; double €24/€27.

Where to eat

Bar Restaurante Hayde Calle Constitución, on the way out of town towards the airport. Venezuelan-run, this place offers an alternative to the usual fare when you have a snack attack. *Empanadas*, *arepas* and *cachapas* are the specialities, though tapas and sandwiches are also available. Service is very friendly.

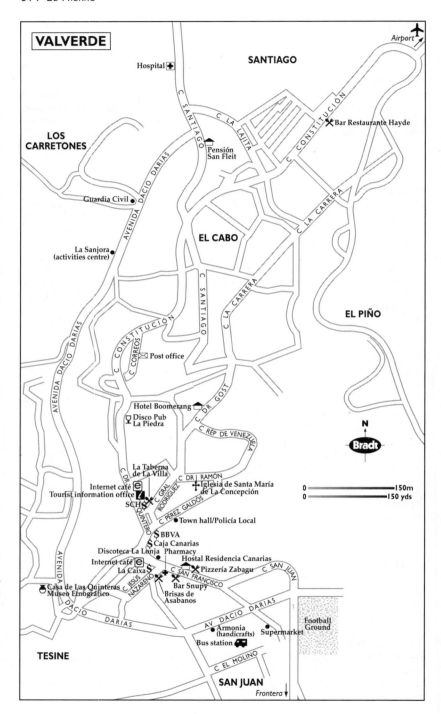

VALVERDE

Airport

SANTIAGO

Hospital

Bar Restaurante Hayde

LOS CARRETONES

C SANTIAGO

C LA LAITA

C CONSTITUCIÓN

AVENIDA DACIO DARIAS

Pensión San Fleit

Guardia Civil

C LA CARRERA

La Sanjora (activities centre)

EL CABO

C SANTIAGO

C LA CARRERA

EL PIÑO

AVENIDA DACIO DARIAS

C CONSTITUCIÓN

C CORREOS

Post office

DR GOST

N

Bradt

Hotel Boomerang

Disco Pub La Piedra

C RÉP DE VENEZUELA

La Taberna de La Villa

C DR RAMÓN

0 ———— 150m

0 ———— 150 yds

Internet café

Tourist information office

SCH

C DR

QUINTERO

C GRAL RODRÍGUEZ

Iglesia de Santa María de La Concepción

C PÉREZ GALDÓS

Town hall/Policía Local

BBVA

Caja Canarias

Discoteca La Lonja

Pharmacy

Internet café

La Caixa

C JESÚS NAZARENO

Hostal Residencia Canarias

Pizzería Zabagu

C SAN FRANCISCO

C SAN JUAN

Bar Snupy

Casa de Las Quinteras Museo Etnográfico

Brisas de Asabanos

AVENIDA DACIO DARIAS

AV DACIO DARIAS

Armonia (handicrafts)

Supermarket

Football Ground

Bus station

TESINE

C EL MOLINO

SAN JUAN

Frontera

Bar Snupy Calle San Francisco. OK for snacks and chatting with the locals.
La Taberna de la Villa To the left of the main square; tel: 922 55 19 07. Without doubt the most atmospheric place in town. They have a reasonable tapas menu and also serve pizzas and good wine. Closed on Sundays.
Restaurante Brisas de Asabanos Calle Jesus Nazareño; tel: 922 55 13 50. Probably the classiest place in Valverde, although the service is bordering on terrible. With a restaurant and separate bar area they offer something for everyone, from tasty fish dishes to tapas and even metre-long sausages. Closed on Mondays. Main courses start at €10; a good-sized plate of tapas is about €4.
Restaurante Pizzería Zabagu Next door to the Pensión Casañas on Calle San Francisco. Always busy and does tasty breakfasts as well as pizzas and the usual tapas and sandwiches.

Nightlife

The very fact you're in El Hierro suggests that other things may be more important than a good night on the town, and this is just as well. There are two discos in Valverde, though they open sporadically. **Disco Pub La Piedra**, on Calle la Constitución, is the more popular place, opening at midnight and playing a variety of music. The other option is **Discoteca La Lonja**, on Calle San Francisco, which plays dance and house music and is open Thursday, Friday and Saturday nights. Don't expect to find anything open if there is a fiesta happening somewhere else on the island. Everyone starts their night in La Taberna de la Villa.

Practicalities

Banks All are on the main street: Santander Central Hispano, open Mon–Fri 08.30–14.00, Sat 08.30–13.00; BBVA, open Mon–Fri 08.30–14.15, Sat 08.30–13.00; Caja Canarias, open Mon–Fri 08.30–14.00, Thu 17.00–19.30; La Caixa, open Mon–Fri 08.15–14.00, Thu 16.30–19.45.
Health The hospital is on Calle Santiago, near to Pensión San Fleit.
Internet There are two internet cafés, one on Calle San Francisco and one on Calle Doctor Quintero; access is €1.50 per hour.
Pharmacy On the corner of Calle San Francisco and Calle Jesus Nazareño.
Police The Guardia Civil is on Av Dacio Darias, the Policía Local is in the Town Hall on Calle Pérez Galdós.
Post office Set back from Calle Constitución on Calle el Correos. Open Mon–Fri 08.30–14.00, Sat 09.00–13.00.
Shopping There is a largish supermarket on Calle San Francisco, near the bus station. Nearby on Av Dacio Darias, Armonia has a good selection of local handicrafts and other Herreño products and there is a handicrafts shop in the Museo Etnográfico (see *What to see and do*, below).
Tourist information On Calle Doctor Quintero, open Mon–Fri 09.00–14.00, Sat 09.30–13.00.

What to see and do

Valverde is not the most exciting of towns and you may find yourself twiddling your thumbs after a few hours. The **Iglesia de Santa María de la Concepción** and the square next to it are worth a visit, as is the **Casa de las Quinteras Museo Etnográfico**. It's a small museum with information and exhibits on the history and culture of El Hierro. There is also a small shop selling handicrafts from across the island. It's on Calle Armas Martel, open Mon–Fri 09.00–14.00, Sat 10.30–13.30, 16.30–18.30; entrance €3.

TAMADUSTE

This is now the summer getaway for the residents wanting to escape the (ahem) bright lights and stress of Valverde. It is by no means a tourist resort, though, more a place to relax and eat some good fresh fish. There is no beach but you can join the locals and sun worship on the rocks. The water is calm and ideal for a dip.

Getting there

There's a bus from Valverde on Sundays at 09.00 which continues to La Caleta. It returns in the evening, leaving La Caleta at 19.00 and passing through Tamaduste about 15 minutes later. A taxi from Valverde would cost around €15.

Where to stay

Apartamentos Boomerang Calle El Cantil; tel: 922 55 02 00; fax: 922 55 02 53. Owned by the same family as the Hotel Boomerang in Valverde, the apartments have the best location in Tamaduste. Balconies overlook the ocean and the apartments are so close to the water that you can hear the waves crashing throughout the night. Apartments for 2 people are €54 and for 4 people €60 per night.

Apartamentos Verode Calle El Verode; tel: 922 55 01 59. A couple of roads back from the water's edge (but let's face it, nothing is too far from the sea in Tamaduste), these apartments are clean and quiet. Apartments for 2 people €40; for 4 people €42 per night.

Where to eat

Bar Restaurante Bimbache Calle Los Cardones. The best place in town to eat. Naturally, they specialise in fish, but also have a good variety of tapas and Canarian specials. Main courses start at €7.

Practicalities

Everything is in Valverde.

What to see and do

Tamaduste is no place for an action holiday. The only things to do here are sunbathe, swim, follow the locals and do some fishing off the rocks or, if that's too much effort, just join them in eating their catch.

LA CALETA

This is another weekend getaway for the capital's residents. There are a couple of 'natural' swimming pools (concrete pools regularly topped up by the ocean) and a kiosk nearby serving cold beers and a couple of tapas dishes. There's a bus between La Caleta and Valverde on Sunday (See *Tamaduste* section for details).

TIMIJIRAQUE AND THE EAST COAST

The road from Puerto de la Estaca hugs the coast, affording vistas of the curious rock formations and the imposing Isora cliffs. This area is ideal for a day trip and has the island's most luxurious hotel, the Parador Nacional. It's also a good place for water babies, the crashing waves a favourite amongst surfers and the waters are clear enough for divers.

Getting there

There are no buses that go further than Puerto de la Estaca, so you need a car to see this part of the island. It's a pleasant drive along the coast, once you get past the road that winds down from Valverde. The road ends at the Parador.

Where to stay and eat

Casa Guayana Tel: 922 55 10 82. Great location, next to Playa del Varadero. Rooms have washbasin, but bathrooms are shared. €15 per person or €12 if you plan to stay a few days. The small restaurant serves hearty local fodder.

Parador Nacional Tel: 922 55 80 36; fax: 922 55 80 86; email: hierro@parador.es; www.parador.es. The island's state-run hotel is in a fabulous location, although not overly convenient for getting around the island. It has a swimming pool and several patios and terraces where you can enjoy a drink and the view. Two of its rooms are specially adapted for disabled guests. Singles €88; doubles €110. Meals are available at an extra cost.

What to see and do

Timijiraque has one of the island's few sandy beaches, which is usually almost deserted – ideal for sun lovers, though the water can be rough and it often gets windy. There are other beaches further down the coast towards the Parador which are less windy but pebbly. Timijiraque is a haven for surfers and is generally considered to be the best place on the island for catching waves.

Timijiraque is also the only place other than La Restinga where you can learn to dive or rent equipment, with **Hierro Sub** (tel: 922 55 04 82; email: hierro_sub@yahoo.es; www.inicia.es/de/hierro_sub). They offer a discovery dive but cater more to the experienced diver, renting out equipment from €30 per person. There are good discounts for larger groups and accommodation can be arranged from €15 per person.

As you emerge from the one-way tunnel, you'll see the much talked about Roque de la Bonanza, an arch-shaped rock that apparently rises 200m from the seabed. Most are a little disappointed with it, having read so much about it in the information from the tourist office, but it is photogenic and impressive to think that it reaches such a depth so close to the shore.

ISORA

Isora is pretty, but the village itself has little more than a couple of very average bars and a rather nondescript church. The main reason you'd come here is to admire the view of the east coast from the Mirador de Isora, which sits atop a 1,000m-high cliff. It's one of the best viewpoints on the island and the starting point for a pretty tough hike down to the coast (and back up if you're feeling strong). The path is clearly marked and the walk down takes about two hours (five hours for the round trip). Bear in mind that there is almost no shade for the whole walk so a hat and plenty of water are essential. Buses between La Restinga and Valverde pass through Isora; ask locally to find out the exact times.

EL PINAR

The only reason you'd be in El Pinar is if you want to explore the south and don't fancy staying in La Restinga (or can't find any available accommodation there). The town is dull and basically consists of one road, though there are a few gems in the surrounding area. There's a decent hotel on the main road, **Hotel Pinar** (tel: 922 55 80 08; fax: 922 55 80 90). It has pleasant rooms with television and bathroom and meals are available. Single €34; double €42. El Pinar is one of the best places on the island to pick up a few handicrafts and has several shops on the main road. The main crafts here are basketry, weaving and woodcarving. It's also an ideal place to explore the nearby pine forest and isn't far from the Hoya del Morcillo picnic and camping area. Buses between Valverde and La Restinga pass through El Pinar: there's one in the morning to Valverde and one in the afternoon to La Restinga; it's best to ask locally to find out what time the buses leave.

LA RESTINGA

Ask an islander for their least favourite town on the island and they're apt to say La Restinga, though I have to disagree. True, it's more built up than most places but it has a lovely atmosphere: laid-back, yet with a bit of life trying to get out. And while it's the island's main tourist centre, it's a far cry from the big resorts in Tenerife and Gran Canaria. Think Playa de las Américas 50 years ago. The clear waters make it ideal for scuba diving (many agree that it's the best place within the Canary Islands) and there are more decent restaurants than in most Herreño towns – there are even a couple of night-time hang-outs. If diving's not for you, just lie on the pleasant black-sand beach and watch the boats come and go. The small harbour was built in 1970 and has since been the island's most important fishing port, so a fresh fish lunch is a must. The town also hosts an annual underwater photography competition, Photo Sub, usually taking place in October or November.

Getting there

Buses leave Valverde for La Restinga Mon–Sat at noon. If you want to head back to the capital, buses leave Mon–Sat at 07.00, stopping at El Pinar and Isora on the way. There is also a bus to get to Pozo de la Salud, Mon–Fri at 08.00, returning at 13.00.

Where to stay

This is one place where accommodation is in abundance (relatively speaking), though it's also in demand. The majority of places don't have a reception so you must call first to book a room.

Apartamentos Mar de las Calmas Av Marítima; tel: 922 55 71 11. Small 1- and 2-bedroom apartments with TV, kitchen and balconies; most have sea views. Apartments for 2 people €42; 4 people €48.

Apartamentos Mareas Brujas, Av Marítima 24; tel: 922 55 71 41; fax: 922 21 08 84. These apartments have sea views and are very clean. Rooms have balconies, TV and kitchen. Studios €36, 1-bedroom apartments €42.

Apartamentos Restinga Calle Los Saltos 16; tel/fax: 922 55 81 70. Fully equipped and with balconies. You might get a sea view if you crane your neck and squint – they're a few rows back from the beach. 2 people €33; 4 people €36.

Apartamentos Rocamar I Av Marítima; tel: 922 55 70 83; fax: 922 55 70 83. All apartments have sea view, TV and kitchen. There is also a reception that's open normal Spanish trading hours. 1-bedroom apartments €33, 2 bedrooms €39.

Apartamentos Rocamar II Calle Las Calmas; tel: 922 55 70 83. Brand new and well equipped with TVs, washing machines and even microwaves. 2 people €36; 4 people €45.

Apartamentos Tanajara Calle La Lapa; tel: 922 55 70 99. Although they don't look much from the outside, the apartments are spacious, well equipped and clean inside. Balconies have a sea view if you stretch your neck a bit. Studios €21, 1-bedroom apartments €30, 2 bedrooms €39.

Pensión Kai Marino Tel: 922 55 70 34. The best location and the lowest prices in town. Kai Marino is next to the beach and has a sun terrace for the truly lazy. The rooms aren't spectacular but they're clean, reasonably priced and in an unbeatable location. Breakfast is available and there is a TV room. The restaurant was closed at time of writing. There are no single rooms. Doubles €18 without bathroom or €23 with bathroom.

Where to eat

Bar Restaurante Tagoror Av Marítima. Snack menu, young lively atmosphere, good place for a few evening drinks.

LA RESTINGA
(SKETCH MAP)

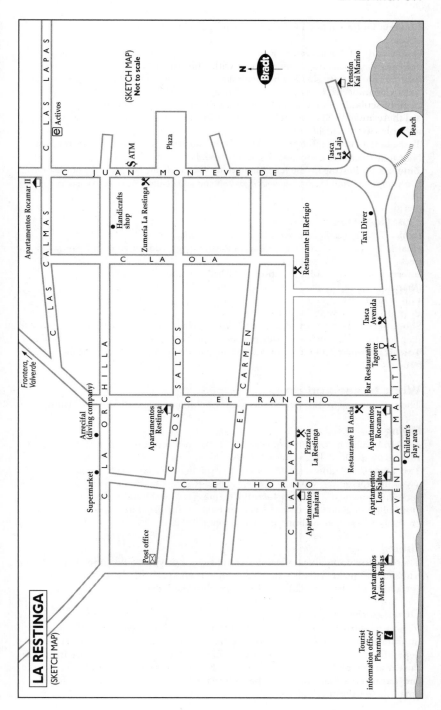

(SKETCH MAP)
Not to scale

N→ Beach

Tourist
information office/
Pharmacy

C L A S L A P A S

Activos

C J U A N M O N T E V E R D E

ATM

Plaza

Apartamentos Rocamar II

C L A S C A L M A S

Handicrafts
shop

Zumería La Restinga

Restaurante El Refugio

Tasca
La Laja

Beach

Pensión
Kai Marino

Frontera,
Valverde

Arrecifal
(diving company)

Supermarket

Post office

C L A O R C H I L L A

C L A O L A

C L O S S A L T O S

Apartamentos
Restinga

C E L R A N C H O

C E L C A R M E N

Taxi Diver

Tasca
Avenida

Bar Restaurante
Tagoror

Pizzería
La Restinga

Restaurante El Ancla

Apartamentos
Rocamar I

Apartamentos
Tanajara

C L A L A P A

C E L H O R N O

Apartamentos
Los Saltos

A V E N I D A M A R Í T I M A

Children's
play area

Apartamentos
Mareas Brujas

Pizzeria La Restinga Calle La Lapa. Friendly service and good pizza at reasonable prices.

Restaurante El Ancla Calle El Rancho. More choice than most, though the main drawcard is still fresh fish. Main meals start at €8. Closed on Tuesdays.

Restaurante El Refugio On a narrow street where Calle La Ola and Calle La Lapa join. The locals' favourite, serving tasty fish and seafood and with typically friendly service. Good home-made desserts too. Main meals are around €6. Closed on Mondays.

Tasca Avenida Av Marítima. The place to go for roast chicken. Tables outside get reasonably lively at night.

Tasca la Laja Really more of a drinking place, though they do have a few tapas choices. Nice atmosphere and a good location just behind the beach.

Zumería La Restinga Calle Juan Monteverde. Definitely the best place for breakfast. Every juice you could want, a few nice pastries and good coffee. Also serve tapas at lunchtimes.

Practicalities

Banks There is a cashpoint on Calle Juan Monteverde.

Health The closest Health Centre is in El Pinar, though a doctor visits La Restinga twice a week.

Internet Access is available at Activos on Calle Las Lapas.

Pharmacy In the complex at the far end of the Av Marítima.

Police In El Pinar.

Post office At the west side of town, on a street yet to be named.

Shopping The best supermarket is on Calle La Orchilla. On the same road there is a small shop specialising in handmade leather goods, particularly shoes.

Tourist information In the complex at the end of the Av Marítima, open Mon–Fri 09.00–14.00.

What to see and do

The two main activities here, other than catching rays, are diving and fishing.

Diving

Arrecifal Calle Orchilla 30; tel/fax: 922 55 71 71; email: arrecifal@arakis.es. A package of 10 dives for qualified divers costs €210. A week-long course for beginners is €300.

Taxi Diver Av Marítima; tel: 922 55 71 42; email: info@elhierrotaxidiver.com; www.elhierrotaxidiver.com. The best outfit in La Restinga, offering a variety of activities. A discovery dive costs €40 while a 4-day PADI course is €360. Dives for those already qualified cost around €20 per immersion, including equipment hire. They also rent out kayaks for €10 an hour and run snorkelling trips for €30.

Fishing

There are no companies offering fishing trips, but you could mooch around the harbour and make friends with a fisherman if you particularly want to head out to sea. Otherwise you can fish off the shore with the locals.

Other activities

If you prefer to stay dry, there are other options. **Activos** offers guided mountain-biking trips, car excursions, hikes and kayak hire. Prices vary depending on the length of the excursion: bike trips and hikes start from €18, car excursions €28 including picnic, barbecue trip €20 (minimum five people) and kayak hire €20. They are based on Calle Las Calmas; tel: 922 55 71 17; email: activos@ya.com.

Cala de Tacorón

This bay is about a 20-minute drive from La Restinga and well worth the petrol. It's a popular swimming and snorkelling area (though not crowded) with barbecuing facilities or, if you don't feel like cooking, there's a lovely open-air restaurant overlooking the bay. They have a tasty, extensive, inexpensive menu that changes daily.

SABINOSA

For many, this is the prettiest village on the island. There's not much going on but a walk through its steep streets to admire the traditional old houses is worthwhile. There's also a tasty local wine to sample.

Getting there

Buses leave Valverde for Sabinosa Mon–Sat at 12.00 and return at 06.30 on Mon, Thu and Sat. There are also buses to Tigaday Mon–Fri at 09.45 and 13.15. Buses leave Tigaday at 09.00 and 13.15 Mon–Fri. Buses to Pozo de la Salud leave La Restinga on weekdays at 08.00, returning at 13.00.

Where to stay

Hotel Balneario Pozo de la Salud Tel: 922 55 95 61; fax: 922 55 98 01; email: balneario@el-meridiano.com; www.el-meridiano.com/balneario. Not in the *pueblo* itself but not far away, on the coast. It's a 3-star hotel offering a wide variety of health treatments, many of which employ the medicinal powers of the water. Single €53; double €70, with breakfast.

Pensión Sabinosa Calle Valentina Hernández; tel: 922 55 93 55. Small, well-kept place with a restaurant serving breakfast and dinner. Single €18; double €24 (with private bathroom), €15/€22 without bathroom. It's signposted from the main road.

Where to eat

Bar Restaurante Sabinosa On the main road. A tidy place offering the usual menu. It opens whenever the chef arrives!

Pozo de la Salud There's a restaurant at the hotel serving healthy dishes, with specials available for diabetics, dieters or those with hypertension.

Practicalities

Banks The closest banks are in Tigaday.
Health There is a Health Centre on the main road.
Police In Frontera.
Shopping There is a supermarket on the main road and a small handicrafts shop on Calle Inocencia Duran Casañas specialising in wicker crafts.

What to see and do

Hike

Sabinosa–Ermita de los Reyes–Sabinosa

Distance: 9km; time: 6 hours (there and back); difficulty: 3–4.

Sabinosa is the starting point for one of the nicest walks on the island; the hike up to the Ermita de los Reyes. From the village square, walk up Calle Hoya del Moral and turn right into Camino de la Dehesa. From here a well-signed path takes you zigzagging up the mountain towards the small whitewashed church at the top. This is the starting point for the Bajada del Virgen, El Hierro's most important fiesta. It's a tough walk because, like many of the walks on the island, you spent half of it constantly walking uphill and the rest slipping back down again. Walking boots with good grips are essential.

Pozo de la Salud

Tel: 922 55 95 61; fax: 922 55 98 01; email: balneario@el-meridiano.com; www.el-meridiano.com/balneario.

This is the place to go if you're not up to a strenuous hike or to reward yourself once you've finished. The waters in this part of the island have long been hailed for their healing properties, though it is relatively recently that the authorities have cashed in on it, building a health spa. Treatments start at €6 for a mud mask and go up to €55 for a rejuvenating facial.

FRONTERA AND TIGADAY

Locals can't tell you where one village stops and the other starts and the two names are used interchangeably. The two villages form a second capital and the main town in the Frontera province of the island. The Iglesia de la Madonna de Candelaria is the dominating sight, with its belltower sitting on the Monte de Joapira, an outcrop of red volcanic rock. There's actually nothing to do here but plenty of accommodation and it's close to many of the island's beauty spots such as Las Puntas, the various natural pools along the coast and El Sabinar.

Getting there

As with all the towns, the buses leave Valverde Mon–Sat at 12.00. Buses leave for Valverde at 06.45 Mon–Sat. There are also buses to Las Puntas Mon–Fri at 09.00 and to Sabinosa Mon–Fri at 09.00 and 13.15. The tunnel, which opened in 2003, cuts the journey time from Valverde to Frontera in half and is a much more pleasurable drive without the endless mountain bends.

Where to stay

All of the accommodation is on Calle Tigaday or the continuation of it, Calle Cruz Alta.

Apartamentos El Valle Calle Tigaday 17; tel: 922 55 94 71. Geared to group travellers with its enormous 3- or 4-bedroom apartments. An apartment for 6 people is great value at €54. At quiet times they will allow smaller groups to stay at €36 for 3 people and €42 for 4 people.

Apartamentos Frontera Calle Tigaday 19; tel: 922 55 92 46. Two-bedroom apartments are €45 and have a fully equipped kitchen, TV and a balcony or terrace with mountain views. Studios for 2 people are €33 and are set around a pleasant courtyard.

Apartamentos Jucar Calle Tigaday 30; tel: 922 55 93 01; fax: 922 55 51 68; email: jucar@elhierro.tv; www.elhierro.tv/jucar. The pick of the bunch. Apartments are large and spotlessly clean, some with a sea view, some looking out on to the street. All have TV and kitchen. €38 for 2 people and €6 for each additional person

Hotelito Ida Inés Calle Belgara Alta 2; tel: 922 55 94 45; fax: 922 55 60 88; email: info@hotelitoidaines.com; www.hotelitoidaines.com. The more upmarket choice, in a very quiet spot opposite the Health Centre (signposted from the main road). Has a swimming pool and sun terrace. Single €63; double €76, including breakfast.

Pensión Guanche Calle Cruz Alta 1; tel: 922 55 90 65. The village's cheapest and least inviting option. Rooms are clean but a bit dingy. Single €15; double €21.

Where to eat

Again, everything is concentrated on the main road.

Bar Restaurante El Cazador Specialises in chicken and pizza, though the former is more highly recommended.

Bar Restaurante Frontera Quite an extensive menu and offers a 3-course *menú del día* for €7.50. Closed on Mondays.

LOOKING AFTER THE LIZARDS

When Roman natural historian Pliny the Elder wrote his description of the Canary Islands in the 1st century AD, he remarked upon an island teeming with giant lizards. He wasn't specific on which island it was, though people tend to narrow it down to either El Hierro or La Gomera. Around the time of the conquest, French chroniclers mentioned lizards 'the size of cats; not harmful nor poisonous, but revolting to look at' living on El Hierro.

Things have changed a lot since the times of the Bimbaches, who appeared to use massive reptiles as food, and these days the El Hierro giant lizard is an endangered species. The average size of the lizards is 60cm, though they are thought to grow to around 75cm in the wild.

Man's interference over the years has led to the considerable reduction in the numbers of giant lizards in El Hierro and in the 1940s they had died out everywhere but Fuga de Gorreta (in El Golfo). They were declared extinct in 1972 but not all were convinced that this magnificent species had been wiped out.

Well-known reptile lover Werner Bings paid a visit to the island in 1974 to hunt for clues as to the existence of the lizards. He tried to bait the lizards but hadn't achieved success by the time he had to return to his homeland to tend to an ill child. Almost as soon as his back was turned, a pair of lizards wandered into his investigation area and were promptly caught by a couple of passing shepherds. Their intentions for the reptiles were unclear, but the authorities wasted no time in confiscating the lizards and returning them to their habitat, declaring it a prohibited zone. A year later Bings returned to El Hierro, revealing the discovery that the giant lizard was not extinct after all.

The recuperation plan started in 1985 with the capture of a male and two females. Soon after, 21 lizards were born in captivity and the authorities turned their attention to protecting the lizards' habitat from human interference and predators. The three main causes of their decline are destruction of habitat, the need to compete for food with the large number of goats on the island and the introduction of wild cats, the lizards' only predator. Once the lizards are deemed fit to survive in the wild, they are tagged and then released.

Today the only colony survives in a virtually inaccessible cliff in the northwest of the island, La Fuga de Gorreta, within the Reserva Natural Especial de Tibataje. Juan Pedro Pérez, grandson of the goat herder who captured the first pair of reptiles, is now the watchman and ensures that no-one gets near the lizards or attempts to take a souvenir.

There are currently 340 examples of the El Hierro giant lizard roaming around and despite the success of the breeding programme, the lizards are considered Europe's most endangered reptile and in the top five in the world. Although you're unlikely to see any roaming free, you can see the lizards at the recuperation centre in Las Puntas.

Bar Restaurante Sosito Next to Apartamentos Frontera, this place sells locally made honey as well as offering staple El Hierro cuisine.

La Taguarita In the arcade. Does tasty breakfasts and has a pleasant terrace outside where you can watch the Tigaday action, such as it is.

Tacos and Pizzas An alternative to the typical bars in the village. Open evenings only, it offers a variety of Mexican dishes as well as pizza. Closed on Tuesdays.

Practicalities

Banks Caja Rural, open Mon–Fri 08.30–14.00, Thu 17.00–19.30, and Caja Canarias, open Mon–Fri 08.30–14.00, Thu 17.00-19.30, are both on Calle Cruz Alta. BBVA, Calle Tigaday, open Mon–Fri 08.30–14.15, Sat 08.30–13.00.

Health The Health Centre is opposite the petrol station.

Pharmacy In the small shopping arcade at the end of Calle Tigaday.

Police Joined to the Town Hall on the corner of Calle La Corredera and Calle El Moral.

Post office On Calle Tigaday, open Mon–Fri 08.30–14.00, Sat 09.00–13.00.

Shopping There are two reasonably sized supermarkets, one on Calle La Corredera and the other on Calle Tigaday. Calle Cruz Alta has a few souvenir shops but your best bet is Casa Nicio on Calle Tigaday, which has a good selection of local handicrafts.

Tourist information On Calle El Hoyo, signposted from the main road, open Mon–Fri 08.00–14.00.

LAS PUNTAS AND PUNTA GRANDE

After La Restinga, Las Puntas is the island's main tourist area. The centre is a small cluster of apartments and fish restaurants at the end of the main road, though there are a few restaurants scattered along the road all the way from Tigaday. Las Puntas has excellent views of the coast and is close to a number of natural pools, some more natural than others.

Getting there

There are buses from Valverde on Wed and Fri at 12.00 and from Tigaday Mon–Fri at 09.00. Buses return to Valverde at 06.30 Wed and Fri and to Tigaday at 09.15 Mon–Fri. Las Puntas is now linked to the north of the island by a tunnel, which means that the journey from Valverde is now just 20 minutes (it used to take an hour).

Where to stay

Apartamentos Noemi Calle Tibataje; tel: 659 693 814. Owned by Noemi, long-time manager of the Hotel Punta Grande, these new apartments are well equipped and spotless. They are signposted from the main road. Apartment for 2 people €40.

Casa Salmor Ctra General Las Puntas; tel: 922 55 93 29. Great value rooms or apartments set around patios and gardens. Rooms have bathroom and fridge while apartments have a full kitchen. There is also a bar and restaurant. Single €15; double €25; studio apartments (2 people) €30; apartments €35/€40 for 2 /3 people.

Hotel Punta Grande Tel: 922 55 92 03. Certified by the Guinness Book of Records as being the smallest hotel in the world, Hotel Punta Grande epitomises the intimacy of the island. Its 4 rooms are popular, so book well in advance. The hotel is in a spectacular location where you can listen to the waves crashing on the rocks as you fall asleep. It also has a small (of course) bar and restaurant. Single €47; double €57, including breakfast.

Where to eat

Bar Restaurante Tejerde Near the Hotel Punta Grande, a busy place offering the freshest (and sometimes largest!) fish around. Closed on Mondays.

Hotel Punta Grande Tel: 922 55 92 03. There's a restaurant specialising in fish at the hotel, but non-residents need to book in advance.

Restaurante Pizzería Las Puntas On the main Las Puntas road. Offers a nice respite from fresh fish. Closed on Wednesdays.

Practicalities

All amenities are in Frontera and Tigaday.

What to see and do
Ecomuseo de Guinea
There are two museums in this complex, the Archaeological Village of Guinea and the Giant Lizard Recuperation Centre. Although there is some dispute over which is the oldest settlement on the island, many agree that it is Guinea, which has been open to the public as an eco-museum since 1995. Knowledgeable guides lead tours around the village giving insights into aboriginal life on the island. It's open Tue–Sat 10.30–14.30, 17.00–19.00, Sun 11.00–14.00.

The recuperation centre is next door and houses some of the island's endangered giant lizards. The centre has a breeding programme to try to prevent the species becoming extinct, as it was thought to be until the 1970s. Open Tue–Thu and Sat 10.30–14.30, 17.00–19.00.

A guided tour around both museums takes 50 minutes and costs €7.25. A ticket for just one of the museums is €4.25.

Swimming
The coastal road passes three of the island's favourite swimming holes: **La Maceta**, **Charco de los Sargos** and **Charco Azul**. La Maceta is the most popular but the least natural as it's a concrete pool with natural water crashing in from the ocean. Charco de los Sargos and Charco Azul are natural pools and both good scuba-diving areas.

DRIVES
Northern circuit
Leave **Valverde** on the road that passes the hospital and head for **Echedo,** a wine-producing village. From here you can take a detour to the **Charco Manso** natural pool or the excellently preserved village of **Pozo de las Calcosas** (which also has pools). They are both worth the detour, or you could carry on to **Mocanal**, a series of houses scattered along the main road; there's nothing of interest here. The road continues to **Los Burros Felices**, a donkey sanctuary which cares for badly treated animals rescued from across the archipelago (see *Giving something back*, page 55). From here it's a stone's throw to César Manrique's contribution to the island, the **Mirador de la Peña**, where there is a restaurant and a magnificent view across El Golfo; you can't enter the restaurant if you're wearing shorts. Continue to one of the island's oldest villages, **Las Montañetas**. The majority of the houses here have been quite recently restored and are now used as *casa rurales* for tourists. If you haven't had enough of the view of El Golfo, stop off at the **Mirador de Jinama** and then head south to the **Mirador de las Playas** for vistas of the island's other coast. The view is even better from the **Mirador de Isora**, which you can get to via the small village of **Isora**. Heading north again you won't find much of interest in **San Andrés** but you'll have to pass through if you want to visit El Hierro's holy tree, the **Garoé**. The tree itself is far from impressive, though the many myths and legends surrounding it are interesting and the staff working there are knowledgeable and helpful (see box, page 309). Open Tue–Sat 10.30–14.30, 17.00–19.00, Sun 11.00–14.00. From here, retrace the dirt track back to the main road and head back to **Valverde**.

Southern circuit
Heading south from **Frontera** you should visit the island's finest natural pool, the Charco Azul. The road down to it isn't great and you have to make your way down a lot of steps but it's worth it for some peace and coastal views. Backtrack to the main road and head for El Hierro's rural gem, **Sabinosa**. Just a few minutes further down the road is the **Pozo de la Salud**, a health spa and hotel. Continuing

past the spa, the road takes you through the dramatic landscape of the lava fields and a short dirt track leads down to **Playa del Verodal**, an unusual red-sand beach and El Hierro's largest. Rejoin the main road and head south until you reach a steep dirt track. It's a terrible road, but there's no alternative if you want to visit Spain's westernmost point and one-time home of the zero meridian, **Faro de Orchilla** (and if you're particularly keen you can get a certificate from the tourist office in Valverde verifying that you've been to the end of the world). Return to the main road, which becomes full of tight bends, towards the **Ermita de los Reyes**. This 18th-century hermitage houses artworks from that era and is home to the island's patron saint, Nuestra Señora de los Reyes. More dirt tracks (although at least here there are no tight bends or steep drops) lead you to **El Sabinar**, the location of one of the island's most photographed sights. The wind-blasted juniper trees make a bizarre landscape and it's hard to believe that they are still alive. There are a couple of short walks you can do here to get up close and personal with the trees. Further down the dirt road is the **Mirador de Bascos**, possibly the finest lookout point on the island. From here you can see the whole of El Golfo and also the island of La Palma if you can stay on your feet: the wind is pretty strong. Heading back towards the Ermita de los Reyes, take the road heading for Valverde, a mountain pass not for the faint-hearted. If you have time, it's worth parking up and hiking down to the **Grabados de El Júlan** (signposted). This is the most important archaeological site on the island, although it's not hugely impressive. It's a tough 16km round trip taking four to five hours. The site is open only Mon–Sat 09.00–15.00 and you're really better off doing the walk with La Sanjora (see *Hiking* in the *Activities* section). If you don't fancy it, then follow signs for **Hoya del Morcillo**, the island's only official camping ground, in the depths of the pine forest. It has a children's play area, toilets, barbecuing facilities and so makes a pleasant stop. From here you could head up through the forest and then back down the hillside to **Frontera** or, if you haven't had enough of those mountain bends, head for the fishing port of **La Restinga**. There's another area of *malpaís* here, known as Los Lajiales and described by a friend of mine as 'the ugliest place I've ever seen'. The badlands were formed around 6,000 years ago and have been left relatively untouched by erosion due to their location in a dry area of the island. The only life that survives here is lichen, so it makes for a barren but striking landscape. Returning along the same road, a ten-minute detour takes you to the natural pools at **Cala de Tacorón**, one of the island's favourite weekend spots and the location of a good fish restaurant.

Appendix 1

LANGUAGE
Pronunciation

Unlike English, Spanish is pronounced as it is written and provided you learn how to pronounce each letter you'll have no problems. Canarian Spanish is a little different to that spoken on the mainland and the information given here generally reflects local pronunciation and grammar. For more detail on Canarian Spanish, see *Language* and box *Papas and guaguas*, page 21.

a	like the 'a' in 'cat'
e	like the 'e' in 'pet'
i	like the 'ee' in 'see'
o	like the 'o' in 'dog'
u	like the 'oo' in 'food'
b	as in 'big'; there is little difference between the pronunciation of 'b' and 'v' in Spanish.
c	hard 'c' (as in 'cat') if followed by 'a', 'u' or 'o', a consonant. Pronounced as 's' if followed by 'e' or 'i' (in mainland Spain the latter is pronounced like the 'th' in 'three').
d	as in 'dog', though a little softer. In mainland Spain it is pronounced as the 'th' in 'that' when in the middle or the end of the word, but Canarians don't pronounce it this way.
g	as in 'get' when followed by 'a', 'o' or 'u'. If followed by 'e' or 'i' it's pronounced like the 'ch' in the Scottich 'loch'. When followed by 'u' and then 'a' the letter is barely pronounced and sounds more like a 'w': *agua* is pronounced 'awa' and *guagua* sounds more like 'wawa'.
h	always silent
j	Similar to the 'ch' in the Scottish 'loch'
ll	Similar to the 'y' in 'yes'
ñ	like the sound in 'onion'
q	is always followed by 'u' and sounds like 'k'
r	lightly rolled, as in Scottish; 'rr' is a longer sound.
v	almost the same as the 'b'
x	like the 'x' in 'extra'
z	in mainland Spain it is pronounced as 'th' (like in 'three'), but in the Canaries it's somewhere between the English 's' and 'z'

Stress rules

Stress is important in Spanish and mispronouncing the word can lead to misunderstandings or amusement. There are three rules to remember:

- If the word ends in a vowel, 'n' or 's' then the stress falls on the second to last syllable.
- With words ending in any other letter, the stress falls on the last syllable.
- Any exceptions to the above carry a written accent (´) on the stressed syllable.

Basic grammar

To make plurals add an 's' if the word ends in a vowel or 'es' for words that end in a consonant. Adjectives and nouns are gender specific and the adjective must agree with the noun – a masculine noun takes a masculine adjective (*un chico bueno*) and a feminine adjective describes a feminine noun (*una chica buena*). When talking about yourself, the adjective must agree with your gender, so if you're male you'd say *estoy cansado* (I'm tired), while if you're female you'd say *estoy cansada*.

Verbs end in *ar, er* or *ir*; the following is an *ar* verb (*comprar* – to buy) in the present tense.

(Yo) compro	I buy
(Tu) compras	you buy
(El/ella/usted) compra	he/she/you (for strangers) buys
(Nosotros) compramos	we buy
(Vosotros) compráis	you (plural) buy
	(this form is not used in the Canary Islands)
(Ellos/as/ustedes) compran	they/you (plural) buy
	(this form is used instead of *vosotros* in the Canaries)

You should address strangers with the *usted* form rather than the familiar *tu*. Pronouns (yo, tu etc) aren't generally used, unless you wish to emphasise them.

Useful phrases
Greetings and small talk

Hello	*hola*
good morning	*buenos días*
good afternoon	*buenas tardes*
good night	*buenas noches*
	(used as both a greeting and a farewell)
goodbye	*adiós*
See you later	*Hasta luego*
How are you?	*¿Qué tal/cómo esta?*
What's your name?	*¿Cómo se llama?*
My name is	*Me llamo*
Where are you from?	*¿De dónde es?*
I'm from London/England/ /USA	*Soy de Londrés/Inglaterra/Estados Unidos*
please	*por favor*
thank you (very much)	*(muchas) gracias*
yes	*sí*
no	*no*

Tricky situations

I don't understand	*No entiendo*
I don't speak Spanish	*No hablo español*
Do you speak English/French/German?	*¿Habla usted inglés/francés/alemán?*
Please speak slowly	*Por favor hable despacio*
Can you repeat that?	*¿Podría repetir?*
Could you write it down?	*¿Podría escribirlo?*
help!	*socorro!*
I'm lost	*Estoy perdido/a*

Finding your way around

Where is…?	*¿Dónde está…?*
(on the) left	*(a la) izquierda*

(turn) right	(gire a la) derecha
(carry) straight on	(sigue) recto
next to	al lado
opposite	en frente
first floor	primera planta
second/third/fourth	segunda/tercera/cuarta
lift	asensor
bank	banco
post office	correos
bus station	estación de guaguas
police station	comisaría
tourist information office	oficina de información turística
hospital	hospital
health centre	centro de salud
pharmacy	farmacia
internet café	ciber or cibercafé
museum	museo
supermarket	supermercado
shop	tienda
public toilets	baños públicos

Shopping

How much is…?	¿Cuánto cuesta…?
cheap	barato/a
expensive	caro/a
Can I try it on?	¿Puedo probarmelo?
Can I taste it?	¿Puedo probarlo?
What time does…..open/close?	¿A qué hora abre/cierra…?
open/closed	abierto/cerrado

Accommodation

Is there a hotel near here?	¿Hay un hotel por aqui?
campsite	camping
guesthouse	pensión/hostal
hostel	albergue
hotel	hotel
cottage	casa rural
Have you got a single/double room available?	¿Tiene una habitación individual/doble libre?
with private bathroom	con baño privado
shared bathroom	baño compartido
air conditioning	aire acondicionado
How much is it per night?	¿Cuánto cuesta por noche?
Is breakfast included?	¿Está incluido el desayuno?
Can I see the room?	¿Puedo ver la habitación?
What time is breakfast served?	¿A qué hora es el desayuno?

Health

I need a doctor	Necesito un médico
headache/stomach ache	dolor de cabeza/de barriga
diarrhoea	diarrea
sunblock	crema solar
aspirin	aspirina

seasickness tablets	*pastillas para el mareo*
plasters	*tiritas*
contraceptive pill	*píldora anticonceptiva*
condoms	*preservativos/condones*

In a restaurant

Can you bring the menu please?	*¿Me trae la carta por favor?*
I'd like…	*Quiero…*
Do you have a three-course set menu?	*¿Tienen un menú del día?*
Can you bring the bill please?	*¿Me trae la cuenta por favor?*
I'm vegetarian	*Soy vegetariano/a*
waiter/waitress	*camarero/a*
My knife is dirty	*El cuchillo está sucio*
fork	*tenedor*
spoon	*cuchara*
plate	*plato*
glass	*vaso*
serviette	*servieta*

Food list
Drinks

sparkling water	*agua con gas*	milk	*leche*
still water	*agua sin gas*	sugar	*azúcar*
orange juice	*zumo de naranja*	red/white wine	*vino tinto/blanco*
soft drink	*refresco*	beer	*cerveza*
milkshake	*batido*	small draught beer	*caña*
ice	*hielo*	large draught beer	*jarra*
white coffee	*café con leche*	rum	*ron*
black coffee	*café solo*	rum and coke	*cubata*

Food

bread	*pan*	meat	*carne*
breakfast	*desayuno*	octopus	*pulpo*
cake	*tarta*	olives	*aceitunas*
cheese	*queso*	orange	*naranja*
chicken	*pollo*	pepper	*pimienta*
chips (French fries)	*papas fritas*	potatoes	*papas*
cream	*nata*	prawns	*gambas*
dessert	*postre*	rabbit	*conejo*
dinner	*cena*	rice	*arroz*
eggs	*huevos*	rump steak	*bistec*
fillet steak	*solomillo*	salad	*ensalada*
fish	*pescado*	salt	*sal*
fruit	*fruta*	soup	*sopa*
ice-cream	*helado*	squid	*calamares*
lemon	*limón*	tuna	*atún*
lunch	*almuerzo/comida*	vegetables	*verduras*
mayonnaise	*mayonesa*		

The following list is to help you understand the average Canarian menu

a la plancha	grilled on a hot plate
adobado	marinated
ali oli	garlic mayonnaise
almogrote	paste made with goat's cheese, garlic and chilli
arroz con leche	rice pudding
asado	roast
bacalao	cod
bienmesabe	sticky dessert made with honey and almonds
cabra	goat
chorizo	spicy sausage
dorada	sea bass
flan	crème caramel
gofio	toasted wheat or maize
gofio escaldado	fish stew with *gofio*
jamon Serrano	cured ham, similar to Parma ham
lenguado	sole
lentejas	lentils
lomo	pork loin
miel de palma	palm syrup, served with desserts
mojo	spicy sauce
mus	mousse
papas arrugadas	new potatoes cooked in their skins with lots of salt
picante	spicy
potaje	thick soup or stew
ropa vieja	chick-pea stew
sancochado	boiled
vieja	parrot fish

Numbers, days and months

one	*uno*	sixteen	*dieciseis*
two	*dos*	seventeen	*diecisiete*
three	*tres*	eighteen	*dieciocho*
four	*cuatro*	nineteen	*diecinueve*
five	*cinco*	twenty	*veinte*
six	*seis*	twenty-one	*veinte uno*
seven	*siete*	thirty	*treinta*
eight	*ocho*	forty	*cuarenta*
nine	*nueve*	fifty	*cinquenta*
ten	*diez*	sixty	*sesenta*
eleven	*once*	seventy	*setenta*
twelve	*doce*	eighty	*ochenta*
thirteen	*trece*	ninety	*noventa*
fourteen	*catorce*	one hundred	*cien*
fifteen	*quince*	one thousand	*mil*

Monday	*lunes*	Friday	*viernes*
Tuesday	*martes*	Saturday	*sábado*
Wednesday	*miércoles*	Sunday	*domingo*
Thursday	*jueves*		

January	*enero*	July	*julio*
February	*febrero*	August	*agosto*
March	*marzo*	September	*septiembre*
April	*abril*	October	*octubre*
May	*mayo*	November	*noviembre*
June	*junio*	December	*diciembre*

Getting around

Where does the bus to…leave from?	*¿De dónde sale la guagua para…?*
What time is the next bus to….?	*¿A qué hora sale la proxima guagua para…?*
Where is the bus stop?	*¿Donde está la parada de guaguas?*
Can you call me a taxi?	*¿Puede llamarme un taxi?*

Money matters

What is the exchange rate?	*¿A cuánto está el cambio?*
Can I change travellers' cheques here?	*¿Puedo cambiar cheques de viaje aquí?*
I'm expecting a money transfer.	*Estoy esperando una transferencia.*

Hiking

Where is the path to…?	*¿Donde está el camino a…?*
Is it safe?	*¿Es seguro?*
How far is it to…?	*¿A que distancia está…?*
Can you show me on the map?	*¿Me lo podría enseñar en el mapa?*

Appendix

FURTHER READING

Publications on the islands in English are not in abundance but if you speak Spanish there are some superb books available. The best place to buy is in the *Cabildo* bookshops – those in Las Palmas and Santa Cruz de Tenerife are superlative. The local libraries also have an excellent range of books on every aspect of Canarian history, geography and culture.

Natural history

Bramwell, David *Flora of the Canary Islands*, Rueda 1997. This is the bible on Canarian flora. The book is written in easy-to-understand language and is fully illustrated.

Hanquet, Sergio *Diving in the Canaries*, Litografía Romero. Available in the Canaries. As well as information on the best dive sites in the islands, the book has a decent guide on sub-aquatic flora and fauna.

Various *Natural Parks on the Canary Islands*, Everest 2001. Fairly in-depth information on each of the islands' four national parks and some details on Gran Canaria's protected spaces. Excellent photographs.

Hiking

Discovery Walking Guides publish up-to-date books covering all seven islands, while Sunflower have detailed guides to most islands. For a detailed hiking guide to one of the finest areas of the islands, try Miguel Pérez Carballo's *Teno Tenerife Walks* (Romero 1999), an excellent guide to walking in the Parque Natural de Teno, northwest Tenerife.

History

Alzola, José Miguel *Brief History of the Canary Islands*, Museo Canario 1989, available in the *Cabildo* bookshops but you'd have to scavenge to find it anywhere else. If you're short on time or only want a *very* brief account of Canarian history, this little book will suffice.

Castellano Gil, José María *History of the Canary Islands*, Centro de la Cultura Popular Canaria 1993. An easy-to-read account of pre-Hispanic Canarias, the conquest and the aftermath. There is also brief information on the politics, economy, legends and culture of the islands.

López Herrera, Salvador *The Canary Islands through History*, 1998. At times this account is a little dubious but the style is lively and there are some interesting opinions.

Torriani, Leonardo *Descripción de las Islas Canarias*, Cabildo de Tenerife 1999. Spanish, available only within the Canary Islands. Accounts of the pre-Hispanic Canarian culture and the conquest, based on the works of Bethencourt's chroniclers.

Viera y Clavijo, José *Noticias de la historia de Canarias*, Cupsa Editorial 1978. Spanish, available in the islands only. Viera y Clavijo's painstaking work, complemented by decent photographs. There are three volumes.

White, Colin *1797: Nelson's Year of Destiny*, Sutton Publishing 1998. The book covers the battle of Cape St Vincent and the fateful attack on Santa Cruz de Tenerife where Nelson lost his right arm. It challenges the usual British accounts of the battle and offers a fresh look at the events.

Geology

Carracedo, Juan Carlos and Day, Simon *The Canary Islands (Classic Geology in Europe)*, Terra Publishing 2002. Authoritative work on the formation of the archipelago and volcanic activity throughout the ages.

Culture

Chela, José *The Flavour of the Islands*, Hecansa 1997. Available in the islands only. An in-depth guide to Canarian cooking with recipes and a bit of history on local cuisine. There are seven volumes, one for each island. Nicely illustrated.

Concepción, José Luis *Typical Canarian Cooking*, Ediciones Graficolour 2002. Of the many Canarian cookbooks, this is one of the most detailed.

De la Nuez Caballo, Sebastián and Bourne, Louis *Contemporary Poetry from the Canary Islands*, Forest Books, 1992. A collection of works from local poets, such as Tomás Morales and Alonso Quesada. The book contains the original texts and the English translations.

Eddy, M *Crafts and Traditions of the Canary Islands*, Shire Publications 1999. A short, concise work looking at the islands' handicrafts.

Various *Gran Enciclopedia de El Arte en Canarias*, Centro de la Cultura Popular Canaria 1998. Spanish. You'll find it in the islands' bookshops and libraries only. Comprehensive guide to architecture, painting and sculpture in the Canary Islands.

General

Hernández, Pedro *Natura y Cultura de las Islas Canarias*, Tafor Publicaciones 2003. Spanish, widely available in Spain. An excellent book with relatively in-depth information on history, geology, geography and culture plus a brief chapter on each island. The only book you'll need if you want to become acquainted with the islands (provided you read Spanish).

Hernández, Pedro *Conocer Canarias: Mil Preguntas y Respuestas para Disfrutar*, Tafor Publicaciones 2002. Spanish, widely available in Spain. This is the shorter version of the above, with 1,000 questions and answers on every aspect of the Canaries.

Macleod, Donald VL *Tourism, Globalism and Cultural Change: An Island Community Perspective*, Channel View Books 2004. A study into the impact of tourism on a relatively small community. It looks at how family life, politics, the economy and local culture in the Canary Islands have been affected by mass tourism.

Stone, Olivia *Tenerife and its Six Satellites*, Marcus Word 1889, out of print. If you can get hold of this early work, it gives a fascinating view of 19th-century Canarias.

Various *Canarias en Imágenes*, Centro de la Cultura Popular Canaria 2002. Spanish, available throughout Spain. The visual encyclopaedia of the islands with some superb photographs to awaken your interest.

Various *Gran Enciclopedia Canaria*, Ediciones Canarias 1994. Spanish and available in the islands only. This set of encyclopaedias is probably the definitive work on the islands, covering every topic in reasonable detail, but it's not exactly bedtime reading.

Various *Los símbolos de la Identidad Canaria*, Centro de la Cultura Popular Canaria 1997, Spanish. Details the symbols that best represent the Canary Islands, such as the *timple*, the *silbo* and of course, *gofio*. It also includes some of the most important legends, like the Garoé tree, the dragon tree and San Borondón.

Maps

Freytag & Berndt publish excellent, detailed maps of each island.

WEBSITES
Tourist information

Each island's tourist information office has a website, though their quality and content vary. Fuerteventura's site **www.turismofuerteventura.com** is excellent, with detailed information on accommodation, transport and a guide to each town on the island.

Other good sites are **www.gomera-island.com** and **www.cabtfe.es** (Tenerife), where you should be able to find a decent amount of background information and particulars for planning your trip. Gran Canaria (**www.grancanaria.com**) and Lanzarote (**www.turismolanzarote.com**) have average sites, though they tend to be heavy on photos and superficial info and a bit light on practical details. Surprisingly, La Palma's site (**www.lapalmaturismo.com**) isn't too informative – it pales in comparison to the excellent information available from the tourist information office on the island. El Hierro's webpage, **www.el-hierro.org**, has not been updated in some time and is lacking in hard facts.

Natural history

www.gobcan.es/medioambiente The Gobierno de Canarias has an excellent website in English and Spanish with information of flora and fauna, protected spaces and endangered species.

General

www.vivecanarias.com In English, Spanish and German. Dates and details of local fiestas, concerts, sports events and exhibitions.

Photographs

If you want a taste of the islands, there are some superb pictures on **www.canarias-foto.com** and **www.canaryphoto.com**.

Press

www.newscanarias.com The online version of fortnightly English newspaper *Island Connections*. Has the most important stories from each island.

www.tennews.com Tenerife News's website, with a fair amount of the newspaper's content published online.

www.powerfmradio.com Power FM is the largest English-language radio station in the islands. The website has news, weather, a guide to the islands and a jobs page.

There are online versions of the Spanish daily newspapers *Canarias 7* (**www.canarias7.es**) and *La Provincia* (**www.editorialprensacanaria.es**) that cover the Las Palmas province.

Finally, **www.eldia.es** and **www.la-opinion.com** are the websites for the Santa Cruz province newspapers.

Bradt Travel Guides

Africa by Road	£13.95	Kabul Mini Guide	£9.95
Albania	£13.95	Kenya	£14.95
Amazon	£14.95	Kiev City Guide	£7.95
Antarctica: A Guide to the Wildlife	£14.95	Latvia	£12.95
The Arctic: A Guide to Coastal		Lille City Guide	£5.95
Wildlife	£14.95	Lithuania	£12.95
Armenia with Nagorno Karabagh	£13.95	Ljubljana City Guide	£6.95
Azores	£12.95	London: In the Footsteps of	
Baghdad City Guide	£9.95	the Famous	£10.95
Baltic Capitals: Tallinn, Riga,		Macedonia	£13.95
Vilnius, Kaliningrad	£11.95	Madagascar	£14.95
Bosnia & Herzegovina	£13.95	Madagascar Wildlife	£14.95
Botswana: Okavango Delta,		Malawi	£12.95
Chobe, Northern Kalahari	£14.95	Maldives	£12.95
British Isles: Wildlife of Coastal		Mali	£13.95
Waters	£14.95	Mauritius	£12.95
Budapest City Guide	£7.95	Mongolia	£14.95
Cambodia	£11.95	Montenegro	£12.95
Cameroon	£13.95	Mozambique	£12.95
Canada: North – Yukon, Northwest		Namibia	£14.95
Territories	£13.95	Nigeria	£14.95
Canary Islands	£13.95	North Cyprus	£12.95
Cape Verde Islands	£12.95	North Korea	£13.95
Cayman Islands	£12.95	Palestine with Jerusalem	£12.95
Chile	£16.95	Panama	£13.95
Chile & Argentina: Trekking		Paris, Lille & Brussels: Eurostar Cities	£11.95
Guide	£12.95	Peru & Bolivia: Backpacking &	
China: Yunnan Province	£13.95	Trekking	£12.95
Cork City Guide	£6.95	Riga City Guide	£6.95
Croatia	£12.95	River Thames: In the	
Dubrovnik City Guide	£6.95	Footsteps of the Famous	£10.95
East & Southern Africa:		Rwanda	£13.95
Backpacker's Manual	£14.95	St Helena, Ascension,	
Eccentric America	£13.95	Tristan da Cunha	£14.95
Eccentric Britain	£11.95	Serbia	£13.95
Eccentric Edinburgh	£5.95	Seychelles	£12.95
Eccentric France	£12.95	Singapore	£11.95
Eccentric London	£12.95	South Africa: Budget Travel Guide	£11.95
Eccentric Oxford	£5.95	Southern African Wildlife	£18.95
Ecuador, Peru & Bolivia:		Sri Lanka	£12.95
Backpacker's Manual	£13.95	Sudan	£13.95
Ecuador: Climbing & Hiking	£13.95	Svalbard	£13.95
Eritrea	£12.95	Switzerland: Rail, Road, Lake	£12.95
Estonia	£12.95	Tallinn City Guide	£6.95
Ethiopia	£13.95	Tanzania	£14.95
Falkland Islands	£13.95	Tasmania	£12.95
Faroe Islands	£13.95	Tibet	£12.95
Gabon, São Tomé & Príncipe	£13.95	Uganda	£13.95
Galápagos Wildlife	£14.95	Ukraine	£14.95
Gambia, The	£12.95	USA by Rail	£12.95
Georgia with Armenia	£13.95	Venezuela	£14.95
Ghana	£13.95	Your Child's Health Abroad	£9.95
Iran	£12.95	Zambia	£15.95
Iraq	£14.95	Zanzibar	£12.95

WIN £100 CASH!

READER QUESTIONNAIRE

**Send in your completed questionnaire for the chance to win
£100 cash in our regular draw**

All respondents may order a Bradt guide at half the UK retail price – please
complete the order form overleaf.

(Entries may be posted or faxed to us, or scanned and emailed.)

We are interested in getting feedback from our readers to help us plan future Bradt
guides. Please complete this quick questionnaire and return it to us to enter into
our draw.

Have you used any other Bradt guides? If so, which titles? . . . .
. . . .
What other publishers' travel guides do you use regularly? . . . .
. . . .
Where did you buy this guidebook? . . . .
What was the main purpose of your trip to the Canaries (or for what other reason
did you read our guide)? eg: holiday/business/charity etc. . . . .
. . . .
What other destinations would you like to see covered by a Bradt guide?
. . . .
Would you like to receive our catalogue/newsletters?
YES / NO (If yes, please complete details on reverse)
If yes – by post or email? . . . .
Age (circle relevant category) 16–25   26–45   46–60   60+
Male/Female (delete as appropriate)
Home country . . . .
Please send us any comments about our guide to Canaries or other Bradt Travel
Guides. . . . .
. . . .
. . . .
. . . .

Bradt Travel Guides

19 High Street, Chalfont St Peter, Bucks SL9 9QE, UK
Telephone: +44 (0)1753 893444 Fax: +44 (0)1753 892333
Email: info@bradtguides.com
www.bradtguides.com

CLAIM YOUR HALF-PRICE BRADT GUIDE!

Order Form

To order your half-price copy of a Bradt guide, and to enter our prize draw to win £100 (see overleaf), please fill in the order form below, complete the questionnaire overleaf, and send it to Bradt Travel Guides by post, fax or email. Post and packing is free to UK addresses.

Please send me one copy of the following guide at half the UK retail price

Title	Retail price	Half price
. . . .	. . . .	. . . .

Please send the following additional guides at full UK retail price

No	Title	Retail price	Total
. . .	. . . .	. . . .	. . . .
. . .	. . . .	. . . .	. . . .
. . .	. . . .	. . . .	. . . .

Sub total . . . .
Post & packing outside UK . . . .
(£2 per book Europe; £3 per book rest of world)
Total . . . .

Name . . . .

Address . . . .

Tel . . . .   Email . . . .

☐ I enclose a cheque for £ . . . . made payable to Bradt Travel Guides Ltd

☐ I would like to pay by VISA or MasterCard

   Number . . . .   Expiry date . . . .

☐ Please add my name to your catalogue mailing list.

Send your order on this form, with the completed questionnaire, to:

Bradt Travel Guides/CAN
19 High Street, Chalfont St Peter, Bucks SL9 9QE
Tel: +44 (0)1753 893444 Fax: +44 (0)1753 892333
Email: info@bradtguides.com
www.bradtguides.com

Index